Jewhooing the Sixties

BRANDEIS SERIES IN
American Jewish History, Culture, and Life

Jonathan D. Sarna, *Editor*
Sylvia Barack Fishman, *Associate Editor*
For a complete list of books that are available
in the series, visit www.upne.com

David E. Kaufman
  Jewhooing the Sixties: American Celebrity and Jewish Identity—
  Sandy Koufax, Lenny Bruce, Bob Dylan, and Barbra Streisand
Jack Wertheimer, editor
  The New Jewish Leaders: Reshaping the American Jewish Landscape
Eitan P. Fishbane and Jonathan D. Sarna, editors
  Jewish Renaissance and Revival in America
Jonathan B. Krasner
  The Benderly Boys and American Jewish Education
Derek Rubin, editor
  Promised Lands: New Jewish American Fiction on Longing and Belonging
Susan G. Solomon
  Louis I. Kahn's Jewish Architecture: Mikveh Israel and the Midcentury
  American Synagogue
Amy Neustein, editor
  Tempest in the Temple: Jewish Communities and Child Sex Scandals
Jack Wertheimer, editor
  Learning and Community: Jewish Supplementary Schools in the
  Twenty-first Century
Carole S. Kessner
  Marie Syrkin: Values Beyond the Self
Leonard Saxe and Barry Chazan
  Ten Days of Birthright Israel: A Journey in Young Adult Identity
Jack Wertheimer, editor
  Imagining the American Jewish Community

Jewhooing the Sixties

American Celebrity & Jewish Identity

DAVID E. KAUFMAN

SANDY KOUFAX, LENNY BRUCE, BOB DYLAN, AND BARBRA STREISAND

60s

BRANDEIS UNIVERSITY PRESS
WALTHAM, MASSACHUSETTS

BRANDEIS UNIVERSITY PRESS
An imprint of University Press of New England
www.upne.com
© 2012 Brandeis University
All rights reserved
Manufactured in the United States of America
Designed by Eric M. Brooks
Typeset in Sabon and Futura by Passumpsic Publishing

University Press of New England is a member of the
Green Press Initiative. The paper used in this book meets
their minimum requirement for recycled paper.

For permission to reproduce any of the material
in this book, contact Permissions, University Press
of New England, One Court Street, Suite 250,
Lebanon NH 03766; or visit www.upne.com

*The publication of this book was generously supported
by the Lucius N. Littauer Foundation.*

Library of Congress Cataloging-in-Publication Data
Kaufman, David, 1959–
Jewhooing the sixties: American celebrity and Jewish
identity; Sandy Koufax, Lenny Bruce, Bob Dylan, and
Barbra Streisand / David E. Kaufman.
    p. cm. — (Brandeis series in American Jewish history,
culture, and life)
Includes bibliographical references and index.
ISBN 978-1-61168-313-4 (cloth : alk. paper)—
ISBN 978-1-61168-314-1 (pbk. : alk. paper)—
ISBN 978-1-61168-315-8 (ebook)
    1. Jews in the performing arts—United States. 2. Jewish
athletes—United States. 3. Jewish entertainers—United
States. 4. Jews in popular culture—United States.
5. Popular culture—United States—History—20th century.
6. Nineteen sixties. I. Title.
PN1590.J48K38   2012
791'.089'792073—dc23   2012014014

5 4 3 2 1

The book is dedicated to

    SANDY (b. Brooklyn, New York, 1935)

    LENNY (b. Mineola, New York; 1925–1966)

    BOB (b. Duluth, Minnesota, 1941)

    BARBRA (b. Brooklyn, New York, 1942)

and Barbra's fellow Erasmus High alum,

    ARNIE (b. Brooklyn, New York; 1932–2007),

    my father

CONTENTS

Preface

Some of my colleagues in the field of American Jewish history will no doubt be surprised by the subject of this, my second book. My first (*Shul with a Pool: The "Synagogue-Center" in American Jewish History*, 1999) was a history of American synagogues, Jewish schools, and community centers—a study of the internal dynamics of institutional Judaism and Jewish communal life in America. How, one might wonder, did I move from that to this inquiry into Jewish celebrity, from the subject of American Judaism to Jews in American popular culture? But as will become clear, this book is likewise a work in American Jewish history, resting on the assumption that certain key tensions characterize American Jewish life, and hence the dynamics of that history are to be found in the various moves toward resolution. The earlier work engaged with the tension between religious Judaism, as embodied institutionally by the synagogue, and social (or ethnic) Jewishness, represented by the communal center. The resolution: the synagogue-center. In this study, the key tension is between American success, as embodied by the famous Jew, and Jewish survival, a chief concern of the Jewish community at large. The resolution here, I shall argue, is a commonplace feature of American Jewish culture: colloquially called *Jewhooing*, it is, simply, Jewish celebrity consciousness.

How did I come to this subject in the first place? Sometime in the early 1990s, when I was a graduate student living in Cambridge, Massachusetts, I stumbled upon a dog-eared paperback in a local used bookstore. It was the 1965 autobiography of Allan Sherman, *A Gift of Laughter*, in which he describes his own amazement at his recent catapulting to major American celebrity. I was a fan of Sherman's parody songs, and their blatant Jewishness (my favorite: "Seltzer Boy," a takeoff of "Water Boy"), but was unaware of how quickly and dramatically he had appeared on the scene. The book alerted me to the significance of the early 1960s as a time when American Jews were just starting to assert their Jewishness in more public fashion—no longer just within the safe confines of Jewish culture and community, but "out" in the popular culture shared by all Americans. Sherman was an important figure in this development, I surmised, but at the same time, I suspected there were other, more critical historical figures and circumstances.

While on the faculty of the Hebrew Union College–Los Angeles from 2000 to 2009, I had the additional pleasure of teaching undergraduate courses at the University of Southern California across the street; and one of the most popular (and enjoyable for me) was a course on Jewish comedy in America. This led, of course, to an appreciation of Lenny Bruce as a key catalyst, even more than Sherman, of that historical moment. Like Sherman, Bruce had became famous rather suddenly, and explicitly as a Jew—thus pointing to the importance of the celebrity-making process per se. Looking for other exemplars of early 1960s Jewish celebrity, I settled on Bruce, Sandy Koufax, Bob Dylan, and Barbra Streisand as the four celebrity figures most worthy of study. All four have had volumes and volumes written on their lives, careers, and accomplishments; but none of the four had yet been treated from the perspective of American Jewish history. This is that book.

A note on research method. As I embarked on this study, I was often asked if I intended to interview the celebrities who were my subjects (at least the three still living). I would invariably answer that I surely would if offered the opportunity (hear that, Sandy, Bob, and Barb?). But truth be told, the figures themselves would have little to say to inform my inquiry into the culture of celebrity surrounding them. Instead, I have relied primarily on the extensive literature—journalistic, biographical, and academic—covering their lives and work; on sites of celebrity worship, such as fan magazines and Internet websites; on interviews with individuals representing or otherwise reflecting the public adulation of the figures; and on graphic images and other visual representations of the figures, a rich source of both positive and negative commentary on their celebrity.

Finally, the most important part of a preface: acknowledgment of those who helped along the way. Due to the vagaries of life, it has taken me several years to complete this project, and my first debt of gratitude is to my cherished colleagues on the faculties of Hebrew Union College–Los Angeles and now Hofstra University, whose forbearance made it possible for me to carve out the time necessary to finish a book. During that time, many friends and colleagues helpfully read parts of the manuscript at various stages of the writing. Needless to say, responsibility for the final product lies entirely with me, but I still owe heartfelt gratitude to them all and will offer appropriate thanks to them individually. Also, special thank-yous to interview respondents Kitty Bruce, Joel Gilbert, Milton Glaser, Deborah Kass, Jeff Klepper, Paul Krassner, Elliot Landy, and Seth Rogovoy. The reviewers of the manuscript—UPNE editor Phyllis Deutsch, Jonathan Sarna, Donald Weber, and Stephen Whitfield— were the first to read it in its entirety, and I thank them for their incisive critiques. The book is much improved as the result. As academic mentor, Jonathan Sarna has steadfastly supported my work and my career, and I am forever grateful. I am also mindful of my debt to my family, who have always been there with their love and support. During the course of writing the book, my beloved father, Arnold Kaufman, passed away. The book is dedicated to his memory.

As I write these concluding words, it is a day before Rosh Hashana, 5772. It also happens to be exactly fifty years to the day since Sandy Koufax set his first strikeout record for a season, and two days before the fiftieth anniversary of Bob Dylan's first newspaper review and Lenny Bruce's first arrest. Feeling a sharpened sense of history is understandable, especially as I've just come home from teaching my Jewish history class at Hofstra. Today my students and I studied the Babylonian Exile by comparing two documents from the time: Jeremiah's letter to the exiles (*Jeremiah* 29), and the famous psalm, "By the rivers of Babylon" (*Psalms* 137). The first was the prophet's call to the exiled Judeans to settle down in their new home and contribute to the society of which they were now a part. The second was a poet's lament upon finding himself in exile, and the resonant pledge of the Jews to never forget where they came from or who they were. Because both texts appear in the Hebrew Bible, both attitudes are enshrined in Jewish tradition—both the confident call to acculturate and accommodate, and the wrenching cry of foreignness and alienation. It's doubtful that Jewhooing was as common in ancient Babylon as today (though an argument could be made for Joseph in Egypt and Queen Esther in Persia as the first objects of the practice), yet the dynamic tension it reflects has been with us for ages—the urge to "make it" in the current culture, versus the imperative to preserve the memory of *Jewish* culture from generation to generation. In American Jewish history, the dialectic reappears as that between American integration and Jewish identity. Jewhooing, in this view, is but the latest expression of an age-old attempt to square the circle of Jewish life in Diaspora. May this book contribute in some small way to the resolution of the Jewish dilemma both ancient and modern—how to honor both sides of the hyphen at once.

David E. Kaufman
Long Island City, New York
September 27, 2011

Jewhooing the Sixties

Jews, Celebrity, and the Early 1960s

In 1961, a whole new world opened up for me.
SANDY KOUFAX, 1966

Well, fortunately, by some twist of Fate it's becoming "in" to be Jewish.
LENNY BRUCE, 1960

Here's a foreign song I learned in Utah: "Ha-vah, Ha-vah Na-gee-lahhhh!"
BOB DYLAN, 1962

Who's an American beauty rose, with an American beauty nose?
BARBRA STREISAND, 1964

This is a book full of lists, and at the most basic level is itself a list—of four famous Jews. It thus exemplifies the very phenomenon it describes: our constant inventorying of, and enduring fascination with, Jewish celebrity. The naming and claiming of famous "members of the tribe"—and the consequent projection of group identity onto them—is a common ethnic practice, certainly not unique to Jews but especially pronounced among them. It's fair to say that the habit of citing Jewish celebrities—"Didja know, Natalie Portman is Jewish!"—is characteristic of many Jews, and the persistent behavioral quirk has even been given a name: "Jewhooing."[1] The puckish term befits an activity that some see as ethnocentric and crass—one might even object that it is not a fit topic for a serious study of American Jewish identity. But this book intends to be just that, proceeding from the assumption that Jewhooing, while embarrassing to some, is really just the tip of the iceberg and points to a deeper relationship between Jews and celebrity overall.

1

2   In the first place, Jews take pride in their fellow Jews who have "made it" in the arena of American popular culture for the simple reason that their idols' success and acceptance reflects their own. In no uncertain terms, the sheer popularity of the Jewish celebrity demonstrates that Jews are *a part of* America. Yet at the same time, the special talent and heightened status of the Jewish celebrity suggests Jewish difference—the notion that Jews, despite their broad integration and participation in American life, nonetheless remain distinctive, even exceptional, and thus stand *apart from* America. The Jewish celebrity embodies both ideas simultaneously, subtly synthesizing them, and for this reason above all, American Jews are prone to point out the famous among them.

The Jewhooing impulse was perhaps more ubiquitous in an earlier time, when most Jewish celebrities were "passing" as gentiles and begged to be outed—yet such habits die hard. Hence "The Chanukah Song," Adam Sandler's playful musical accounting of "people that are Jewish like you and me" became a sort of Jewhooing anthem in the mid-1990s.[2] The song's lyrics humorously enumerated Jewish celebrities of the past—for example, Kirk Douglas, Dinah Shore, the Three Stooges—while its performance highlighted the Jewishness of Sandler himself. Like him, many celebrities today seem far more comfortable in their Jewish identities, no longer changing their names or otherwise evading ethnic identification, so we might reasonably expect Jewhooing to be in decline. Yet the tendency to cite famous Jews is still quite common and easily observable. As the editor of Los Angeles's *Jewish Journal* puts it, "I check surnames. It's a reflex, and I can't help it. If you're like most Jews I know, you do it too."[3] Though some call it shallow, the reflex is lodged deep in the psyche of the American Jew. Jewhooing—or Jewish celebrity consciousness—provides a novel way to study American Jews and Jewish identity, and is treated here with seriousness and nonjudgment. It is, moreover, the linchpin of the central theme of this book: the interrelationship of Jews and celebrity. *Jewhooing the Sixties: American Celebrity and Jewish Identity* is a full-length study of this relationship, viewing it through the prism of four case studies of Jewish celebrity, and situating it within the broader field of American Jewish history.

Insofar as American Jewish history represents the confluence of American history and Jewish history, its major theme is the tension between American assimilation and Jewish identity, between social integration and group preservation. Though both *assimilation* and *Jewish identity* are somewhat hackneyed terms, the dialectic they represent, between American Jews' enthusiastic embrace of the general culture and their continued engagement with Jewish culture, has been a characteristic tension of the American Jewish experience.[4] As historian Jonathan Sarna explains, "[T]his tension pits the desire to become American and to conform to American norms against the fear that Jews by conforming too much will cease to be distinctive and soon disappear." Sarna further comments that such themes "characterize all minority group history in America."[5] The relationship between Jews and celebrity reflects these themes well. By their very nature as popular figures, Jewish celebrities must appeal to the widest possible audience, having to "play in Peoria." Yet at the same time, they grapple with the *otherness* implied by their Jewish origins, often resolving the dilemma by incorporating some token element of Jewish identity into an otherwise assimilated public image. One example is the actor Edward G. Robinson, who added the letter *G* to his stage name to recall his original Jewish surname, Goldenberg; another is Bob Dylan (born Zimmerman), who, in the midst of his early pretense of gentile origins, included a "Talkin' Havah Nagilah Blues" in his coffeehouse set. As I have suggested, Jewish fans of celebrities likewise exhibit the tension between assimilation and identity—cheering the popular success and widespread social acceptance of their heroes on the one hand, while projecting Jewishness onto them (through the practice of Jewhooing) on the other. This inquiry into the nature of Jewish celebrity is thus a study of the challenge of balancing universalist and particularist concerns—a challenge crystallized by the phenomenon of Jewhooing, as it uniquely combines the universal appeal of celebrity with the more particular identification of celebrities as Jews.

The relationship between Jewish life and celebrity culture cuts deeper still, for in a more figurative sense, the two groups may be analogized. Jews and celebrities alike are small minorities of the population who tend to live in urban centers, especially the media capitals of New York and Los Angeles.[6] As conspicuous elites, both are often objectified in the public eye and stereotyped in the popular imagination. Jews, like celebrities, are subject to love-hate reactions for their apparent claim of exceptionalism; and celebrities, like Jews, are outsiders who nonetheless embody the deepest values and aspirations of the majority. Perhaps most intriguingly, both are characterized by an intrinsic paradox. Author Norman Mailer, a Jewish celebrity himself, once defined a *minority* as someone who "live[s] with two opposed notions of himself. What characterizes a member of a minority group is that he is forced to see himself as both exceptional and insignificant, marvelous and awful, good and evil."[7] Jews, ever the model minority, are often said to manifest both a sense of their own specialness *and* a deep-seated insecurity. To the degree that this is true, such a contradictory nature may be understood as a legacy of the traditional belief in divine chosenness on the one hand and a collective memory of victimization on the other. Conditioned both by Judaism and by antisemitism, the image of Jews is alternately exalted and demeaned, and so paradoxically, Jews occupy a high and low status at once. Celebrities, too, have the dualistic nature of a minority and exhibit a similar internal contradiction. From one angle, they are idolized and revered as transcendent beings, looming larger than life and living larger than their many fans; while from another, they seem quite ordinary and accessible, entering our lives and our collective psyche in a relationship of intimacy—we feel we *know* them, often calling them by their first names. Both Jews and celebrities are in a sense "chosen people"—seemingly "chosen" by some higher power, but at the same time "people" like everyone else. This study of their interrelation will further illuminate their social and symbolic function within American life—and more specifically, within the context of the American "religion" of popular culture.

To gain better insight into the intersection of Jews and celebrity, I have chosen to concentrate on four figures who occupy both categories at once: Sandy Koufax, Lenny Bruce, Bob Dylan, and Barbra Streisand. All four are Jews—third-generation American Jews, to be exact. All four became extraordinarily famous at the same historical moment—their careers can therefore be viewed in parallel. And all four expressed some measure of Jewishness in their public personae—but in widely varying ways. Baseball pitcher Koufax famously sat out a World Series game for the Jewish holy day of Yom Kippur, and became an iconic Jewish hero as the result. Standup comic Bruce was the opposite of Koufax, a Jewish antihero—his subversive comedy contained a great deal of insightful observation on the Jewish condition, yet his celebrity was sullied by his reputation for unlawfulness. Singer-songwriter Dylan first attempted to hide his Jewish roots but then, once revealed as a Jew, continued to confound his fans with ever-shifting identities. And stage and screen star Streisand embraced her Jewish persona from the start, becoming the rare Jewish celebrity with *both* Jewish content and Jewish image. Koufax had the latter but not the former, Bruce the former but not the latter, and Dylan—well, Dylan is enigmatic on both counts. As models of American Jewish identity, the four celebrities thus represent a range of possibilities: Koufax represents religious propriety, Bruce ethnic sensibility, Dylan the elusiveness of identity, and Streisand, in a sense, represents Jewish representation. They are four very different kinds of Jews, and in sum may be said to reflect the very diversity of American Jewish life.

Yet despite their differences, the four share one key feature: they all attained their fame at the same moment in American history—the early 1960s. Focusing on the early 1960s as the critical era for our inquiry suggests a turning point in the history of both American celebrity and Jewish identity. As I will explore further, the period of the early 1960s, specifically the five years from 1961 to 1965, was a time of transition for both America and its Jews—and indeed, Jewish celebrity played a significant role in both American and Jewish historical development of the time. One unifying theme of this book, then, is the pivotal role of the early 1960s in American Jewish culture. Until now, that role has been largely overlooked in favor of the later, post-1967 period usually intended by the phrase "the Sixties." *Jewhooing the Sixties* offers the revisionist view that the earlier part of the decade, sometimes called the "Kennedy years" or the "civil rights era," is of vital importance in the history of Jewish popular culture and in the greater scheme of American Jewish history. *Jewhooing the Sixties* is a study of the special relationship that American Jews have with celebrity, interwoven with a look at the broader social and cultural role that Jewish celebrity played in the 1960s. The four case studies, though contrasting and divergent, together illustrate the nexus between Jews, their celebrities, and the Sixties era in American history.

On September 27, 1961, Sandy Koufax set his first National League strikeout record—in just a few years, he would attain sports immortality as one of the greatest pitchers of all time. Two days later, on September 29, Lenny Bruce was arrested for the first time, beginning a downward spiral that would result in his premature death—yet the impact of his words would long outlast his lifetime. On the very same date, the *New York Times* published the first review of a new talent in town—Bob Dylan—a twenty-year-old unknown who would soon become the most influential musical artist of his generation. Parallel to Dylan, another young phenom appeared in Greenwich Village: Barbra Streisand, who made her off-Broadway debut in October and then auditioned for her first Broadway role in November of 1961. Only nineteen, Streisand rocketed to stardom and found herself playing the White House in just two years' time. Four very different celebrity figures, with four distinct paths to fame—yet they appeared on the scene almost simultaneously. As one of them would later recall, "In 1961, a whole new world opened up for me."[8] And the same might have been said of an entire generation.

Today, when we celebrate them, when we affirm their stardom through various forms of celebrity worship and adulation, we simultaneously shine a light on the time they represent in our collective experience. As it turns out, that brief era was especially important in the history of Jews and celebrity. So the title of this book, *Jewhooing the Sixties*, has multiple meanings: first, it refers to the pointing out of famous Jews from the 1960s; second, it points to the Jewishness *of* the Sixties, asserting a special *Jewish* significance of the era for both Jewish and American history; and last, it suggests an integral relationship between Jewish celebrity and American popular culture on the whole.

Accordingly, the four main chapters of *Jewhooing the Sixties* examine the key themes of pop celebrity and Jewish identity through the prism of the careers and personae of the four figures. Each chapter considers one figure's initial rise to fame during the early 1960s, and then proceeds with a review of his or her Jewish celebrity—that is, the Jewish implications of that celebrity image—to the current day. More than a study of four famous American Jews, the book is a broader reading of American fame and Jewish celebrity writ large. If celebrity figures such as Koufax, Bruce, Dylan, and Streisand can be said to be emblematic of their time, then their appearance on the scene has much to tell us regarding the history of both America and American Jews at the same moment. In the chapters that follow, I delve respectively into the lives, careers, art, and images of the four stars. Though each of the case studies may be read alone, the book as a whole is conceived as a study of the interrelation of three discrete subjects: American celebrity, Jewish identity, and the early 1960s.

American Celebrity

In his 1998 film *Celebrity*, Woody Allen has a character remark, "It's interesting to see who we choose as our celebrities, y'know, and why, what makes them tick. You can learn a lot about a society by who it chooses to celebrate."[9] With that principle in mind, *Jewhooing the Sixties* is a study of celebrity in America. Written from the perspective of American Jewish history, it presumes that celebrity must play some important role in American Jewish life, and further suggests that Jews must play some important role in American celebrity—notions I will develop more extensively later. But first we must simply ask, "What is *celebrity*?" In 1961, Daniel Boorstin defined "the celebrity [as] a person who is known for his well-knownness."[10] That description certainly applies to the Paris Hiltons and Kim Kardashians of our time, celebrities with no discernible reason for being celebrated. In its pejorative application, "celebrity" is attached to the most inconsequential public figures, so "celebrity worship" tends to be denigrated as a trivial and even venal pursuit, a form of modern idolatry.[11] In colloquial usage, *celebrity* thus often takes on a belittling quality, especially in contrast to its near synonym, *fame*. Fame implies greatness based on talent and achievement—the word derives from the Latin for "manifest deeds"—whereas celebrity is a less weighty term, evoking the public adulation, whether deserved or not, accorded the very well-known individual.[12]

But this common and colloquial usage is too limiting, as Boorstin's notion of "well-knownness" may apply equally to the talentless and to the genius, to both the profoundly unimportant personage and to the figure of true greatness. If there is any meaningful distinction between fame and celebrity, it is that the latter focuses less on the underlying reasons for one's fame, the achievement, and more on the quality of fame itself, or as Bob Dylan once put it, "famiousity"[13]—that is, the nature of one's public image. As employed here, the term celebrity refers not just to the well-known figure per se, nor is it to be confused with the cultural products of such figures—the art, entertainment, or other noteworthy activities of the famous. Instead, celebrity refers to a set of complex relationships: between famous individuals and their public, between the image and reality of such individuals, and between the media-driven creation of fame and its unintended social consequences. As students of popular culture remind us, our lives and our very consciousness are shaped in significant ways by celebrities—the select individuals we choose to reward with extraordinary public recognition. Celebrity, in this view, has historical salience. The term encompasses both the famed ones and the culture of idol worship formed around them (hence, "celebrity culture"), and here will principally concern the *relationship* between the famous and the rest of us.

Oddly, given how pervasive a cultural factor it is, celebrity has not been a favorite subject of historians; more typically, it is the province of popular biographers and scholars of popular culture.[14] This may perhaps be related to the rejection by contemporary historians of the traditional emphasis on "great men," and the topic of celebrity may smack of the same. Its denigration is also a sign of the times, as the subject has been further trivialized by the antics of such Hollywood celebrities as Lindsay Lohan and Charlie Sheen. It may be due as well to the naked exposure of the celebrity manufacturing process by the contemporary trend of "reality TV."[15] In truth, the trivialization of celebrity is a long-standing trend, parallel to the growth of mass media over the past century. The formerly wide gap between the famous and us, and hence the preservation of celebrities' elevated status, was greatly narrowed first by the tabloid press, then by the intrusion of radio and later television into our living rooms. That distance has been further diminished by the information technology revolution at the turn of the twenty-first century. As Norman Mailer put it so piquantly, "In the age of television we know everything about the great but how they fart."[16] In the present moment we are witnessing Andy Warhol's prophecy of "fifteen minutes of fame" fulfilled, a time in which the stature of celebrity has declined precipitously.

Yet celebrity, for better or worse, still exerts tremendous power in our culture. In his ambitious world history of fame, *The Frenzy of Renown*, cultural historian Leo Braudy casts celebrity as popular mythology, and examines the effect "they" have on "us." Absorbing the images and narratives of the famous in ways equivalent to the ancient apprehension of myth and folklore, we shape our own image and self-understanding. A form of cultural transmission, Braudy describes this popular mythology as "the inheritance we all share, wittingly or unwittingly, from those figures," and kabbalistically points to "the shards of [their] individual nature embedded in our own."[17] Like fictional characters, we project our own inner lives onto the famous; and like historical actors, they help shape the structure of our lives and of society overall. In this way, the phenomenon of celebrity combines fictive power with historical agency. The famous have the capacity to affect the culture in deep ways, not through their actual persons so much as by our perceptions of them; and the greater their fame, the deeper their influence. In a study of female Jewish stars, June Sochen makes the point well: "Entertainers become 'texts' in American popular culture and therefore are figures that become influential in the popular imagination. Their very beings, in addition to their work, become part of the collective identity they project to the public."[18]

Beginning with Richard Dyer's pathbreaking work of the late 1970s, the thrust of celebrity studies has been to describe the power dynamic whereby "stars" exercise influence over the public. Much of this "star power" is derived from the dialectic between perceptions of the celebrity's public and private personae, between their performative roles and their "true" selves. Citing Dyer, J. Hoberman and Jeffrey Shandler make the following observation: "At once fictional representations and actual people, stars effect a 'magical reconciliation' of seemingly contradictory states. Thus, while some stars verge on mythic stereotypes (the vamp, the Latin lover, America's sweetheart, the bitch goddess, the teen heart-throb, the good bad-boy), stars can also seem familiar, even intimate presences."[19] By reconciling such opposite qualities, celebrities attain a kind of magical or even religious power, and may accrue even more cultural influence than social and political leaders per se.

Richard Schickel, in his compelling study *Intimate Strangers*, also reads celebrity in terms of its power dynamics. He describes celebrity as "the principal source of motive power in putting across ideas of every kind—social, political, aesthetic, moral," and further explains that "famous people are used as symbols for these ideas, or become famous for being symbols of them." Schickel's analysis turns darker still: "From this it follows that various institutions have found it convenient to play up and play off these figures—and not just for something as simple as advertising a product. They are turned into representations for much more inchoate longings; they are used to simplify complex matters of the mind and spirit; they are used to subvert rationalism in politics, [and] in every realm of public life."[20]

Both Braudy and Schickel recapitulate the history of American celebrity, and each locates its initial rise in the aftermath of World War I—Braudy, with the heroic exploits and rugged individualism of Charles Lindbergh and Ernest Hemingway; and Schickel, with the newly conceived star power of Hollywood figures such as D. W. Griffith, Errol Flynn, and Mary Pickford. In the first case, celebrity culture in twentieth-century America is said to start with those stars of the twenties whose "fascination as self-made men . . . expressed a self-sufficiency deeply indebted to professional craft. Crucial to their public images was a publicized aloneness, an exemplary solitude, that yet required an audience to give it life."[21] Their fame reflected something deep in the American character, so Braudy begins the story with them. On the other hand, Schickel's thesis of a Hollywood genesis for celebrity requires little elaboration, as it is the reigning approach in celebrity studies. It rests on the inarguable premise that Hollywood-manufactured film stars are the deities of modern American life, godlike in their perceived perfection, communicative power, transcendence of ordinary reality, and need for our worship.

These two perspectives may be combined, just as two other compelling candidates for pioneers of American celebrity merged American individualism and Hollywood spectacle: Harry Houdini and Charlie Chaplin, who each came on the scene in the early 1900s and reached phenomenal heights of fame by World War I. Houdini—unnecessary to add "the great escape artist," so familiar is the name—garnered so much public attention in the first two decades of the century that George Bernard Shaw would wryly rank him with Jesus Christ and Sherlock Holmes as one of the three most famous figures in history. His biographer further elaborates that "Houdini found that his escapes had earned him a degree of fame beyond which celebrity, the adoration of the moment, passes into mythology, celebrity etherealized by historical memory."[22] Beyond his own status as a famous figure, the word *Houdini* entered the English language.[23] Chaplin, likewise, achieved a level of worldwide fame unheard of before the age of mass media. But these celebrities' extraordinary fame rested on more than simply the new channels of communication. Where Lindbergh and Hemingway reflected the manly heroism of the Teddy Roosevelt era, Houdini and Chaplin represented a still greater American ideal: the triumph of the immigrant era "little guy," and the subversion of the powerful by the powerless. Moreover, Houdini was a rabbi's son who few knew was Jewish, and Chaplin was a gentile Englishman who many imagined to be a Jew.[24] Their celebrity thus reflects yet another core principle of American life: the interchangeability of identity. This theme runs throughout the history of American popular culture—as memorably exemplified by Woody Allen's 1983 film *Zelig*—and is a cultural phenomenon that has often implicated Jews and Jewishness.

America's preoccupation with fame and celebrity continued to grow through midcentury, and would reach still greater heights in the post–World War II era. With the chilling political aftereffects of a world war and the anxieties of domestic affluence combined, Americans of the 1950s looked for distraction to movie stars and popular entertainers, and were primed to move to a higher plateau of idol worship. Just a decade earlier, GIs had pinned up Betty Grable and bobby-soxers had mobbed Frank Sinatra, yet the new intensity of adulation would eclipse even the enthusiasm of the war years. In the 1950s, the popularity of Sinatra would yield to that of Elvis Presley, just as in the 1960s Elvis would yield to the Beatles—and each step represented an exponential advance in celebrity worship and fan obsession. This can be attributed, at least in part, to the enterprise of celebrity promotion—more familiarly called PR (public relations)—which attained far greater sophistication in the postwar decades. Advances in public relations, together with the growing influence of the mass media, prepared the way for an explosion of celebrity consciousness. As Schickel observes, "We were witnessing in the fifties the birth of what we now think of as 'superstardom' . . . a quantum change in the institution [of celebrity] . . . was taking place before our very eyes, that it was now possible for stars to escape the categories of their origins, to take on both a wider public life and to make a profound emotional impact on the individual's inner life than had ever been possible before."[25]

Perhaps the best exemplars of the new celebrity culture were four monumentally famed figures of post–World War II America: Elvis Presley, Marilyn Monroe, John F. Kennedy (JFK), and Rev. Martin Luther King Jr.—luminaries, respectively, of music, film, politics, and social activism. There were no bigger names in the America of the late 1950s and early 1960s, and of course all four died tragically early in life, freeze-framing their fame in perpetuity and carving a new Mount Rushmore on the cultural landscape. More than just exemplars of a particular field of endeavor, Presley, Monroe, Kennedy, and King represented elemental forces in our society, and embodied ideal aspects of our character. All of them, through their iconic personae, refracted some inner revolution in the collective mind, enabling us as a nation to see the world anew.

As suggested earlier, the stardom of such figures, abetted by innovations in communications technology, set the stage for a new era in celebrity culture. Celebrity consciousness reached a new level of intensity at the turn of the 1960s largely due to the media revolution of television—although only 9 percent of American households owned a television set in 1950, this would jump to 90 percent by 1962. The devastating losses of Monroe in 1962 and Kennedy in 1963 were thus experienced all the more immediately and universally, as the images of these tragic events were brought directly into the American home. Moreover, they presaged the untimely deaths of numerous other popular figures of the 1960s era: Malcolm X in 1965, Lenny Bruce in 1966, Robert F. Kennedy and King in 1968, Jimi Hendrix and Janis Joplin in 1970, Jim Morrison in 1971, Phil Ochs in 1976, and Presley in 1977. And these repeated tragedies further demonstrate the pivotal nature of the early 1960s, in this case for the history of American celebrity.

In this study of celebrity, both famous figures and the public's adoration of them will be understood as key constituents of popular culture—the conglomerate of media images and entertainment that both mirrors and influences greater historical development. For in addition to the words and acts of the famed ones among us, we are deeply affected by their very personae, their projected selves. In the end, it is the *reception* of celebrity by the public which deserves our attention. As Sean Redmond and Su Holmes write in the introduction to their reader *Stardom and Celebrity*, "Fame matters on one level because of our status as

11

audiences for celebrity (we have all been, or are, a fan of someone). Stars and celebrities are consumed and appropriated by fans in ways which have a profound effect on their identity, self-image and sense of belonging."[26] This study of four Jewish celebrities moves beyond their work to look at their lives; beyond their lives to look at their representations; and finally, beyond such images to look at their fans, who respond to both the celebrity achievement and image at once.

Jewish Celebrity in America

Jewhooing the Sixties proposes the notion that Jews—and Jewishness—play an outsized role in the history of American celebrity. Though relatively few sports stars or Hollywood screen idols have been Jews, celebrities come in many varieties: politicians and activists, intellectuals and artists, journalists and other media figures, and so on. Once we take into account the full array of celebrity-making fields, it becomes evident that American popular culture has a disproportionately high percentage of Jews. Moreover, those in the business of celebrity production and promotion are often Jews—the producers, agents, public relations people, gossip columnists, and other entertainment professionals. But beyond the individuals we may count, there is also something in the nature of American celebrity that corresponds to the Jewish experience. In the figurative sense noted earlier, the phenomenon of celebrity has a certain "Jewish" quality in that celebrities, much like the popular image of American Jews, are outsiders who have made good, embodiments of the Horatio Alger myth of American life—the promise that anyone can make it to the big time. Certainly, the dream of "making it"—or, as Jonathan Sarna calls it, the "quest for success"[27]—has pulsated throughout the American Jewish narrative, and one result has been a glut of famous Jews.

A history of American Jewish celebrity has yet to be written, but in brief it may be said to have started in the turn-of-the-twentieth-century immigrant era[28] with several rabbinic and cantorial figures in the religious sphere, and a number of theatrical personalities in the secular sphere. Religious figures such as "chief rabbi" Jacob Joseph and the star cantor Yossele Rosenblatt quickly became "culture-heroes" within the Jewish community, as did the newly anointed stars of the Yiddish theater such as Jacob Adler, Molly Picon, and Boris Tomashevsky—all of whom can be seen as precursors of American Jewish celebrity. One oft-cited indication of their popularity is the attendance at their funerals, exemplified in a comment by drama critic (and Adler's onetime son-in-law) Harold Clurman: "When Jacob Adler died, two hundred thousand people came to his funeral. The image he created has never been forgotten."[29]

Using this measure, the biggest immigrant idol of all was neither a rabbi nor an actor, but the greatest Jewish writer of the time, Sholom Aleichem—whose 1916 funeral attracted hundreds of thousands of Jews to watch the procession make its way through the streets of New York City. One writer makes a telling comparison: "A large part of the eastern European Jewish community of the city came into the streets in a state of mourning comparable to that which would follow the death of Rudolph Valentino, the film star."[30] It wasn't the first time that Sholom Aleichem had been compared to an American celebrity. Just ten years before his death, he had arrived in the United States for the first time and was immediately hailed by the New York press as the "Jewish Mark Twain." Already a culture-hero within the Jewish community, but now linked in the popular imagination with a bona fide American icon, Sholom Aleichem became the first major celebrity in American Jewish history—the first figure to attain an iconic, larger-than-life stature, and the first to attract legions of fans.

But if Sholom Aleichem was celebrated as the embodiment of Jewish culture, most subsequent Jewish celebrities would better exemplify assimilation, that is, the *escape* from Jewish culture—for example, the great escape artist himself, Harry Houdini (for this reason, Houdini is better grouped with Chaplin as an exemplar of early twentieth-century *American* celebrity). The subsequent era in American Jewish celebrity would see figures who, like Houdini, personified American assimilation; but at the same time, these figures would often interpolate some form of Jewish identification within their public image. During the 1920s and 1930s, popular entertainers such as Al Jolson, Fanny Brice, Eddie Cantor, Sophie Tucker, the Marx Brothers, Jack Benny, and George Burns would all achieve enormous popularity. None were Jewish culture-heroes in the Sholom Aleichem sense, yet all at times would inject some element of Jewishness into their performance and persona. For example, Al Jolson starred in *The Jazz Singer*, the seminal 1927 film talkie about the son of a cantor struggling to reconcile show business success with loyalty to his Jewish heritage. Fanny Brice, coached by Irving Berlin, learned to sing with a Yiddish accent. Though playing to a general audience, Brice, Cantor, Tucker, and others learned to wink at their fellow Jews in the seats by throwing in an occasional Yiddish expression.

The Marx Brothers are perhaps the best example of stars masking their identities only to turn the subterfuge on its head. A key scene in

14 this regard is from their 1930 film *Animal Crackers*, in which Chico and Harpo taunt a high-society art dealer, Roscoe W. Chandler (implicitly a gentile), by revealing his true identity as Abie the fish-man, an immigrant from Czechoslovakia (implicitly a Jew).[31] But just as Roscoe is recognized as Abie only by the Marxes, all of these celebrities were known to be Jews primarily by other Jews. To most Americans, Jack Benny seemed just as "white bread" (that is, non-ethnic) as Bob Hope. Cultural historian Henry Bial has termed this phenomenon *double coding*, the process by which a celebrity can be read in two ways simultaneously—by the general populace as a fellow American, and by co-ethnics as one of their own.[32]

For this reason, the effect of the American Jewish celebrity is multiplied inasmuch as the American Jew responds to the famous on two levels at once: both as an American and as a Jew. While all baseball fans thrilled to the exploits of Hank Greenberg, seeing him as a new Babe Ruth, Jewish fans saw him additionally as a new Moses, a "Jewish star" leading them to the promised land of America.[33] The same duality applies to other Jewish heroes of World War II era America, figures as diverse as Albert Einstein, who won the Nobel Prize in Physics in 1922 and spent the last twenty years of his life (from 1935 to 1955) in the United States; and Bess Myerson, who won the Miss America beauty pageant in 1945. Both as Jews and as Americans, American Jews would be doubly proud of such heroes.

On the other hand, the reaction to the 1950 arrest and subsequent trial and execution of Ethel and Julius Rosenberg reflected the potential tension between American and Jewish concerns. Whereas many immigrant Jews and their children continued to believe in the Rosenbergs' innocence, more Americanized Jews tended to distance themselves from the accused spies. Indeed, the 1950s was a time of contrasts for American Jews in the public eye. Today it is hard to imagine, in this age of Spielberg and Seinfeld, the fearfulness evoked when a name like Rosenberg was linked to high treason. Conversely, other Jewish-sounding names were cause for ethnic pride: baseball star Greenberg, Gertrude Berg (and the beloved character she created for radio and television, Molly Goldberg), and Benny Goodman, to name but a few. Thus, identification cut both ways. While many Jews' heads swelled over the scientific advances of Jonas Salk and Albert Einstein,[34] many also experienced anxiety over the all-too-apparent Jewishness of the atomic bomb makers—with names such as Oppenheimer, Teller, and Feynman.

In the decades preceding the 1960s, Jewish celebrity figures mostly fell into one of two distinct camps: (1) those who were seen in no uncertain terms as Jews—for example, Berg, Greenberg, the Rosenbergs, Myerson; and (2) those who, while prominent in the public eye, were not necessarily perceived as Jewish—for example, Houdini, Jack Benny, Danny Kaye, Dinah Shore, Lauren Bacall, Kirk Douglas. Notwithstanding the high-profile conversions of Sammy Davis Jr. and others, the boundaries between Jew and non-Jew remained firm in the 1950s, and anxiety over any public avowal of Jewish identity remained the norm. At the turn of the 1960s, this would begin to change as a new type of Jewish celebrity began to emerge, combining American acculturation with Jewish identification—neither one nor the other, but now representing some new merging of formerly opposite tendencies.

As such, the new Jewish celebrity of the 1960s would be implicated in broader societal changes. Just as Jewish intellectuals were indispensable in challenging the white Protestant hegemony of American intellectual life,[35] so too did Jewish celebrities play an important part in breaking up the homogeneous nature of American popular culture. Through the medium of celebrity, Jews have helped to make these United States less united and more diverse, less static and more dynamic. The major turning point here was the era of the 1960s, when the contours of American society were reshaped to be more inclusive of ethnicity and other forms of outsider identity—a trend in which Jewish celebrity played its part. As a culture, we could not have gone from Kate Smith and Doris Day to Madonna and Lady Gaga without the revolutionary rise of Barbra Streisand in between. Just one year after the 1963 civil rights march on Washington, her star-making turn in *Funny Girl* offered its own form of social protest, as her character boasted of her "American beauty nose" after her Jewish mother opined, "Is a nose with deviation such a crime against the nation?"[36] Streisand, through her celebrity persona as a Jewish *other*, helped achieve greater acceptance for all outsiders in America. Jews did not accomplish this cultural transformation alone, of course; they were joined in the effort by African Americans. Parallel to the pathbreaking careers of 1960s black celebrities such as Sidney Poitier, Harry Belafonte, Diana Ross, and Cassius Clay/Muhammad Ali (Ali changed his name in 1964), Jewish celebrities of the era likewise added their own complexion (and complexity) to the lily-white coloring of postwar American culture.

Nevertheless, the subject of Jews and celebrity is not as well covered as one might expect. By contrast, African American history is replete with studies assessing the cultural significance of African American celebrities—for example, the four just noted, as well as Jack Johnson, Joe

Louis, Louis Armstrong, Lena Horne, Jackie Robinson, Martin Luther King Jr., Michael Jordan, Bill Cosby, Oprah Winfrey, Michael Jackson, and Barack Obama—all iconic figures who have blackness attributed to them as an elemental aspect of their public personae, and each of whom is said to have influenced the nature of blackness in America.[37] On the other hand, American Jews in the public eye have no such unanimity or certainty of Jewish identification and are rarely, if ever, said to have shaped the Jewish experience writ large.

American Jewish studies, unlike African American studies, has relatively little work analyzing the contribution of famous Jews to Jewishness in America. Although there exist voluminous listings of Jews in American popular culture, few are much more than exercises in hagiography, and fewer still offer any useful analysis of the figures and their meaning as Jewish celebrities. Most scholarly accountings of significant American Jews focus on the intellectual elite: for example, Suzanne Klingenstein's study of Jews in the academy, Andrew Heinze's study of Jews in American therapeutic culture, and Kirsten Fermaglich's study of Holocaust imagery in the work of select Jewish thinkers. But as insightful as these studies may be, they represent a clear preference for elite over popular culture. Certainly, there are ever-multiplying studies of the Jewish contribution to popular culture, that is, studies whose primary interest is the work of art, performance, or other cultural product—in short, the *text*.[38] A smaller, but growing literature is beginning to treat celebrity figures *themselves* as texts—some noteworthy examples being Michael Alexander's *Jazz Age Jews* and J. Hoberman and Jeffrey Shandler's *Entertaining America: Jews, Movies, and Broadcasting*.[39]

Yet despite the relative dearth of studies attesting to the phenomenon, American Jews clearly have a special relationship with celebrity—a relationship that is often more intense, more layered than the analogous relationship of other ethnic groups with their icons. Perhaps the only other group to have a similar level of celebrity consciousness is the gay community, whose position in American society resembles that of Jews in many ways.[40] Both Jews and gays have contributed heavily to popular culture, and both have often had to hide their true identities to do so— and thus both have developed a hyper-consciousness of celebrity identity. As the lesbian Jewish artist Deborah Kass told her mother, "We talk about who is gay in Hollywood, the way you talk about who is Jewish in Hollywood."[41] For understandable psychological reasons, all minority groups take great pride in the accomplishments and the celebrity of their famous members. The satisfaction derived from admiring the famous figure of the same background helps to offset feelings of inferiority stemming from minority status—and all minorities do it. But Jews, like gays, obsess over their celebrities all the more so. This can be attributed to two interrelated factors:

1. *Jews have a lot of celebrities.* For a group comprising less than 2 percent of the U.S. population, it is remarkable how many well-known figures in America are Jews—a phenomenon due to the numerically disproportionate entry of Jews into the popular arts and mass media during the twentieth century. Some commonly offered historical explanations include the timing of Jewish immigration; the skill set and value system of the immigrants and their children; and an entrepreneurial orientation combined with the openings provided by the parallel development of popular culture during the same years as Jewish adjustment to America (for example, vaudeville and early Hollywood developed during the first generation era, radio and comic books during the second, and television and nightclub performance during the third). The most widely cited explanation suggests that as upwardly mobile Jews sought entrée into the American economy, the only fields open to them were those in which the established elite had no interest—in particular, the "marginal" arena of popular culture. Still, a more fully satisfying explanation has yet to be offered.

What can be asserted here, with only slight exaggeration, is that musical theater and the comedic arts have been nearly monopolized by Jews; American popular music owes at least as much to Jews as to African Americans; and the Hollywood film industry was the creation of immigrant Jews and continues to be dominated by Jewish executives, writers, and agents. Each of these areas has yielded a bumper crop of Jewish celebrities. For example, Broadway musicals gave us Irving Berlin, George Gershwin, and Richard Rodgers; comedy gave us Jack Benny, George Burns, and Jerry Lewis; popular music gave us Artie Shaw, Dinah Shore, and Herb Alpert; and Hollywood film production gave us Samuel Goldwyn, Jack Warner, and Robert Evans.[42]

Beyond such widely acknowledged "Jewish" fields, Jews have also tended to overpopulate (relative to their numbers) a diverse array of culturally conspicuous and media-exposed professions such as advice (Abigail Van Buren, Ann Landers, Suze Orman); architecture (Denise Scott Brown, Gordon Bunshaft, Frank Gehry); celebrity interviews (Larry King, Barbara Walters, James Lipton); comic books (Stan Lee, Jack Kirby, William Gaines); fashion (Ralph Lauren, Calvin Klein, Donna

Karan); film criticism (Pauline Kael, Jeffrey Lyons, Kenneth Turan); film direction (George Cukor, William Wyler, Billy Wilder); gossip (Walter Winchell, Rona Barrett, Matt Drudge); liberal politics (Paul Wellstone, Bernie Sanders, Barney Frank); magic (David Copperfield, Ricky Jay, David Blaine); media moguldom (William Paley, Walter Annenberg, David Geffen); music promotion (Clive Davis, Bill Graham, Phil Spector); photography (Diane Arbus, Richard Avedon, Robert Capa); political columns (William Safire, Michael Kinsley, David Brooks); pop psychology (Werner Erhard, Dr. Joyce Brothers, Dr. Drew); sports reporting (Howard Cosell, Marv Albert, Al Michaels); sports team ownership (Robert Kraft, Fred Wilpon, Mark Cuban); talk shows (Sally Jessy Raphael, Jerry Springer, Kathy Lee Gifford); and television news (Mike Wallace, Ted Koppel, Andrea Mitchell). The notion that American Jews have an extraordinary number of celebrities, out of all proportion to their numbers, ought to be beyond dispute.

2. *Jewish celebrities are prone to assimilation and are not easily identifiable as Jews.* That the lists in number 1 contain few recognizably Jewish names is no coincidence. With some significant exceptions, the majority of Jews in the public eye have little to no public Jewish identification (identity as perceived by others). They are, at least in an external sense, assimilated Jews. The chicken-and-egg question of whether the attainment of celebrity is enabled by assimilation or further encourages it is not my main concern here. More critical to this inquiry is the public perception of the celebrity in question. Here, we may again distinguish between the pre- and post-1960s eras. In the earlier period, Jewish celebrities were more likely than not to change their names, disassociate from Jewish life, and marry out of the faith. By and large, Jewishness was not part of their public personae—there is a long list of public figures who were such "hidden" Jews. On the other hand, as I have already noted, the period also saw many celebrities widely identified as Jews: for example, Greenberg, the "great Jewish" baseball hero, and Myerson, the first (and so far only) Jewish Miss America.

Yet even when perceived as Jewish, the midcentury Jewish celebrity still tended to be highly acculturated in lifestyle and behavior. Even Gertrude Berg, creator of the popular character Molly Goldberg, was far more Americanized in her personal life than her highly ethnic characterization may have suggested. Today, the reverse circumstance often holds true, in which the celebrity may have a more substantial Jewish identity in private but is still publicly perceived as non-Jewish. The fact that movie star Natalie Portman is a Hebrew-speaking, self-identifying Jew of Israeli parentage matters far less than the fact that her name and face are not readily identifiable as Jewish, so she is not seen as Jewish by the wider film audience. For every Steven Spielberg and Jon Stewart—celebrities broadly identified as Jews—there are dozens of public figures far less identifiable. As a general rule of thumb, American celebrity and Jewish identity do not accord well together, co-existing in a state of tension, not harmony.

The two phenomena I have outlined together account for the fact that Jews tend to be especially interested in their celebrities. Given that many celebrities are Jews, but that few explicitly read as Jewish, it is left to the wider Jewish public to take notice of the Jewishness of its public representatives. As noted earlier, such celebrity consciousness among Jews has been given a name—*Jewhooing*.

The phenomenon of Jewhooing will be explored in each of the chapters to come, including a more thorough historical analysis in the epilogue (Chapter 6), but suffice it to say for now that Jewhooing sits at the intersection of celebrity and Jewishness. To the degree that it fulfills psychological needs of self-definition and group identification, we turn now to a discussion of the second major theme of *Jewhooing the Sixties*, Jewish identity.

Jewish Identity

Beyond its examination of American celebrity, *Jewhooing the Sixties* is also a study in the history of Jewish identity. Just as the nature of celebrity underwent some profound change in the postwar era, so too did the nature of being Jewish. The four celebrities profiled will be seen to represent four distinct iterations of Jewishness, collectively representing a transformation in Jewish identification. But first, the term *Jewish identity* requires some preliminary definition and analysis. A commonplace, even hackneyed phrase in contemporary Jewish discourse, its exact meaning is obscured by its multiple usages. Generally speaking, Jewish identity is employed in one of three distinct ways, alternately denoting (1) identification as a Jew based on familial descent, and supposedly, therefore, an objective and quantitative measure; (2) identification with Judaism, the Jewish people, or Jewish culture, related to communal imperatives for group survival and thus an ideological and value-laden criterion; and (3) identification of Jewishness, postmodern in its plurality and subjectivity, and hence qualitative and (ostensibly) value-free. As it turns out, all three versions came into popular usage at just about the same time, the early 1960s—suggesting that it was a key turning point in the history of Jewish identity in America.

In the first instance, Jewish identity is a matter of categorization, referring to the insider/outsider distinction between who is Jewish and who is not. This usage is parallel to the age-old question, "Who is a Jew?" That is, who is considered *by others* to be a Jew? Or, how can one be objectively *defined* as Jewish? Since the rabbinic era of late antiquity, the answer has been principally determined by biological descent—according to *halacha* (Jewish religious law), a Jew is defined as the child of a Jewish mother. Though the ancient rabbis added the possibility of religious conversion, the prevailing norm has long been a parental determinant of identity.[43] Today, many contemporary Jews and others chafe at the notion that once born a Jew, the designation is fixed and permanent, disallowing a more self-determined identity—it is the objection of modern individualism.

Assigning Jewish identity primarily by descent is also sometimes denigrated as a form of racial thinking; for the emphasis on parentage implies to some that Jews are a biological group, a "race." One scholar has called this "blood logic," and others point to the recent interest in "Jewish genetics"[44] as evidence of the same. But such a stark emphasis on biology—*nature*—obscures the crucial element of parental influence—*nurture*. Although some continue to see "Jewish identity by descent" solely in biological terms, believing that Jewishness is conferred genetically, a more accurate assessment points to the deep psychological impress made by Jewish mothers and fathers as the chief transmitters of identity. Simply put, the child of Jews becomes a Jew through parental nurturing and Jewish identity is created through a process of socialization, not genetic inheritance. Yet whether understood as nature or nurture, this common usage is an either/or proposition: either you are or aren't a Jew; either you have or don't have Jewish identity. Because the main criterion is descent from other Jews, this version of Jewishness purports to be a quantitative measure of identity. Thus, for example, the designation "half-Jew," referring to someone with one Jewish parent, treats identity in purely quantitative terms.

Such zero-sum determination of Jewishness serves many purposes. In political discourse, it relates primarily to the State of Israel, where the question of identity is generally couched in public debate around inclusion in the Jewish polity.[45] As scholar Gad Barzilai notes, "In Israel, the question of 'who is a Jew' is as much about power as it is about religion."⁴⁶ The contemporary "who is a Jew" debate was first sparked by a public query issued by Prime Minister David Ben-Gurion in 1958 and has continued to provoke controversy to the present day. Outside of Israel, the question further resonated within the context of intrareligious controversy over intermarriage and conversion. Hence, Jewish identity in the definitional sense has been applied by custodians of religious boundaries, as in the title of Baruch Litvin and Sidney Hoenig's 1965 collection of responses to the Ben-Gurion query, *Jewish Identity: Modern Responsa and Opinions on the Registration of Children of Mixed Marriages*.⁴⁷ In a more secular vein, demographers of Jewish life must routinely decide "who is a Jew" for the purpose of measuring the Jewish population. For most such studies—and in discussions like this of Jews in popular culture—a Jew is defined as anyone born to (either one or two) Jewish parents, and who is thus assumed to have been raised under the influence of Jewish family and culture. But this relatively straightforward method of determining identity suggests that "Who is a Jew?" can be easily and summarily answered. The very question itself conveys the more enigmatic nature of Jewish identity.

But what has all this to do with Jewish celebrity? This first question of Jewish identity—"Who is a Jew?"—is in fact often expressed as celebrity consciousness, since the question can also refer to the act of determining who is Jewish in the public sphere. (This also applies to one's own interpersonal experience—the practice sometimes described as "Jewish radar" or "Jewdar." When directed toward popular culture, the same impulse is called Jewhooing.) Two of the most commonly employed indicators of Jewish identity in this regard are related to family descent: (1) physical characteristics associated with Jews, so-called "Jewish looks"; and (2) Jewish names, especially surnames. In both cases, one derives these features from one's forbears.

But such external markers of Jewish descent are highly unreliable. Many Jews do not fit the stereotype of looking Jewish, and many people who do fit the stereotype aren't in fact Jews (such cases of mistaken Jewish identity have been described as "virtual Jews," for example, Charlie Chaplin, Valerie Harper, Jason Biggs⁴⁸). Likewise, many Jews do not have Jewishly identifiable last names, and many with such names are not Jewish at all (for example, Caspar Weinberger, Whoopi Goldberg, Mike Myers). Both names and looks, therefore, can be deceptive and misleading as determinants of identity. Names can be easily changed, of course, and physical appearance is even less dependable a marker because many, if not most Jews do not "look Jewish." Moreover, what constitutes Jewish looks is a highly subjective and slippery subject itself.[49] It is precisely this lack of clarity on the matter that makes the attempt to ascertain Jewish identity—to figure out who's Jewish and who's not—so commonplace a behavior. That is to say, the frequency of Jewhooing is increased by the very difficulty of identifying who is a Jew. And, as we shall see, our perception of Jewish celebrity addresses many of the quandaries of Jewish identity in this first sense.

In its second application, *Jewish identity* is an ideologically charged term implying a positive affirmation of Jewish group belonging, often used as a synonym for Jewish pride or Jewish engagement. Jewish identity in this sense is not the answer to "Who is a Jew?" but to "Who is a *good* Jew?" In this regard, it is much like a cognate term, *Jewish identification*.[50] Both terms are directly related to the communal challenge of *continuity*, and are most often employed in the fields of Jewish education and Jewish sociology. The term appeared in this vein as early as 1944, when Rabbi Max Arzt confronted "the problem of Jewish identity" in the journal of the Reconstructionist movement. The thrust of his article was a staunch opposition to the "negative program of Jewish *extinctionists*" and a strident call for asserting "the Jew's right and duty to *survive* as a *distinct* recognizable entity among the peoples of the world," a group distinguished by Judaic content and purpose.[51] Though employed throughout those years, the term came into vogue in the early 1960s, when anxiety over assimilation began to rise dramatically, in what one historian has called "the first Jewish continuity crisis" (the second would follow the National Jewish Population Survey of 1990).[52]

Just as ethnic consciousness was on the rise in the civil rights era in America, the moment also saw a notable rise in the rate of intermarriage, as revealed by two eye-opening articles by sociologists Erich Rosenthal and Marshall Sklare, in 1963 and 1964 respectively.[53] The emerging concern for Jewish group survival—or *survivalism*—was therefore a direct response to the growing fear of assimilation and group disappearance. Responding to the new awareness of intermarriage as a problem, American Jewish Committee leader John Slawson issued a 1963 broadside titled "The Quest for Jewish Identity in America," in which he noted "the intensity of this new interest," and stated that "defense against assimilation now seems more urgent than defense against discrimination."[54] The concern peaked in the following year, when rabbis began to give high holiday sermons with titles such as "Jewish Identity Today" and "The Search for Jewish Identity."[55] And not incidentally, 1964 was also the year when Milton Gordon published his influential study *Assimilation in American Life,* and *Look* magazine ran an article with the unnerving title "The Vanishing American Jew."[56]

Pioneering American Jewish sociologist Marshall Sklare, who would later help popularize the term, tended to use the bulkier "Jewish identification" rather than "Jewish identity" in his earlier work of the 1950s.[57] But then, in 1967 he issued the results of a decade's worth of research as *Jewish Identity on the Suburban Frontier,* a now classic work. There, Sklare describes "the problem of Jewish identity" for American Jews as "the question of how to guarantee their survival in a society which is on the one hand pluralistic but on the other hand is so hospitable as to make group survival difficult."[58] Working along similar lines today, sociologist Bethamie Horowitz makes the following statement: "Jewish identity is now seen as the fulcrum of a vibrant Jewish life in North America, where the continuity of the Jewish group as a collective has come to be seen as dependent on the expression of strong individual identity. Low Jewish identity of individuals is seen as resulting in poorer prospects for Jewish continuity, while high or strong identity is seen as strengthening group continuity."[59] Horowitz, like Sklare, links individual Jewish identity to Jewish group continuity. Because the latter is a primary goal of organized Jewish life, Jewish identity in this sense becomes a key indicator of Jewish prospects for the future, and is therefore measured and assessed and quantified, rated from high to low. Indices of identity include religious practices, values, and beliefs, as well as social attitudes and cultural behaviors associated with Jewish life. In this common and still popular usage, as an assessment of who's a "good Jew,"[60] Jewish identity is seen as the main factor in ensuring Jewish "survival" and serves as the counterpoint to "assimilation."

As a measure of religious devotion and cultural engagement, Jewish identity also becomes a factor in the role that celebrities play in the collective Jewish psyche. Gauging their own position on the continuum between assimilated and identified, American Jews are keenly aware of the Jewish image of their celebrities—are they good Jews or not? And as such, do they represent their fellow Jews in a positive light or not? Because most Jewish celebrities tend to score low in such measures of Jewish identity (as noted earlier), this most often takes the form of a negative judgment—for example, the widespread condemnation of Philip Roth as a "self-hating Jew" following the publication of his first collection of short stories in 1959.[61] More commonly, Jewish celebrities are taken to task for assimilatory behaviors such as changing their names or marrying gentiles—Lenny Bruce, for example, did both. Barbra Streisand's

Jewish fans were cheered when she married Elliott Gould (Jewish) and disappointed when she married James Brolin (not Jewish). More rarely, a Jewish celebrity will go beyond mere cultural assimilation and commit religious apostasy—as in the case of Bob Dylan, who became a "born-again" Christian for a few years in the late 1970s. Such "traitors to their people" are implicitly measured against those who exhibit a more positive Jewish identity, such as Sandy Koufax, who became a Jewish icon for choosing not to play baseball on a high holiday, and Streisand, who attained a similar heroic stature for choosing not to fix her nose. That such minor gestures are enough to catapult one into the ranks of Jewish heroes betrays the anxiety many Jews feel over their own degree of Jewish identity in this second sense.

A third usage of *Jewish identity* has become more common in recent years and is the one most directly relevant to this study. As increasingly used by students of Jewish culture, it evokes the variable nature of Jewishness—in fact, *Jewishness*, a rather vague term itself, is best understood as a synonym for this sense of Jewish identity.[62] Both terms signify the qualitative and psychological state of being Jewish—or the subjective perception of another's Jewishness—and so reflect the ever-changing and enigmatic nature of the Jewish experience. Above all, it is the quality of changeability that distinguishes this understanding of Jewish identity from its predecessor. Identity in the "good Jew" sense relies on the notion of a fixed standard, a normative culture that many imagine to be "essential and unchanging in a group's identity"; whereas Jewishness in this third usage rejects such "essentialist conceptions of identity" in favor of a more fluid and potentializing "process, a matter of 'becoming' rather than being."[63]

Subject to varied cultural influences throughout their lengthy history, Jews have generated a multiplicity of Jewish cultures, Judaisms, and Jewish identities. Still, the diversification of Jewishness has accelerated all the more in the modern age.[64] The critical break in the nature of Jewishness occurred in the era following the French Revolution, when the holistic Jewish community of the European ghetto was eliminated and Jews were emancipated as individuals with the right to define themselves in relation both to the state and to the Jewish community. One key effect of this historic rupture was to dissolve the unity between religion and peoplehood inherent in traditional Judaism, splitting the Jewish atom, as it were. Only in the modern world is it possible to be a Jew without Jewish religion (that is, a "secular" or "cultural" Jew), or conversely, to be a Jew by religion who rejects the notion of Jewish peoplehood (an ideological stance less common today, but historically represented by the "classical Reform" Jew). Hence much contemporary teeth-gnashing over Jewish identity concerns the enduring question of whether Jews should be understood as a religious or an ethnic group.[65]

But this third notion of Jewish identity extends beyond the religious/ ethnic divide. The very vagueness of the term *Jewishness* indicates a form of Jewish identity dependent on neither religious nor ethnic culture. In her classic study of totalitarianism, German Jewish philosopher Hannah Arendt suggests a specifically modern definition for the term, asserting that Jewish identity in this sense is itself the product of the modern age. Describing the rapidly assimilating Jewry of nineteenth-century Germany, she writes, "Instead of being defined by nationality or religion, Jews were being transformed into a social group whose members shared certain psychological attributes and reactions, the sum total of which was supposed to constitute 'Jewishness.' In other words, Judaism became a psychological quality and the Jewish question became an involved personal problem for every Jew."[66] Whereas earlier generations of Jews defined themselves both by nationhood and by religion, modernizing Jews began to shed both forms of Jewish identity, the first through political emancipation and integration, and the second through intellectual enlightenment and secularization. For those who continued to see themselves and be seen by others as Jews, what remained was only a vague sense of being different, a vestigial form of identity called Jewishness.

But then we might ask: for the Jew who no longer observes the Jewish religion in any fashion, or who no longer engages in Jewish culture in any form, what is there to identify *with*? As exemplified by Arendt, it is often the Jewish intellectual who, having rejected the particularism of Jewish religion and culture, self-consciously grapples with this problem. In the April 1961 issue of *Commentary* magazine, new editor Norman Podhoretz convened a symposium on "Jewishness and the Younger Intellectuals," in which thirty-one respondents contemplated the complexities of American Jewish identity. Two issues later, noted sociologist Daniel Bell added his own piece, "Reflections on Jewish Identity," in which he poignantly asks, "What is left, then, for one who feels himself to be a Jew, emotionally rather than rationally—who has not lost his sense of identification with the Jewish past and wants to understand the nature of that tie?" Having rejected both the religious formalism of Orthodoxy and the religious moralism of Reform, Bell concludes, "For me, therefore, to be a Jew is to be part of a community woven by memory."[67]

More psychological than political, and more impressionistic than ideological, this new form of Jewish consciousness—based almost exclusively on "memory"—has become a norm of the modern age, and is nowhere more evident than in the American experience. In America, the quintessential open society, the dilemma of Jewish identity goes beyond "Who is a Jew?" and "Who is a good Jew?" to "What is the meaning of being Jewish?" Or, more to the point, what is the meaning of being Jewish once biological, familial, religious, and cultural distinctiveness decline and disappear? Jewish identity, in this sense, is not quite so concrete an issue as in the European past or the Israeli present, but is rather a more subtle, internal, and personal phenomenon. The title of an authoritative study of contemporary American Jewish identity captures this internality well: *The Jew Within*.[68]

Of course, the "Jew within" remains dependent on external expressions of Jewish religion, culture, and community in order to construct an internal Jewish life. For one's personal identity is ultimately a reflection of social relationships and political realities, as Simon Herman explains in his "social psychological" study of Jewish identity: "The individual's self-identity is influenced by subjective public identity, i.e., by the way he believes others see him. What is crucial here is not simply whether he sees himself classified as a Jew—this in most cases is not open to question—but how he believes others view the Jew and the value they attach to that identity."[69] Herman's insight begins to explain how and why Jewish celebrities play such an important part in the construction of individual Jewish identity. For if, in fact, the famous Jew in American life helps determine the way Americans see all Jews, then it follows that individual Jews would take their cues from such widely disseminated images in the construction of their own sense of Jewishness. The Jewish celebrity, in short, is a source of Jewish identity for all.

Thus Jewish celebrity consciousness becomes a means by which Jewish identity in this third sense is evaluated and enacted. For some, as Susan Glenn suggests by her notion of "blood logic," Jewhooing reasserts the meaningfulness of genetics in Jewish identity, a return to seeing Jewishness in racial terms. Madeleine Albright became a Jew in the eyes of the world the moment her Jewish ancestry was discovered; that is, her Jewishness is entirely a matter of descent, and is mainly a function of other Jews' projection of identity onto her. Such thinking also explains why the Jewhooing habit is so distasteful to many Jews and others, who see it as the basest form of group identification. Yet at the same time, the citing of Jewish celebrities is an affirmation of Jewish ethnic culture. As much a statement of "culture" as of "race," Jewhooing identifies Jews in the popular culture not for their biological roots, but for their representation of Jewish values, traits, and other cultural characteristics. When Jews engage in Jewhooing, they are asserting the existence of a shared Jewish culture, both searching for evidence of its distinctiveness and constructing such an identifiable culture simultaneously.

As I will discuss at length in the chapters to come, Sandy Koufax attained *Jewish* celebrity by casually honoring the Jewish religious tradition; Lenny Bruce turned traditional Jewish humor into modern social critique; Bob Dylan tried to evade Jewish identity while continuing to be seen as a Jew, evoking the paradox of assimilation; and Barbra Streisand made Jewishness fashionable. When American Jews look to these figures and other celebrity Jews, they see in them all the complexities and contradictions of their own experience of Jewish identity. Jewhooing is not merely reductive racializing, but a cultural expression evidencing the wide range of possibilities of Jewishness. At a time when religion often defines the public image of Jews, the practice of Jewhooing is a contrarian assertion of *ethnic* culture and identity. And as an ethnic behavior, it is itself a form of Jewish "memory," a project of cultural construction.

As I have already noted, the term *Jewish identity* came into widespread use in the early 1960s, a period when notions of Jewishness came to be contested in new ways. Social and cultural changes wrought by suburbanization, together with the rise of a new generation, set the stage for new forms of Jewish consciousness—just when the term *Jewish identity* came into more widespread use. The popularization of the phrase at that time suggests three basic shifts in the understanding of Jewishness. First, the very word *identity*[70] indicates a shift away from outward modes of Jewish identification—ethnic markers such as physical appearance, residential concentration, cultural practices, religious behavior, and institutional affiliation—to a more inward experience, to a "state of being" Jewish. In this sense, Jewish identity refers to the interiorization of Jewishness, the move from "doing Jewish" externally to "feeling Jewish" internally.

Second, the meaning of *Jewish* became evermore contested, as some Jews continued to identify through religious affiliation and behavior, while others moved toward a more secularized, ethnic form of Jewishness. Outwardly, suburbanizing Jews seemed to be reviving religious Judaism through their construction of new synagogues and emphasis on holiday observance. Yet as Will Herberg explained in his 1955 classic *Protestant, Catholic, Jew*, such seemingly religious behavior wasn't truly religiosity, but ethnic survivalism.[71] The main consequence of this shell game of identity was to further confuse the matter for American Jews—no longer thinking of their group identity in racial terms, they nonetheless continued to ask, were they Jews by religion or Jews by ethnicity? The term *Jewish identity*, indicating neither religious nor ethnic identification per se, reflects this state of confusion. Little wonder that social scientific studies of Jewish identity proliferated during this period.

Third, the popularization of Jewish identity marks a significant shift in our understanding of the immutability of Jewishness, or as cultural historian Stephen Whitfield phrased it, "the essentialism long entwined in Jewish identity."[72] Once Jewish identification is seen as an autonomous choice rather than an inherited and fixed definition of self, once the implicit claim of constructedness is made, Jewishness comes to be understood as fragmented, conditional, and changeable—and the phrase Jewish identity captures this amorphous quality well. By the 1960s, the experience of being Jewish in America was becoming ever more complicated and elusive. As playwright Daniel Goldfarb puts it, "Being Jewish provides endless confusion. It's not about going to shul or keeping kosher. If you are in the process of trying to figure out what it means that you're Jewish, then you're Jewish."[73] *Jewish identity*, then, associates to both a historical moment—the early 1960s—and a new form of Jewishness—one more conflicted, contested, and confused than that which came before. *Jewhooing the Sixties* attempts to clarify our understanding of the often perplexing nature of modern Jewish consciousness by viewing the subject of identity through the prism of celebrity.

The Early 1960s

As our discussions of celebrity and identity have indicated, the third major theme of this book is a historical period: the early part of the 1960s. In the popular mind, the decade of the 1960s has by now been thoroughly mythologized as *the Sixties*, an era of tumultuous social and political change. In academic history as well, the Sixties looms large as a period of broad cultural transformation whose galvanizing and polarizing effects have lasted to this day. Yet until recently, historians have rarely noted how integral a role American Jews played in the 1960s era.[74] Michael Staub's 2004 sourcebook, *The Jewish 1960s*, was among "the first to acknowledge the decade's significant Jewish dimension." And, playing on Lenny Bruce's famous distinction between Jewish and "goyish," Staub goes so far as to suggest that "the 1960s were *very* Jewish" as opposed to the goyish 1950s. He further argues the centrality of Jews in the Sixties, stating that "no other American decade during the twentieth century has been so strongly defined by Jewish-led and Jewish-sponsored social activism or so deeply informed and influenced by Jewish culture." He concludes by noting how the Sixties deeply affected Jews, in that "the very meaning and content of American Jewish identity went through a dramatic shift during the 1960s."[75] While demonstrating the critical relationship between Jews and the 1960s, Staub exhibits a common bias— his collection of sources overwhelmingly tilts toward the latter part of the decade. Except for several selections from the early years of the civil rights movement, the majority of sources come from the post-1965 era, especially the years following the Six Day War of 1967—coincidentally, also the height of the Sixties counterculture.

Indeed, the focus of most American Jewish historiography remains on the late 1960s and beyond, as conventional accounts of postwar American Jews almost universally cite 1967 as the genesis of a new Jewish consciousness, the beginning of a Jewish cultural revival. Jewish historians routinely point to the Six Day War as *the* watershed event in the contemporary history of American Jews; and in many ways it was, turning many toward renewed Jewish purpose. Typical are statements by Arthur Hertzberg: "After 1967 the Jews in America were freer, bolder, and more powerful than any community of Jews had ever been in the Diaspora"; Edward Shapiro: "Nineteen sixty-seven was a watershed year in the history of American Jewry"; and Jonathan Sarna: "The Six-Day War of June 1967 marked a turning point in the lives of many 1960s-era Jews . . . [striking] deep emotional chords among American Jews . . . [and] something of a spiritual revival washed over the American Jewish community after 1967."[76]

According to this conventional wisdom, the jolting trauma of Israel's near defeat and then miraculous victory unleashed a flood of emotions among Jews, sparking a new era of ethnic pride and religious revival. For more than half a century prior to 1967, so the narrative goes, American Jews were subject to the dominant strains of assimilation and acculturation. But following that historic rupture, the pendulum between Americanization and Jewish survival finally swung the other way. Jewish distinctiveness at last gained some greater acceptance in America, prompting many Jews to express their identity openly and assertively, and giving renewed energy to American Jewish life. For just as the Sixties counterculture spurred greater ethnic identification across the board— one need only recall slogans such as "Black is beautiful" and "Kiss me, I'm Irish"—so too would Jews emerge from the decade more Jewishly identified than before. The year 1967 is viewed as the pivotal moment in this development, due to the increased Jewish identification and activism following the Six Day War, and also to the advent of a communitarian Jewish youth culture, both principal manifestations of Jewish revival in the late 1960s and beyond.

And yet an equally compelling case can be made for a somewhat earlier turning point, of another kind altogether—premised not on the experience of a foreign war, but on cultural rumblings here at home. Although it is well established in general American history that the countercultural Sixties had its origins in the early 1960s and before, most histories of America's Jews pay relatively little attention to the first half of the decade. Until recently, only the occasional comment challenged this orthodoxy: for example, "The events of 1967 answered some questions that the mainstream of the community had been asking themselves for the several years before: how to define Jewishness in America's open society."[77] One of the few full-length works to claim the importance of the period is Kirsten Fermaglich's *American Dreams and Nazi Nightmares*. As Fermaglich compellingly argues, the several years around "the turn of the 1960s" ought to be appreciated as a discrete period, neither the popularly conceived 1950s nor the mythic 1960s, but rather "a bridge that transformed the quietism of the early McCarthy years into the angry radicalism that dominated headlines in 1968." Her book follows a trend in American history toward establishing a greater sense of continuity between the oft-contrasted eras. Fermaglich emphasizes the background of the Cold War and the civil rights movement, and further reviews the "political, intellectual, and cultural trends that made the years between 1957 and 1965 a distinct era": for example, "the rise of liberalism, and an upsurge in political radicalism," a "preoccupation with the dangers of mass society for individual autonomy," and a renewed "emphasis on universalism." More relevant to this discussion, she also notes a new "spirit of cultural transgression" characteristic of the time. Finally, she observes the "social transformations that integrated Jews more fully into a newly important academic and professional class"—such a significant shift in the social prominence of Jews in the early 1960s is basic to my argument as well.[78]

Here I will make a case for the importance of the early 1960s period in the history of American Jewish celebrity, and hence in the development of Jewish identity and Jewish life overall. On closer examination, we will see that a vanguard of American Jews in the period that Fermaglich calls "the turn of the 1960s" laid the groundwork for the post-1967 Jewish revival. That intermediary period began in the late 1950s with the demise of McCarthyist blacklisting and the rise of the civil rights movement. Both held profound implications for American Jews: McCarthyism had not only effectively quelled Jewish radicalism, but also inhibited other expressions of Jewish difference; and civil rights had deflected many Jews' attention away from more particularly Jewish concerns, while establishing a critical precedent for the revival of Jewish particularism in the years to come (also providing the model for a later movement of Jewish liberation, the campaign to rescue Soviet Jewry). The sense of new possibility—a "new frontier"—for outsider groups in this country reached its apogee with the presidential election in 1960. The examples of the black community and an Irish Catholic president both fighting for acceptance in America affected Jews in powerful ways—as evidenced by the heavy Jewish participation in both of these campaigns. Against this background, and spurred by developments internal to Jewish life as well—most critically, a burgeoning pride in Israel and an ever-increasing consciousness of the Holocaust—they began to reengage with their own Jewishness. Several years before the Six Day War, therefore, American Jews had already begun to recover a sharper sense of their common peoplehood. Both external and internal factors were at play, and change was in the air.

Perhaps the best indicator of this new tendency lay in the nexus of internal and external, the arena in which Jews aired their particular experience for a universal audience—the arena of popular culture. Shifting away from Staub's focus on Jewish politics and Fermaglich's interest in intellectual culture, *Jewhooing the Sixties* reveals how the Jewish ethnic revival of the post-1967 era had its roots in the popular culture of the early 1960s. In one of the great ironies of American Jewish history, the very cultural space in which so many Jews attempted to "make it" in America—show business—became the medium through which they injected an explicit Jewishness into the general culture, a development which then eased the way for other Jews to return to Jewish identification. As film critic and historian J. Hoberman comments, "[I]t's fair to say that popular culture plays a leading role in defining what being Jewish is for many American Jews."[79] Some of the pop cultural landmarks of the period include the Hollywood blockbuster film *Exodus* in 1960, the wildly popular song parody albums of Allan Sherman in 1962 and 1963, and the Broadway smash hit *Fiddler on the Roof* in 1964. Through its four studies of individual Jewish celebrities, this book explores four principal cultural arenas of the early 1960s: sports (as represented by Sandy Koufax), comedy (Lenny Bruce), popular music (Bob Dylan), and stage/film performance (Barbra Streisand). Yet as central as these figures and the areas they represent may have been to the creation of a new Jewish consciousness, the period saw several other relevant developments in popular culture as well, providing an essential context for this study of Jewish celebrity. So a brief summary of some of the main trends of the time is in order.

The first and perhaps most important element of the Jewish revivalism of the early 1960s was an increasing awareness of the Holocaust. As historians have now demonstrated, the production of Holocaust memory commenced early on. Historian Hasia Diner in particular has effectively debunked the myth of Jewish inattention to the Holocaust through the 1950s. As Diner describes at length, from the end of the war in 1945 and well before the term *Holocaust* entered popular usage, Jewish educators and leaders in numerous sectors of the community attempted as best they could to introduce the subject to their fellow Jews and, to a lesser extent, the general population.[80] But Holocaust education and commemoration within the Jewish community do not equate to mass consciousness. It was not until the turn of the 1960s that a broader awareness of the Holocaust pervaded the consciousness not only of Jews, but of the greater population—this in turn enabled a psychological shift whereby the Jewish minority was given greater license to engage with its own history *by virtue of* the engagement of the American majority.[81] It was a change that would only occur with the increasing appearance of Holocaust representation in popular culture, a trend climaxing at the turn of the 1960s.

The *Diary of Anne Frank* is a case in point. First published in English in 1952, it was dramatized on radio and on television later that same year. The stage version premiered on Broadway in 1955, Anne and her diary made the cover of *Life* magazine in 1958, and her story was ultimately made into a major Hollywood film in 1959, directed by George Stevens and starring Millie Perkins as Anne. In the role of Mrs. Van Daan, Jewish actress Shelley Winters won an Oscar for best supporting actress. Anne Frank had arrived in American popular culture, and we might even say that she had become a full-fledged American celebrity.[82] By 1963, one observer could state, "I move through a country where the secular sanctification of Anne Frank has been utterly astonishing."[83] And the Holocaust had penetrated the inner lives of far more Americans, especially Jewish Americans, as the result. In subsequent years, other Holocaust-themed films arrived, most notably *Exodus* (1960), *Judgment at Nuremberg* (1961), and *The Pawnbroker* (1965).[84]

As with the diary, however, Holocaust memory often first appeared in literary form. In 1959, a young Jewish writer named Philip Roth published his first book, *Goodbye, Columbus and Five Short Stories*, a collection that included "Eli, the Fanatic," the story of a suburban Jewish community confronted with the presence of a group of Holocaust survivors in its midst. Holocaust literature gained its seminal work when Elie Wiesel published an English edition of his memoir, *Night*, in 1960; and in the following year, Raul Hilberg published the first major history of the Nazi genocide, *The Destruction of the European Jews*.[85] Popular awareness of the Holocaust reached its apogee in 1961 with the trial of Adolf Eichmann in Jerusalem, a shattering, revelatory event for television viewers around the world.[86] In the United States, the event was echoed and further magnified by the December release of the film *Judgment at Nuremberg*. Stanley Kramer's star-studded dramatization of the American trial of Nazi war criminals would be nominated for Academy Awards for best picture and best director. As the first major Hollywood film to address the crime of the Holocaust in its totality, the film had a particularly galvanizing effect on American Jews.[87]

Concurrent with the rise in Holocaust consciousness, American Jews became evermore focused on the existence of Israel—again, a trend fostered by popular culture. In 1958, Leon Uris had published a riveting novel about the birth of the Jewish state. *Exodus* was an immediate bestseller, ranked number one for nineteen straight weeks, and ultimately sold over one million copies. The novel told the story of the Jewish underground resistance in British Mandate Palestine and its fight to establish the independent State of Israel. The images the book conveyed to an American public were of Jews hardened by historical circumstance and empowered as an unyielding fighting force—in stark contrast to the popular image of American Jews. Historian Deborah Dash Moore notes, "Its vision of the creation of the State of Israel influenced an entire generation of American Jews," and she quotes a book critic who explained its appeal as telling "a new kind of story about a *new kind of Jew*."[88] Similarly, journalist David Twersky remembered the impact of the best-selling book on his Bronx Jewish neighborhood and beyond: "*Exodus* became something of a watershed in the evolving cultural identity of American Jews. Before that, our cultural role models were brainy types like Louis Brandeis and Albert Einstein, clowns like Milton Berle and pampered arrivistes like the fictional Marjorie Morningstar. Uris invited us to identify with the warrior heroes who had created Israel. He taught us to stand tall."[89] And in the most exhaustive history of *Exodus* to date, M. M. Silver concludes, "Something fundamental changed among American Jews as a result of Uris's book. One heavy layer of inhibition about being 'too Jewish' was peeled away, and an articulated sense of connection with the state of Israel forever thereafter became part of the ethnic identity of the American Jew."[90]

Those who didn't read the book likely saw the film version of *Exodus* released on December 15, 1960—just a month after the barrier-breaking election of John F. Kennedy. A Hollywood movie about the post-Holocaust birth of Israel, its success proved to be a powerful demonstration of the acceptance of Jews in America. Directed and produced by the German-Jewish Otto Preminger and starring Paul Newman (whose father was Jewish), the film was a major hit and, perhaps even more so than the book, a cultural touchstone for American Jews. Central to the film's appeal was the performance of Newman as Ari Ben-Canaan, the archetypal *sabra*—the "new Jew" of modern Israel. In the role, Newman combined the dashing heroism of Errol Flynn with the angry intensity of James Dean—defining a new American masculinity ("new man") in his own right.

At the same time, Newman's character represented the Jewish objection to American universalism, a stubborn insistence on cultural survival and group difference. The key moment in this regard was a scene between Newman's Ben-Canaan and his American love interest, the very blonde and very gentile Kitty, played by Eva Marie Saint. Showing Kitty the biblical landscape, Ben-Canaan proclaims, "I just wanted you to know I'm a Jew. This is *my* country." Saint's character replies with a typically American sentiment: "All these differences between people are made up. People are the same no matter what they're called." To which Newman emphatically responds: "Don't ever believe it. People are different. They have a right to be different. They *like* to be different. It's no good pretending that differences don't exist. They do. They have to be recognized and respected."[91] The exchange echoed the classic dialectic between "melting pot" assimilationism and cultural pluralism, and Newman's words prefigured the growing ethnic pride and communal confidence of American Jews.

In the 1950s, such a staunch defense of ethnic pluralism and the preservation of identity was not yet commonplace among American Jews. But in the wake of the electrifying election of JFK and the popular success of *Exodus*—and several years before the Six Day War—the early 1960s would see the stirrings of a new consciousness, reflected by two intersecting trends: the elevation of many talented and ambitious young

Jews to new heights of success (and therefore celebrity), and a remark-able change in the nature of public Jewish expression. Regarding the former, Roth would state in late 1960, "I find that I am suddenly living in a country in which the Jew has come to be—or is allowed for now to think he is—a cultural hero."[92] As to the latter phenomenon, Leslie Fiedler could write in 1963, "There has occurred a Judaization of Ameri-can culture which is beyond belief."[93]

Both Jews and Jewishness had dramatically entered the realm of American culture. The interrelation of the two trends is evidenced by the following statement by Lenny Bruce, one of the four figures profiled in this book, and a perfect illustration himself of the nexus between Amer-ican popular culture and Jewish celebrity. In his monthly column for *Rogue* magazine, Bruce noted the tendency toward a more pronounced public Jewishness as early as March of 1960—prior to both the JFK election and the *Exodus* movie:

> Well, fortunately, by some twist of Fate it's becoming "in" to be Jewish. Sammy Davis Jr., started it and now all the hippies dig it . . . Even Baby Doll Carroll Baker and Elizabeth Taylor. Even the Vikings were Jewish: Tony Curtis and Kirk Douglas. The only Gentile was Ernest Borgnine, and he got killed. To quote one of the most brilliant comedians of all time, Irwin Corey, "I play Jewish chess. We use Rabbis instead of Bishops." Seriously, though, even the best-sellers in books are Jewish, such as *Exodus* and *Only in America*. And the best Broadway shows like Paddy Chayefsky's *Tenth Man* are Jewish. The capper is a Jewish repertory company in Los Angeles that did a Yiddish version of *My Fair Lady*. A YIDDISH *My Fair Lady*! I can't wait to see it. I know I'll flip when I hear Eliza Doolittle's old man sing, "Get Me to the Shul on Time."[94]

By humorously observing how "in" it was to be Jewish at the turn of the 1960s, Bruce inadvertently contextualized his own performance of Jewish identity. In so doing, he quite rightly pointed to popular culture— film, comedy, literature, and theater—as the media fomenting the trend. What all had in common was the celebrity personage embodying the newly acceptable Jewishness. Intriguingly, Bruce points to the stars of the 1958 film *The Vikings* to illustrate the point—in the film, Kirk Douglas and Tony Curtis played Viking warriors Einar and Eric, the "Mightiest Of Men." Bruce found this amusing because the actors' actual back-grounds belied this image of machismo—Douglas and Curtis had grown up as Jewish kids named Izzy Demsky (born Issur Danielovitch) and Ber-nie Schwartz. Neither were new on the scene, however, as both had been movie stars since the early 1950s (their film debuts were in 1946 and 1949 respectively). What changed in the early 1960s was not the popular success of such Jewish celebrities, but rather their observable Jewishness and hence the willingness of others to point it out—or perhaps it was the other way around. In either event, Bruce's citing of these Jewish movie stars marked a new trend in Jewish celebrity consciousness. It wasn't entirely new, of course, as jazz critic and radical journalist Nat Hentoff recalls: "When I was a boy in the 1930s, a recurrent source of neighborhood pride was the high percentage of reigning comedians who were Jews—Jack Benny, Joe Penner, Milton Berle, Eddie Cantor, George Burns, among them." But note, Hentoff made that statement in 1961.[95]

As Bruce also noted, the dawn of a new age of Jewish celebrity in the early 1960s was foreshadowed by an extraordinary turn of events during the 1950s: the highly publicized Jewish conversions of several popular stars. In an era when most Hollywood Jews sought to avoid public Jewish identification, some high-profile non-Jews actually joined the fold by converting to Judaism. The famous new recruits were Carroll Baker, who converted in 1955, Marilyn Monroe in 1956, Elizabeth Taylor in 1959, and Sammy Davis Jr. in 1960—together, very publicly suggesting that Jewish identification was a respectable and acceptable option for all. Of course, starlets Baker, Monroe, and Taylor converted expressly for the purpose of marrying Jewish men (Jack Garfein, Arthur Miller, and Eddie Fisher respectively), so their newfound Jewishness should be read primarily as an endorsement of such marital choice—and we are led to wonder whether their examples may have helped prompt the later dramatic rise in the rate of intermarriage.

In the 1950s, such rarified Jewish matings were more harbingers of the future than signs of the times.[96] Yet because they took place on the public stage of celebrity, the Hollywood conversions most certainly made a strong impression on American Jews of the time. They demonstrated that Jewish identity was something that could be chosen, adopted, put on like an article of clothing, thereby undermining the ethnic essentialism that had prevailed in previous Jewish generations. The conversions of Monroe, Taylor, and others ought to be seen therefore as more than just an adumbration of the later Jewish revival—they may very well have contributed to its emergence. In evidence of what he called the "Judaization of American culture," Fiedler marveled: "I live in a country which has witnessed the strange conversions to Judaism of the mythical, erotic figures we see on the screen, Marilyn Monroe and Elizabeth Taylor."[97]

In the late 1950s, Jewish periodicals began assigning reporters to cover Jewish celebrities, most notably writer Herbert G. Luft of the Jewish Telegraphic Agency. Under the byline "Our Film Folk," Luft profiled Jewish film and comedy stars such as Jerry Lewis, Mort Sahl, and Danny Kaye.[98] In a 1959 column titled "The Jewishness of Eddie Fisher," he details the singing star's recent marriage to Taylor, and describes a Fisher performance in Las Vegas: "Eddie brought the house down with his rendition of 'Hava Nagila' done in perfect Hebrew, a medley of Al Jolson numbers and finally Eddie Cantor's 'Whoopee.'" Luft further assures his readers that "for the first time in public, [Fischer] referred proudly to his Jewishness." In his interview with Fisher, Luft interrogates the star's turn toward Jewish identification and prompts Fisher to cite "three specific factors that inspired his religious fervor in recent years, though he wants the readers of this column to know that he has always regarded himself as a good Jew." The three factors were "first and foremost his trip to Israel in July of 1957 . . . Second, there came his friendship of three years with Rabbi Max Nussbaum; and last, not least, the impact of Leon Uris' *Exodus* which made Eddie Fisher proudly confess in song and words, 'I Am a Jew.'"[99] Left unstated is the influence that public interest in the Jewishness of stars, as expressed by this Jewhooing reporter and his readership, may have had as well.

The turn of the 1960s would see the emergence of numerous other Jewish public personalities, together hailing a new era of ethnic acceptance in America. Lenny Bruce's biographer, Albert Goldman, asserted a connection between Holocaust/Israel consciousness and the efflorescence of Jewish celebrity, and would go so far as to call the 1960s "the Jewish Decade," explaining,

> Overnight, the Jew was raised from his traditional role of underdog or invisible man to the glory of being the most fascinating authority in America. Benefiting from universal guilt over the murders by the Nazis, stiffening into fresh pride over the achievements of the State, Israel, reaping the harvest in America of generations of hard work and sacrifice for the sake of the "children," the Jews burst suddenly into prominence in a dozen different areas of national life. They became the new heroes of commerce, art, and intellect. They scaled the social heights.[100]

A new generation of talented Jews was entering the fray of American culture in the early 1960s, together attracting the bright glare of celebrity. In politics, for example, the Kennedy administration included several prominent Jews, most notably Secretary of Labor Arthur Goldberg and Health, Education and Welfare (HEW) Secretary Abraham Ribicoff. The two were not just of Jewish origin, but were as often noted "Jewish Jews," sons of East European immigrants with recognizable Jewish names.[101] Goldberg, who was shortly appointed to the Supreme Court and ultimately became US Ambassador to the United Nations, was highlighted in a 1966 sermon by one prominent Reform rabbi:

> In America in the 1960's one need not accept the testimony of rabbis as evidence of the amazing record of American Jewry . . . What has taken place is astonishing, even in America, where we are accustomed to remarkable success stories . . . Even political life, although hardly a Jewish province, has seen a substantial Jewish contribution, especially in the judicial area. The son of a Jewish immigrant peddler represents the United States in the United Nations. As if to dot the last "I" and cross the last "T," the 1960's have brought us not only Goldberg in the U.N., but Koufax on the mound.[102]

Beyond politics, noteworthy careers in several other areas of the culture also had their start in the early 1960s. In television journalism, for example, Barbara Walters started her career at NBC's *Today Show*, and David Susskind's local talk show *Open End* (later renamed the *David Susskind Show*) went national—both in 1961. Mike Wallace, already an established television personality, began hosting the CBS Morning News two years later. In popular music, Mitch Miller first appeared on television as the host of the *Sing Along With Mitch* show in 1961, and in the following year Herb Alpert made his first Tijuana Brass recording, *The Lonely Bull*. Also in 1961, the *Joey Bishop Show* first aired on television and Neil Simon staged his first Broadway play, *Come Blow Your Horn*. All of these individuals were born in the quarter-century from 1910 to 1935; they came of age during World War II, and began their careers in the decades following. Though all were Jews, Jewishness played little if any role in their public lives. Politics, journalism, television, and other public media were not yet accommodating to overt ethnicity.

Likewise, Hollywood films of this period still did not treat explicit Jewishness very often—unless the setting was ancient Palestine or modern-day Israel. But in films set in contemporary America, Jewishness was nonetheless introduced thematically—through the metaphor of the alienated outsider. In Hollywood movies of the early 1960s, the director's chair was often filled by a Jewish auteur, while the projection of filmic manhood, the movie hero (or antihero), was often played by a Jewish star. Through these screen images, a new American man was envisioned for the American public. The trend was epitomized by Jewish directors such as Stanley Kubrick and Martin Ritt; and by Jewish movie stars such as Paul Newman and Kirk Douglas. Almost as a rule, the main theme of these films would be the travails of the alienated outsider. This was already a central Hollywood theme of the 1950s, in such memorable works as *On the Waterfront* (1954), *Rebel Without a Cause* (1955), and *Marty* (1955). With the arrival of a new generation of Jewish directors at decade's end, the theme took on added resonance. In 1958, for example, Stanley Kramer made *The Defiant Ones* with Tony Curtis (and Sidney Poitier), and Richard Brooks made *Cat on a Hot Tin Roof* with Newman. In the following year, Billy Wilder wrote and directed the comedy classic *Some Like It Hot*, with Curtis (and Marilyn Monroe); and in 1960, the same year as *Exodus*, Kubrick directed the historical epic *Spartacus*, starring both Douglas and Curtis.

As the new decade progressed, these contemporary Jewish directors became keenly interested in the changing mores of their time. Hence Kubrick gave us two more classics with *Lolita* (1962) and *Dr. Strangelove* (1964), both starring Peter Sellers (who, like Newman, had one Jewish parent). Another Jewish auteur deeply affected by his Cold War context was John Frankenheimer, who made *The Manchurian Candidate* (1962) with Laurence Harvey (a Lithuanian-born Jew), and *Seven Days in May* (1964) with Kirk Douglas. Yet another notable director of the period was Sidney Lumet, who gave us *Fail-Safe* (1964) with Walter Matthau, and *The Pawnbroker* (1965) with Rod Steiger, a non-Jew playing the part of a Jewish Holocaust survivor. Martin Ritt made several films with Paul Newman, including *Paris Blues* (1961), *Hud* (1963), *The Outrage* (1964), and *Hombre* (1967). *The Outrage*, a western remake of Akira Kurasawa's *Rashomon*, had the unique distinction of an all-Jewish cast, including Edward G. Robinson, Claire Bloom, Howard Da Silva, Laurence Harvey, and William Shatner in addition to Newman. And the list goes on, with Jewish-directed Newman vehicles such as Robert Rossen's *The Hustler* (1961), Richard Brooks's *Sweet Bird of Youth* (1962), and Stuart Rosenberg's *Cool Hand Luke* (1967). The pivotal year of 1967 also yielded the film epitomizing "the alienated young man as seen through Jewish eyes" genre: *The Graduate*, directed by Mike Nichols (born Peschkowsky), written by Buck Henry (born Zuckerman), scored by Paul Simon, and starring Dustin Hoffman. Critic J. Hoberman posits Nichols's hit film as initiator of a trend in Hollywood film that he calls the "Jewish new wave," lasting from 1967 to 1972. But as a film that only hints at the Jewishness of its protagonist, *The Graduate* belongs as much to the preceding period of the early 1960s.[103]

Notwithstanding the reluctance of television and film to be "too Jewish," more explicit evocations of Jewishness did begin to appear in some other areas of American culture. As often observed, the 1950s had seen the entry of a cadre of Jewish writers into the literary arena—Saul Bellow, J. D. Salinger, Bernard Malamud, Norman Mailer, and so on—but only at the turn of the 1960s would many of them begin to engage with explicitly Jewish themes. The best-known example is Philip Roth, who published his first collection of short stories and a novella, *Goodbye, Columbus*, in 1959. In that same year, Herman Wouk—who had previously written novels with Jewish characters (*The Caine Mutiny* in 1951 and *Marjorie Morningstar* in 1955)—offered a very personal work of nonfiction titled *This is My God: The Jewish Way of Life*. Two years later, Leon Uris followed up his epic of Israel's history with a Holocaust-themed novel, *Mila 18*, a dramatization of the Warsaw ghetto uprising. A war story of another sort, Joseph Heller's *Catch-22* also came out in 1961—though its main character, Yossarian, was identified as Assyrian, its absurdist humor was unmistakably Jewish (Heller's giving the character as obscure an ethnicity as Assyrian is a Jewish joke itself).

Poet Allen Ginsberg contributed to the trend with a poem written in memory of his mother, titled "Kaddish"—after the Jewish prayer of mourning. Composed between 1957 and 1960, and published in 1961 as the lead in the collection *Kaddish and Other Poems 1958–1960*,[104] it is recognized as one of Ginsberg's finest works and his best-known poem after "Howl." Coincidentally or not, musical composer Leonard Bernstein followed with his own *Kaddish*, his third symphony, begun in the summer of 1961 and finished in 1963; after its completion, he dedicated it to the memory of the slain JFK.[105] But back to literature per se: in 1962, Bruce Jay Friedman published *Stern*, the first of his eight novels; and in 1963, Malamud included a story titled "The Jewbird" in a collection of his works. In that year, Bellow edited *Great Jewish Short Stories*, in which he anthologized the works of Aleichem, Peretz, Agnon, Singer, and other classic Jewish writers together with the American newcomers Malamud, Roth, Grace Paley, and so on—making the point that the new crop of American writers were heirs to a longer-standing tradition of Jewish letters. Not insignificantly, in the following year, 1964, Bellow published his first novel with a Jewish name, *Herzog*. All told, the vaunted incursion of Jews into American literature took a decidedly more Jewish turn at the start of the 1960s.

Beyond literature, Jewishness came to the fore during the early 1960s in a more popular arena of American culture: comedy. As Fiedler noted, "I turn on radio or television and I hear Jewish comics—Jewish American comics, let's say—bringing to the great multitudes the kind of humor which was built by the Jews at the point of ultimate desperation."[106] The history of American Jews and comedy in the postwar period can be summarized by noting two successive stages: the move from the ethnically segregated "Borscht Belt" circuit into the mainstream by numerous Jewish comedians during the 1950s; followed by the injection of an explicit Jewishness into their comedy beginning at the turn of the 1960s—a trend more apparent in some comedic media than in others. Perhaps the most popular format was the comedy record album, as surveyed in a recent book by Roger Bennett and Josh Kun. Simply by recovering the lost world of Jewish recordings and record covers, Bennett and Kun have made a remarkable contribution. But their study also inadvertently highlights the early 1960s—for many, if not most, items in their collection date to what seems, in retrospect, a golden age of Jewish-themed record albums. Of the hundreds of titles they list, many are dated "c. 1960." Those with a more certain date include *Connie Francis Sings Jewish Favorites* (1960); Juan Calle and his Latin Lantzmen's *Mazel Tov, Mis Amigos* (1961); Marv Kurtz's *Sing-along in Yiddish* (1962); the Barry Sisters' *Shalom* (1962) and their live recording *The Barry Sisters in Israel* (1963); *Shlomo Carlebach at the Village Gate* (1963); Joey Adams and Sholom Secunda's *Jewish Folk Songs* (1964); Effi Netzer and Regina Zarai's *Folk Dance in Israel Today* (1965); and Zero Mostel's *Songs My Mother Never Sang* (1966).[107]

In addition to telling the story of Jewish musical recordings of the time, the co-editors also devote a chapter to "the vinyl world of comedy."[108] Their story begins with the "milestone" 1959 album *Inside Shelley Berman*, which, according to Bennett and Kun, "was the first solo comedy LP to go gold and become a major national hit."[109] Berman had been preceded by the prolific Mickey Katz, but a key distinction between them was popular, crossover success. As Herbert Gans points out, "The Jewish underground culture has traditionally been created only for in-group consumption, as in the case of Mickey Katz, whose parodies were originally recorded on RCA's foreign language label."[110] Whereas Katz had a devoted audience of urban Jews, Berman and those who followed managed to project their Jewish humor (and neuroses) into the general realm of American popular culture—somehow, that is, they "played in Peoria."

Comedy will be discussed at greater length in my chapter on Lenny Bruce, but two prominent examples of the Jewish comedy album trend ought to be noted here: Mel Brooks and Carl Reiner's *The 2,000 Year Old Man* (1961) and Allan Sherman's *My Son, the Folk Singer* (1962). Both had their origins in the 1950s, when Brooks, Reiner, and Sherman would perform their patently ethnic material at private parties; and both were emblematic of the new trend toward public Jewishness in the early 1960s. Brooks and Reiner have often recalled how they believed the material would appeal only to fellow Jews (and sympathetic gentiles) and never to a broader audience. But then, prodded by show business personalities George Burns, Edward G. Robinson, and Steve Allen, Brooks and Reiner were persuaded to put the informal routine on record—and the rest is history, as the bit became a hit. Brooks's 2,000-year-old man channeled the quintessential *alter kocker* (Yiddish term for an old-timer), speaking in a thick New York Jewish accent and complaining about his thousands of children who "never once come to visit!" As he later recalled, the character was in reality "the East European immigrant Jew," and in his Yiddish-inflected characterization, he "was doing [his] grandparents."[111] Reiner, playing the straight-man role of interviewer, represented the assimilated younger generation, and though not recognizably Jewish himself, his polished cadences helped to set off Brooks's accented ethnicity all the more. Despite, or perhaps because of, this explicit Jewishness, the record was a runaway success and made instant celebrities of Reiner and Brooks in the early 1960s.

One year later, Sherman became an overnight sensation as well. In good Jewish humor, his recording of song parodies was titled *My Son, the Folk Singer* (a spoof of the Jewish parent's favorite claim: "my son, the doctor"). Released in October 1962, it included such clever send-ups as "The Ballad of Harry Lewis" (to the tune of "The Battle Hymn of the Republic"), "Sarah Jackman" ("Frère Jacques"), and "Seltzer Boy" ("Water Boy"), all descriptive of contemporary Jewish life in America, with lyrics full of Jewish references. In "Shake Hands With Your Uncle Max," Sherman lists all the Jewish-sounding names in his old Brooklyn neighborhood. In "Sir Greenbaum's Madrigal," his not-so-chivalrous knight laments, "That's no job for a boy who is Jewish." And in a wicked parody of Harry Belafonte's "Matilda" called "My Zelda," he sings, "Oh, why did she go and fall in love / I haven't seen her since Tisha B'ov." Like Reiner and Brooks, Sherman had been concerned that the material was "too Jewish." Yet his hit albums of the early 1960s dispelled the anxiety—his Jewishly flavored tunes became so widely popular, even President Kennedy was a fan. In dazed wonderment, Sherman relates in his autobiography how "my son, the [blank]" became a catchphrase across the country, how Kennedy was overheard singing "Sarah Jackman" (later telling Sherman in person, "I've got your record and I like it very much"), and how a Harvard graduate student's thesis explaining the record's success was that "all over America people were expressing their secret wish to be Jewish."[112]

The apotheosis of the Judaizing trend—now combining literature, theater, music, dance, and comedy—was the 1964 Broadway production of *Fiddler on the Roof*. The first musical theater production to employ Jewish themes explicitly, not merely as subtext, *Fiddler* opened in September of that year and went on to become one of the most popular Broadway shows of all time, and moreover, the epitome of American Jewish nostalgia.[113] Its creators, Sheldon Harnick and Jerry Bock, had begun shopping it around in 1961, understandably worried that it would be received as "too Jewish"—in fact, one producer famously turned them down by wondering who would come after the Hadassah groups. But then, with choreography by Jerome Robbins and starring Zero Mostel, the musical opened on September 22, 1964, to widespread public acclaim. Any question of the acceptability and appeal of its Jewish subject matter was soon dispelled as the hit Broadway musical ran for over 3,000 performances, winning nine Tony Awards in the process. Apparently, something in the culture had shifted between 1961 and 1964.

The cause of the shift is complex, of course, but one factor stands out above all. In addition to the cultural developments discussed earlier, and beyond the move of many notable Jews into American popular culture, the early 1960s saw the merging of the two trends into a new type of Jewish celebrity—now embodying both Jewish social success *and* the public expression of Jewishness. Emerging during a period of heightened emotions and perceptions, their celebrity would be further magnified by the expanded role of the media and the ever-increasing acuity of the public eye. But it was Jewish celebrity with a difference: though Jews were well represented in American popular culture before then, only rarely had an acknowledged Jewishness been so pronounced a part of their public personae. Collectively, they represented the first time that Jews—recognizable as such—indelibly engraved themselves into the American consciousness as *both* fully-fledged Americans and ethnically identifiable Jews.

No longer reflecting the tension, but now embodying a synthesis, this was nothing less than a paradigm shift in the American Jewish experience. Several years before the dramatic events of June 1967, therefore, a newly assertive Jewishness had already entered the American public sphere, fostered by the radical notion that one could succeed in America, could become an insider—*as* an outsider, that is, while retaining one's identity as a Jewish *other*. This pointed message was conveyed by a specific medium: the public images and popular representations of certain famous Jews—well-known figures who were well known to be Jewish. There are numerous representative figures, including Woody Allen, Leonard Bernstein, Theodore Bikel, Mel Brooks, Shlomo Carlebach, Howard Cosell, Neil Diamond, Jules Feiffer, Betty Friedan, Allen Ginsberg, Arthur Goldberg, Buddy Hackett, Nat Hentoff, Jackie Mason, Zero Mostel, Don Rickles, Joan Rivers, Philip Roth, Neil Sedaka, Beverly Sills, Shel Silverstein, Neil Simon, Allan Sherman, David Susskind, Barbara Walters, Elie Wiesel, and others. All of them exemplified contemporary American Jewish celebrity, and all emerged in the early 1960s.

Sandy, Lenny, Bob, and Barb

Of the new Jewish celebrities of the period, four stand out for both their archetypal fame and their cultural influence. Like John F. Kennedy, Martin Luther King Jr., Elvis Presley, and Marilyn Monroe on the general scene, postwar American Jewish culture had its own Mount Rushmore of fame—four celebrated individuals who made their impact on American life, but also impressed themselves on the Jewish psyche. Caught in the spotlight of history, their idealized lives and pathbreaking personae may be read as key "texts" in the narrative of American Jewish life. They are baseball pitcher Sandy Koufax, comedian Lenny Bruce, folk/rock musician Bob Dylan, and film/musical star Barbra Streisand.

Just as Presley, Monroe, Kennedy, and King had reshaped American society and culture through their iconic fame, so too would Dylan, Streisand, Koufax, and Bruce reshape the image of the American Jew. Through these figures' public lives, Americans saw a new kind of Jew, and Jews saw themselves projected into the consciousness of all Americans. These four possessed something few before them had—extraordinary success in the American arena and, at the same time, identifiable public profiles as Jews. To varying degrees and in sometimes contrasting ways, these figures evinced a newly explicit Jewishness. All four rose to prominence in the early 1960s; all became extremely famous in their respective fields; all had some measure of publicly acknowledged Jewish identity; and all four thereafter became icons of American Jewish culture.

At the same time, each embodied a distinct and idiosyncratic celebrity persona. Akin to Kennedy, Koufax was an outsider in his profession, embodying the cool masculinity of the Hollywood antihero. Like King,

Bruce harnessed the power of the spoken word and was a fearless challenger of the status quo, martyred in the course of upturning the culture in defense of freedom. Echoing Presley, Dylan used music to shake up the world, and modeled a radical style of personal rebellion to a new generation of American youth. And after the fashion of Monroe, Streisand redefined beauty, femininity, and female stardom for her era. All had a more "primitive" identity preceding and underlying their public personae—Kennedy the wealthy Irish Catholic, King the southern black preacher, Presley the hillbilly trucker, and Monroe the brunette Norma Jean. Koufax, Bruce, Dylan, and Streisand, on the other hand, were all Jews.

And yet the four represented Jewishness in very different ways. Koufax was a secular, "cultural" Jew who ironically became a religious symbol, idolized by other Jews for his casually inadvertent observance of a religious holiday. Bruce was an assimilated and iconoclastic soul whose outsider's interest in religion led to polemical tirades against its manifest contradictions, as well as to comedic routines exploring the complexities of Jewish identity. Dylan did his best to hide his ethnic roots for the first three years of his career, but after being exposed as a Jew named Zimmerman in November of 1963, he came to personify Jewish assimilation and the lack of a fixed identity, Jewish or otherwise. Streisand turned her conspicuous ethnicity to her advantage, playing up the stereotype of the brash Brooklyn Jew during her early career, helping to create a new model of Jewish womanhood in the process. Together, the four became archetypes for emergent forms of Jewish identification in post-1960s America.

OUR FIRST CELEBRITY STUDY, profiled in Chapter 2, is Sandy Koufax. Born in 1935, Koufax was a "nice Jewish boy" from Brooklyn who happened to be athletically gifted. Well before his celebrated refusal to pitch on the high holidays of 1965, he had become a Jewish icon for his superhuman ability on the mound as well as his gentlemanly demeanor off the field. Though he had been a major leaguer since 1955, it was not until spring training of 1961 that Koufax finally found his pitching form—and a new Jewish star appeared on the horizon. In the view of baseball fans, he became one of the all-time great players in the history of the game. In the eyes of his many Jewish fans, he came to embody a new model of American Jew—identifiably and unashamedly Jewish, yet suave, well mannered, and deeply respected at the same time. Yet the so-called "super Jew" had his areas of vulnerability. From early on, Koufax was criticized for being intellectual and aloof, for not being "one of the guys." Retiring early due to a sore pitching arm, he briefly tried broadcasting, but ultimately retreated into what seemed to many a Greta Garbo–like isolation, a futile attempt to escape his celebrity. Yet Jews especially would never forget him, and he remains an iconic figure without peer.

Chapter 3 engages another darkly handsome Jewish boy, Lenny Bruce, who developed a less savory reputation. Where Koufax was the archetypal good Jew, Bruce came to represent just the opposite. Annointed "king of the sick comics" by *Time* magazine in 1959, Bruce attained fame as a comic provocateur and transgressor of social norms. In retrospect, he is considered by many to have been one of the most influential performers in American cultural history, and, as a martyr to the cause of freedom of expression, a key inspiration for the cultural revolutions of the later 1960s. Less well known is his role in changing the public expression of Jewishness in America. Alone among 1950s standup comedians, Bruce introduced into his performances the subject of being Jewish. By ignoring the unwritten rule not to speak of Jewishness openly, and thus subverting the "too Jewish" taboo, Bruce helped tweak the new Jewish identity of his generation. On the downside, his commitment to obscenity may be linked to his Jewishness as well, as a recent PhD dissertation argues—hence the antisemitic epithet "dirty Jew" suits him all too well. Yet his place in the history of American Jewish comedy is assured, as is his role in the history of the Sixties. Unquestionably, therefore, Bruce deserves his place alongside Koufax in the pantheon of American Jewish icons—Koufax, the "good Jew" who held the line of Jewish difference as Jews' assimilation in America reached new heights; and Bruce, the "bad Jew" who, come to think of it, did the same.

Chapter 4 moves from the "dirty Jew" to the "wandering Jew." On the same day as Bruce's first arrest, a music review appeared in the *New York Times*. Written by critic Robert Shelton, it heralded "a bright new face in folk music." The article was titled "Bob Dylan: A Distinctive Folk-Song Stylist," and it was the first public notice of the man who would become his generation's muse, Irving Berlin and Elvis Presley rolled into one. Among other things, the review notes a comic number Dylan often performed, called "Talkin' Havah Nagilah"—Shelton offhandedly remarks that by it, the singer was lampooning himself. That's as close as Shelton or anyone else would come to identifying the twenty-year-old Dylan as a Jew. Like Bruce, who was born Leonard Alfred Schneider, Dylan had changed his Jewish name upon entering show business. Yet the former Robert Zimmerman had no intention of acknowledging his heritage, and kept his identity hidden until November 1963, when *Newsweek* magazine outed him in an infamous article. Thereafter, Dylan became a Jewish icon despite himself; and, like both Koufax and Bruce, he modeled a new form of Jewish identity—his based on fierce individualism and resistance to being defined by anyone else's norms. Dylan's relation to Jewish identity may be the most enigmatic of our group, as he consistently shied away from any fixed identity throughout his protean career. It may well be this challenge to the very notion of identity that constitutes Dylan's contribution to the ever-evolving identity of American Jews.

Chapter 5 explores the extraordinary celebrity of the one woman in the group. Like her contemporary Dylan, Streisand also refused to conform to the expectations of others; in her case, however, she did so with an unabashedly Jewish demeanor. Also like Dylan, she invented fanciful origins at first, claiming to have been born in Burma or in Turkey. Yet unlike Dylan's more extreme deception, Streisand then added the more truthful information that she had attended Erasmus Hall high school in Brooklyn. First attracting notice in Greenwich Village nightclubs in the spring of 1960, by the following year she was appearing regularly on Mike Wallace's television program *PM East*. Then, in November 1961, just as Dylan was recording his first album for Columbia Records, nineteen-year-old Streisand was cast in her first role on Broadway, playing Miss Marmelstein in *I Can Get It for You Wholesale*. Dylan had attained fame by masking his Jewishness—"Einstein disguised as Robin Hood," according to his own lyrical imagery—whereas Streisand would claim her celebrity through a series of explicitly Jewish impersonations, from Fanny Brice to Yentl to, most recently, Ben Stiller's Jewish mother in the 2004 and 2010 film sequels *Meet the Fockers* and *Little Fockers*. Not only on stage and screen, but also in the celebrity persona she projected to the public, Streisand represented herself as a "nice Jewish girl" from Brooklyn. In this sense, she may truly be described as the quintessential "Hollywood Jew," performing Jewishness in what is perhaps the greatest performance American show business has yet seen. Thus, what Streisand shares with Koufax, Bruce, and Dylan is a refusal to play by the established rules of American Jewish identity. Instead, these four created their own rules, and helped usher in a new era for all American Jews.

In 1966, Koufax retired from baseball due to a sore arm. Bruce died tragically of a drug overdose. Dylan had a motorcycle accident and disappeared from public view. Streisand had a baby, moved to Hollywood, and began to make movies. In the very next year, a Jewish revival began. Coincidence? Well, yes, but still, it is clear that we cannot **47**

48 properly understand the Jewish revival of the late 1960s without more carefully reviewing and analyzing the prior period, when these four Jewish stars shot across the horizon of American popular culture. Koufax was a sports star whose American Jewish celebrity rested in large part on his reputation for religious loyalty—yet neither his sports success nor his legendary no-show on Yom Kippur had very much meaningful Jewish content, as we shall see. Bruce was a famous comedian whose American Jewish celebrity was mitigated by his reputation as a dangerous character, certainly not a fitting role model—nevertheless, he did serve as an important model for a generation of young Jews (especially for Jewish hippies and comedians). And, unlike Koufax's, Bruce's career had significant Jewish content; as we shall further explore, Bruce plumbed a deep well of Jewish material in his seminal work as a pioneer of Jewish stand-up comedy. Both Dylan and Streisand were major musical talents whose American Jewish celebrity is more complex than might first seem apparent. Dylan changed his name and invented himself anew, leaving little room for Jewish identity in any sense, yet the remarkable amount of Jewishness projected onto him suggests that there may be more here than meets the eye. Streisand's celebrity may be opposite—whereas she is understandably read as very Jewish, both in life and in her art, at least some measure of this overt identification may be instrumental, that is, not entirely "authentic."

In sum, the four represent the vagaries of identity among American Jews of the baby-boom generation. Throughout this study, all four will be seen to be emblematic of American celebrity, just as all four exemplified the reconceptualization of Jewish identity in the early 1960s. Seen together, their American Jewish celebrity has much to tell us about America and its Jews. To quote yet another culture-hero of the era, "Now vee may perhaps to begin—yes?"[114]

Super Jew

Sandy Koufax! The closest thing to a Jewish messiah since Jesus! There isn't a young Jewish male out there that wasn't regaled to the tales of the great Koufax. Unhittable as a pitcher. Unimpeachable as a Jew (he didn't play on Yom Kippur, donchaknow). Does there even need to be a discussion?

JEW OR NOT JEW WEBSITE

At 4:27 p.m. on May 27, 2010, the president of the United States strode to the podium of the East Room to welcome a select group of Jewish notables to the White House. In his opening remarks, President Obama singled out one guest in particular:

> THE PRESIDENT: (Applause.) Thank you so much. It is wonderful to see all of you, and I am proud to welcome you to the first ever event held at the White House to honor Jewish American Heritage Month. (Applause.) This is a pretty, pretty fancy group here, pretty distinguished group. We've got senators and representatives. We've got Supreme Court justices and successful entrepreneurs, rabbinical scholars, Olympic athletes—and Sandy Koufax.[1]

It was a terrific line, garnering both laughter and applause—as did the joke the president then added: "Sandy and I actually have something in common—we are both lefties. He can't pitch on Yom Kippur; I can't pitch."[2] Without doubt, all assembled understood the reference to Koufax's main claim to Jewish fame; as journalist Debra Rubin noted, the former baseball star was "a hero to many in the Jewish community for his refusal to pitch on Yom Kippur [during the World Series of 1965]." In her article "Koufax Wows White House Reception," Rubin observes **49** how Koufax's celebrity outshone even Obama's: "Forget the president. Baseball great Sandy Koufax was the draw at Thursday afternoon's White House reception in honor of Jewish American Heritage Month. Those attending swarmed Koufax . . . and he was the only guest President Barack Obama singled out in his remarks."[3]

The White House also gave Koufax an honored place in the assembly, seating him immediately next to the president in a front row including First Lady Michelle Obama, Vice President Joe Biden, Supreme Court justices Ruth Bader Ginsburg and Stephen Breyer, Senator Arlen Specter (who had co-authored the bill instituting Jewish American Heritage Month), and Theodore Bikel. All in all, it was a remarkable display of favoritism, highlighting the unique celebrity of Sandy Koufax. The president's privileging of the pitcher anticipated the reaction that many of the invited guests would have toward Koufax. Rabbi Brad Hirschfield, for example, writes of his White House experience:

> As far as Sandy Koufax goes, I can tell you what I said to him when we finally got a chance to chat at the end of program. I asked him what it felt like to be both a Hall-of-Famer and one of the most important rabbis of the 20th century. He looked at me a little funny and said, "Believe me, I'm no rabbi." I explained that there was probably no person who empowered a certain generation of Jews, especially young men and boys, to claim their Jewishness with pride, confidence and joy, and if that isn't being a great rabbi, I didn't know what was. His eyes welled up with tears and he said, "Thank you rabbi for putting me in your club."[4]

Hirschfield's anecdote reveals something of the extraordinary celebrity American Jews have bestowed on Koufax, a phenomenon that has become all the more evident in recent years. Yet the same anecdote also points to some internal contradiction in the Koufax myth. Although elevated in the eyes of many Jews to the level of religious icon, Koufax in reality was never terribly religious—as he honestly put it, "Believe me, I'm no rabbi"—nor was his choice to miss a game on Yom Kippur the heroically pious act it has been puffed up to be. Koufax was a great baseball player, certainly; but he has entered the realm of collective memory as a great Jew. As this chapter will further explore, this is but one of the many anomalies contained in the American Jewish celebrity of Sandy Koufax.

Any consideration of Koufax's celebrity has to begin with his athletic accomplishment. The youngest man ever to be inducted into the National Baseball Hall of Fame in Cooperstown, New York, his plaque sums up his career as a pitcher for the Dodgers (in Brooklyn, 1955–1957; and in Los Angeles, 1958–1966): "Sanford Koufax 'Sandy' . . . Set all-time records with 4 no-hitters in 4 years, capped by 1965 perfect game, and by capturing earned-run title five seasons in a row, 1962–1966. Won 25 or more games three times. Had 11 shutouts in 1963. Strikeout leader four times, with record 382 in 1965. Fanned 18 in a game twice. Most Valuable Player 1963. Cy Young award winner 1963–65–66."[5]

But statistics and awards alone cannot convey the myth and mystique of Sandy Koufax. In the first instance, there is the remarkable transformation he underwent midway through his career. Signed by the Dodgers in 1955 at the tender age of nineteen, Koufax soon earned a reputation as a hard thrower lacking in control. After struggling without success for the first several years of his contract, he suddenly found his pitching form in the spring of 1961. At last able to hit the strike zone and strike out batters with regularity, the second half of his career consisted of six superlative seasons (1961–1966), establishing him as one of the most dominating pitchers in baseball history. Hitters of that era, including all-time greats such as Mickey Mantle and Willie Mays, would speak of his pitching with profound respect and awe. Slugger Willie Stargell cracked that facing Koufax was like "trying to drink coffee with a fork."[6] But then, at age thirty, Koufax shocked the sports world by retiring from baseball seemingly at the height of his powers. He had overused his arm, he explained, and had been pitching in intense pain; yet the timing of the decision still baffled many observers and only added to the air of mystery around the man. After a brief second career as a baseball announcer, Koufax retired to a quiet life out of the spotlight—or at least as much anonymity as the world would allow. Since his induction into the Baseball Hall of Fame in 1972 at age thirty-six, his myth has grown with each passing year.

All of this begins to explain Koufax's elevated stature among baseball fans—but what of his *Jewish* celebrity, the undying adulation of his fellow Jews? At first glance, Koufax's popularity among the Jews of his generation seems perfectly logical—he was a "nice Jewish boy" who became a famous baseball player, one of the greatest of all time. He was the rare Jewish professional athlete, and the even rarer sports superstar of Jewish birth. This anomalous status alone would have ensured his celebrity among Jews. But unfailingly, the Jewish legend of Sandy Koufax is pinned to one particular moment in his storied career—his decision not to go to work on *the* high holy day of Judaism, despite the fact that it fell on the first game of the World Series, the "high holy days" of baseball. In that one momentous act, Koufax seemed to privilege his Jewish identity over his commitment to his sport. No matter that his own religious feelings were minimal—the mere public acknowledgment of the Jewish calendar was viewed as a symbolic act of great import. Recited almost ritualistically by those recalling his significance, it has passed into the realms of myth and collective memory.

Beyond the Yom Kippur gesture, several other elements of the Koufax image have endeared him to fellow Jews. One was simply his choice of sport—while in his youth, Koufax had excelled in basketball, but he ultimately chose baseball, a sport occupying a special niche in both the American and Jewish imaginations. Cherished as the "national pastime" for much of the twentieth century and thoroughly identified with American culture and identity, baseball has served as a kind of proxy for American society on the whole; and as such has played a vital role in the process of Americanization for immigrant communities such as the Jews.[7] As Jewish baseball fan Robert Gurstein observes, "No sport entered the American Jewish psyche more than baseball. Hank Greenberg, Sandy Koufax—these were super athletes and *ipso facto* super Jews."[8]

As a Jewish baseball player, and much like his predecessor Hank Greenberg (baseball star of the 1930s and 1940s, as we will discuss), Koufax's stellar career and celebrity dispelled the notion that Jews were outsiders to America and spurred young Jews to move more confidently into the American mainstream. But Jews have gravitated to baseball for other reasons as well. Baseball is a relatively genteel team sport, far less violent than others, and has fostered a culture of fair play and personal dignity. Squarely within this tradition, and again like Greenberg, Koufax was not only a talented ballplayer, but also a consummate gentleman. His biographer Jane Leavy describes Koufax as a true *mensch* in the vein of Lou Gehrig and Jackie Robinson. Yet unlike Greenberg, Koufax found success not as a hitter, but as a pitcher—a highly specialized position in baseball, occupying an elite status on every ball club. As a pitcher, Koufax embodied the "Jewish" quality of intelligence—he was a gentleman *and* a scholar—a trait valued in baseball far more than in other sports. This was true both on the field in his role as a pitcher, the thinking man's position; and off the field, as when he joined with fellow pitcher Don Drysdale to negotiate his own contract (a first in baseball). In a sport with a literary tradition rivaling that of the people of the book, Koufax was known as an avid reader and wrote his baseball memoir while still a player. In the postwar era, he provided a singular link between Jews and baseball, and consequently, between Jews and America. In sum, his symbolic role as a "Jew in baseball" is unparalleled.

But not just any Jew in baseball, Koufax was one of the greatest pitchers of all time, a superbly gifted athlete whose physical prowess was evident every time he took the mound. Thus, beyond exemplifying Jewish inclusion in America, Koufax also became a potent symbol of Jewish masculinity. This aspect of the Jewish athlete is especially significant to Jewish men, as it counters the negative stereotype that they are unathletic and unmanly. As Norman Kleeblatt puts it, "Visible and heroic, such sports champions as Koufax and Hank Greenberg broke the traditional (and stereotypical) image of the Jewish male as weak or feminine, forging an American version of Max Nordau's concept of a 'muscle-Jew' and creating a fresh American Jewish identity wherein Jews assimilated into 'tough, fighting men.'"[9]

Yet Koufax and Greenberg attained their sports stardom in vastly different eras. In Greenberg's case, the 1930s and 1940s were an era when American sports, especially boxing and basketball, had their fair share of Jewish stars. Jewish men, therefore, were as likely to be seen as "tough, fighting men" as the contrary stereotype of the nice Jewish boy (or n.j.b.). In the decades following World War II, the latter image took over, as the image of the Jewish male trended away from the sporting arena and into the professional realm of lawyers, doctors, and accountants—occupations thought more suitable for nice Jewish boys of the postwar generation. An archetypal n.j.b. himself, Koufax confounded the stereotype and entered the profession of baseball instead. He was the first and greatest sports star of his generation, and he became a lightning rod for the worshipful feelings many Jews have toward Jewish athletes. Yet beneath the surface, Koufax's celebrity reflected many of the identity dilemmas of his generation of American Jews; this makes him the perfect illustration of the thematic tension between American celebrity and Jewish identity. The height of his fame, moreover, coincides perfectly with the period under discussion, the early 1960s. As his biographer observes, "Koufax is the sixties before the sixties became the sixties. He is celebrity before celebrity became an entitlement."[10]

Greenberg versus Koufax

To better demonstrate the more complex quality of Sandy Koufax's Jewish celebrity, let us compare the mythologizing of Koufax with that of his earlier compatriot on the baseball diamond, Hank Greenberg. Often cited together, both appear on a timeline in the American Jewish Historical Society (AJHS) magazine; Greenberg's entry reads, "1934—American Jews cheer Detroit Tigers' Hank Greenberg (1911–1986) when he refuses to play ball on Yom Kippur . . ."[11] The two often compete for the title of all-time greatest Jewish baseball player, as Greenberg's historian writes: "Except for Sandy Koufax, the pitching sensation of the 1960s, no rivals challenge this Hall of Famer's status as baseball's premier Jewish player."[12] On the opposing side, Koufax's entry on the (no longer active) Jewhoo! website hyperbolized: "What can we say? Koufax holds a place so deep in the hearts of Jewish baseball fans that words are not enough. In our humble opinion, he narrowly edges out Hank Greenberg as the greatest Jewish baseball player ever."

Similarly, in Philip Brooks's 1988 publication *Extraordinary Jewish Americans*, the section on Koufax begins, "Jewish Americans have always been especially proud of great Jewish athletes. For Jewish immigrants, such sports heroes seemed proof that they were truly a part of their adopted country. No Jewish athlete ever aroused more pride than Sandy Koufax."[13] Brooks's logic is a bit faulty, however, because by the 1960s, American Jews were no longer insecure immigrants. Koufax's appeal to his generation of Jews would have to be of a different nature than the more straightforward ethnic pride evoked by Greenberg in the 1930s and 1940s. In fact, the dissimilarities between the two Jewish baseball stars far outweigh their commonalities. As we shall see, compared to Greenberg, Koufax was neither a very good representation of "tough, fighting" manliness, nor was he a particularly good symbol of American inclusion for the Jewish outsider. Though they are justifiably linked as the two greatest Jewish players in the history of baseball, the comparison obscures the more significant differences between them.

In many regards, the difference boils down to context: Greenberg attained his sports celebrity during the Depression era of the 1930s, whereas Koufax reached public consciousness in a radically different historical environment, the early 1960s. Peter Levine, author of a book on sport and the American Jewish experience, employs such historical context to distinguish between Greenberg's and Koufax's high holiday decisions. On the former, he writes, "Greenberg's choice appeared as critical dilemma—how to balance loyalty to parents, religion, and tradition with commitment to his American profession and his desire to fully participate in his American life. Equally important, he made it at a time when American Jews still did daily battle with stereotypes about their weakness in a world full of real threats to Jewish existence." Whereas on Koufax, Levine perceptively adds:

By the time Koufax chose not to play, Greenberg's dilemma no longer existed for most American Jews. While they proudly acknowledged Sandy's decision, it hardly signaled hope for their own American ambitions or symbolically challenged insistent anti-Semitic claims of Jewish inferiority. Their own remarkable success in the decades since World War II and the appearance of a new breed of Jewish hero [the Israeli] far more capable of countering such charges than any baseball player both figured in their response.[14]

In the earlier, prewar period, many Jews felt themselves to be outsiders in American society—and thus Greenberg represented the possibility of inclusion. As Levine puts it, "Hank Greenberg became important as a symbol of Jewish strength and survival at a time when such images served the needs of American Jews."[15] While Jews of the 1930s collectively played the role of the other, the individual baseball hero subverted the norm, offering some hope of redemption. Koufax, on the other hand, played during the heady decades following World War II, a time when antisemitism was in steep decline in America, and Jewish social integration was sharply on the rise. By the 1960s, Jews had already begun to succeed in America—therefore, while "a symbol of Jewish strength" to a degree, Koufax was not playing against a background of perceived Jewish victimhood and inferiority. As *the* Jewish sports hero of the latter period, it stands to reason that Koufax represented something else as well.

Press coverage of the two baseball stars differed accordingly. From Greenberg's rookie season in 1933, newspaper coverage rarely failed to note his ethnicity, calling him the first "really great Jewish player," "that long-sought Hebrew star," "the Tigers' great Jewish first baseman," and "the Jewish slugger."[16] William Simons observes that sportswriters of the era tended to note the ethnic background of baseball players across the board—as demonstration of the "melting pot" process of American assimilation at work. So while still seen as part of an outsider group, the ethnic baseball star was imagined to be the harbinger of a more homogeneous society. But in Koufax's time (and also, note, in the latter phase of Greenberg's career, following World War II), conspicuous mention of ethnicity was no longer considered good form. For one thing, race had overtaken ethnicity as the outside boundary of "white" American society. In the 1940s and 1950s, Jackie Robinson served the same lightning-rod function as had Greenberg in the 1930s—a role no longer asked of Koufax in the 1960s.

Closer examination of the high holiday question may further illuminate the issue. According to the popular conception, both Greenberg and Koufax elected to sit out ball games falling on Yom Kippur, and thereby demonstrated their commitment to their religion, loyalty to their people, and some deeper understanding that however important their role as baseball star, it was ultimately trumped by being a Jew. The symbolic value of the act is evident in the constant reference made to it by American Jews, often citing it in support of their own Jewish choices. Koufax's most recent biographer, Jane Leavy, claims it motivated her own decision not to work on the Jewish holidays. But the myth is problematic, as again, there are distinctions to be drawn between the Jewish communities of the two eras. In Greenberg's time, secularism was in ascendance. Like the baseball player himself, many second-generation Jews had rejected synagogue Judaism altogether during the Depression years. Greenberg's 1934 decision not to play on Yom Kippur, and thus to respect the sanctity of a religious holiday, may be seen as a harbinger of the turn from ethnicity to religion coming to fruition in the postwar years; or else perhaps, it may have helped advance the trend toward one-day-a-year synagogue attendance that also came to predominate in postwar suburbia—the precise environment in which Koufax made his choice.

When Koufax took off work for the Yom Kippur of 1965, such "religious devotion" was already the norm for most American Jews. By the 1960s it had become commonplace for suburban Jews to affiliate with synagogues, but then only to attend services on the high holidays. In this context, Koufax's action held little extraordinary significance. It was, rather, an affirmation of the status quo. Koufax himself insisted that it was no big deal, as he explained in his memoir (written the year following the event in question): "There was never any decision to make, though, because there was never any possibility that I would pitch. Yom Kippur is the holiest day of the Jewish religion. The club knows that I don't work that day."[17]

There are also certain differences in the baseball circumstances of the two Yom Kippur events. For one, in Greenberg's case, it was an inconsequential, late-season game after the pennant had been clinched; whereas just ten days earlier, he had in fact played on Rosh Hashanah when the pennant was on the line, amid much controversy and publicity. Koufax, on the other hand, missed the first game of the 1965 World Series, ostensibly a far more critical absence from the lineup. And yet, as any baseball fan knows, Koufax was a pitcher and not an everyday player—like Greenberg—and choosing to pitch on one day rather than another entailed a lesser sacrifice than would the loss of a star hitter. This was especially true in the Dodgers' case, because Koufax's stand-in would be an equally dominating pitcher, Don Drysdale (who nevertheless pitched poorly and lost the first game, telling his manager upon exiting, "Bet you wish I was Jewish too"). Just prior to the World Series that year, *Newsweek* magazine weighed in on the issue, noting that "with Drysdale pitching the first game, and Koufax the second, it still will be possible for the artful left-hander to work three times if the series goes the full seven games."[18] It did, and Koufax did pitch three times, winning the critical final game of the series. Though an argument could be made that pitching the first game of a World Series provides a special advantage, Leavy puts it plainly: "So you pitch a day late. Big schmeer."[19]

So in neither the 1934 Greenberg case nor the 1965 Koufax case was the actual decision to sit out for Yom Kippur as great a sacrifice as it may have appeared. Moreover, it should be recalled that during the rest of the year, both Greenberg and Koufax were marginal Jews, religiously inactive and liable to intermarry. Both players later made it clear that their high holiday decisions were motivated not by any religious propriety of their own, but rather out of deference to their Jewish fans. Yet while Greenberg's appearance in a Detroit synagogue that Yom Kippur has become the stuff of legend, Koufax spent the day in his hotel room—directly contradicting the memories of fans who insist they saw him attending services that day.[20] Though he never denied his Jewishness, neither did he embrace it in any meaningful way. Yet the myth lives on, serving the identity needs of the faithful.

Over and above the myth of the Yom Kippur absence lies the no less significant question of the two men's greater symbolism as Jewish sports heroes. Greenberg played during an era of boundary breaking for minorities in the public spotlight of sports. In the decade following World War II, Jackie Robinson broke the color barrier in the national pastime, which led ineluctably to Bill Russell, Wilt Chamberlain, Muhammad Ali, Jim Brown, Hank Aaron, Bob Gibson, and myriad black sports stars of the post-1950s era. Greenberg, though identified with Robinson as a fellow victim of on-field abuse and discrimination (and famously offering Robinson some on-field encouragement during the one year they overlapped as players), played no similar role for Jews in professional sports—he was not fated to become the pioneer of a new generation of Jewish sports stars. Nevertheless, in that more innocent time, American Jews could be forgiven for looking to Greenberg as "the great Jewish hope," the one who would prove the stereotype false—because by his example, he demonstrated that Jews were athletic after all and could become sports heroes like any other American.

In the 1930s and 1940s, the fantasy was not so far removed from reality because certain sports—principally boxing and basketball—had their fair share of Jewish athletes. By the 1960s, however, Jewish athletic participation in professional sports was in rapid decline. Whereas Greenberg served as a potential harbinger of future Jewish glory, Koufax represented the end of an era and the demise of such dreams. Despite understandable Jewish hopes, Koufax, far more than Greenberg, was the exception who proved the rule—thus *confirming* the stereotype that Jews aren't athletic. As historian Stephen Whitfield quips, "it is no secret that Jews in the major leagues have been almost as rare as a double steal."[21] Might it be that it was Koufax's *un*representativeness that appealed to his many Jewish fans of the 1960s and beyond? For just beneath the veneer of the Jewish sports fan's adulation of a figure like Koufax lies the knowledge of an all-too-apparent set of facts: few pro athletes are Jewish, and Jews do not generally excel in sports. Can it be that American Jews are secretly proud of their image of unathleticism?

In the end, the Yom Kippur myth might actually serve to obscure the real reason for Koufax's popularity among Jews of his generation. It may seem paradoxical, but let me suggest that his appeal lies only initially in his athletic prowess and in his consequent acceptance as a Jew in a non-Jewish field. Beyond all of that, Koufax's appeal may also reside in the very opposite—in his persona as an outsider. Despite his success in the sport, Koufax was commonly perceived as standing apart from the world of baseball. In this regard, he was once again diametrically opposed to Greenberg. Greenberg, indelibly marked as a Jew, represented the promise of inclusion for the (explicitly Jewish) other—that is, Jews too can play baseball, Jews too can be big and strong and hit home runs, Jews too can serve in the army, and Jews too can be regular guys like everyone else in the locker room. Koufax, as it turns out, was just the opposite: the consummate insider who nevertheless continued to be seen as an (implicitly Jewish) outsider—a man at the top of his sport who represented the persistence of otherness and difference throughout his career.

The Koufax Persona in the 1960s

By contrast with the rather simplistic view of Koufax reflected in his current celebrity, his public image and persona during the 1960s was really quite complex. He gives some indication of this himself, when, at the very start of his 1966 autobiography, he unburdens himself of a complaint that must have been eating at him for some while:

> I have nothing against myths. But there is one myth that has been building through the years that I would just as soon bury without any particular

honors: the myth of Sandy Koufax, the anti-athlete. The way this fantasy goes, I am really a sort of dreamy intellectual who was lured out of college by a bonus in the flush of my youth and have forever after regretted—and even resented—the life of fame and fortune that has been forced upon me. Since I have never done a thing to indicate that I don't like being a ball-player, the myth also has to say that I am mightily concerned about projecting a sparkling All-American image—presumably so that nobody will suspect how much I really dislike what I am doing. . . . What offends me about the myth, aside from its sheer falsehood, is that it makes me sound as if I feel I'm above what I'm doing, which is an insult not to me but to all ballplayers.[22]

And so Koufax, prodded perhaps by his co-author, sportswriter Ed Linn, sets the tone for his memoir: self-justifying, defensive, prickly. What he did not, indeed would not acknowledge was the role his Jewish background and others' bias against Jewishness might have played in the creation of an image he so clearly resented. In reviewing the book, Canadian author Mordecai Richler—who once revealed that, "like most Jewish novelists, he would rather have been Sandy Koufax"[23]—suggested the possibility of antisemitism as the true basis of "the myth of the anti-athlete," noting, "Anti-Semitism takes many subtle shapes and the deprecating story one reads again and again, most memorably recorded in *Time*, is that Sandy Koufax is actually something of an intellectual. He doesn't mix. Though he is the highest-paid player in the history of the game, . . . he considers himself above it."[24]

In fact, an essential part of the Koufax persona was his purported intellectuality: here was a ballplayer who read books and listened to classical music. The negative implication, of course, was that there was something different, something suspect about this Jewish baseball player—Koufax, no dumb jock, but a scholar and a gentleman; not a regular American as the uniform might suggest, but really a Jew underneath. As his reputation grew, the mythology developed that Koufax didn't really like baseball—after all, he had never aspired to it, wanted to be an architect instead. Again, the implication was that he wasn't really one of the guys, wasn't a team player. Such negative stereotyping began early in his career, when he was often resented by other players for having been signed as a "bonus baby," a privileged rookie playing for higher pay and under special protection. Later in his career, he made baseball history for walking out of salary negotiations and forming a "union" with a fellow pitcher, Don Drysdale—all before baseball became unionized and agents became the norm. Finally, Koufax set himself apart by retiring early, at the age of thirty, due to severe arm pain. The ultimate act of self-centeredness, came the accusations.

Again and again in the press coverage of the time, Koufax was described as aloof, an intellectual snob, smugly superior, and self-serving, and one's imagination need not be stretched very much to see the encoded antisemitism in such put-downs. Revealing some deep schism in the culture, the public image of Koufax was divided between glowing encomia on the one hand and thinly veiled character assassinations on the other. It was clear to Richler at the time, and seems even clearer in retrospect, that such denigrating descriptions were in some way related to Koufax's Jewishness. As many of his teammates testify, he was all too often the object of antisemitic taunts and other ill-willed comments. Yet Koufax himself somehow missed this entirely; or else, perhaps he knew, but just didn't let on.

The closest he ever came to acknowledging antisemitism was in the spring of 1964, when the *Los Angeles Herald-Examiner*'s Bob Hunter wrote that Koufax had played hardball in his salary negotiations with the Dodgers. The headline read, "$90,000 OR I QUIT." Koufax responded with indignation, denying that he had said anything about $90,000, or that he had threatened to quit at all. He seemed especially incensed by the harm such publicity might do his public image, charging "the Los Angeles front office with shattering ('in one minute,' lamented the pitcher) the image he had worked all year to build, the things he had done to bring credit to himself, to the Dodgers, and to baseball." Moreover, Koufax accused Dodgers management of having planted the "phony story about his contract demands," and by doing so, having "marked him as 'greedy' and 'money-hungry.'" In this, Koufax was certainly aware of the relevant negative stereotypes of Jews. But though deeply affected by the incident—"Koufax, as sensitive as he is articulate, said he was unable to sleep, unable to talk without a tremor and—pointedly—unable to pitch properly"[25]—he made no overt reference to antisemitism per se.

If Koufax didn't acknowledge anti-Jewish biases, his teammates did —especially the black players, such as Roy Campanella and Don Newcombe, who took the rookie under their wing when he first arrived in the big leagues. As quoted by Jane Leavy, Newcombe recalled what motivated them:

> We had our reasons, our one reason—it was because he was a Jew. Some of the players did not like him because he was a Jew . . . I couldn't understand

the narrow-mindedness of these players when they would come to us and talk about Sandy as "this kike" and "this Jew bastard" or "Jew sonofabitch that's gonna take my job" . . . And saying it in front of us about Sandy! They hated Jews as much as they hated blacks. I don't know if Sandy ever knew that, but that's why we took care of Sandy.[26]

But none of this is the antisemitism of which Richler speaks. The Canadian Jewish novelist was onto something other than the base prejudices of small-minded men. More reflective of the time, and more relevant for our purposes, was a subtler form of antisemitism found in the descriptions of contemporary sports reporters. In the name of journalism, Koufax came to be described as an anomaly in his chosen field, an "antiathlete"—whether he was seen as too cerebral, or else not manly enough to be a ballplayer, both implications echoed standard negative stereotypes of Jews. The tendency began as far back as Koufax's first spring training in 1955, when Bill Roeder of the *New York World-Telegram* submitted an article titled "Koufax, Unorthodox, Reads Books."[27]

In 1962, just as Koufax was rocketing to stardom, Melvin Durslag described him in the *Saturday Evening Post* as "one of baseball's most mysterious performers," adding, "Baffling as an athlete, Sandy also is enigmatic as a person," further explaining, "He lives by himself . . . [and] reads Thomas Wolfe, George Santayana, Aldous Huxley, and other writers of substance. He takes solitary drives in the country, collects symphonic albums and spurns the affections of the Sandy Koufax Fan Club." In the same article, Durslag also made note of Koufax's Jewishness, writing,

> One day last year when [manager] Alston had scheduled Sandy to start, it turned out to be Yom Kippur. Since Koufax is Jewish, he asked to be excused. Williams replaced him—and again the Dodgers were beaten. Alston was criticized sharply for not having planned his rotation to make allowances for Jewish holy days. At the start of the 1962 season, a fan sent him a subtle reminder—a Hebrew calendar. "There'll be no slipups this time," the skipper promised.[28]

But with comments such as "he is known as a fellow who moves about mostly by himself," Durslag's focus was clearly on depicting the young pitcher as a loner and an outsider.

Similarly, Jim Murray of the *Los Angeles Times* described Koufax in 1963 as "a captive of baseball, trapped by his talent and his instincts," and further opined, "Sandy Koufax belongs in baseball about the way

Albert Schweitzer belongs in a twist joint." Finally, the infamous *Time* magazine story of 1965 depicted Koufax's apparent aloofness as an intrinsic part of his personality: "Just because a man does his job better than anybody else doesn't mean that he has to take it seriously—or even like it. . . . Alone among ballplayers, Koufax is an anti-athlete." The article went further still: "Dodger vice president Fresco Thompson considers him a heretic. 'I don't think he likes baseball,' mutters Thompson. 'What kind of a line is he drawing anyway—between himself and the world, between himself and the team?'" The basic implication of the negative press, Leavy concludes, was that "Koufax was tortured with a gift that compelled him to do something he really didn't like. He would have been happier as a doctor, a lawyer. He was a nice Jewish boy. In a word, different."[29]

Yet another manifestation of such subtle antisemitism can be found in the myriad photographic representations of Koufax made by reporters and other observers of the time. Though friendly with the black members of his team, Koufax is rarely depicted with them. Instead, he is far more often shown in the company of the typically sun-bleached, blonde-haired, middle-American farm boys who populated baseball at the time. The intended effect of these photographs, usually posed by the newspaper photographer, may have been to show Koufax's easy camaraderie with and mutual respect for his fellow baseball players; yet the actual visual effect is to emphasize his own dark-featured ethnicity, his Semitic otherness. By constantly posing him next to the Don Drysdales and Whitey Fords, the photographers subtly portrayed him as "other" than white, a non-*goy*. Similarly, an oil painting by artist Phil Hanks was used as the cover of the 1990 centennial edition of the *Dodgers Blue Book*—it depicts three players from Dodgers history: Zack Wheat, Sandy Koufax, and Jackie Robinson. Suggestively, Koufax is given the same skin color and tone as Robinson. The effect of the three figures together, surely unintentional but evocative nonetheless, is to portray Koufax as neither white nor black but something else, belonging in a different category altogether—Jewish, perhaps?

Koufax's response to all of this other-ing was to assert his normalcy, that is, his *sameness*. In a 1963 interview with Milton Gross, sportswriter for the *New York Post*, he protested: "I'm just a normal twenty-seven-year-old bachelor who happens to be of the Jewish faith. I like nice clothes. I like comfort. I like to read a book and listen to music and I'd like to meet the girl I'd want to marry. That's normal, isn't it?"[30] His memoir was written in direct response to the *Time* article that he called

Koufax posing with teammate Don Drysdale—the very image of
Jewish-gentile brotherhood.

"one great orgy of mythmaking." Contrary to its insinuations, Koufax
writes, "I *like* what I'm doing. I find that pitching, both as an art and
a craft, is endlessly demanding and endlessly fascinating." To the accusation that he had betrayed his parents' ambitions, he counters, "My
parents, they decided, were 'a little taken aback when Sandy decided to
spend his life throwing a ball around.' 'To this day,' they said, 'baseball
is never discussed in the Koufax household.' . . . To this day, little else
is discussed in the Koufax household. . . . I assure you that my mother
and father take the same pleasure in my success that your mother and
father take in yours." He was especially bothered by the implication that
he was an outsider among his teammates: "What griped me about their
story was that they painted me as a stranger in my own clubhouse." Instead, he compares the "camaraderie of the locker room" to "the *esprit*
of the members of an infantry platoon" whose members are bonded in
deep and profound ways.[31]

What seems to have vexed Koufax most of all was the idea that he
was too intellectual for the sport of baseball: "The whole meaning of
the anti-athlete myth I've been talking about here is that I do not like   **63**

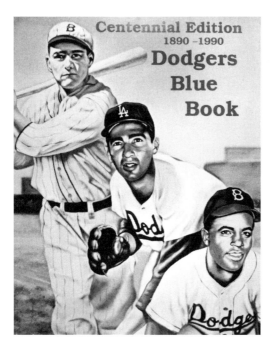

Dodgers Blue Book (1990) cover illustration by Phil Hanks showing all-time great Dodgers players Zack Wheat, Sandy Koufax, and Jackie Robinson—nicely portraying the ethnic diversity of baseball, America's national pastime.

baseball because it is an essentially adolescent game that does not satisfy some kind of intellectual curiosity I'm supposed to possess."[32] The thirty-year-old memoirist then launches into a labored defense of the seriousness with which he approaches his sport, arguing that (1) baseball's not a game, it's work; (2) you don't play for money, but for pride; and (3) baseball isn't a simple game, but subtle and complex. Rather than attempt to demonstrate his own lack of sophistication, therefore, he chooses instead to assert the cerebral capacity demanded by the sport of baseball. Nowadays, the affinity that many intellectuals have for the game is commonplace, as demonstrated by baseball aficionados such as Bart Giamatti and George Will. But in this regard, Koufax was ahead of his time. And ironically, he had tried to counter the charge of intellectualism by making an intellectual argument that baseball was, at least in part, an intellectual exercise. It was almost as if he subconsciously agreed with the assessments of him as an outsider to baseball. On the surface, of course, his protestation was simply a defensive measure against the negative implications of being called an egghead ballplayer.

In sum, the accusations tend to support Richler's suggestion of subtle antisemitism, yet Koufax himself seemed either oblivious or else just uninterested in this aspect of his image. Throughout his memoir the subject of his Jewishness is rarely mentioned and never thoughtfully considered. Early on, he muses somewhat humorously, "I sometimes feel that I should have said originally that I wanted to be a doctor [as opposed to an architect] so they could use all the jokes." He reminisces fondly about his Brooklyn background and family history, giving special attention to his grandfather, Max Lichtenstein, yet once again he ignores the Jewish element. At one point, he recalls how his grandmother used to call their "nutty" next-door neighbor (who grew up to become the comedian Buddy Hackett), a "meshugana." But otherwise, Jewish terms and references are nearly absent from his discourse—except when absolutely necessary, as in his recollection of playing basketball at the Jewish Community House on Bay Parkway. Tellingly, one incident requiring some reference to his ethnic identity occurred when the New York Yankees attempted to sign the young pitcher: "A pair of Yankee scouts even came to my house two or three times to talk to my folks. When it came to the point of trying to get our names on a contract, though, they sent an entirely different scout, a Jewish scout. It offended us. It was just a little too obvious."[33]

In accord with this desire not to be "too obvious," not to be overly conspicuous as a Jew or overly conscious of being Jewish, Koufax treats his Jewishness as a minor detail. He even downplays it in his description of the famed Yom Kippur incident:

> I had already pitched and lost the second game because of the coincidence of the opening game falling on Yom Kippur, a situation which I think was played all out of proportion. I had tried to deflect questions about my intentions through the last couple of weeks of the season by saying that I was praying for rain. There was never any decision to make, though, because there was never any possibility that I would pitch.
>
> Yom Kippur is the holiest day of the Jewish religion. The club knows that I don't work that day. When Yom Kippur falls during the season, as it usually does, it has always been a simple matter of pitching a day earlier, with two days' rest, when my turn happened to be coming up.
>
> I had ducked a direct answer about the World Series because it seemed presumptuous to talk about it while we were still trying to get there. For all I knew, I could be home watching on television.[34]

Note how he leaves out any sense of his own responsibility or personal feelings regarding the issue. The only emotion he purports to have experienced came on the day following the famous missed game:

The surprise of the day, as far as I was concerned, came the next morning when I was reading the report of the game by Don Riley, the columnist of the St. Paul *Pioneer Press*. His column took the form of "An Open Letter to Sandy Koufax," in which he was kind enough to tell me how badly we had been beaten in the opener. . . . I found it vastly amusing, until right at the end. "Spitballs dissolved Tuesday," he wrote. "And the Twins love matzoh balls on Thursdays." I couldn't believe it. I thought that kind of thing went out with dialect comics.[35]

His only "Jewish" response was to express indignation that a reporter had referenced his Jewishness at all.

Though Jewishness may not have been part of Koufax's self-image, it certainly colored others' perceptions of him. Assessing a century of pitching excellence, baseball sage Casey Stengel once said, "Forget the other fellow, Walter Johnson. The Jewish kid is probably the best of them." In 1963, Stengel also offered this: "If that young fella was running for office in Israel, they'd have a whole new government over there and he'd boss it just like he bosses practically every game he pitches." In October 1965, just prior to the famous Yom Kippur World Series, *Newsweek* magazine put Koufax on its cover. The article referred to him as "the Jewish star" and quoted him self-deprecatingly saying, "I can't make up my mind whether I'm a *schlemiel* or a *schlamazel*" (referring to his recurring injuries and setbacks). It was, the magazine explained, "a piece of classic Yiddish humor."[36] Koufax's fellow players often referred to him as "Super Jew," and contemporary magazines began to call him "the world's most eligible Jewish bachelor." Milton Berle called him "the greatest Jewish athlete since Samson."[37] Despite his own best attempts to assimilate, to fit in, Koufax was fated always to be seen not just as a great baseball player, but as a great *Jewish* baseball player—which is to say, an outsider in his sport.

As noted earlier, Richler argues that all such marking of Koufax's Jewish otherness was a form of antisemitism. However, I would make the case that his elitist reputation also served Jewish fans in a more positive sense—it provided a welcome reminder of their own difference in a time of rapid acculturation and widespread acceptance of Jews. Koufax clearly stood apart in terms of his enormous talent and his reserved nature, his supposed aloofness. But as Leavy makes abundantly clear in her portrayal of the man and his milieu, Koufax also stood apart as a gentle soul and a man of unusual politeness, humility, and dignity—the ultimate *mensch*. He thus shattered the stereotype of the loud, whiny, and crass New York Jew. Though born and raised in Brooklyn, he had no discernible accent and could easily pass for gentile in terms of social behavior.

Yet in his life as a baseball player, Koufax stood out as a Jewish other in some additional ways. Unlike many athletes, he was articulate and thoughtful in his interviews. Unlike other power pitchers, he never tried to intimidate or embarrass hitters. Unlike other baseball superstars, he never cashed in on his celebrity. And so on. But such differentiation is precisely the secret of his appeal. Though an anomaly in the world of professional sports, he would become a ready model for American Jews. Without any intention on his part, Koufax had become the ultimate symbol of American Jewish success, powerfully demonstrating that Jews could succeed in a non-Jewish world while retaining the best of themselves as Jews: integration without assimilation, Americanism without goyism—the highest ideal of the 1960s generation of American Jews.

Koufax and American Jewish Masculinity

The celebrity of Sandy Koufax also provided a compelling new model of Jewish masculinity.[38] As many have noted, manhood is a fraught subject for Jews, torn between traditional Jewish ideals of male gentility and scholarliness on the one hand, and modern Western ideals of male power and competitiveness on the other. Daniel Boyarin in particular has compellingly argued that gentility, or *edelkayt* in Yiddish, *was* the ideal masculinity of Ashkenazic Jewish culture. Only in modern Europe did Jewish *menschlichkeit* (literally, "manliness," but in Jewish culture, denoting goodness and thoughtfulness) come into conflict with a variant ideal of manhood—embracing war and sport and other pursuits characterized by Boyarin as *goyim naches* (literally, "gentile pleasures").[39]

From the Western point of view, Jewish men looked unmanly, even feminine, and hence negative stereotypes emerged; whereas in Jewish culture, the ideal of *edelkayt* survived. Caught in between, acculturating Jewish men have experienced the dilemma of masculinity in profound and often painful ways. This is evident in the history of American Jewish celebrity, including as it does figures who conformed to the Jewish stereotype of intellectual ineffectuality (for example, Woody Allen); those who conformed to the Western ideal of "masculine" toughness (for example, Norman Mailer); and, in certain instances, individuals who managed to reconcile the extremes. As I argue here, Koufax was the rare instance of such an exquisitely balanced Jewish masculinity—and as such became *the* great culture-hero for American Jewish men.

For Jewish and non-Jewish fans alike, Koufax represented a certain ideal of manliness not generally associated with Jews. He was a great athlete, and thus a "real man," that is, masculine in the normative sense of big and strong, powerful and dominant. On the most basic level, his athletic prowess countered negative images of Jewish weakness and physical uncoordination. The feeble-bodied Jew is a long-standing anti-semitic notion—a self-fulfilling notion, in fact, as whatever truth is in it was the consequence of the oppressive conditions of Jewish life in pre-modern Europe (for example, banned from army service, Jews did not learn to be fighters). The modern Jewish response to both the image and the reality was most often couched in terms of Zionism.

To undo the perception of male Jews as effeminate weaklings, turn-of-the-twentieth-century Zionist leader Max Nordau proposed the development of a new Jewish type—the "muscle-Jew"—and modern-day Israel has certainly followed through on the promise. Jewish participation in sports offers a similar argument, in which the athletic exploits of Jewish strongmen and boxers (for example, Siegmund "Zishe" Breit-bart, Barney Ross), football and basketball players (Sid Luckman, Dolph Schayes), and swimmers and wrestlers (Mark Spitz, Goldberg) are cited to give the lie to the myth of Jewish unathleticism.[40] As the only major Jewish sports star of his era, Koufax was a principal example of this "real man" phenomenon. And his was an especially potent example, for he was more than a baseball star—Koufax was a sports *super*star with seemingly unnatural abilities, appearing to transcend most other players in some herculean way. He was seen not just as a *real* man but as a *super* man, and consequently, as a "super Jew."

But in addition to such images of athletic masculinity, Koufax also embodied a more contemporary version of maleness, corresponding to changes in the image of the American man during the postwar era.[41] In the wake of the "greatest generation" of World War II era military men, the reigning image of American manhood moved away from its traditional profile of stoic strength and toward a more complex and con-flicted persona. Once again, this was a cultural shift that can be seen in the history of celebrity. Whereas masculinity during the war years was defined by supremely confident, self-contained and unflappable movie stars such as Gary Cooper and John Wayne, the subsequent pe-riod would see the rise of more troubled and impassioned actors such as Marlon Brando and James Dean. The latter were no less sexually appeal-ing as Hollywood movie idols, but now embraced a greater emotional complexity. The same years saw similar shifts in other areas of popular culture, moving, for example, from Dwight D. Eisenhower to John F. Kennedy, from Joe Louis to Muhammad Ali, and from Bing Crosby to Elvis Presley.

In each case, the new type of American male was a more layered and divided personality than his predecessor. He was perceived as an outsider even after his social success, and his seemingly tough exterior contained a more sensitive soul within. It was a masculine persona deepened by some inner turmoil; and, softened by qualities of emotionality and sensitivity, a male image that had become more feminine. It was, in short, an American masculinity closer to the conflicted, feminized image of the male Jew. Not surprisingly, then, the postwar generation these men reflected was often demeaned in comparison with their fathers. Middle-class American men growing up in the 1950s and 1960s were more at home on the local college campus than on foreign battle fields. Lacking the experience of war to establish their manhood, they looked instead to a new breed of male celebrities as models for a new brand of American masculinity. Koufax was one of those figures.

We might even view Koufax—the great Jewish idol of the time—in conjunction with the great American idol of the time, John F. Kennedy. It may seem farfetched to compare a baseball player with a president—and at first glance, Koufax appears to resemble Kennedy no more than Barbra Streisand mirrors Marilyn Monroe. One might joke that the only thing the Jewish athlete and the Irish Catholic politician had in common was that one was born in Brooklyn, the other in Brookline. But upon further examination, some intriguing parallels emerge: both were minorities in their respective fields, initially treated as underdogs but ultimately victorious, and thus represented the emergence of the ethnic outsider. Both occupied the dominant position in their fields—the presidency and the pitching mound—and thus represented the combination of control and power, each in his own way: one with hardball politics, the other with fastball and curveball. Both were perceived as handsome, glamorous men in what had been, until they came along, rather unglamorous professions. Both were distinctly seductive personalities, subtle combinations of the inscrutable "strong, silent type" with intellectual depth and complexity, and thus represented a new style of American masculinity, defined by the cool charisma of controlled power. Like Kennedy, Koufax's public persona combined images of power, glamour, strength of character, intelligence, and integrity—the very opposite of immigrant insecurity. And like Kennedy's rapid ascent, Koufax's extraordinary success surprised everyone—both made it to Camelot, a mythic realm of **69** charmed perfection. Then, almost as suddenly as the Kennedy era came to its tragic end in 1963, the career of Sandy Koufax ended summarily just three years later. But the powerful resonance of his persona would outlast his career, and, like that of Kennedy, shape the consciousness of a generation.

Alongside changes in American masculinity, the image of Jewish men was also transformed during the same years. Koufax, again, gave visible demonstration that a Jew could be as physically adept, and thus as manly, as any gentile. But he was not alone in this; in fact, Koufax's star began to rise at the very moment that another image of Jewish manhood entered popular consciousness: the tough, combative *sabra*, the native-born Israeli. As discussed earlier, most influential here was the one-two punch of Leon Uris's best-selling novel of 1958, *Exodus*, and Otto Preminger's film version of 1960 starring Paul Newman as Ari Ben-Canaan. Yet the Israeli hero of *Exodus* represented something more than *sabra* toughness. To a Jewish generation dominated by Americanization and assimilation, Ben-Canaan also represented the opposite principles of ethnic pride and Jewish survival. During the transitional period of the 1960s, American Jews would be poised somewhere between the two extremes—and Koufax was a key figure pointing toward some form of synthesis. In his public persona, one can almost see Kitty, the American universalist, and Ari, the Jewish particularist, combined. Like the one, Koufax reflected social inclusion and personal accommodation; and like the other, he represented persistent difference and stubborn stoicism. He thus embodied, in the world of professional baseball, the myth of the conflicted antihero, combining the alienation of the outsider with the allure of the leading man.

As I discussed in Chapter 1, the same myth was simultaneously being propagated by Hollywood filmmakers. In the early 1960s, Jewish directors such as Sidney Lumet, Richard Brooks, and Martin Ritt often worked with Jewish actors such as Kirk Douglas, Tony Curtis, and Paul Newman, and in the process helped to construct a new American masculinity. Comparing such cinematic projections of manhood with the popular image of Koufax points first of all to the Hollywood-like celebrity he had attained. In a 1964 article, "The Koufax Nobody Knows," Milton Gross phrases it as follows: "Los Angeles is a city built on celluloid dreams, part fact, part fiction, part fantasy. Understandably, the latest glamour boy in the land of make-believe is Sandy Koufax, the Dodgers' left-handed pitcher, who seems to have been created out of a script writer's imagination. . . . When Sandy won twenty-five games for the Dodgers last season, . . . he was elevated roughly to the status symbol of Elizabeth Taylor in the movies and Frank Sinatra in show biz.[42]

The comparison further suggests a parallel between the subtle effect of such movies and the impact of Koufax's fame on the American Jewish public. Koufax's celebrity reached its pinnacle at the same moment in American culture when some of his fellow Jews in Hollywood—located, not incidentally, just a few miles west of the new Dodger Stadium—were busily projecting their self-image as outsiders onto the white screen of America's consciousness. Of course, by romanticizing the outsider, the Hollywood auteurs were asserting their own desire to "make it" in America, to erase their own marginalization and become insiders. More often than not, both their antiheroic characters and they themselves ended up frustrated in their ambitions, never fully arriving at the desired destination. Like them, and much like celebrity in general, the Koufax persona was characterized by a basic duality. Neither insider nor outsider, neither an ultra-macho John Wayne nor an ultra-sensitive James Dean, Koufax betrayed elements of both, standing somewhere in between.

A transitional figure in more ways than one, Koufax also stands between two sharply contrasting conceptions in the popular image of Jewish men. Before Koufax, the reigning stereotype of the Jewish male was the anti-WASP: weak and uncoordinated rather than strong and athletic, emotive and neurotic rather than reserved and controlled. This stereotypical image was echoed and reinforced by postwar Jewish celebrity. In the era preceding the arrival of Koufax, Jewish male celebrity in America was largely associated with music (Jascha Heifetz, Benny Goodman, Leonard Bernstein), science (Jonas Salk, Albert Einstein, Robert Oppenheimer), and literature (Saul Bellow, J. D. Salinger, Bernard Malamud)— all fields privileging brains over brawn, intellectuality over physicality.

The stereotype of the Jewish egghead and milquetoast grew especially common following World War II, despite the fact that so many young Jews were emerging from their wartime experience battle hardened and with a newly heroic self-image.[43] As if to offset this very reality, popular culture persisted in portraying Jewish men as "nice boys." Jewish comedy stars of the 1950s who were physically agile (for example, Danny Kaye and Jerry Lewis) or physically strong (for example, Milton Berle and Sid Caesar) often hid behind neurotic or effeminate characters to deemphasize or diminish their masculinity. As Jews in the public spotlight, they simply could not allow themselves to seem too manly. And conversely, to be convincing as "tough guys," movie stars such as Edward G. Robinson, Kirk Douglas, and Tony Curtis had to disguise their Jewish

71

ethnicity altogether. As a general rule, Jewish men in the public spotlight could be either "Jews"—whether in the form of intellectuals or comedians—or "men," but almost never both at once.

In the 1950s, the most significant exception to this rule may have been playwright Arthur Miller, who transcended his image as a meek and mild-mannered Jewish intellectual by capturing *the* sex symbol of the era. As argued by Jonathan Freedman, Miller was transformed into a major celebrity by his 1956 marriage to Marilyn Monroe, and in the process, helped transform the image of Jewish men: "For what is crucial about it is not just that Miller is the man who succeeded with the woman who dumped Joe DiMaggio and whom countless other American men wished to win, but he succeeded *because* of his status as an awkward, nervous, press-shy, artistic, sensitive, man: all the things that defined the Jewish man as effeminate or at least nonmasculine in the American popular imaginary."[44] Freedman adds that "Miller was transformed into a figure of such potency in the media—the entertainment industry—to which Jewish men turned for their models of American masculinity."[45] But as much press attention as Miller attracted for marrying Monroe, he never rivaled her star power as a movie star.

In this regard, there was a far more compelling image of the male Jew in 1950s popular culture—an image generated by the Hollywood trend of biblical epics, in which Jews were often depicted as mythical heroes. The key figure in this trend was, rather incongruously, a non-Jewish actor, Charlton Heston. In *The Ten Commandments* (1956) and *Ben-Hur* (1959), both Oscar-winning blockbusters, Heston respectively played the archetypal Jewish hero, Moses, and a Jewish prince contemporary with Jesus, Judah Ben-Hur. In each film, the tall and strapping actor played an explicitly Jewish character as a bold and charismatic leader of men. Granted, it had little to do with the contemporary image of Jewish men as good citizens and good husbands, subsidiary and deferential to their fellow citizens and to their wives (for example, the male leads of television's *The Goldbergs*). But still, Hollywood's flirtation with biblical epics in the 1950s, and the consequent heroic treatment of ancient Jews, must be taken into account in assessing images of Jewish masculinity at that time. If not a reflection of reality, such images constituted an aspirational ideal, a fantasy of what Jewish men had been and could become again—but prior to Koufax, only the Israeli *sabra* offered any such satisfaction in real life.

In the period following the 1960s, post-Koufax, American Jewish masculinity suffered further diminishment when popular film images of

Jewish men devolved to a state of neurosis and weakness. This was the Hollywood heyday of the American *shlemiel*, as exemplified by Jewish actors such as Dustin Hoffman, Peter Sellers, and Gene Wilder; and by their memorable characterizations of Benjamin Braddock in Mike Nichols's *The Graduate* (1967), Harold Fine in Paul Mazursky's *I Love You Alice B. Toklas* (1968), and Leo Bloom in Mel Brooks's *The Producers* (1968). But the type was epitomized by Woody Allen. Having started as a standup comedian in early 1960s Greenwich Village, Allen established a persona as an urban Jewish neurotic through a series of films he wrote, directed, and starred in, beginning with *Take the Money and Run* (1969) and *Bananas* (1971). Because Allen's *shlemiel* character appeared repeatedly in his films, it became indelibly associated with his own celebrity image; and thus Allen, attaining his greatest popularity in the 1970s, became the quintessential representation of the American Jewish male as *shlemiel*.[46] The contrast between Charlton Heston and Woody Allen—as representative figures of Jewish manhood—is startling to say the least.

But as suggested earlier, Koufax represented a new profile of American Jewish maleness—conforming to neither the biblical nor the comedic stereotypes of the time—and therefore directly challenged the persistent critique of Jewish masculinity during the postwar era. In addition to his image as a super Jew, his appeal also lay in the fact that he was a "nice Jewish boy." In this regard, the Koufax persona echoed contemporary comic book superheroes all the more—for he projected an image of Jewish masculinity that was as much the mild-mannered Clark Kent as it was the muscle-bound Superman. The original Superman character was conceived in 1932 by two young Jewish men, Jerry Siegel and Joe Shuster; and it was their ingenious innovation to give the superhero an alternate persona, a "secret identity." Siegel and Shuster's creation has been interpreted as a reflection of their own American-Jewish duality, as the fantasy of a nerdy and bespectacled Jew to be a strong and powerful gentile.[47] The doubled character of Superman/Clark Kent combined both attributes, being superheroic and an ordinary human simultaneously. That Koufax was a super/man in this sense helps further explain his popularity among Jews. Both physically powerful and temperamentally gentle, he would come to be seen as the ideal American Jewish male—for Jewish men who embody strength *and* refined behavior have been few and far between.

Prior to Koufax, images of powerful Jewish men in America were found mainly in the unrefined lives of Jewish gangsters such as Meyer

Lansky and Bugsy Siegel. Whereas the Jewish man seen as an ineffectual intellectual is a common stereotype—as noted, a stereotype epitomized by Woody Allen, who attained his celebrity in the period immediately following the Koufax era, the late 1960s and 1970s. But Koufax—the key figure in the transitional era of the early 1960s—balanced both extremes, almost uniquely combining the opposite qualities of a superstar athlete and a "nice Jewish boy" from Brooklyn. Even his name contains the duality: "Sandy," the soft, friendly, non-gender-specific first name; and "Koufax," the surname he adopted from his stepfather, all hard consonants and harsh sounds.[48]

The Koufax story demonstrates the extent to which Jewish masculinity has been conditioned by the American experience. Like African American men and other minority males, Jewish men have often had to "emasculate" themselves so as not to pose too great a threat to the gentile majority[49] (and also, perhaps, to Jewish women). Hence the stereotype of a nice Jewish boy arose to quash any potential for Jewish male empowerment. As the English equivalent of the Yiddish *mensch*, the phrase may seem innocuous enough; but in effect it is a backhanded compliment, demeaning the male Jew as less than a man and thereby "cutting him down to size." Writing in the 1970s, Philip Roth would describe "nice Jewish boy" as an "epithet" implying "repression, respectability, and social acceptance."[50] Such an image both engenders and reflects a social-psychological dynamic whereby Jewish men must avoid any display of "masculine" assertiveness or aggression, and instead conform to a more "feminine" image of niceness and gentility—a narrative that, once again, has played out in the history of American Jewish celebrity.

In the early 1960s, several famous or almost-famous Jews offered their own solutions to the problem of Jewish masculinity. Norman Mailer, confronting the dilemma, chose to embrace an image of machismo—but to do so, he was forced to erase his Jewishness as far as possible. Another Norman, Podhoretz, says of Mailer, "He spent his entire life trying to extirpate what he himself called the 'nice Jewish boy' from his soul, which is one of the reasons he has done so many outrageous things and gotten into trouble, including with the police. It's part of trying to overcome that life-long terror of being a sissy."[51] Woody Allen moved in the opposite direction. Although he had been quite athletic as a youngster growing up in Brooklyn, he buried that side of himself entirely as he created the familiar comedic character of a Jewish nerd, a modern-day *shlemiel*. Still other Jewish men chafed against this image of pusillanimity, as Philip Roth's character Alex Portnoy importunes his psychiatrist:

"Doctor, I can't stand any more being frightened like this over nothing! Bless me with manhood! Make me brave! Make me strong! Make me *whole*! Enough being a nice Jewish boy . . ."[52] Tragically, the American Jewish male finds it nearly impossible to be a *mensch* and a man at once. In his era, Koufax was the one great exception to the rule.

The Jewhooing of Sandy Koufax

We are now in a better position to explain the extraordinary Jewhooing of Sandy Koufax—that is, specifically Jewish adulation and celebration of the baseball star—and to see why it began so early in his career. He first began to draw attention with his breakout seasons of 1961 and 1962 (the latter being cut short by a finger injury), when he set a new National League record for strikeouts in a season and when he pitched his first no-hitter. By the spring of 1963, Koufax's early feats inspired cousins Jesse and Roy Silver to imagine an "All-Time, All-Jewish" team, a "big league minyan of stars." As they explained, "Even if Koufax never pitches again, he already has established himself as one of the outstanding Jewish players of all time. His future, understandably, has triggered many discussions about an All-Star Jewish Team, a berth on which he is assured."[53] The attention would only increase with his spectacular record of 25-5 (games won-lost) in 1963. In September, as he passed the 20-game mark, the *National Jewish Post and Opinion* put the achievement in perspective by noting that Koufax "became only the second Jewish pitcher in the history of major league baseball to attain that magic figure."[54] In both cases, the arrival of a new Jewish star prompted the memory of *all* Jewish baseball players—principally as a way of contextualizing the event, but also perhaps to defend against the implicit message of Koufax's success: its exceptionalism. The rise of Koufax paradoxically served to remind Jewish fans what a rarity the Jewish athlete had become.

More than any other event, one would expect the Yom Kippur game of 1965 to have elicited an impassioned response from the Jewish community. In fact, at the precise moment when Koufax stated "I am a Jew" in no uncertain terms, at least some of his fellow Jews responded, "Yes, but first we are American." One week after the World Series, the *Detroit Jewish News* published a tribute to "Sandy Koufax, an American Hero." The Jewish editorialist saw "an important moral lesson for Americans" in the recently concluded series: "that it is possible for people of all faiths, of all races, to meet on equal ground." Koufax's avowal of his Judaism thus made an unequivocal statement in support of American pluralism, baseball, and the "spirit of good will, . . . fair play and mutual respect" that America and baseball have in common. Ironically enough, Koufax's public demonstration of his ethnic *difference*—by choosing to absent himself from a game—was used to highlight the *inclusivity* of both baseball and American life. His Jewishness per se was secondary; though clearly not "an observant Jew," the piece notes, Koufax was nevertheless "respectful in relation to his ancestry."[55] Interestingly, this particular article was later selected for inclusion in a sourcebook of "the Jewish 1960s"—canonization, of a sort.

As early as 1948, Harold Ribalow initiated the trend of canonizing Jews in professional sports with the publication of *The Jew in American Sport*. The work has been a perennial favorite of Jewish readers (and those looking for a suitable bar mitzvah gift), earning multiple reprintings and new editions. Koufax was first included in the third revised and enlarged edition of 1966. In forty-eight detailed pages, Ribalow summarizes the career of the man he calls "the Jewish southpaw star of the Los Angeles Dodgers," and makes the case for Koufax as "The World's Greatest Pitcher."[56] Anticipating the speculation that would accompany Koufax's name to the present day, Ribalow wonders whether "there ever had been a better pitcher in baseball," and further contemplates the extent of his celebrity:

> He had won almost every award in the game that a pitcher could win. He had achieved miracles . . . He had captured the imagination not only of the baseball world but of millions to whom baseball was of small importance. He had had books written about him, thousands of articles and hundreds of feature stories. He had had his picture on the cover of the leading magazines in the United States and he had become one of the best-known names in the United States. Thus, he had also become one of the most famous Jews in America.[57]

In place of the journalistic intimations of Koufax's otherness, Ribalow stresses his statistical superiority and cites contemporary players to bear witness to his ability. He quotes the great St. Louis Cardinal hitter, Stan Musial, to the effect that "Koufax is the most overpowering pitcher I ever faced. He overpowers you with both his fastball and his curve . . . Sandy throws as hard as any pitcher I ever saw." Ribalow also spends some time documenting the first half of Koufax's career, the period *before* he was great. In addition to making the case for Koufax's greatness, therefore, Ribalow also mounts a defense of his early struggles, for example, noting his lack of experience when he first signed with the Dodgers and explaining the disadvantage he faced: "being a bonus player, he could not be farmed out to the minors. He had to learn his craft the hard way, in the majors, with veteran players looking askance at bonus rookies."[58] When his breakout season came in 1961, it was overshadowed by the record-breaking exploits of the Yankees' Roger Maris.

Koufax's own sense of history comes through in Ribalow's account. In a 1959 game against the Giants, Koufax became aware that with fifteen strikeouts, he was on the brink of making history: "In the ninth, Koufax realized that if he fanned the side he would shatter the National League record of seventeen, held by Dizzy Dean, and the major league mark of eighteen by Bob Feller would be equaled." He struck out the side and captured the record. After his first no-hitter in 1962, he was quoted as saying, "It doesn't happen very often. A lot of great pitchers never got one. Sal Maglie had to wait almost to the end of his career to get his."[59] And earlier that year, Koufax gave an interview to a reporter in which he reminisced about the first Dodgers game he ever attended, as a small boy with his father. This offers a quite dissonant view from the press portrayal of him as a disinterested baseball player.

On Jewish issues, Ribalow is matter-of-fact. He notes as unremarkable, for example, Koufax's 1963 decision to have "altered his pitching schedule to avoid working on the Jewish High Holidays. He had pitched in Philadelphia with two days rest and in St. Louis with three days off so that he could miss working during the holidays." Following Koufax's starring performance in the World Series of that year, Ribalow tells us that the Los Angeles County Supervisor "proposed that Fairfax Avenue be renamed Koufax Avenue," without explaining that Fairfax was the heart of a Jewish neighborhood. Regarding the 1965 World Series, Ribalow writes,

> Normally, Koufax, the Dodger ace, would have been the first Dodger pitcher to take the mound. But it was Yom Kippur and Sandy already had told Alston—and the sports world—that he would not play ball on the Jewish holiday. This act of faith made for a good deal of discussion throughout the nation, but Koufax won the admiration of almost everyone by making clear he did not think that even a baseball game, a World Series game at that, was as important to him as observing Yom Kippur.[60]

Ribalow adds further perspective, stressing its normalcy, as he concludes:

> Koufax also had been aware of his image as an American-Jewish sports star. And he always made a point of observing Jewish holidays, regardless

of baseball schedules. He told many reporters that this was nothing new with him. Since 1955, he had followed this discipline. Once, his manager had scheduled him to pitch on a Jewish holiday and Sandy asked to be excused. Alston then began to check the Hebrew calendar to make sure that he worked out his rotation in such a fashion that Koufax would not lose a turn on the mound and, at the same time, not have to miss marking a holiday.[61]

In 1966, therefore, the Yom Kippur incident of 1965 had not yet acquired the mythic quality it would have in later years. A year after his induction into the Baseball Hall of Fame in 1971, an entry on Koufax appeared in the authoritative *Encyclopedia Judaica*, which briefly notes, "Koufax would never play on Rosh Ha-Shanah and Yom Kippur."[62]— with no mention of the 1965 event per se. Nor was it considered worthy of note by the Jewish Sports Hall of Fame, founded in Los Angeles in 1974 (later renamed the International Jewish Sports Hall of Fame, it is currently located in Israel). Koufax's entry cites all the key points of his career, especially his record-breaking exploits of 1963, and also highlights the question of his Jewishness. Regarding his feat of setting a new record for shutout games in a season:

> Koufax notched his 11th shutout after careful planning. Although he was involved in a heated pennant race, he arranged his pitching rotation so that it would not conflict with the Jewish holidays. The day after he notched the victory he flew to Los Angeles to be with his parents. His observance of religious holidays was noted editorially in papers throughout the country. However, Koufax, a member of B'nai B'rith, said: "It's nothing new. I've done it every year since 1955 when former Brooklyn Dodger coach Jake Pitler [who was Jewish] told me to do it if I felt strongly enough about it." Koufax's Jewishness brought into clearer focus a 1961 incident when Dodger manager Walter Alston was roundly criticized for scheduling the southpaw to pitch on Yom Kippur Day. Alston had to change pitchers at the last moment and Los Angeles lost. Since that time the Dodger skipper had a Jewish calendar on his desk . . .[63]

The Jewish Sports Hall of Fame entry adds that "Koufax was baseball's top attraction," repeats Casey Stengel's quip, and ends by noting his perfect game—with no mention of Yom Kippur.

This would change dramatically beginning in the 1980s, when the Yom Kippur myth began to take center stage. In his 1982 compilation of *American Jewish Biographies*, Murray Polner writes of Koufax, "In the 1965 World Series, one of the games fell on Yom Kippur. The club indicated its respect for Koufax by acceding to his request to stay away from the ballpark on this most sacred day and thereby skip his place in the pitching rotation. Because the team lost that day, he received a lot of criticism in the southern California press, but Koufax insisted that his personal beliefs took priority over business. And the Dodgers did go on to win the series, anyway."[64] In the following year, Robert Slater followed in Ribalow's tradition with the publication of *Great Jews in Sports*, adding, "A host of stories, many of them simply not true, have developed surrounding Sandy Koufax's relationship to his Jewish faith. One which appears true is that the Dodgers took the Jewish High Holy Days into consideration so that Koufax could pitch as much as possible during September or October. Another that Sandy himself denies has it that because of Koufax, the Dodger clubhouse was stocked with bagels, lox, and chopped chicken liver, all traditional Jewish foods."[65] On the other hand, notes Slater, Koufax did confirm the Yom Kippur story of 1965 to be true.

Yet another compendium of Jewish athletes was published at decade's end. In *The Jewish Athletes' Hall of Fame*, Buddy Robert S. Silverman ups the ante on the question of Koufax's Jewishness. Having noticed that Koufax's 1972 induction into the Baseball Hall of Fame followed by a month the infamous massacre of Israelis at the Munich Olympics, Silverman surmised that the pitcher's "unique aura of fear and anticipation" might somehow be linked to his Jewish identity. In 1973, Silverman contacted Koufax "and posed questions to him regarding the impact of the Munich murders of Israeli athletes on American Jewish athletes, disparate treatment he may have experienced because of his being Jewish, and the appropriateness of Jewish athletes using their fame to promote the public's support of Jewish causes."[66] But Koufax, protective as always of his privacy, politely refused to reveal his personal feelings about such matters. In the absence of corroboration from the only authoritative source, Silverman felt free to conjecture, and indeed, he created his own *midrash*, or Jewish gloss, on Koufax's career. For example, he provocatively relates the Yom Kippur incident of 1965 to the Yom Kippur War of 1973:

> The publicity surrounding Koufax's decision not to open the World Series in 1965 because it fell on Yom Kippur helped demonstrate the sanctity of that day for a public opinion that would react with shocked horror at the unified attack of Israel eight years later without provocation by Arab forces. Perhaps if Koufax had pitched that day, President Richard M. Nixon might

not have understood the despicability of the Arab attack and might not have been as quick to put American forces on alert. And today, ordinary working Jewish people might experience more difficulty when attempting to take time away from their jobs in observance of the Day of Atonement.[67]

The second suggestion seems far more plausible than the first, in which we are asked to accept that the United States' military response to the Middle East war could have been influenced by the memory of an un-pitched baseball game. But Silverman isn't quite done—his next suggestion is even more farfetched, and I quote in full:

> In 1960, Sandy Koufax had not yet arrived as baseball's greatest pitcher. But that year—on among the greatest of Jewish days, one even perhaps as heroic as the subsequent rescue of Israeli hostages in the now legendary raid on Entebbe—Koufax celebrated with his first one-hitter. The date was May 23, 1960. Hours before the game, Israeli Prime Minister Ben-Gurion, in a voice full of emotion, read the following statement: "Adolf Eichmann is already under arrest in Israel and he will shortly be brought to trial in Israel under the Nazis and Nazi Collaborators Law of 1950." In the second inning of a game between the Pittsburgh Pirates and Los Angeles Dodgers that night, Pirate batter Benny Daniels slapped a clean single. The pitcher was Sandy Koufax. That would be the only hit Koufax would give up that night.
>
> Until now no comparison had ever been made between the simultaneous announcement of Eichmann's capture and the extraordinary accomplishment by this Jewish pitcher. Whether the breakthrough coup de grace by Nazi hunter Simon Wiesenthal in outsmarting the German bureaucrat responsible for contributing to the murder of six million Jewish people inspired Sandy Koufax is purely a matter of conjecture. But, on that night—after learning with the rest of the world of Adolf Eichmann's capture—Sandy Koufax was not to be denied. This was a turning point in Jewish history. Eichmann was eventually executed; and Sandy Koufax became immortal.
>
> Linking the emergence of Sandy Koufax to the highly publicized heroic capture of Adolf Eichmann by Simon Wiesenthal might conflict with the pitcher's own humble assessment. But, at the time of Eichmann's capture, Koufax had an inauspicious record of 28 games won and 31 games lost. The night Eichmann was apprehended, Koufax pitched a spectacular one-hit shutout. From that point on—including the one-hitter—Sandy Koufax compiled an astronomical 119-43 won/lost record. Just about then, his self-confidence began to blossom. Whether the greatness of Simon Wiesenthal inspired Sandy Koufax to recognize his own enormous talent—whether that special sense of pride and extended feeling of personal accomplishment

swelling so many Jewish people had an effect on Sandy Koufax—is some-thing perhaps that even Koufax could not answer.[68]

The idea that Koufax was so deeply affected by news of the apprehen-sion of the Nazi war criminal that he began to pitch brilliantly from that time on is nothing short of ludicrous. Nevertheless, some relation-ship might be posited between collective memory of the Holocaust and the ethnic pride inspired by Koufax, as demonstrated here by Sandor Slomovits, in a reminiscence of his survivor father's appreciation for the American sports star:

> Now, thirty five years later, I've come to understand my father much better than I did then. I know that he had perhaps more powerful reasons than many Jews in this country for appreciating Sandy Koufax's public stand—and for taking his own. Before moving to the United States, he'd lived most of his life in Hungary, in a society where it was often dangerous and some-times lethal just to be a Jew—much less be very public about it. During wwii he had barely survived several years in forced labor camps and had lost, among others, both his parents and his first wife and three children in Auschwitz. To him, a Jew who did not hide his Jewishness, was willing to declare it in as public a way as Sandy Koufax did, was willing to sacrifice something important for his Jewishness, was heroic beyond words.[69]

Though the notion of any direct relationship between Holocaust con-sciousness and the hall of fame career of Koufax is itself specious, Silver-man may inadvertently have hit on a greater truth. As he implies, the capture of Eichmann and the subsequent internationally broadcast trial in Jerusalem did, in fact, have a profound effect on many American Jews. It simultaneously reminded them of the vulnerability of Jewish existence, as embodied in the victims of the Holocaust; and, at the same time, of the post–World War II emergence of Jewish power, as embodied in the State of Israel. This new dual consciousness, of Jewish vulnerability *and* power—both, it must be noted, functions of Jewish *difference*—condi-tioned the American Jewish mindset of the early 1960s. It was against this background that Koufax came to prominence; and it is in this context that the impact of his persona on his fellow Jews must be understood.

Contemporary Images of Koufax

Recent years have seen renewed attention to the Jewishness of Sandy Koufax. Ken Burns, for example, in his acclaimed 1994 documentary on the history of baseball, titles the section on Koufax simply and affectionately "The Jewish Kid," borrowing the phrase from Casey Stengel's famous assessment of Koufax's standing in baseball history: "Forget the other fellow, Walter Johnson. The Jewish kid is probably the best of them." The talking heads gathered by Burns to praise Koufax invariably describe him in terms connoting virtuosity and rarefied talent. For example, longtime Dodgers announcer Vin Scully reverently calls him "a genius" and compares his reception upon walking out of the dugout to that of a symphony conductor. Writer Gerald Early similarly calls him "an extraordinary artist," "a kind of Picasso on the mound," and further notes his "cerebral" quality, having a "sort of artistic flair about him."[70] That all of this is prefaced by a title like "The Jewish Kid" suggests that such indications of Koufax's otherness, a form of subtle antisemitism during the 1960s, has by now transformed into a celebration of his specialness—demonstrating how philosemitism is sometimes just the other side of the coin of antisemitism.

Such Jewish celebration of Koufax became commonplace in the 1990s. The decade was marked by the Kennedy-esque presidency of Bill Clinton (whose cabinet was stocked full of Jews—Rubin, Reich, Glickman, and so on); the appearance of yet another crop of Jewish celebrities (Spielberg, Drescher, Seinfeld, and so on); and a rise in Jewish survivalist anxieties—all echoing the early 1960s. Not surprisingly, a trend toward the teaching of Jewish heroes took hold in educational circles, and Koufax often took center stage. He appears prominently, for example, on the covers of two publications intended for a young audience: *Jewish Heroes & Heroines of America: 150 True Stories of American Jewish Heroism* (1996) and *Extraordinary Jewish Americans* (1998). Their portrayals of Koufax are telling. Author Seymour Brody concludes his portrait: "Koufax will always be famous for breaking records as a pitcher in baseball and not playing baseball on Yom Kippur and Rosh Hashana."[71]

But the cover art of the two books is even more revealing. *Jewish Heroes & Heroines*, stressing women's contributions, depicts four figures on its cover: astronaut Judith Resnik, Albert Einstein, Barbara Walters, and the young Sandy Koufax, wearing a Brooklyn Dodgers cap. Of the fifty-plus figures celebrated in *Extraordinary Jewish Americans*, six are depicted on the cover: Groucho Marx, Sandy Koufax, Betty Friedan, Barbra Streisand, Steven Spielberg, and, perhaps to add some sense of history, Meyer Guggenheim. The juxtaposition of six black-and-white photographs of *yiddishe punim* (Jewish faces) makes a subtle point— Jews are an *ethnos*, family members, a people. Nestled between the cigar-chomping Marx and feminist matriarch Friedan, as if to suggest he was

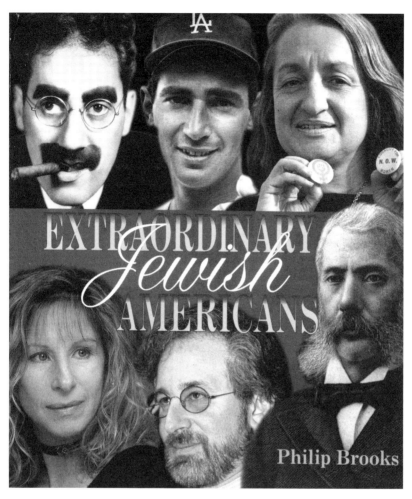

Extraordinary Jewish Americans (1998), a graphic example of the Jewhooing of Sandy Koufax.

their secret love child, Sandy Koufax has never looked more stereotypically Jewish, with protruding ears, dark eyes, large nose, and imperfect teeth. It's almost as if the photo was retouched to make him look more like a member of the tribe.

A turning point of a sort came with the 1996 publication of an encomium to Koufax written by a prominent rabbi. Published in the *Northern California Jewish Bulletin*, Rabbi Lee Bycel's article, "Sandy Koufax Taught Pride to Generation of Young Jews," marked a new willingness to claim the baseball star as a Jewish icon. Demonstrating the truth of **83**

Rabbi Hirschfield's comments to Koufax at the White House, Bycel reminisces about his own youthful adulation of the Jewish sports hero, writing, "As a Jewish boy and an ardent baseball fan, I had a great need for Jewish heroes—especially on the playing field. Koufax's refusal to play on Yom Kippur filled me with pride. I realized that day that no one should ever be embarrassed when practicing one's religion or identifying with one's ancestral culture. Ethnic and religious identity should engender fulfillment and hope." Speaking for many of his generation—and to a new generation at the same time—Bycel further sermonizes: "It was a courageous act for Koufax to abstain from playing in an era that preferred to sanitize difference. His decision not to pitch that Yom Kippur served as an important reminder that America shelters many different faiths and religious practices. Koufax taught me that I could hope to take an active part in American life without compromising my religious convictions. This lesson has remained, and has solidified my commitment to make it accessible to all people." And Bycel concludes, "He was a great baseball player and a Jew, but who could have imagined that his not playing would inspire a generation of youth to embrace their distinctive identity? . . . Koufax's act gave me and a great many in my generation a renewed determination to assert our Jewish identity . . . Sandy, I thank you for the inspiration and the example you provided. Today, 31 years later, your decision shines brighter than ever."[72]

Thirty years after the event, Koufax's decision not to play ball on Yom Kippur had become the stuff of Jewish legend—an inspirational tale for an entire generation, and hence a milestone in Jewish history. Jewish filmmakers Joel Coen and Ethan Coen acknowledge as much in their 1998 comedy *The Big Lebowski*, in which John Goodman's Jewish-by-choice character describes Judaism as "three thousand years of beautiful tradition: from Moses to Sandy Koufax." Koufax's symbolic value and appeal to Jewish youth is put to further service in the 1996 curricular guide *Jewish Heroes, Jewish Values*, whose chapter on Koufax is titled "A Pitcher Goes to Synagogue." An image of Koufax occupies the center of the cover illustration, surrounded by fellow Jewish heroes such as Albert Einstein, Golda Meir, Steven Spielberg, Anne Frank, and Hannah Senesh. The book tells the story of each so as to exemplify a cardinal Jewish value; in Koufax's case it is "K'lal Yisrael, the mitzvah of Jewish solidarity."[73]

As the twentieth century drew to an end, the Jewish idolization of Koufax dovetailed with a more general appreciation of his sports greatness. In the summer of 1999, *Sports Illustrated* chose Koufax as its "favorite athlete of the century." Chosen over other all-time greats, such as basketball's Bill Russell and hockey's Wayne Gretzky, Koufax was so honored for having certain admirable personal qualities in addition to his athletic prowess. Its feature article, "Our Favorite Athletes," praises Koufax for putting "team before self, modesty before fame and God before the World Series"; and the piece devoted to him captures both his supernatural athletic ability and the religious reverence he inspired in its title, "The Left Arm of God."[74] Similarly, the sports cable channel ESPN broadcast its list of the "50 Greatest Athletes" of the twentieth century that same year, and the only baseball pitcher to make the cut was Koufax. Its profile covers the usual bases, emphasizing the pitcher's private nature. Following the 1963 World Series, the narrator intones, "Sandy Koufax would never be at peace with his new celebrity." The profile then delves into the Jewish issue in some depth, and as usual, begins with "the first game of the 1965 World Series against the Twins. It was Yom Kippur. He spent the day in a synagogue."[75] Fascinatingly, public reaction to the event is represented by the unlikeliest of Koufax fans, Rev. Jesse Jackson. The black Baptist preacher and civil rights leader simply *kvells* (gushes) over the Jewish pitcher's courageous decision: "The cameras are rolling, the crowds are cheering, and the rulers [?] are waiting, but he had to draw a line on his sense of religion and dignity and heritage. He would not violate that, even for the glory of a ballgame. I thought that was one of the great statements in American athletics."[76]

The Jackson quote reveals how Koufax's Yom Kippur stand played in the non-Jewish, Christian world. Apparently, gentiles as well as Jews— especially people of faith—took pride in Koufax's seeming religious loyalty. Echoing Jackson, Wladyslaw Pleszczynski writes, "Koufax is best known today for declining to pitch the 1965 World Series opener because it fell on Yom Kippur. In my [Catholic] parochial school world— and I suspect most American precincts—that was the first anyone had heard of that holy day. (The Yom Kippur War in Israel was a distant eight years away.) The liberating decision clinched his standing as the greatest Jewish sports hero ever. But more typical must have been the reactions I experienced: whatever Koufax wants to do is fine by us."[77]

In both cases, Christian observers see Koufax's decision not to play on Yom Kippur as a public display of faith and loyalty to one's "church"— and also, perhaps, as evidence of the religious, "Judeo-Christian" basis of American life. Of course, many American Jews feel rather uncomfortable with such characteristically Christian sentiments; and yet, such Christian acceptance of Jews and Judaism—expressed here by their recognition of

Koufax as a religious hero, as well as their exposure to elements of Judaism such as Yom Kippur—can only serve to gladden the hearts of Jews, who, despite their social and economic success, remain an insecure religious minority in an overwhelmingly Christian country. Isn't it possible, then, that the Koufax myth derives at least some of its appeal from this simple fact: that his ostensibly religious statement casts Jews in a favorable light in the eyes of their more religiously inclined fellow citizens?

As discussed earlier, however, Koufax's actual motives were not so very devout. Following Jackson, therefore, ESPN interviewed another member of the clergy who reflects on this question. Hillel Silverman, rabbi of Los Angeles's Sinai Temple from 1964 to 1980, spoke with Koufax and took the opportunity to ask him about the famous decision of 1965: "I discovered that he was not necessarily a religiously observant Jew. And I asked him about it. I said, 'if you yourself didn't frequent the temple for services so often, why did you do it?' And he said to me very humbly, 'I felt I was a role model for Jewish children. And I felt that it would be good for them to see somebody who respects himself.'"[78] One cannot help but notice the discrepancy between Koufax's explanation here and his earlier public position of nonchalance. While in his autobiography and elsewhere he downplays the whole affair, claiming no significance for it at all, here he pitches his Yom Kippur "observance" as a moral lesson for young people. Koufax's new sentiment—at least as remembered by Rabbi Silverman—reflects the typically American notion that loyalty to one's group is a form of self-respect. And, as in Rabbi Bycel's sermon, the symbolic importance of the Jewish baseball player's actions to Jewish youth is highlighted as well.

But young people grow up, and so more recent offerings on Koufax have been intended for an adult audience. The new century has seen the appearance of two new biographies by sports journalists: Edward Gruver's *Koufax* (2000) and Jane Leavy's *Sandy Koufax* (2002). Both, as distinct from the spate of Koufax biographies of the 1960s,[79] now include lengthy discussion of the Jewish issue. Gruver writes, "Like DiMaggio, like Jackie Robinson and Roberto Clemente, Koufax was a significant ethnic figure in major league baseball. He was a star of Jewish heritage, and in the socially conscious sixties, his observances of High Holy Days had a tremendous impact on Jews across the country."[80] Gruver seems especially interested in Koufax's holiday observance, devoting several pages to describing how "Koufax's decision to remain faithful to his religion even though it could cost his team a World Series win inspired a generation of youths to embrace their religious identity."[81] Regarding the 1965 series, he theorizes, "The fact that Koufax was beaten by the Twins in Game Two may have had something to do with his being weakened by a lengthy fast in the two days prior to his start."[82] Gruver again assumes Koufax's observance of the Yom Kippur fast, in reference to a 1961 extra-inning game on the evening following the holy day: "what makes Koufax's performance so incredible is that he was able to work as many innings and throw as many pitches as he did coming off a 25-hour fast."[83] Beyond this spurious surmise, Gruver further offers that "while he never pitched on Passover, Rosh Hashanah, or Yom Kippur, research of his career reveals he pitched on Shavuot eight times and Sukkot/Shemini Atzereth twice."[84] He later refines the observation: "While Koufax never pitched on the Passover Seder that occurs the first evening of the holiday, he did pitch on this holiday four times in his career."[85] Not exactly typical fare for a baseball biography, and perhaps the only known instance of sports commentary on the Jewish holiday of Shemini Atzereth.

Citing Harvey Frommer,[86] Lee Bycel, and Aviva Kempner's documentary on Hank Greenberg at some length, Gruver also quotes a number of Jewish fans to the effect that "Koufax's willingness to publicly declare that he was a Jew brought enormous pride to the Jewish community." But beyond this commonplace observation, he also makes two more idiosyncratic points. First, he reminds us of the ethnic orientation of the Dodgers' fan base. Once Koufax joined the club, many Jewish fans began to see the Dodgers as the "Jewish team" (especially as opposed to the "goyish team," the Yankees): "Jewish families identified with the Dodgers. They saw in them a team whose cry of 'Wait 'til next year!' played into the Jews' messianic hope of looking to the future." Second, Gruver quotes Roger Kahn concerning Koufax's reticence on Jewish topics: Koufax reportedly told the well-known sportswriter that "he thought too much was made of his being a Jewish pitcher, and not enough as just a pitcher." Gruver then concludes, "Koufax's reluctance to be portrayed as anything special . . . extended not only to his athleticism but also to his Judaism."[87] On the one hand, Koufax was seen as the epitome of Jewishness; on the other, he himself made little of his Jewish background. Perhaps, we might suggest, it was his very blankness regarding his own identity that enabled so many to project onto him their most impassioned feelings of Jewish pride and identification.

Leavy's book received far more attention and ultimately had a greater impact on Koufax's celebrity image. *Sandy Koufax* was a *New York Times* best seller for much of 2002–2003 and was widely reviewed. For the first time, a Koufax biographer received direct access to the reclusive hall of famer, and the resulting sense of authenticity and intimacy gives the book its added value. Leavy's principal theme is not the man but the image—that is, the mystique and allure of the Koufax persona in the public mind. In the words of one reviewer, "THE PROBLEM is not to figure out why Sandy Koufax was a great pitcher. The problem is to figure out why he was Sandy Koufax—the stuff of myth."[88] Hence, where Gruver devotes several pages to this topic, Leavy sprinkles her work throughout with anecdotes, quotes, and other references to Koufax's amazingly broad following, from poet laureate Robert Pinsky to a teen-aged groupie named Eileen Rogow. Though not originally a Dodgers fan herself, Leavy includes her own adulation of the man—like so many of his fans, "Sandy Koufax had made himself at home in [her] soul."[89] As he did for so many other Jews, Koufax provided the author, "the grandchild of Jewish immigrants, with an unlikely barometer of [her] own assimilation into mainstream American culture."[90]

While referencing Koufax's Jewishness throughout her narrative, Leavy also notes the low profile of the issue early in his career: "Koufax didn't trumpet his background, nor did he hide it." And she quotes Tom Villante, the team's broadcast coordinator: "It wasn't as though Sandy had a Star of David on his sleeve. Some people thought he was French."[91] That would change, of course, with the Yom Kippur series. In a chapter titled "King of the Jews"—a sly comparison of Koufax with Jesus Christ—Leavy details both the pivotal event of October 1965 and the Jewish adoration stemming from it. She records businessman George Blumenthal's acquisition of a precious item of sports memorabilia—Koufax's rookie jersey—and his use of it to raise funds for a Jewish cultural institution. She records future rabbi Bruce Lustig's youthful embarrassment when caught listening to the Dodgers broadcast in the middle of the Yom Kippur service. And she records Alan Dershowitz's mistaken memory that Koufax had once appeared together with his father in a Brooklyn synagogue.

Throughout her book, Leavy makes two salient points—one, that while clearly not religiously observant, Koufax was a typically cultural Jew of his generation. As childhood friend (and Mets owner) Fred Wilpon explains, "His Jewishness has nothing to do with whether he wears a yarmulke every day. And I will tell you this—he is very Jewish. He is a Jewish being. And unlike most of us who aren't very religious, he is very Jewish in his thinking because he's very New York in his thinking and his background."[92] Leavey sums up the Jewish mythos of Sandy Koufax:

On October 6, 1965, Koufax was inscribed forever in the Book of Life as the Jew who refused to pitch on Yom Kippur . . . In that moment, he became known as much for what he refused to do as for what he did on the mound. *By refusing to pitch, . . . [h]e became inextricably linked with the American Jewish experience* . . . In Jewish households, he was the New Patriarch: Abraham, Isaac, Jacob, and Sand*ee*. A moral exemplar, and single too! (Such a catch!) He was every Jewish mother's dream.[93]

Yet despite being showered with all this attention, Koufax himself has remained close-mouthed on the subject of his Jewishness—Leavy's second point. As she attempts to explain, "Some have attributed his silence to modesty; others to the realization that nothing he could say would improve upon what he did. But this too is true. It's embarrassing being a religious icon, especially an inadvertent one." And somewhat enigmatically, she concludes, "Koufax refused to be a Jew's Jew or a gentile's Jew. He may have been different but he refused to be anything other than himself."[94] One is left with the impression that even after 469 interviews, Leavy remains just as puzzled as ever regarding Koufax's Jewish identity.

In a chapter added to the 2003 paperback edition, Leavy extends her coverage of the widespread adulation of Koufax—especially in the Jewish community where, apparently, she did most of her post-publication book touring. She breathlessly describes the *yentas* and *kibitzers* she met at various Jewish events, all claiming some prior connection to their idol or else attempting to connect to him through her. Through it all, she maintains her own admiration for Koufax, consistently describing him as a man of great dignity and humanity, the ultimate *mensch*. The summary effect of all this idolizing is a work that, while attempting to be critical, succeeds in becoming the ultimate example of Jewhooing. Practically screaming "He's one of us!" through much of the book, Leavy betrays her journalistic objectivity with a patently Jewish veneration of her own. It is the greatest love letter to Koufax ever written.

Many reviews of the Leavy book echo the idea of a Koufax cult of idolization. *Time* magazine writes, "As one of the very greatest of living ballplayers, [Koufax is] still venerated by fans—especially Jewish fans, who embraced him with a fervor bordering on idolatry." And similarly, "The impact of Koufax goes beyond baseball alone . . . His quality playing made him a baseball icon. His decision to not play a game made him a religious icon."[95] Another reviewer compares him to yet another famous Jew: "Dodgers Hall of Fame pitcher Sandy Koufax is a figure so legendary for his talent and his reclusiveness that he could well be considered baseball's J. D. Salinger . . . Many American Jews still idolize him for placing his religious beliefs above baseball in the 1965 World Series."[96]

Nevertheless, some of the response is less than favorable. Reviewing the book for the *Los Angeles Times*, Brooklyn-bred screenwriter Walter Bernstein takes the biographer to task for her lack of critical objectivity: "[Leavy's] Koufax is pretty much perfection all around. If you pricked him, there is an even chance he wouldn't bleed. He has no discernible flaws; everyone speaks well of him. It all seems deserved but makes the book monochromatic . . . [quoting Leavy,] 'You don't need to know everything to write the truth.' Maybe not, but if you want to know the man whose biography you are writing, it's nice to know a bit more than this."[97]

A few of the more critical reviewers thus point to some overlooked aspect of the Koufax myth. J. Bottum, for one, revisits the issue of Koufax's seeming inscrutability, what even his teammates called "his aloofness, his distance, his aura of impenetrability." After asserting that "Leavy cannot quite explain . . . why the sun always seemed to center its rays on him," the reviewer adds, "A deeper problem with *Sandy Koufax: A Lefty's Legacy* is that Leavy proves unable to penetrate what Ed Linn (who helped produce Koufax's 1966 autobiography) called the pitcher's 'wall of amiability.' She is hardly alone. After interviewing hundreds of Koufax's friends and acquaintances, Linn came to the conclusion that none of them knew him at all." Koufax's coolness during his playing days and his reclusiveness during the years of his retirement combine to form an image of an unknowable man, a blank slate. Bottum also questions the popular view of his physical appearance:

> People always described Koufax as handsome, but he was not, really, and especially not while he was pitching. . . . People may have called him handsome because they lacked any other word to describe what they saw in him. The reason Koufax seemed so distant was the same reason fans and players alike were so fascinated by him: he felt, and they could see him feel, the burden of something given to very few human beings—the chance to be great at what he was good at.

In the end, Bottum reaches the same reverential conclusion as most others: "Sandy Koufax was an Achilles figure—and . . . we cannot keep our eyes off such men. How can it be otherwise? The sun shines on them, and for a moment in their lives greatness shimmers into view."[98] Like so many others, he is simply awestruck by Koufax's mythic stature.

In the wake of Jane Leavy's hagiographic biography—and the near-unanimous praise it garnered—came a blatant attack on both the book and Koufax himself. On December 19, 2002, three months after the publication of *Sandy Koufax*, the *New York Post* gossip column reported that an unnamed "Hall of Fame baseball hero" had "cooperated with a best-selling biography only because the author promised to keep it secret that he is gay."[99] Both Koufax and Leavy denied the rumor, but the flap was enough to cause Koufax to sever his ties with the Dodgers; the team was owned by the same media conglomerate as the *Post*. Whether true or not the report was a malicious intrusion into Koufax's cherished privacy. Moreover, it can also be seen as a response to the problem noted earlier: Leavy had not gotten to the deeper truth of Koufax's persona, so imagination was given free reign. And perhaps the accusation of hidden identity recapitulated something essential about the popular image of Koufax—its irreducible otherness. Though Koufax loyalist Leavy had trumpeted his "just one of the boys" normalcy, the fact remains that Koufax has always been seen as an outsider. And in this regard, perceptions of Jewishness and rumors of gayness really amount to the same thing—othering.

Artists, responsive to the ambiguities of the man, have gravitated to Koufax as a subject; their artistic representations of the baseball pitcher offer graphic demonstration of both his mythic status and conflicted image. In 1967, noted Jewish painter R. B. Kitaj was commissioned by the art director of *Sports Illustrated* magazine to create an insert for a piece on Koufax. Kitaj complied with an abstract work ironically titled *Upon Never Having Seen Koufax Pitch*. But then, thirty years later, ostensibly better aware of Koufax's prowess, Kitaj would supply a likeness of the pitcher in a 1998 composition titled *Koufax*. In 1994 another Jewish artist, Deborah Kass, reimagined Andy Warhol's *Baseball* (1962), a composition of repeated images of slugger Roger Maris, by replacing Maris with Koufax.[100] Included in the provocative museum exhibition *Too Jewish? Challenging Traditional Identities*, the piece was described by the curator: "*Sandy Koufax* (fig. 14) is a celebrity portrait of the Jewish pitcher on the mound a la Warhol. (Koufax also happens to be related to Kass.) Through the image of the Jewish baseball hero, one is made to remember how vital such idols were to Jews in postwar America."[101] Yet Kass, an artist with penetrating Jewish sensibilities, chose not to signify Koufax's Jewishness in any explicit way. For example, the artist avoided portraying Koufax's facial features and thus exploring his Jewish identity or its meaning to others (as she would do with Barbra Streisand; see Chapter 5).

Double portrait by
Nicholas Volpe (1964),
revealing two sides of the
elusive Koufax persona.

It is instructive in this regard to compare Kass to the official Dodgers artist, Nicholas Volpe, whose 1962 and 1964 portraits of Koufax are deeply personal and unmistakably ethnic in their portrayal. The latter work juxtaposes two Koufax likenesses—one the suave celebrity, the other the intense ballplayer—together evoking the complexity of his identity. In the case of both Kitaj and Kass, however, as in numerous contemporary images of Koufax by artists such as Stephen Holland, Randsom Keith, LeRoy Neiman, Robert Simon, and Richard Wallich, portraits of the athlete most often depict Koufax's uniformed body, on the mound, in the midst of his pitching motion—legs akimbo in forward stride, arching his back and cocking his left arm to fire the next pitch. Though every baseball pitcher approximates the same motion, the image is nevertheless immediately recognizable as Koufax—slightly awkward, yet devastatingly effective. Only Kitaj's 1998 work combines the two perspectives, portraying Koufax in mid-pitch, with a seemingly off-kilter head, in Semitic profile, perched precariously atop his off-balance body. All these works of art are vivid reminders of why Koufax is so universally revered: he was a unique figure, one of a kind. As in these artistic images, Koufax stands alone, both on the mound and in Jewish memory.

In popular culture, Koufax's name is more often linked to expressions of contemporary Jewish celebrity. In 2003, for example, the popular animated television series *The Simpsons* paid satirical homage to Koufax. In an episode titled "Today I Am a Clown," Krusty the Clown (the *Jazz Singer*-inspired Jewish character of the series) rediscovers his roots while visiting the old Jewish neighborhood. As Krusty enters the ethnically marked space, he encounters a "Jewish Walk of Fame" (modeled after the Hollywood Walk of Fame, which has stars' plaques embedded in the pavement), and the first plaque he sees belongs to none other than Sandy Koufax. His comically exasperated reaction—lamenting a wager he lost when Koufax refused to pitch on Yom Kippur—only deepens the satire, and further mocks the American Jewish proclivity to lionize figures such as Koufax.

The scenario may have been inspired by the real-life Los Angeles, city of Koufax's baseball success. In contemporary LA, his image pops up repeatedly, in obvious places such as Dodger Stadium, but in less obvious venues as well. A landmark of the Jewish community, Canter's Deli on Fairfax Avenue has a 1985 mural on its outside wall depicting Los Angeles Jewish history; Koufax on the pitching mound is prominently displayed at its center. Elsewhere in LA one encounters images of the local hero, sometimes unexpectedly, as in the collection of Koufax photos displayed in the Brooklyn Bagel store on Beverly Boulevard, and among the religious icons adorning the wall of a drugstore in downtown LA—Koufax's image tops them all.

In 2004, Jewish adulation of Koufax reached a high point—six years prior to the White House reception—when Jewish Americans commemorated the 350th anniversary of their arrival in America. One of the most common activities of the yearlong celebration was the making of timelines, and the appearance of the 1960s Dodgers pitcher on timelines of American Jewish history was striking. In May 2005, for example, the American Jewish Historical Society published a special issue of its *Heritage* magazine to commemorate "350 years of American Jewish life." The requisite timeline includes an entry for Koufax, inserting an especially noteworthy pitching performance as a discrete historic event between two larger trends of the 1960s, the Jewish counterculture and the student movement for Soviet Jewry. The intervening caption reads simply, "Sandy Koufax, Los Angeles Dodger pitcher, sets a baseball record when he pitches his fourth no-hitter in four years."[102] A notable sports feat, certainly, but a highlight of American Jewish history? In fact, such a simple accounting of athletic achievement is anomalous. Other citings of Koufax as a Jewish historical figure do not fail to mention the principal reason for his elevated status among his fellow Jews—as for example, the 1971 entry on a timeline published by the American Jewish Committee: "Sanford 'Sandy' Koufax, *who refused to play on the High Holidays*, is initiated into the Baseball Hall of Fame."[103]

In the process of becoming an iconic celebrity himself, Koufax's name came to denote the very notion of Jewish sports celebrity. In a 2004 *Heeb* magazine article titled "Where Have You Gone, Sandy Koufax?" (alluding to the Paul Simon song "Mrs. Robinson," and playing on its famous lyric: "Where have you gone, Joe DiMaggio? A nation turns its weary eyes to you"), Allen Salkin reports on the phenomenon of Jew-hooing of Jewish athletes. It is, he writes, on the rise: "Four decades after Los Angeles Dodger Sandy Koufax refused to pitch on Yom Kippur during the World Series and ignited Jewish pride, the Jewish-athlete-obsession business is red hot. But times have changed since 1965. Now every Jew who lifts a dumbbell at a Muscle Beach competition or warms a bench as a third-string professional is benighted by sports fans as a mini-Koufax."[104] Salkin tells us of the eighteen Jewish Sports Halls of Fame, dozens of websites, and numerous publications dedicated to the "sport" of identifying Jews in sports. Of them all, the most highly publicized has been the American Jewish Historical Society's limited-edition commemorative set of baseball cards, collecting (read: Jewhooing) all 142 Jews who have played professional baseball throughout its history. The project's initiator is Martin Abramowitz, president of "Jewish Major Leaguers, Inc., a not-for-profit organization dedicated to documenting American Jews in America's game." Explaining his motives, Abramowitz writes, "Everyone knows legends Sandy Koufax and Hank Greenberg . . . But what about the other Jewish players who played between 1871 and 2002? Why do we know so little about them?"[105]

The publication of such a set raises some thorny questions. How is it, to commemorate the 350th year of American Jewish life, that the American Jewish Historical Society chose to honor the history of Jews in baseball? As the set itself demonstrates, Jewish players in the national pastime have been a statistical rarity (142 Jews out of approximately 16,700 players overall). Jews, as a group, do not excel on the baseball field. Yet Jews have excelled in other fields, yielding more than their share of all-stars in show business, law, journalism, literature, academia, science, medicine, and so on. So why not issue card sets—as the ultra-Orthodox have done with great rabbis—of "great Jewish lawyers," or "great Jewish intellectuals," or better yet, "great Jewish sportswriters"?

Because, when it comes to Jews in sports, there is an additional boost to the Jewhooing urge—the anomalous condition that the figure not only represents success in the public arena, but success in a field usually dominated by gentiles—hence the excitement surrounding anomalies such as beauty queen Bess Myerson, soldier Mickey Marcus, vice presidential candidate Joe Lieberman, Olympic swimmer Mark Spitz, and the "great Jewish baseball player" Sandy Koufax. The excitement is further heightened if the figure embodies a widely acknowledged success *with* difference preserved, a conspicuous pulling back from the borderland of assimilation, and public proof that social integration does not erase social otherness after all. The Jewish celebrity of Sandy Koufax was all that.

How ironic that the commemorative card set actually downplays the stardom of Koufax. True, of the 142 players listed, place of honor is given to the Dodger pitcher, who merits card number 1. The photo on the card is of a young and innocent-looking Koufax, circa 1960, thus prior to his celebrity; and the text on the back of the card is the contribution of Marc Brettler, professor of Bible at Brandeis University, who opens, "Sandy made his major league debut with the Brooklyn Dodgers at 19," and closes, "Sandy's rookie card was a 1955 Topps, #123."[106] The commemorative card, on both sides, attempts to normalize our image of the hallowed ballplayer. Moreover, the net effect of canonizing every Jewish player in baseball history is to reduce the centrality of Koufax overall.

In 2010, a new documentary film titled *Jews and Baseball: An American Love Story* gave Koufax his due. Combining the comprehensive approach of the card set with more focused attention on Greenberg and Koufax, the documentary effectively highlights the two stars within the context of "all Jews in baseball." Containing a rare interview with Koufax, the film has become the definitive statement on the subject of Jews in baseball;[107] yet it is worth noting that Sandy Koufax himself has as yet inspired no film treatment of his own (unlike Hank Greenberg, Gertrude Berg, Woody Allen, Lenny Bruce, and Bob Dylan, all of whom have been profiled in film documentaries).

A recent book by American Jewish historian Jeffrey Gurock also downplays Koufax, this time in favor of more Jewishly engaged Jewish athletes. In a thorough survey of *Judaism's Encounter with American Sports*, Gurock barely mentions Koufax and devotes no discussion at all to the famous Yom Kippur incident of 1965.[108] Gurock also neglects to tell perhaps the most amazing story about Koufax and religious

Judaism—perhaps because the story never happened. It is the story of a young Hasidic rabbi visiting Koufax and giving him a set of *tefillin*, the leather phylacteries worn by observant Jewish men during the weekday morning prayer. As best as I can reconstruct it, two weeks after the Yom Kippur of 1965, the Lubavitcher Rebbe, Rabbi Menahem Mendel Schneerson, added the following narrative to his *Simchat Torah* homily:

> There was a young man, and in fact he had a beard, he went to see the pitcher that wouldn't pitch on Yom Kippur and he told him that he does not play baseball on Rosh Hashanah either. The young man told the pitcher that he would like to give him a present. He gave him a pair of *tefillin*. The pitcher told him that he still remembers *tefillin*, however, he did not want to put them [on] at that time. The young man left, and that day the pitcher lost the game . . . But at the end it turned out that he won the World Series, and on his table there were the *tefillin*. In the end, even "a distant individual will not be distanced" and he will merit to put them on, and another Jew will be added to those who have donned *tefillin* . . .[109]

The young man was purportedly Rabbi Moshe Feller, who may have been the one to inform the rebbe of Koufax's act of religious loyalty. The rebbe's story of a meeting with Koufax, however, was in all likelihood a fantasy. In the ancient Jewish tradition of *midrash*, the initial event of Koufax's sitting out Yom Kippur was embellished with further detail in order to make a homiletical point—it is an axiom of Lubavitch theology that the *mitzvah* (commandment) of donning *tefillin* is especially vital because it will hasten the coming of *moshiach* (the messiah). With the impetus of the rebbe's *drash*, the story then developed that Feller had actually visited Koufax in his hotel room, given him a set of *tefillin*, and thereby enlisted the rising celebrity in the Hasidic cause. Though even in his own telling, he never saw Koufax actually wearing the *tefillin*, Feller is now known as "the man who put *tefillin* on Sandy Koufax." In subsequent years, he quickly discovered how effective the story was in promoting Jewish identity and observance:

> Rabbi Feller also shared the story with the Anglo Jewish paper in his community and it created a lot of good feeling and Jewish pride. "When I saw how many kids loved the story and how thrilled they were that baseball was associated with *yiddishkeit* [Jewish culture], I knew we had a mission and we started to go to the games and seek out the Jewish players. We've put *tefillin* on Mike Epstein of the Oakland Athletics and Ken Holtzman of the New York Yankees."[110]

Of course, it is possible that Feller's story is true and that he did in fact visit Koufax in his hotel room and leave a pair of *tefillin* behind—but call me a skeptic. Factual or not, the story is an excellent example of myth making. Witnessing the inadvertent religious act of "the most famous Jew in America" (in Feller's description), the Jewish educational leader succeeded in exploiting the incident for the ideological end of promoting Jewish identity. It was a marvelous use of celebrity, and, its probable dishonesty notwithstanding, a perfect illustration of how the images of famous Jews become potent symbols for the consumption of the Jewish public.

As amply demonstrated in this chapter, the myth of Sandy Koufax—and its role in American Jewish consciousness—is formidable and lasting. Rising as an ethnic baseball star in the wake of Hank Greenberg and Jackie Robinson, Koufax also reflected the universal appeal and charisma of 1960s icons John F. Kennedy and Paul Newman. He attained American fame through his unique athletic ability, and gained Jewish immortality through his casual decision to avoid offending fellow Jews by pitching on Yom Kippur. As in Pharaoh's dream, he followed six lean years with six fat ones—and came to represent the ultimate late-bloomer, the embodiment of second efforts. Already a sports legend by the end of his career, Koufax sealed his elite reputation by retiring at the height of his powers, and then, nearly disappearing from public view. Yet despite his own desire to not stand out, he continues to stand apart in the eyes of most others, from fellow players calling him "Super Jew" to yellow journalists calling him gay. In a sense, Koufax was the archetypal American Jew—the outsider who made good and thought he'd joined the club. Though persisting in his claim to (American) normalcy, he was ultimately unsuccessful in the attempt to dispel the popular perception of his (Jewish) otherness.

In all of this, Koufax mirrored the American Jewish experience. Like the rising young baseball star, American Jews of the postwar generation were on the move, away from enclaves such as Brooklyn, and out to the greener pastures of suburbia (with its ubiquitous baseball fields). Like Koufax, acculturating Jews of the 1950s and early 1960s remained shy about public Jewish identification, anxious about being perceived as "too Jewish." But then, echoing the experience of Koufax, some event or series of events served to redraw those boundaries. Whether it was the media sensation of *Exodus*, or the election of Kennedy, or the Eichmann trial, or *Fiddler on the Roof*, or Koufax's refusal to pitch on Yom Kippur—the early 1960s gave Jews a collective kick-start, stimulating their dormant sense of Jewishness.

97

Just as Hollywood filmmakers fashioned mass entertainment from an underlying experience of alienation, the mass appeal of Koufax derived in part from an image of Jewish otherness underlying his public persona. As distinct from the Jewish actors and directors discussed earlier, Koufax had found success in the public arena while being perceived as a Jew. Far more than the Hollywood Jews of the era, he continued to stand apart while fitting in, maintaining a Jewish image while entering the American scene. Likewise, he managed to project an image as a "nice Jewish boy" while at the same time establishing a new model of Jewish masculinity as a sports superstar. It was precisely this dual character that gave his persona its special magic for American Jews. Like him, Jews of the 1960s generation would often find success in the American marketplace; and like him, they mostly would abandon the more explicit Jewishness of their parents along the way. Yet also like him, they would continue to feel themselves outsiders in America, a perpetual minority despite their upward mobility. The Koufax persona perfectly encapsulated these contradictions, and in the process, Sandy Koufax became an American Jewish icon.

Dirty Jew

Bruce was a Jewish comic who embarrassed older Jews because he dared use Yiddishisms usually only heard on stages at the Catskills and Miami Beach— or anywhere two or more Jews gathered. At one performance, a woman said, "He looks like such a nice Jewish boy—until he opens his dirty mouth."

GERALD NACHMAN, *Seriously Funny*

To the best of our knowledge, Lenny Bruce never once skipped a club date to observe Yom Kippur. Yet much like Sandy Koufax, the comedian is remembered by fellow Jews for a particular aspect of his storied career: one of his standup routines, "Jewish and Goyish," is cited repeatedly, having attained legendary status for its incisive deconstruction of modern Jewish identity. "Jewish and Goyish," it can be said, is his 1965 World Series. Bruce himself is less fondly recalled—belying his status as a famous Jew, and distinctly unlike Koufax, he doesn't show up on many Jewish history timelines. While the baseball player was hailed as a hero, a source of Jewish pride, Bruce was more often feared as an upstart, evoking anxiety rather than adulation.

Still, the two had more in common than one might expect. Both Koufax and Bruce were third-generation American Jews who came of age in the post–World War II era. The only sons of divorced parents, they similarly grew up shuttling between homes in Brooklyn and Long Island. Launching their careers in their native city, they each endured several lean years while trying to make it in their respective fields, and then moved to the West Coast, where they found success at last. Both became extremely famous in the early 1960s, and then had their careers end abruptly in 1966. And both were often described as darkly handsome and glamorous Jewish men—super Jews. But that's where the parallels end. Koufax's glory years, from 1962 to 1966, were Bruce's years of decline. After several remarkable years of skyrocketing fame as a standup comic and creative brilliance as a social satirist, Bruce began a downward spiral of mounting legal troubles and eroding comedic skills, a sad decline ending tragically in death at age forty. While Koufax went out on top, cementing his fame through early retirement, Bruce bottomed out at the end, his death by drug overdose only enhancing his notoriety.

But there remains a more critical distinction between the two men. As discussed in the previous chapter, Koufax excelled in a sport—baseball—not known for a preponderance of Jewish players, and he was consequently lionized by his fellow Jews. By contrast, Bruce excelled in a field nearly monopolized by Jews—comedy—and yet has been largely ignored by the Jewish community. One need only compare the Jewish response to Bruce with that to more recent Jewish comedians such as Billy Crystal, Adam Sandler, and Jerry Seinfeld—these congenial funnymen are routinely claimed by other Jews; but not so Bruce. Like Larry David and Sarah Silverman today, Bruce's off-color offensiveness and ambivalent Jewishness made his fellow Jews squirm. The polar opposite of "nice Jewish boy" Koufax, Bruce was a discomfiting figure—misbehaved at best, depraved at worst, a "bad boy" in any event—and therefore an undesirable representative for the Jews.

And yet despite such a negative image, Bruce was a figure of major significance in American cultural history. In the late 1950s and early 1960s, the freethinking and outspoken comic served as a sort of court jester in a postwar culture stifled by social conformity and personal inhibition. As is true of many male comedians, his persona both onstage and off was that of an immature man-child, and Bruce, especially, betrayed the arrested development of a "momma's boy." His very persona, therefore, prefigured the adolescent rebelliousness that marked the Sixties generation of baby boomers. He was, moreover, a recognizably *Jewish* figure. Fearlessly challenging the puritanical streak in American (Christian) culture, Bruce was the (Jewish) antibody, promoting freedom of expression, lack of inhibition, and its logical extension, sexual liberation; thereby tying the pleasure principle to Jewishness. To paraphrase Philip Roth, he put the "id back in yid." As the Jewish alter ego of *Playboy* publisher Hugh Hefner, Bruce became a symbol of unbridled sexuality—and together with Hefner, helped inspire the sexual revolutions of the Sixties. Hippie leaders, most of whom were Jewish themselves, acknowledged him as their patron saint. To this day, standup comics and other practitioners of the comedic arts see him as their Galileo. He was, without question, a uniquely influential figure.

So Koufax, who never produced anything of Judaic significance, is a hero to the Jews—a bona fide Jewish celebrity with little Jewish content. Yet Bruce, who played a pivotal role in the history of American popular culture—and therefore in American *Jewish* culture—is full of Jewish content with little Jewish celebrity. Hence we have two central questions to address regarding Bruce: First, how do we understand the extraordinary Jewish substance of his work? And second, what do we make of his relative lack of Jewish celebrity? The contradiction here is really quite striking, given the amount of patently Jewish material in his standup comedy. As we shall see, his act was permeated with Jewish references, placing him in a unique position for the time; for alone among Jewish comedians of the 1950s, Bruce explored onstage the subject of being Jewish.

In addition to his pioneering role in the general arena of popular culture, Bruce also broke new ground in the introduction of Jewish culture—that is, explicit Jewishness—into the public realm. The point has been made before. Darryl Lyman, compiler of *The Jewish Comedy Catalog*, claims that "Bruce was among the first entertainers to use 'Jewish' material in front of audiences that were not exclusively Jewish."[1] In a 2003 book on "the rebel comedians of the 1950s and 1960s," Gerald Nachman notes that "Jewishness had seeped into the routines of Shelley Berman and Nichols & May, and had infiltrated Jules Feiffer and MAD magazine cartoons. It had been a secret subtext in the humor of everyone from Milton Berle to Groucho Marx and Sid Caesar, but Bruce dragged it out of the comedy closet kicking and kvetching. He was followed not long after by Woody Allen, Allan Sherman, and Mel Brooks."[2] And writing for the New York *Jewish Week*, Jonathan Mark adds this:

> If Elvis brought black music out of the segregated South and onto the Hit Parade, Lenny Bruce brought "Jewish" into the world of cool at a time when other Jewish comedians never used Jewish words or topics. It was a time when even Jewish newspapers were afraid of "talking Jewish," using words like phylacteries instead of tefillin. But there was Bruce onstage, on TV, saying shul, emes, bubbemeyseh, goyish, rachmonis, and he wouldn't bother to translate. He made his audiences feel hip, and if you were hip, you got it.[3]

Indeed, Bruce was the first major celebrity in American show business to pull off the mask of assimilation and challenge the idea that one's public identity could be "too Jewish." In his blisteringly honest standup routines, magazine columns, and appearances, he cried out for all to hear, "Look at me, I'm a Jew!" Of course, he did not do so in total isolation. In the late 1950s and early 1960s, the culture of conformity in America was beginning to change, assaulted by the civil rights movement on the one hand and beat bohemianism on the other, but in no small measure also due to the effects of Jewish comedy—a cultural arena in which Bruce was *the* central figure.

The Jewishness of Lenny Bruce

Though many have argued Lenny Bruce's historical importance in American popular culture, far fewer have essayed the analogous point regarding Jewish culture. Over the past forty years, the image of the man has been refracted in many ways: king of the sick comics, a countercultural guru, a cuckolded husband, a drug and sex addict, a religious martyr, a crusader for free speech, a pioneering standup comedian, and a great American artist—but not as a great *Jewish* artist, not as a Jew. This is remarkable for at least two reasons. First, as we'll see, Bruce's comedy is chock-full of Jewish content, absolutely unique for its time. This content included Yiddish words and expressions, Jewish characters and scenarios, irreverent critiques of both Judaism and Christianity, and most important, the correlation of Jewish otherness with a subversive, iconoclastic attitude part beatnik and part hippie. Second, Bruce's singular career fits squarely within the historical frame of American Jewish comedy, situated midway between the Marx Brothers' movies of the thirties and the *Seinfeld* sitcom of the nineties. But the relevant literature only hints at this essential context.

As historians of popular culture have demonstrated, neither Hollywood nor broadcast television was very hospitable to Jewish ethnicity prior to the 1960s.[4] But during the post–World War II era, from 1945 to 1960, many ambitious young Jews were entering show business as aspiring nightclub entertainers, a trend coinciding with the emergence of a new form of comedy in which comedians did not merely stand up and tell jokes, but instead spoke uninhibitedly about the world around them and about themselves. The confluence of the trends would produce a boom in Jewish standup comics. Many had begun in the insular world of the "Borscht Belt," the Catskill Mountains hotel circuit catering almost exclusively to Jews, and at first, their Jewishly inflected material played only in such ethnic enclaves. But over the course of the 1950s, as these performers made their way into more mainstream venues, such as Las

Vegas nightclubs and television talk shows, the nature of standup comedy would begin to change as they brought their Jewishness with them.

In an enlightening 1971 study, Sig Altman describes "the Jewish Comedian" as "typically a 'stand-up' comedian, a man who . . . stands and addresses the audience as 'himself.'"[5] This suggests that standup might ultimately lead to more explicitly Jewish subject matter. Though not yet open to uninhibited Jewishness himself, the pioneer of such comedic self-revelation was Mort Sahl, who, beginning in 1953, introduced a new style of standup: discursive, political, satirical, and unflinchingly honest. Gerald Nachman gives him pride of place, claiming, "It all started with Sahl, whose entire act, demeanor, language, look, and wardrobe warred against almost everything that had come before . . . Sahl challenged and changed all that, simply by the unheard-of comic device of being himself and speaking his mind onstage."[6]

By the end of the decade, Sahl was no longer alone, and chief among his fellow comic observers of the human condition were Shelley Berman, Mike Nichols and Elaine May, and Lenny Bruce—all Jews. Though very different in style and sensibility, they would still be lumped together as a new breed of comedian, espousing an observational comedy that would prove uncomfortable for some. In its issue of July 13, 1959, *Time* magazine described the new humor as "sick" and the new comedians as "sickniks." As noted by Richard Corliss, *Time* had "coined the phrase . . . after beatnik, itself inspired by the 1957 Soviet satellite Sputnik."[7] In March of 1961, *Playboy* magazine followed suit with a panel discussion on "Hip Comics and the New Humor," moderated by Paul Krassner and adding Steve Allen, Bill Dana, Jules Feiffer, and Jonathan Winters to Bruce, Nichols, and Sahl.[8] Though all but Allen and Winters were Jewish, the otherwise in-depth conversation doesn't address the question of their shared heritage—but others soon would. Shortly after the *Playboy* article, Kenneth Allsop, writing for "England's leading politico-literary quarterly," explained "why so many 'Sicknik' comedians are Jews"; and in September 1961, jazz critic Nat Hentoff published a short but incisive article, "Yiddish Survivals in the New Comedy," in which he profiled Sahl, May and Nichols, Berman, and Bruce.[9] Allsop ascribes the coincidence of Jewish comedians to "the truth that the Jew, with as much experience of grief and damage as any race on earth, should be the tutor of mortified candour."[10] Whereas Hentoff notes that "it cannot have escaped even the most nominal Jew that a . . . high percentage of the 'new' comedians—the social and political satirists—are Jewish," and attributes the phenomenon to the precedent and influence of Yiddish humor.[11]

Yet of all the Jewish comics of his generation, only Bruce made the subject of Jewishness a staple of his nightclub routines. True, he was preceded in his use of Jewish language and otherwise familiar subject matter by in-group comedians such as Myron Cohen and Sam Levenson; and he was preceded in his use of scatological language and otherwise transgressive subject matter by "blue" comedians such as B. S. Pully and Belle Barth (both Jewish). But Bruce was the first to combine the two, to employ Jewish material in a transgressive vein. According to Hentoff, "Oddly, the most daring and, to some, the most outrageously unprecedented of all the new comedians is the one who uses the most Yiddish words in his act as well as those sweeping gestures that used to be endemic to the Yiddish stage. Lenny Bruce . . ."[12] Bruce's example gave rise to the more explicitly Jewish musings and references of 1960s comedians such as Shecky Greene, Buddy Hackett, Jackie Mason, Mel Brooks, and Woody Allen. To this list, comedy historian Richard Zoglin adds later Jewish comedians Robert Klein, Richard Lewis, David Steinberg, Barry Levinson (who did standup before becoming a film director), Joan Rivers, Albert Brooks, Andy Kaufman, and even Jerry Seinfeld as prominent examples of those directly influenced by Bruce.

But Bruce's influence extended beyond the confines of standup comedy. He was a key player in a broader trend toward free expression, and thus toward more openly *Jewish* expression in general. As his biographer would later claim, "Lenny's obsession with Jewishness proved prophetic of the whole period of the sixties: the Jewish Decade."[13] All of this raises the "Jewish question," or really, several questions regarding the Jewishness of Lenny Bruce: What was his place in the history of Jewish comedy in America? How, after all, does Bruce fit into the grand tradition of Sholom Aleichem, Molly Picon, Fanny Brice, Eddie Cantor, Jack Benny, George Burns, the Marx Brothers, Jerry Lewis, Sid Caesar, and others?[14] How might his subversively comedic perspective have emerged from his experience as a Jew in 1950s America? What was the significance of Jewish subject matter and other Jewish allusions in his comedy? And what impact, if any, did he have on American Jewish culture in the 1960s and beyond?

To address these questions is to raise the more general issue of the Jewish role in American comedy. As often claimed, Jews have dominated the field at least since World War II. Already in 1956, non-Jewish comedian Steve Allen could state that "most comedians are Jewish,"[15] later elaborating, "American comedy, you understand, is a sort of Jewish cottage industry. By this I mean that the overwhelming majority of

American comics and comedy writers are Jewish."[16] Likewise, Sig Altman asserted in 1971 that the Jewish comedian "has become a cultural institution in American society," further noting the close association between Jewishness and comedians: "The Jew and comedy are officially married; if the Jew, as a Jew, has any role to play in the media, it is comedy, and if comedy has any *special* label, it is most often Jewish."[17] Though the ratio of Jewish to non-Jewish comedians may have leveled in recent years, the Jewish presence in comedic performance, writing, and production has remained conspicuously high. So how are we to account for this phenomenon, the disproportionate number of Jews in comedy? Why, after all, are Jews so funny?

Perhaps the most common theory combines some notion of Jewish *intelligence* with the idea of Jewish *suffering*. In the first instance, the theory goes, the premium placed upon education in Jewish culture fosters complexity of thought—that is, "talmudic reasoning"—and general cleverness, which then yield comedic ability. In the second case, Jews, as perpetual victims of antisemitic persecution, are thought to have developed their humor as a form of consolation—that is, "laughter through tears"—and as a defense, to have turned feelings of hostility toward the oppressor into comic barbs, and then redirected those barbs against themselves for safety's sake.[18] Jewish tradition taught that Jews were God's chosen people; yet historical experience taught that Jews were powerless and vulnerable—and thus was born a sharp sense of Jewish irony. Although there is some modicum of truth in such broad generalizations, they cannot fully account for the explosion of Jewish comedians in a particular time and place—mid-twentieth-century America—nor do they tell us much about the biting modern Jewish humor of Bruce.

A somewhat more grounded historical explanation points to the legacy of the immigrant generation of Jews, a generation noted for its "proliferation of entertainers—comics, singers, dancers."[19] According to Irving Howe, the infusion of Jewish talent into American show business derived from several factors: East European traditions of humor, the Jewish involvement in the theatrical business and vaudeville, and above all, the urgent drive to succeed characteristic of second-generation Jews. The earliest Jewish comedians were children of foreign-born Jews eager to escape the immigrant ghetto and "make it" in America. Show business seemed to offer a way out to many in that generation, and thus were born the careers of all the great entertainers of the immigrant era: stars such as Al Jolson, Fanny Brice, Eddie Cantor, and Sophie Tucker. But this theory would seem to better apply to Bruce's mother, Sally Marr (born Sadie Kitchenberg), than to Lenny. In the Bruce story, it was Sally who appeared so desperately eager to achieve fame and fortune, trying any number of strategies for success in show business. Howe notes "the eclecticism of the aspiring Jewish entertainers, their readiness to try 'almost anything,'"[20] a description perfectly suited to Bruce's show business mother, who sang, danced, burlesqued, acted, and told jokes. Sally never made it to the big time, as her son, following her into the family business, later would.

There are at least three other explanations for the heavy Jewish representation in comedy, and each one better illuminates Bruce's career. One is the American experience of assimilation—the erasure of ethnic identity by changing names, fixing noses, marrying *shiksas* (Yiddish term for non-Jewish women), and so on—a behavioral pattern characteristic of many Jews in mid-twentieth-century America, epitomized and even pioneered by the Jewish entertainer. Due to the effects of antisemitism and ambition combined, and therefore even more avidly than other ethnics, Americanizing Jews did what they could to escape their origins, not only changing their names and appearances, but mastering new cultural codes of language and behavior. Such assimilatory strategies would contribute greatly to the ironic sensibility characteristic of the Jewish comedian, as we shall see.

A second explanation is an often overlooked legacy of the immigrant generation: an explicit, if ambivalent, Jewishness. Whereas the second generation was marked by rampant assimilation, many of those Jewish children of immigrants were still deeply affected by their parents' culture of *Yiddishkeit*. Though their reaction was often one of embarrassment, some aspects of immigrant Jewish culture nevertheless persisted, thereby heightening the tension with the trend toward assimilation. Together with assimilation, therefore, Jewishness too became fodder for the Jewish comedian. And third, the post–World War II comedian also embodies an age-old Jewish archetype—the iconoclast—the irreverent breaker of taboos and subversive smasher of idols. Here, above all, the comedy of Lenny Bruce will be seen to be Jewish to the core.

The Comedy of Assimilation

The comedic equivalent of assimilation is masking, impersonation—the humor comes from our apprehension of the mask and the simultaneous knowledge of the true identity behind it. Jews, who assimilated into American culture with such great enthusiasm, developed the skills necessary to "pass" or to impersonate a non-Jew, and also a healthy skepticism of the attempt to alter one's identity. Both these traits contribute to the making of a Jewish comedian. In the first case, masking and impersonation were classic stratagems of American minstrel shows and immigrant era vaudeville, and thereafter became central elements of the comedian's repertoire. To make the point, one need only think of the Marx Brothers' (born Julius, Leonard, and Arthur) personae of Groucho, Chico, and Harpo; Milton Berle's cross-dressing; and the alternate identities of comic stars such as Fanny Brice, Danny Kaye, Jerry Lewis, Sid Caesar, and Mel Brooks. Exemplified by Bruce, vocal impersonation is often the foundation of a standup comedian's act—we shall see how Bruce employed other types of comic masking as well.

As for the second trait, skepticism about assimilation, American Jewish humor is replete with jokes skewering the process of passing, ranging from changing the old country name to joining a new country club. One famous example: Sean Ferguson, an immigrant Jew, is asked how he came to have an Irish name. He replies, "At Ellis Island, when the official asked my name, I was so nervous I blurted out, 'shoyn fergessen!' ['I already forgot' in Yiddish]." In another well-known example, Woody Allen opens his 1977 film *Annie Hall* by quoting Groucho Marx's quip that he would never join a club that would have someone like him for a member. The classic Jewish joke betrays the outsider's desire to join the majority at the same time that he or she adopts the majority's exclusionary attitude *toward* the outsider—it is the paradox of assimilation, and perfectly illustrates the comedic potential of the assimilatory experience.

In the case of Bruce, this experience shot through his early life, and would later inform his comedy profoundly. Bruce was born Leonard Alfred Schneider, son of Myron Schneider and Sadie Kitchenberg—and certainly, the personal names they bestowed on their only child betray the assimilatory impulse. As did Myron and Sadie, legions of interwar Jewish parents would choose regal-sounding names such as Leonard, Alfred, Milton, Arthur, Morton, Arnold, Gerald, or Bernard, trying to give their precious sons a boost toward upward mobility in America. Of course, when all these Jewish boys were later more familiarly called Lenny, Al, Miltie, Artie, Morty, Arnie, Jerry, or Bernie, the names took on a distinctly middle-class Jewish tinge. Pinned with such a name himself, Albert Goldman relates how Rodney Dangerfield (born Jacob Cohen) once told Bruce, "All you guys who try to get away from being Jewish by changing your last name always give the secret away by forgetting to change your *first* name. What kinda *goy* has a first name Lenny?"[21]

Bruce himself would later make the same point regarding Barry Goldwater. Nevertheless, the generational trend had its intended effect.

Raised in an assimilated environment on Long Island, Bruce became estranged from his father and eventually came to live with his show business mother, renamed Sally Marr. As his ex-wife Honey Bruce later recalled, "Her real name was Sadie Kitchenberg and then, let me see, Sally Marr, and then she changed it to Boots Malloy. She'd been in show business too, vaudeville, clubs, won Charleston contests: she'd work as a crazy-leg dancer. She had nice legs. From Sadie Kitchenberg to Boots Malloy you better have nice legs. That's quite a switch, huh?"[22] When, in 1947, the twenty-one-year-old Bruce decided to enter show business as well, it was only natural that like his mother, he changed his family name—and thus Leonard Schneider became Lenny Bruce. Photographs from this period reveal his attempts to forge a new identity. In one, he strikes a Rudolph Valentino–like pose, and in another he seems to impersonate an Arab sheik.

As a struggling young comedian in 1951, Bruce met the woman he would marry: Honey Harlowe, a beautiful redheaded Irish Catholic striptease dancer. Although intermarriage between Jews and non-Jews is commonplace and generally accepted today, in the early 1950s it was still anathema to most Jews and relatively rare. Its occurrence, therefore, was an unequivocal move toward assimilation. Though intermarriage is not a form of impersonation per se, in the 1950s it did serve the psychological function of allowing one to feel as if he or she were joining the majority. By capturing the "*shiksa* goddess," the Jewish man eats the forbidden fruit of *goyish*-ness and achieves a higher degree of social integration. Made familiar by authors such as Philip Roth, the phenomenon certainly applies to the young Lenny Bruce.

At the same time, Bruce did engage in more literal acts of impersonation. One of his earliest routines, for which he won the talent competition on the Arthur Godfrey radio show in 1948, was called the "Bavarian mimic"—a double impersonation, really, because the act had him playing a German comedian doing heavily accented impressions of American movie stars—a clever send-up of conventional standup mimicry. Moreover, according to Goldman, "the bit was a variation on a variation: adapted from Red Buttons' routine called *The Jewish Mimic*. Red actually complained to mimic Will Jordan that Lenny's German was *his* Yiddish—but he conceded that it didn't really matter because Lenny was no threat to anyone."[23] In fact, it was a quadruple impersonation insofar as Bruce had borrowed the routine directly from Sally Marr—so

Publicity photo of a baby-faced Lenny Bruce as an aspiring young comic, circa 1947.

in the one routine he was "doing" Humphrey Bogart, a Bavarian mimic, Red Buttons, and his own mother.[24] Such a multiple personality imper-sonation would become a staple of Bruce's act and demonstrates the comedian's uncanny ability to switch back and forth between identities.

Frank Kofsky, in his revealing study *Lenny Bruce: The Comedian as Social Critic and Secular Moralist*, devotes considerable space to discuss-ing the question of Jewish assimilation, and notes that "again and again, Lenny plumbed his own pain at trying to come to terms with being a **109**

Jew in a society that reserved all the major manifestations of its approval for those who could conform to non-Jewish patterns of appearance and behavior." Kofsky further suggests that Bruce's disinclination to fully assimilate contrasted with most other Jews of the time: "Regardless of the degree to which Lenny might have envied the WASPs . . . regardless of how self-conscious or maybe even ashamed of his Jewishness he may sometimes have been, it was a foregone conclusion that he would not—indeed, could not—ape the bulk of the Jewish educated classes in their mindless scramble after the supposed goodies of the affluent society." But Kofsky concludes by emphasizing Lenny's remarkable ability to impersonate comedically:

> I say this not because Lenny lacked the ability to "pass." Quite the contrary. His work preserved on tape and record reveals that Lenny was an incredibly gifted, even brilliant, mimic. In one and the same bit, he could take on in rapid succession three or four different characters each with a distinct voice and accent pattern, render each part with absolute fidelity, and never once get the characters confused . . . Certainly, if any Jew had the talents required for getting on in the gentile world, Lenny was the one.[25]

But rather than pass, that is, assimilate into non-Jewish society by impersonating a gentile, Bruce instead turned his talent at impersonation to comic effect. Intriguingly, two of his most flamboyant impersonations were performed offstage, in real life. During World War II, he joined the navy and served on a battleship (ironically, the USS Brooklyn) in the European theater. In a sense, military service itself is a form of assimilation, with its uniform dress and penchant for conformity, and Bruce patriotically complied. But as soon as the war ended, he itched to get out of the service and hatched an ingenious plan for early dismissal: he would earn a dishonorable discharge by faking a sexual aberration. According to his biographer, he feigned homosexuality;[26] but his memoir offers a more vivid account of his attempt to escape the navy by pretending to be a WAVE, a female sailor—that is, by cross-dressing, acting as a transvestite. Understanding the symbolism of the uniform, Bruce writes, "I figured that if I could demonstrate to the Navy that I still had a great deal of patriotism and loyalty to the uniform, the old *esprit de corps*—rather than indulging myself with the obvious sort of feather-boa negligee and gold-lamé mules drag outfit—then maybe instead of booting me out, they'd open the door politely and escort me out like an officer and a lady."[27]

Whether factual or not, Bruce's account of his transvestism unwittingly tapped into a rich vein of cultural and comedic challenges to assimilation. In her exhaustive study of the subject, Marjorie Garber describes "cross-dressing as an index, precisely, of many different kinds of 'category crisis' . . . By [which] I mean a failure of definitional distinction, a borderline that becomes permeable, that permits of border crossings from one (apparently distinct) category to another: black/white, Jew/Christian, noble/bourgeois, master/servant, master/slave."[28] Garber's notion of "category crisis" demonstrates how transvestism may be taken as a metaphor for assimilation in all its complexity, and further suggests why the device has been such a constant in the history of American Jewish comedy.

Though Shakespeare certainly predates them, the employ of cross-dressing by Jewish comedic figures such as Molly Picon (in *Yidl mitn Fidl*), Milton Berle, the Three Stooges, Billy Wilder and Tony Curtis (in *Some Like It Hot*), Sydney Pollack and Dustin Hoffman (in *Tootsie*), and Barbra Streisand (in *Yentl*—a text discussed at length by Garber and further explored in Chapter 5, on Streisand) suggests a tradition of their own. By adopting the device himself, Bruce abandoned the conformity of the naval ship—that is, his assimilation—in favor of boundary transgression and identity confusion, the very stuff of comedy, especially when offered by a Jewish comedian. To wit, a young Jewish writer for the Sid Caesar show, Larry Gelbart, would later write and produce the hit sitcom *M*A*S*H* and create a character inspired by Bruce's wartime remembrance—Corporal Klinger, who spent the Korean War vying for a Section 8 discharge by virtue of his incessant cross-dressing. And the tradition lives on.

In a second real-life impersonation, Bruce later adopted the guise of a man of the cloth—a Catholic priest. Around the time that he married the Catholic Honey (in 1951), he created a charity organization purportedly to help lepers in Africa, legally chartering it as the Brother Matthias Foundation. As its lone representative, Bruce donned the garments of a priest and went door-to-door in wealthy suburbs of Detroit and Miami soliciting donations. Though claiming that some donations actually went to legitimate charity cases, he admits that it was mainly a ruse for his own benefit. More than money motivated him, however, for it seems that he also did it for his own entertainment; in fact, he simply delights over the successful deception through three chapters of his autobiography.[29] Although his account sounds rather fantastical at times, some proof of the exploit can be found in the mug shot taken after his arrest for the fraud (he was charged with vagrancy)—in it, his bearded profile looks positively rabbinical. But of course, Bruce was

111

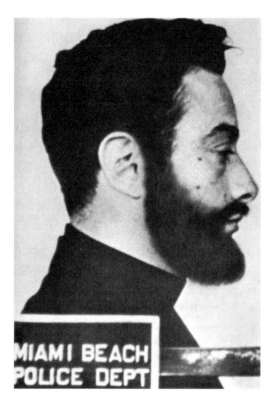

Mugshot of a bearded
Lenny Bruce circa 1951,
after his Miami arrest for
impersonating a priest.

playing the role of a priest, a Jew playing a Catholic, a schlock comedian
pretending to be a holy man. Perhaps even more than the US Navy WAVE,
it was a pretense meant to shock our sense of propriety, to subvert our
notion of what properly belongs where—it was, again, a classic comedic
ploy. Not surprisingly, Bruce later incorporated the story into his act: "I
really am Father Flotsky. Yeah, I was a Catholic priest for about two and
a half years. *Emmis*. And I really dug it. The only hangup is that—well,
the religion is consistent, but the confessions are really a bore. *Whew!
Ridiculous*, man. It's the same scene again and again." [30]

Through the mid-1950s, Bruce struggled to make it in show business,
working sleazy dives and strip clubs, feuding with his wife, and getting
involved with drugs and the underworld. His greatest claim to fame during that period was the night when, working as emcee in a strip club,
he walked onstage entirely in the nude. The incident gave him a certain
admiring notoriety among show people, but for our purposes might be
seen as yet another comedic impersonation—he was simply "assimilating" into the strip-club culture, cross-*dressing* as a stripper. Building on

the ad-libbing he'd done in the looser environment of the strip joints, and after divorcing Honey (in 1956), Bruce began to develop the comic style that would make him famous.

The breakthrough year was 1957, when he began working "straight" (that is, non-strip) clubs with his new material and delivery. As his star began to rise, and contemporary with Shelley Berman's success, he also made a foray into comedy albums, recording four LPs for the Fantasy label from 1958 to 1961. The first, *Interviews of Our Times* (1958) included a cut titled "Interview with Dr. Sholem Stein." Next came *The Sick Humor of Lenny Bruce* (1959), *I Am Not a Nut, Elect Me!* (1960), and *Lenny Bruce: American* (1961). The 1959 album included his classic routine "Religions, Inc.," and the 1961 record his equally famous "How to Relax Your Colored Friends at Parties." But notwithstanding the Sholem Stein interview, these records contained none of the explicitly Jewish material he was offering nightclub audiences from the stage. Even Bruce—or more likely, his record company—was susceptible to the "too Jewish" anxiety.

Onstage, however, Bruce had begun to offer a sharp satirizing of assimilation. He began, for example, to reveal his own change of name and mock it for its patent phoniness. Gerald Nachman reminds us of the common (and today, commonly observed) phenomenon of name changing in show business: "Most comics had their Jewish names—Kominski, Kubelsky, Levitch, Chwatt—bobbed like noses to Kaye, Benny, Lewis, and Buttons."[31] But Bruce was no longer the show-biz hack who had changed his name in 1947. By the late 1950s, he began to make his own name-change—and its implicit evasion of Jewishness—an explicit topic of his standup routine, confessing to the audience, "Louis. That's my name in Jewish. Louis Schneider," and then extending the revelation into a bit of comic dialogue: " '[So w]hy haven't ya got Louis Schneider up on the marquee?' 'Well, cause it's not show business. It doesn't fit.' 'No, no, I don't wanna hear that. You Jewish?' 'Yeah.' 'Why you ashamed you're Jewish?' 'I'm not anymore! But it used to be a problem.' "[32] Of course, by that very routine Bruce announced and emphasized his own Jewishness, while lambasting his fellow comedians for their hypocrisy in hiding theirs. And he was unique in this regard—try to imagine any of the Buddys or Sheckys or Joeys of the time similarly exposing themselves to the public. Bruce would expose his own Jewishness with regularity. His influence on younger Jewish comedians can be heard today on a regular basis—as for example, in Jeffrey Ross's line that "my original name is Lifschultz, which is ancient Hebrew for, 'you need to change that.' "[33]

Later in his career, during the presidential campaign of 1964, Bruce began applying the assimilation critique to the Republican candidate, Barry Goldwater, who was of Jewish descent. He first expresses his feelings, as a Jew, about the possibility of electing a president of Jewish background (remember, the recently assassinated JFK had been the first non-Protestant president) and then echoes Rodney Dangerfield's comment on first names: "Goldwater, how amazing. Having a Jewish president really knocks me out. Can't believe that there. Too much. And tell me, has there been much Jewish support? Singing in Jewish? Forget 'Goldwater.' 'Barry?' '*Barry*!' Are you kidding with that? Mogen David. Barry! Where is there one goy with the name of Barry? It's the most Jewishjewishjewish . . ."[34] Bruce also draws a distinction between his own form of assimilation and Goldwater's: "Not many Jews feel hostility towards Goldwater cause he is Jewish and changed his religion. See, *all* Jews did that. I'm Leonard Alfred Schneider, not Lenny Bruce. I'm Lenny Bruce, legally, but it was a pain in the ass, man. A lot of dues. So dig. Goldwater lives in Arizona. He did a switch, man. He says, '*Frig* it. I'll *keep* my name and I'll change my *religion*.' That was his bit."[35]

The key line here is, "See, *all* Jews did that." In the early 1960s, it seemed as if all Jews had assimilated in one way or another. The controversial stance was to say something about it. But in the end, Bruce's most shocking—and comically effective (that is, funny)—bit had Goldwater revealing his true identity after election:

> That's weird, you know? Finally we have a man in—that's going to be Goldwater's last step: gets in, gets before the T.V. camera for the acceptance speech, and *he rips off the mask and you see the big nose and the semitic look and the spittle coming out* and [*Goldwater screaming vindictively*]: YAHAHAHAAAAAAAA! WE'LL BURN ALL THE CHURCHES![36]

The joke is bitingly effective due to the underlying anxiety of the assimilated—that their "deception" will be discovered, that the truth of who they are will out. (Of course the joke also references the antisemitic notion that Jews hate gentiles, but that will be addressed later on.) Bruce thus played on the inherent problem of masking—the fear of being unmasked—a motif that applied all too well to assimilated Jews, and one that would reappear in many of his routines. Invariably, it was an American cultural icon who proved to be a secret Jew, as in Bruce's 1961 bit, "Dick Tracy is an Orthodox Jew,"[37] or the better-known routine "Thank You Masked Man," in which the true identity of the Lone Ranger is revealed. Explaining why he never waits around to be thanked:

LONE RANGER: Now I've had my first thankyou, and I dig it, and I'm riding all around: "Thank you!" "Don't mention it, donmentionit." "Thank you, thankyouthankyou." But the real reason is [*voice changes, becomes an old Jewish man*] I sent two boice to collich.

HICK: Whassat?

LONE RANGER: Dots right.

HICK: Well, goddamn, maw, the massed man's Jewish!

LONE RANGER: Of course, *schmuck*! Dots vy, ven I tuk on the radio, dots all you hear, is HHHHHHHHHHHHAAAAAAA, SSSSSSUUUUU. You vanna svitch it ova from sefenty-eight to toity-tree-und-a-toid? You'll hear [*imitating slowed-down record*], HIGHH YOOOSILLL BERRRR. I sent two boice to collich. You tink dey even sent me a pustul cud? Hmmm. I got tebble bucitis of my yarm. Alotta *tsuris* I have, mine friend. *Zugnicht* and *goyim*.[38]

Bruce would take the conceit to its further possible extreme when, in his signature routine "Religions, Inc.," he applied the same comedic idea to the most non-Jewish figure imaginable. The heart of the routine has religious leaders such as Bishop Sheen, Cardinal Spellman, Rabbi Steven H. Weiss (sic), and popular preacher Oral Roberts "exposed" as show-biz hucksters and publicity hounds. To close the routine, Lenny-as-Oral-Roberts takes an important phone call:

ROBERTS: Alright . . . Ah got a lawng distance cawl in heah from headquarters, the Vatican—ah'll tawk to yew boys latuh . . . Yes, opuratuh, this is Oral Roberts. . . . Yes, yes, alright, ah'll take the charges . . . yeah . . . yeah . . . HELLO JOHNNY! WHAT'S SHAKIN, BABY? . . . yeah . . . Meant to congratulate you on the election . . . yeah . . . That puff of white smoke was a genius stroke. Was in the papuhs faw six days heah . . . Great! . . . We got an eight-page layout with Viceroy—"The New Pope Is A Thinking Man." Ah'll send ya a tear sheet on it . . . yeah . . . yeah . . .

Same old jazz . . . How's your Old Lady? . . . No, nobody's onna phone. . . .[39]

And so on, until the conversation ends as follows:

When ya comin' to the coast? I can get ya the Steve Allen Show the nineteenth . . . Matinee Theatre dropped . . . Jus wave, thass awl. Wear the big ring . . . yeah . . . yeah . . . yeah . . . yeah . . . O.K., Sweetie . . . yeah . . . Yew cool it tew . . . NO, NOBODY KNOWS YOU'RE JEWISH![40]

The idea that the Pope is really a Jew is absurd, of course, but the notion that a notable figure in the public eye could be passing as a non-Jew **115** wasn't at all farfetched at a time when Jack Warner, Jack Benny, George Burns, Edward G. Robinson, Dinah Shore, Lauren Bacall, Jeff Chandler, Melvyn and Kirk Douglas, Tony Curtis, Walter Winchell, William Paley, Mike Wallace, and so many others were doing just that. By unmasking the Lone Ranger and the Pope as Jews who hid their identities in order to make it in show business, Bruce exposed the anxieties of all those who assimilated to get ahead, and chastised them for their supposed hypocrisy. He reserved a special animus for those who denied their identities through the pretext of religious devotion. Combining his critique of assimilation with his irreverence toward religion (a critical aspect of Bruce's outlook, further discussed later), he would sharply satirize a Judaism he saw as assimilated—mocking modern temples and ridiculing Reform rabbis in the course of his famous routine, "Christ and Moses":

> I bet you, when Christ and Moses return, the *shules* have had it first.
> Saturday they would make every kind of shule—a drive-in *shule*, Frank Lloyd Wright *shule*, West Coast *shule*. West Coast? Santa Monica—there is that A-frame *shule* that they just put the statues in:
> "Are you putting a *madonna* in the *shule*?"
> "Yes, it's contemporary, that's all."
> "Whew! Don't figure out, man . . . that's, uh, they *supposed* to have one?"
> West Coast reform shule. Reform rabbi. So reformed they're ashamed they're Jewish. Rabbis that had this kind of sound:
> *"Heyy, mein Liebe, heyyyyy . . ."*
> These rabbis have turned into doctors of law. And they've lost their beards, because they were called beatniks. And now they have this sound:
> REFORMED RABBI [clipped, hearty, good-fellow British articulation]: Ha ha! This Sabbath we discuss Is-roy-el. Where is Is-roy-el? Quench yon flaming yortsite candle! Alas, alas, poor Yossel . . . Deah deah deah! Today, on Chin-ukka, with Rose-o-shonah approaching, do you know, someone had the chutzpah to ask me,
> "Tell me something, doctor of law, is there a God, or not?"
> What cheek! To ask this in a temple! We're not here to talk of God— we're here to sell bonds for Israel! Remember that! A pox upon you, Christ and Moses! Go among them and kiss your empty *mezuzahs*.
> JEW: Rabbi, that was a beautiful speech!
> RABBI [Jewish accent]: Danksalot. Ya like dot? Vat de hell, tossetoff de top mine head, dot's all. *Und tsi gurnischt.*
> So Moses is depressed. The shules are gone. No more shules. He breaks open a mezuzah—nothing inside!

"GEVULT!"
But a piece of paper that says
"Made in Japan."[41]

Moses, in this case, represents not the lawgiver of ancient Israel, but rather Bruce's idea of the authentic Jew, the "real" Jew lamenting the corruptions of contemporary Judaism. It was the final condemnation of assimilation, moving beyond the straightforward indictment of the "Jew who is no longer a Jew" to a more scathing denunciation of the "Jew who thinks he's still Jewish but isn't really." To make this kind of accusation, Bruce had to have internalized some degree of Jewishness himself. But because he had no Jewish upbringing to speak of, such cultural consciousness would have to be secondhand, a memory of an experience that never was.

The Comedy of Jewishness

The *memory* of Jewishness—the legacy of immigrant Jewish culture, and in many ways the flip side of assimilation—deserves separate treatment as the second key to understanding the Jewish element in Lenny Bruce's comedy. As Bruce developed his comedic style through the late 1950s, he peppered his routines with Jewish language—yiddishisms such as *emmis* and *gurnisht*—and Jewish themes—most famously, the parsing of distinctions between "Jewish and Goyish" mentioned earlier, which began: "Dig: I'm Jewish. Count Basie's Jewish. Ray Charles is Jewish. Eddie Cantor's *goyish*. B'nai B'rith is *goyish*; Hadassah, Jewish," and so on.

That he had his own idiosyncratic way of defining *Jewish* may be related to the fact that Bruce did not come by his Jewishness naturally. Raised in the largely non-Jewish environment of Mineola, Long Island, he acquired his familiarity with Jewish culture only later, under the tutelage of his comic mentor, amateur funnyman and street corner *shpritzer* Joe Ancis.[42] According to Gerald Nachman, "Ancis gave Bruce his Jewish soul, the *Yiddishkeit* that he was denied as a boy growing up in a marginally Jewish family."[43] Fact is, Bruce was a thoroughly acculturated American Jew who nevertheless chose to incorporate Jewish material into his act. This is significant insofar as it reveals his use of Jewish subject matter as an artistic device. He intuited early on the comedic possibilities of Jewish stereotypes, Jewish-gentile differences, antisemitism, and even the Holocaust, and thus adopted the stance of "Jewish" comic observer—but ultimately, Jewishness became something more for Bruce. As he reached his artistic peak, the guise of a Jew became more stage

117

persona than real-life personality—an abstract impersonation (yet another) rather than an experiential identity. As explored further in Chapter 5, this phenomenon may be described as "Jewface," the performance of Jewishness.

A perfect illustration of such a put-on Jewish identity is found in a regular column Bruce wrote for *Rogue* magazine during the course of 1960, under the byline "Bruce Here." In the March issue he dissembles as follows:

> My Mother and Father have been fanatically devoted to me all my life, but their devoted fanaticism is dwarfed by their addiction to Judaism. They are devout orthodox Jews. This has been a big divider between my parents and myself for years. They are in their twilight years now and I realize, according to their standards, the disgrace and humiliation I must have caused them.
>
> I refused to become *bar mitzvah*. I disgraced the rabbinical teacher by disclosing the fact that he was an out-and-out nut who used to expose himself on the subway platform at 59th Street in Brooklyn during the rush hour. He used to flash just before the doors closed . . .
>
> Getting back to being Jewish, my Father didn't give up, however; he drilled me with the Talmud, daily. Things were looking up brighter until I fell in love with a girl—horror of horrors—who wasn't Jewish. But I thought the fact that her Father was a Doctor would only soothe my family. He was the only colored doctor in Freeport, Long Island . . .
>
> But now that my parents are going down the home stretch, I am really trying to be Jewish.[44]

And on he went, continuing in this vein with one fabrication after another. Bruce's parents, for example, were far from being Orthodox Jews. So why, one might ask, would an acculturated Jew choose to portray himself as more Jewish than he really was? In Bruce's comedy, such pretense was a device, allowing him to sharply distinguish himself from 1950s American bourgeois society—"Jewish" as metaphor for "hip"—and, at the same time, it was a handy way to convey the shallowness of "Jewish" show business. In either case, the Jewish stance became a form of critique, and Bruce was the comedic social critic par excellence (with apologies to Mort Sahl).

Just as he turned his own experience of assimilation on its head, Bruce would invert Jewish memory as well, using Jewish language and perspective in order to subvert it. As the decade of the 1960s dawned, it became clear that a new style of comedy had arrived, and that most of its practitioners were Jewish. As cited earlier, Nat Hentoff attempted to explain the phenomenon by attributing the confluence of Jewish comedians to "Yiddish survivals" evident in their comedy. For Sahl, Nichols and May, and Berman, this meant certain Jewish "mannerisms and . . . the sardonic stance of the outsider," but in Bruce's case it was something else again: "What most firmly links Bruce, however, to that Jewish tradition which predates Jews in show business, is his fierce sense of moral outrage. . . . In Bruce, the residue of Judaism is more his implacable morality than the high percentage of Jewish slang he uses."[45] Jewish humor is said to have an ethical dimension, and like Hentoff, contemporary observers often explained Bruce's satirical humor in terms of the Jewish tradition of liberalism. Thus, Frank Kofsky suggests that "Lenny was blessed (or cursed, depending on one's point of view) with the kind of abiding moral sense that made it impossible for him to still his conscience in the name of expediency."[46] And Steve Allen adds, "American comedy generally has nothing whatever to do with morals. But Bruce was, among other things, a moralist."[47]

But a closer study of Bruce's comedy reveals another set of explicitly Jewish themes. Take his use of Yiddish, for example. In Albert Goldman's account, Bruce's embrace of Yiddish was merely reflective of Joe Ancis's influence and thus the Jewish identity conferred on him secondhand. According to Goldman, "Lenny had come to Broadway a veritable goy, without the slightest genuine knowledge of Jewish life, Jewish customs, beliefs, values, words or mannerisms. He was this pretty little goy from Long Island . . ." Only through Ancis, says Goldman, would Bruce encounter "authentic" Jewish culture and by osmosis become a Jew:

There was one other vital matter in which Joe furnished Lenny instruction. Re: Jewishness . . . From Joe, Lenny got the real flavor of the Jewish lower classes. Joe came from the real old-country Yidden. His family spoke Yiddish at the dinner table. He knew *all* the words . . . He spoke the kind of Yiddish that readers of the *Daily Forward* or *Der Tog* or the *Morgen Freiheit* recognized. Hanging around with Joe, you got precious insights into Jewish life. . . . He was the perfect naar, the meshugana, the tummuler who is recognized in the Jewish world as a necessary companion to the rav and wiseman. Bizarre as Joe Ancis must appear to any goy, he always made perfect sense to Jews. Hanging out with him was as good as a pidyan a ben, a bar mitzvah and a Jewish wedding. After knowing Joe, Lenny Bruce could say: *Ich bin ech a Yid*—I too am a Jew.[48]

Kofsky, on the other hand, assigns ideological intent to "Bruce's constant employment of Yiddish." He sees it "as another indication of his opposition to the assimilationist impulses of the educated, middle-class Jews of his generation." Kofsky describes Bruce's use of Yiddish as nothing less than a *"manifesto of Jewishness*, announcing his refusal to be perceived in public as anything but a Jew." And he goes on to suggest, rather provocatively, that Bruce's "assumption was not that he, as a Jew, should learn to conform to the expectations and mores of the gentiles, but rather that the gentiles should be exposed to some of the time-honored ethical values of Jewish life and thought . . . and that *they* should assimilate *that*."[49] Although portraying Bruce as an advocate for Jewish values is rather farfetched (Kofsky goes so far as to suggest that "there is a good prima facie case to be made for considering Bruce a functioning rabbi in secular drag"[50]), the basic argument here does concur with my earlier discussion of Bruce's critique of assimilation.

Nevertheless, both Goldman and Kofsky miss the essential point regarding Bruce's use of Yiddish onstage. Simply put: Lenny Bruce was a comedian, and Yiddish is funny. Thus Sig Altman attributes the trend of "Yiddish being used for comic effect" to the "inherent comicality of Yiddish."[51] Other Jewish comedians had incorporated the occasional Yiddish word into their patter, either as an insider's nod to an all-Jewish audience, as in the Catskills' Borscht Belt, or else a wink to those Jews in the seats who would get the reference, as in Groucho Marx's famous lyric aside, "Did someone call me *schnorrer*?" But Bruce was the first to fully exploit its effect on mixed audiences—just hearing Yiddish made them laugh, whether they were Jewish or not. According to William Novak and Moshe Waldoks, "Yiddish has frequently been celebrated for being so rich in comic possibilities that even those who don't understand it are apt to chuckle at many of its terms; F. Scott Fitzgerald, so the story goes, used to wander into a Jewish delicatessen just to hear the word 'knish.'"[52]

But why this occurred, what made Yiddish sound so funny—especially to audiences of the 1950s and 1960s—is not quite so easy to explain. When asked this very question (in a documentary on Jewish humor), Billy Crystal seemed perplexed, answering, "I'm not sure why [Yiddish is funny], it just is." His combined confusion and certainty may actually provide some clue to the mystery. Yiddish is at once foreign and familiar: strange-sounding and incomprehensible to the acculturated American, while also fondly recognizable to Jews, recalling both the lost civilization of European Jewry and the lost world of one's childhood. Hearing it evokes both the knowledge of one's distance from old-world culture (and perhaps some guilt over the abandonment) and a nostalgic

longing for its folksy and nurturing ways. Third-generation Jews of the
1950s and 1960s were caught between these conflicting emotions, so for
them, Yiddish embodied a tension they knew all too well. Non-Jews, too,
resonated to the tension between assimilation and cultural memory, and
laughed along with the Jews in their embarrassment at hearing the secret code language of their grandparents. Besides, non-Yiddish speakers
knew that if they didn't laugh, they'd be branded as outsiders—outside
the charmed circle of Bruce's "inside" humor.

For Bruce, therefore, Yiddish was primarily a laugh-getter, playing on
the anxieties and tensions of his 1950s/1960s audiences. He understood
its mix of foreignness and familiarity, and he used Yiddish as an integral
part of his hipster lingo, inviting his audience to be—like him—an outsider and insider at once. After one of his arrests for obscenity (in October of 1962, at the Troubadour in Los Angeles), he turned the experience
into the following bit:

> Dig. This last arrest—two weeks ago—I was arrested by a *Yiddish under-
> cover agent*. Isn't that a slap in the face? *Emmis*. Somebody wrote the thing
> up. Dig this:
>
> Sick comic Lenny Bruce, out on bail on a narcotics charge, was arrested
> by a Yiddish[-speaking] undercover agent who had been placed in the club
> several nights running to determine if Bruce's constant use of Yiddish terms
> was a cover for profanity. The officer said it was. Lenny asked the judge if
> he could bring his aunt to court to cross-examine the officer to determine
> how fluent the officer was in Yiddish.
>
> Dig what I got arrested for saying: *schmuck*. And the word *schmuck*—
> well, I was arrested by an illiterate undercover agent. The word *schmuck* is
> a German word and it means, literally—and I'm sure you'd insist on the
> literal meaning, not hearsay—it means a man's decoration, in German, as a
> boutonniere or lapel watch. The Yiddish dictionary, the Harcoff dictionary:
> *schmuck*, "a yard, a fool." So there we have the literal and the colloquial. I
> don't think any Jew ever neologized and said,
>
> "You're acting just like a man's penis!"
>
> Did you? No. It's,
>
> "We drove in from Yonkers. Who did all the driving?"
>
> "*Me*, like a *schmuck*."
>
> Now, "Me, like a *schmuck*" doesn't mean "Me *like* a *schmuck*"—unless
> you're a faggot Indian:
>
> "Ho white man! Me like a *schmuck*."
>
> "Well, if you do, don't bring it in here."

"You no like a *schmuck*, eh?"

"Well, once in a while."[53]

The internal contradiction here—what makes you laugh—is between the use of the word *schmuck* in its original sense and the altered meaning of the word in colloquial usage. To some, it remains obscene no matter the context, whereas to others, it has varying definitions in different cultural contexts. In a sense, the tension here parallels that between assimilationist universalism (that is, we're all the same) and pluralist multiculturalism (that is, we're all different).

By presenting elements of the older Jewish culture—such as Yiddish—and offering them up for the consumption of an American audience, Bruce was playing on this very dichotomy for comic effect. He would do this with other traits of the older Jewish generation as well: for example, their acute awareness of the differences between Jews and gentiles, the related tendency to stereotype the goy, and likewise, a heightened consciousness of antisemitism. In each case, Bruce would first instruct the audience on a particular aspect of Jewish culture—repeating it and thus reaffirming it—and then use it as the premise of a comedic routine, ultimately subverting the original intent. Here, for example, is a straightforward bit about Jews' awareness of ethnic difference:

> Up to about six or seven years ago, there was such a difference between Christians and Jews, that—maybe you did know—but, forget about it! Just a line there that would, *whew!* And the "Brotherhood of Christians and Jews" was like some fifth column bullshit. I don't know, it was like a phony dumb board.
>
> No, I don't think so—I don't think Christians did know it. Because only the group that's involved—it's like: the defense counsel knows it because he has a narrow view, where the D.A. he's hung up with a bigger practice. So it's the same: the Jew is hung up with his shit and maybe the Christian—because, when the Christians say, like, "Oh, is he Jewish? I didn't know. I can't tell when somebody's Jewish."
>
> I always thought, "That's bullshit."
>
> But he can't. Cause he never got hung up with that shit, man. And Jews are very hung up with that, all the time.[54]

So Jews, according to Bruce, were very nearly obsessed with policing the dividing line between themselves and others, between what's Jewish and what's goyish. But rather than dismiss the archaic mindset altogether, he cleverly adapted it to his own way of thinking and made it his own. In discussing the dirty-word concept, for example, he offers the following comparison: "To a Jew f-u-c-k and s-h-i-t have the same value on the dirty-word graph. A Jew has no concept that f-u-c-k is worth 90 points, and s-h-i-t 10. And the reason for that is—well, see, rabbis and priests both s-h-i-t, but only one f-u-c-ks. You see, in the Jewish culture, there's no merit badge for not doing that. . . . And since the leaders of my tribe, rabbis, are *schtuppers*, perhaps that's why words come freer to me."[55]

To a degree, Bruce accepted the idea of Jewish difference—he himself was different due to his Jewishness. But ultimately, he presented the Jewish/non-Jewish divide in order to upend it. Hence, one of his most famous routines, "Jewish and Goyish"—certainly the best known among Jews—goes as follows (in one of many versions):

> See, I neologize Jewish and *goyish*. There's like, the literal meaning—first I'll start with *goyish*, cause it'll really knock you out. Dig this. *Goy*—"one who is not civilized, one who is not Mormon, one who is not Jewish." It's "heathen," that's what *goyish* means. Now, a Jew—dictionary style—"one who is descended from the ancient tribes of Judea, or one who is regarded to have descended from that tribe."
>
> Now I neologize Jewish and *goyish*. Dig: I'm Jewish. Count Basie's Jewish. Ray Charles is Jewish. Eddie Cantor's *goyish*. B'nai B'rith is *goyish*; Hadassah, Jewish. Marine corps—heavy *goyim*, dangerous. Koolaid is *goyish*. All Drake's Cakes are *goyish*. Pumpernickel is Jewish, and, as you know, white bread is very *goyish*. Instant potatoes—goyish. Black cherry soda's very Jewish. Macaroons are *very* Jewish—very Jewish cake. Fruit salad is Jewish. Lime jello is *goyish*. Lime soda is *very goyish*. Trailer parks are so *goyish* that Jews won't go near them. [The] Jack Paar Show is very *goyish*. Underwear is definitely *goyish*. Balls are *goyish*. Titties are Jewish. Mouths are Jewish. All Italians are Jewish. Greeks are *goyish*—bad sauce. Eugene O'Neill—Jewish; Dylan Thomas, Jewish. Steve [Allen] is *goyish*, though. It's the hair. He combs his hair in the boy's room with that soap all the time.[56]

In constructing such a routine, Bruce first accepts the basic premise of the older Jewish mindset—that there is a distinction to be drawn between Jews and non-Jews, a distinction captured in the Yiddish term for non-Jewishness, *goyish*. Yet he very quickly turns it around, subverting our expectations by claiming that black musicians Count Basie and Ray Charles are Jewish, whereas the Jewish entertainer Eddie Cantor and the Jewish organization B'nai B'rith are not. He then develops this premise by applying the distinction to food, body parts, and other cultural figures. In all, he is attempting to suggest that *Jewish* is a sensibility, an ineffable quality, rather than something more concrete and observable, like religion or race. In Bruce's usage, Jewish became a stand-in for hip or cool—for what is socially desirable. In this, he directly challenged a cultural norm of the time: the deeply engrained idea that Jewishness is uncool and undesirable, that it is somehow lesser than other cultural and religious identities—a common bias that is not antisemitic per se, but rather a fainter echo of outright antisemitism, an unfortunate legacy of Western (that is, Christian) civilization.

At the same time, Bruce was lampooning the traditional Jewish bias against the *goyim*. Here's his straightforward reporting of the phenomenon:

> A *schicka* is a *goy*. That's right. That was the concept in the late thirties, that was the Jewish phrase. It meant, literally, a Christian is a drunk. That was the concept of all Jews that I knew then, that Christians were drunks. And that Jewish mothers were the only mothers, and Christian mothers sold their children for bottles of whiskey . . . I'll bet you that if I got a chance to listen at the Christian window I would have heard some "*schicka* is a *goy*" in reverse. But I never got a chance to pass, cause you never catch them without the mask on. . . . Once in a while you hear, "You *mockie* bastard!" Or, "The *goyim*!" But just once in a while.[57]

Bruce draws the obvious conclusion that Jewish prejudice against non-Jews is simply the mirror image of antisemitism. But characteristically, he makes a subtler point as well in his comment that he "never got a chance to pass, cause you never catch them without the mask on." Here, the mask refers to the pretense of civility in the hiding of one's prejudice, and once again Bruce plays the role of the unmasker.

In a far more complex rendering of the stereotypical views of Jews and non-Jews, Bruce reacts to the killing of Lee Harvey Oswald as follows:

> You know, [Jack] Ruby did it, and why he did it was because he was Jewish—and the villain was his grandmother. . . . Why Ruby did it. You see, when I was a kid I had tremendous hostility for Christians my age. The reason I had hostility is that I had no balls for fighting, and *they* could duke. So I disliked them for it, but I admired them for it—it was a tremendous ambivalence all the time: admiring somebody who could do that, you know, and then disliking them for it. Now the neighborhood I came from there were a lot of Jews, so there was no big problem with a balls-virility complex. But *Ruby* came from *Texas*. They're *really* concerned with "bawls"—

they got ninety-year-old men biting rattlesnakes' heads off! And shooting guns! And a Jew in Texas is a tailor. So what went on in Ruby's mind, I'm sure, is that

"Well, if *I* kill the guy that killed the President, the Christians'll go:

'*Whew!* What bawls he had, hey? We always thought the Jews were chickenshit, but look at that! See, a Jew at the end saved everybody!' "

And the Christians'll kiss him and hug him and they'll lift him on high.
A JEWISH BILLY THE KID RODE OUT OF THE WEST!

But he didn't know that was just a fantasy from his grandmother, the villain, telling him about the Christians who punch everybody.

Yeah. Even the shot was Jewish—the way he held the gun. It was a dopey Jewish way. He probably went "*Nach*!" too—that means "There!" in Jewish. *Nach!*[58]

In this account of mutual stereotyping, Jews are mild-mannered tailors in the eyes of non-Jewish Texans, and non-Jews are belligerent bullies in the eyes of Jewish grandmothers; the resulting ambivalence of assimilated Jews such as Lenny Bruce helps to explain the actions of Jack Ruby. The routine both plays on and subverts the stereotypes at the same time. It was the perfect comedic rendering of the deep anxieties and ambivalence affecting American Jews—and moreover, it afforded early 1960s audiences the opportunity to laugh at an all too somber subject, the Kennedy assassination and its aftermath.

Bruce's use of traditional Jewish thinking reached its apogee in his comic commentary on antisemitism. Though antisemitic attitudes in America had declined precipitously in the years following World War II, American Jews still retained their consciousness of it, a habit engrained by centuries of exposure to the social disease of Jew-hatred. In Bruce's hands, the Jewish memory of antisemitism became occasion for contemporary social comment. One of his favorite impersonations was of the "redneck" conservative American, invariably southern, and invariably an antisemite. In his brilliant satire of American racism, "How to Relax Your Colored Friends at Parties," he plays the part of a typical bigot who, in the midst of his faux-friendly conversation with a token African American (of course, the accepted term then was *Negro*) party guest— that is, while hiding his racism—obliviously reveals his antisemitism:

WHITE: You know, I did all the construction here, you know?

NEGRO: Oh, you did?

WHITE: I did all except the painting, and these Hebes—[*whispers*] you're not Jewish, are you?

125

NEGRO: No, man, I'm not.

WHITE: You know what I mean?

NEGRO: Yeah, I understand.

WHITE: Someone calls me a Sheeny I'll knock em right on their ass . . . I wanna tell you sometin. I don't care what the hell a guy is so long as they keep in their place, you know?

NEGRO: Right.[59]

Later in the routine, the white bigot tells his new friend approvingly, "You know, you're a white Jew, you're O.K." Hilariously, he believes he's complimenting the black guy by calling him a "white" (read: good) version of a "Jew" (read: an undesirable outsider; because after all, he's black). Bruce was often at his best when skewering racism, and here we see how he used his understanding of antisemitism to twist the knife. The routine concludes with a painfully funny segment in which the bigot hesitantly invites his new friend over to visit:

WHITE: Awright . . . Now, I wanya to comover the house, but I gotta tell ya somtin cause I know you people get touchy once in a while.

NEGRO: Oh, umhm?

WHITE: Yeah, ahhh, I gotta sister, ya see?

NEGRO: Yeah?

WHITE: Well now, cummere. [whispers] You wouldn't wanna Jew doin it to your sister, wouldja?

NEGRO: It doesn't make any difference to me, just as long as he's a nice guy.

WHITE: Whattayou, on the weed or somtin? Look, nobody wants a Sheeny plowin' their sister, an I don't want no coon doin' it to my sister. What the hell, that makes sense. You can come over my house if you promise you don't do it to my sister. Promise?

NEGRO: O.K.[60]

Bruce not only brought up the subject of antisemitism in his act, he plumbed the reasons for its existence. Here's one example:

The Puerto Ricans are bad, bad, bad. We were bad, once, too, the Jews. Bad Jews once. Our bad label was that we were capable of screwing everyone.

You know why Jews are the smartest people in the world? Cause everybody told them that, for years:

"They'll screw ya, you can't trust em, they'll screw everybody!"

And the schmucks really believed it:

"That's right. We're the smartest people—screw anybody! Goddamn right, we're smart! We'll screw everybody. Boy, we'll screw them all. We're so smart."[61]

According to this bit of comedic analysis, antisemitism consists of the belief that clever Jews are out to cheat the hapless gentiles. Once again, the observation combines gentile bias against Jews with Jewish prejudice against gentiles—for sadly, the idea that Jews are smarter than others did have some currency in the older Jewish culture, as embodied in the phrase *goyishe kop*, meaning a stupid gentile. So rather than make the obvious point that antisemites are foolish to believe it, Bruce turns it around to accuse Jews themselves for buying such malarkey, believing it until they make it true.

In a far more damning appraisal of antisemitism, Bruce discusses the age-old Christian accusation of deicide, that the "Jews killed Christ," a routine made famous by Dustin Hoffman's portrayal in the 1974 film *Lenny*:

I am of a Semitic background—I assume I'm Jewish. A lot of Jews who think they're Jewish are not—they're switched babies. Now, a Jew, in the dictionary, is one who is descended from the ancient tribes of Judea, or one who is regarded as descended from that tribe. That's what it says in the dictionary; but you and I know what a Jew is—*One Who Killed Our Lord*. I don't know if we got much press on that in Illinois—we did this about two thousand years ago—two thousand years of Polack kids whacking the shit out of us coming home from school. Dear, dear. And although there should be a statute of limitations for that crime, it seems that those who neither have the actions nor the gait of Christians, pagan or not, will bust us out, unrelenting dues, for another deuce.

And I really searched it out, why we pay the dues. Why do you keep breaking our balls for this crime?

"Why, Jew, because you skirt the issue. You blame it on Roman soldiers."

Alright. I'll clear the air once and for all, and confess. Yes, we did it. I did it, my family. I found a note in the basement. It said:

"*We killed him.*

signed,

Morty."

And a lot of people say to me,

"Why did you kill Christ?"

"I dunno . . . it was one of those parties, got out of hand, you know."

We killed him because he didn't want to become a doctor, that's why we killed him.[62]

128 Only Lenny Bruce could find the humor in this ugly but persistent belief, the basis of much of historical antisemitism. And what *chutzpah* (effrontery) on his part, because raising this aspect of antisemitism is necessarily an affront to Catholicism. How could devout Christians have believed such nonsense, he seemed to imply, and how could their leaders have allowed it to persist? When Bruce first performed this routine, the Catholic Church had yet to repudiate the deicide charge—as it did in the Second Vatican Council of 1965. Prior to that historic decision, therefore, it was a legitimate critique, but one that could only have been made comedically. In the film version, "Lenny" adds a final thought to the routine: "It's a good thing we killed him when we did, because [if it had been] today, we'd have to contend with generations of Catholic schoolkids with little electric chairs hanging around their necks!"— making the uncomfortable point that Jesus's death on the cross (and hence the implicit murder) is the central symbol of Christianity. As Bruce later described it, "I'll say to an audience—you and I know what a Jew is: one who killed our Lord. Now there's dead silence after that." As "the laughs start to break through," he explained, "now they know— the laughter's all there—but I'm *not* kidding, because there *should* be a statute of limitations for that crime."[63] A taboo subject—antisemitism— mined for laughs, albeit a nervous laughter. Vintage Lenny Bruce.

In the end, Bruce presented Jewish material and represented himself as a Jew for one basic reason: in the late 1950s and early 1960s, it shocked. To be "too Jewish," as the show business admonition had it, was risqué at the time, even subversive. Writing for the men's magazine *Rogue* in 1960, he describes the inhibition: "For a while, and it's still prevalent, mention of Jews or being Jewish was a sticky subject. Miami Beach, which is at least 75 percent Jewish during the season, is so sick that owners who are Jewish request the performers, who are usually Jewish, 'not to work so Jewish. The people want to get away from that.'"[64] Further explaining the effect on the audience, Bruce writes in his autobiography, "Now I'll say 'a Jew' and just the word *Jew* sounds like a dirty word, and people don't know whether to laugh or not. [They're afraid] they'll seem so brazen. So there's just silence until they know I'm kidding, and then they'll break through."[65] By transgressing the unwritten rule not to speak of Jewishness openly, and thus subverting the "too Jewish" taboo, Bruce helped to tweak the Jewish consciousness of his generation.

The Comedy of Transgression

Lenny Bruce's rise to stardom occurred between 1958 and 1961. In 1958 he first began to attract large audiences to his nightclub act, and it was then that he recorded his first LPs. In the following year, he was offered a television appearance—his first exposure to a mass audience—on the *Steve Allen Show* on April 10, 1959. Allen introduced him with fanfare, announcing, "Ladies and gentlemen, here is a very shocking comedian, the most shocking comedian of our time, a young man who is skyrocketing to fame—Lenny Bruce!" Apparently, the show's producers had been nervous about Bruce's reputation for outrageousness and unpredictability and had carefully reviewed the routines planned for the show. But Bruce could not be contained—he was compelled, by his own comedic persona, to say something, do something outlandish. So, defying the censor and departing from the rehearsed script, he walked onstage and opened with this line: "Will Elizabeth Taylor become bar mitzvahed?" (Taylor had just married Eddie Fisher and converted to Judaism.) With millions watching and his career at stake, Bruce couldn't take the same liberties on television that he would onstage—but he could still flout convention and twit taboo through Jewishness. Making direct reference to Jewish anxieties, specifically to those concerning celebrity intermarriage and questionable conversion, Bruce found an acceptable surrogate for obscenity.

On his very next appearance on the *Steve Allen Show*, he once again opened with an unrehearsed Jewish joke. He began by citing a number of negative newspaper reviews of his previous appearance on the show. Then, the punchline: "Finally, a newspaper with some integrity came forth" (holding up a copy of the Yiddish *Daily Forward*, and reading): "Last night, a star was born!" Once again, Bruce exploited the mild shock value of Jewish subject matter to skirt the boundaries of acceptability; and at the same time, he subtly ridiculed Jewish ethnocentrism, that is, Jews' proclivity to favor their own. The use of such Jewish references on television would thereby substitute for the obscene language he used onstage—though it was still transgressive, it would get by the censors.

As it turns out, there is an even better backstory to the *Steve Allen Show* appearances. Before going on the show, Bruce first had to clear his material with the show's producers to make sure it was "kosher" for television. As he relates,

> They sat me down there, and I'm doing the bit for 15 guys. And I got into material that they wouldn't let me do on the *Allen Show*. I have a tattoo on

my arm, and because of this tattoo, I can never be buried in a Jewish cemetery. That's the Orthodox law. You have to go out of the world the same way you came in—no marks, no changes.

Anyway, I told how, when I got back from Malta and went home to Long Island, I was in the kitchen, washing with soap, and my Aunt Mema saw the tattoo. So she flips. A real Jewish yell.

"Look what you did! You ruined your arm! You're no better than a gypsy!"

So the producer says that I can't do this on the show because it would definitely be offensive to the Jewish people.

"You're out of your *nut*," I responded.

No, he said, every time we get into a satire of any ethnic group, we get a lot of mail. You can't talk about that.[66]

Lenny argued his case, explaining that he was simply relating a true-life experience. But after deliberating further, the producers respond:

> "We talked it over, Lenny. You know, it's not only offensive to the Jewish people, but it's definitely offensive to the Gentile people too."
>
> "Oh, yeah—how do you figure that?"
>
> "Well, what you're saying in essence is that the Gentiles don't *care* what they bury."[67]

By telling this rather funny story, Bruce is mocking the oversensitivity and timidity of the television producers; yet despite his protestations to the contrary, he had no choice *but* to offend. It was, after all, the very essence of his work—to break the rules, to transgress social norms. As he would explain, "I satirize many subjects that are particular sacred cows. In other words, I am a satirist basically. I am irreverent politically, religiously, on any things that I think need discussing and satirizing."[68]

Thus, after assimilation/impersonation and explicit Jewishness, irreverence is the third key to understanding Bruce as a Jewish comedian. As co-authors and legal scholars Ronald Collins and David Skover comment offhandedly, "He was *the* confrontational comic. The need to be outspoken, even offensive, was part of Lenny's genetic makeup."[69] They may not have intended it as such, but the comment suggests that the source of Bruce's irreverence lay in his Jewish roots. After all, the traditional *midrashic* depiction of the first Jew, Abraham, has him as a child smashing the idols in his father's idol shop, an archetypal killer of sacred cows, the original iconoclast. Jews, for centuries the only non-Christians in Christian Europe, have often occupied this quintessential outsider's role in world history; and in this view, Bruce would seem to be one in a long line of Jewish truth-tellers, gadflies, and social critics.

But once again, the specific context of mid-twentieth-century America adds a more nuanced perspective. Jews of Bruce's generation, characterized by high upward mobility, may not seem the best candidates for rebels and outlaws. Yet these same middle-class strivers were often filled with a sense of embarrassment and even anger toward their parents and their old-world ways. Prefiguring the "generation gap" of the Sixties, American Jews experienced profound generational tensions almost from the moment they arrived as immigrants. No less an authority than Irving Howe tackles the issue in his monumental history of the Jewish immigrants, *World of Our Fathers*:

> Reflecting and exploiting the psychic uncertainties of the sons and grandsons of immigrants, the Jewish humor of the fifties and sixties spoke most painfully about the difficulties of overextended adolescence, the sense of disablement by parents who loved too much and demanded too much. From such dilemmas, and the embarrassments they spawned, some Jewish comics wove fantasies of loathing, which could bring a big-city audience with many middle-class Jews to shocked laughter because it uncovered a kinship in the forbidden.[70]

Historians of American Jewish life have yet to fully excavate the many layers of such familial and communal conflict—yet the reality, and the pain, of such tensions is beyond dispute. The relevant question here is how the inner turmoil of postwar Jews translated into the biting satirical humor of comedians such as Bruce. In a late chapter, Howe traces the history of Jewish entertainers from Al Jolson to the Marx Brothers, claiming that the humor of post–World War II comedians still "stemmed from the culture of immigrant streets," and ends the chapter with a discussion of Lenny Bruce:

> The momentum of fury which had been gathering in the work of some Jewish performers—comic simulations, but sometimes real fury—came to a head in the work of Lenny Bruce, a performer intent upon leaping out of performance, a prophet corrupted who ranted against corruption, a lacerated nihilist at once brilliant and debased . . . Having stored up a bellyful of Jewish humiliation, Bruce cast it back onto his audiences. The laughter he won was a nervous laughter, tingling with masochism; it was like the laughter of convicts caught in a scheme to escape. Humor of this kind bears a heavy weight of destruction; in Jewish hands, more likely self-destruction,

for it proceeds from a brilliance that corrodes the world faster than, even in imagination, it can remake it. A corrupt ascetic is a man undone. . . . Toward the end, his performances sputtered out in dry rage, quasi-legal ramblings against district attorneys who were persecuting him. He became a *magid* (preacher) without a message, a martyr without a cause. He fell back, deeply back, into a Jewish past that neither he nor his audiences could know much about—a reborn Sabbatai as stand-up comic.[71]

Provocatively comparing Bruce to Sabbatai Tzvi, the false messiah of seventeenth-century Ottoman Turkey, Howe places Bruce into Jewish historical context and indicates the extremity of his iconoclasm at the same time. In his era, Sabbatai claimed to speak the divine truth and abrogated Jewish law; in his time, Bruce claimed to speak ultimate truth as well, and in a more secular vein challenged the norms of "Judeo-Christian" America. Both men shocked the sensibility of their contemporaries, and both became cult figures. But such macro-historical comparison does not suffice for explanation; Howe adds the more immediate context of twentieth-century American Jewish life, attributing the "shrunken messianism" of Bruce's generation to "stored-up resentments"[72]—resentments toward Jewish parents and gentile society, the one for having made them feel "too Jewish," and the other for not allowing them to forget it.

All of this helps to explain Bruce's irreverent and rebellious attitude, both religious and political. He disclaimed any messianic intentions, though, explaining, "The kind of comedy I do isn't, like, going to change the world; but certain areas of society make me unhappy, and satirizing them—aside from being lucrative—provides a release for me."[73] In terms of religious satire, we've seen how he impersonated a Catholic priest, lambasted assimilated Reform Jews, and joked that the Pope was Jewish. Clearly, he had no hesitation about offending religious sensibilities. Some of his most famous routines—"Christ and Moses" and "Religions, Inc." in particular—took on organized religion, brashly criticizing the Catholic Church for its supposed hypocrisy in building opulent cathedrals while claiming concern for the poor.

As many have observed, it was this transgression—religious blasphemy—that sealed Bruce's fate with the authorities. He himself admitted, comically of course, that "the reason I got busted—arrested—is I picked on the wrong god . . . the Western god—the cute god, the In-god, the Kennedy-god—and that's where I screwed up."[74] Here we're more concerned with the *source* of Bruce's irreverence. As suggested earlier, there is a Jewish historical element to such a critical stance toward religion: from Baruch Spinoza to Sigmund Freud, Jews have been some of Western civilization's greatest secular critics of religion. Bruce was particularly susceptible to religious skepticism as a modern Jew, certainly, but also as a nightclub comedian and urban intellectual. In any event, he evinced both a disdain for religious belief *and* a sincere interest in religion at the same time. He explains it as follows:

> Now, the reason, perhaps, for my irreverence is that I have no knowledge of the God, because the Jews lost their God. Really. Before I was born the God was going away.
>
> Because to have a God you have to know something about him, and as a child I didn't speak the same language as the Jewish God.
>
> To have a God you have to love him and know about him as kids—early instruction—and I didn't know what he looked like. Our God has no mother, no father, no manger in the five-and-ten, on cereal boxes and on television shows . . .
>
> The Christian God, you're lucky in that way because you've got Mary, a mother, a father, a beginning, the five-and-ten little mangers—identity. Your God, the Christian God is all over. He's on rocks, he saves you, he's dying on bank buildings—he's been in three films. He's on crucifixes all over. It's a story you can follow. Constant identification.
>
> The Jewish God—where's the Jewish God? He's on a little box nailed to the door jamb. In a *mezuzah*. There he is, in there. He's standing on a slant, God. And all the Jews are looking at him, and kissing him on the way into the house:
>
> "I told the super *don't paint God*! Hey, Super! C'mere. What the hell's the matter with you? I told you twenty times, that's *God* there. What're you painting God for? . . ."[75]

Whether fair or not, the routine accurately reflects the fact that most American Jews of Bruce's generation grew up without much religious knowledge or feeling. Yet notice how Bruce seemingly mocks Judaism's lack of a conspicuous God-image and its trivialization of God in the *mezuzah*; but right below the surface is a still sharper critique of the Christian tendency to "market" their God as concrete symbol—the classic Jewish charge of idolatry. In the end, Bruce wasn't interested in any particular criticism of religion so much as in defending his *right* to criticize religion. The following routine, in which he takes on the voice of the religious "Protestant," makes this abundantly clear:

But as far as *disgusting* is concerned—the reason we left England was just for that right, to be disgusting. . . . In fact, that's why we left England years ago—because we couldn't bitch about the church, the Anglican Church, we Protestants. And we had underground meetings.

"I'm tired of this shit, let's get somewhere else, let's go to a different country where we can have our meetings and be Protestants. Let's go somewhere else so we can be disgusting. And do disgusting shows. No one can stop us—flaunt it in their faces."

"*How* disgusting?"

"Well, go in front of a synagogue and sing about pork."

"*That* disgusting? What about the Moslems?"

"Fuck 'em. The Jews too, and the vegetarians."

Cause that's our right—to be disgusting.[76]

In his inimitable way, Bruce makes the valid observation that the American experiment was born in the search for religious freedom—a freedom that necessarily includes the right to be "disgusting," that is, to offend other people's religious sensibilities. It was his First Amendment–granted right to be able to sing about pork in front of a synagogue—not that he meant to do such a thing, but the combined absurdity and offensiveness of the suggestion made his satirical point. Bruce's use of obscene language was not merely for shock value, therefore, but was intended to challenge the prurience and repressiveness of American society.

Like so many other Jewish liberals of the time, he also challenged the status quo of American racism. Besides his routines about religion, his most famous bits concerned prejudice against blacks, for example, "Are There Any Niggers Here Tonight?" Like his contemporary Don Rickles, Bruce would similarly shock his audience by pointing out their ethnic or racial identities, but he went so much further:

By the way, are there any niggers here tonight? . . . I know that one nigger who works here, I see him back there. Oh, there's two niggers, customers, and ah, *aha*! Between those two niggers sits one kike—man, thank God for the kikes! Uh, two kikes. That's two kikes, and three niggers, and one spic. One spic—two, three spics. One mick. One mick, one spic, one hick, thick, funky, spunky boogey. And there's another kike. Three kikes. Three kikes, one guinea, one greaseball. . . .[77]

As dramatized in the film *Lenny*, the opening line of the provocative routine creates a sense of menace and, at first, stark silence. But then, as the auctioneer's rhythm kicks in the laughs begin to come, and the comedian-philosopher breaks the tension entirely with the denouement:

The point? That the word's suppression gives it the power, the violence, the viciousness. If President Kennedy got on television and said, "Tonight I'd like to introduce the niggers in my cabinet," and he yelled "niggernigger-niggerniggerniggerniggernigger" at every nigger he saw, "boogeyboogey-boogeyboogeyboogey, niggerniggerniggernigger" till nigger didn't mean anything any more, till nigger lost its meaning—you'd never make any four-year-old nigger cry when he came home from school.[78]

This is a word, of course, that has remained taboo into the twenty-first century.[79] Though Bruce's advice to repeat it aloud shouldn't be taken literally, his explanation that "the word's suppression gives it [its] power" is the real point. His stock in trade, therefore, was exposing taboo subjects to the light of day. Whether the topic was religion, sex, drugs, the JFK assassination, racism, or obscenity itself, his constant intent was to combat suppression of speech and of thought—a rather lofty goal for a nightclub comic, true, but not entirely surprising in the context of the subversive comedy of the 1950s and 1960s, of which Bruce was the avatar.

As a subversive *Jewish* comedian, however, Bruce introduced comedic discussion of one other forbidden subject, perhaps the most difficult topic for Jews of the time to speak of and think about—the Holocaust. Lawrence Epstein, historian of American Jewish comedy, suggests that Bruce's Holocaust humor "was deliberately shocking," and cites the following examples: "In one bit, using a salesman's voice, Bruce would say: 'Here's a Volkswagen pickup truck that was just used slightly during the war carrying the people back and forth to the furnaces.' He would hold up a paper with the headline 'Six Million Jews Found Alive in Argentina.'"[80] Epstein further explains that "the shock of such 'jokes' came not only from the inappropriateness of joking about the Holocaust, but also from the fact that very few people even discussed it at all."[81] Whereas Jewish educators and rabbis began to broach the subject soon after the war, the majority of American Jews in the 1950s had yet to fully absorb the catastrophe when, around 1960, a number of cultural events coincided to bring the Holocaust to mass consciousness (see Chapter 1). By that time, American Jews could ignore the subject no longer. Just as it had intruded upon the myth of Sandy Koufax, and just as it would show up in some early Bob Dylan songs (see Chapter 4), the Holocaust inevitably found its way into Lenny Bruce routines.

Bruce had developed a series of sketches about the venality of show business, most notably his classic routine about a hack comedian desperate for success, "The Palladium."[82] In this vein, his bit about two MCA

(Music Corporation of America) talent agents looking to book a dictator and discovering "a guy who has never played San Francisco, wonderful performer, the wonderful Adolf Hitler"[83] is really more of a satire of the agents than of Hitler. Bruce claimed that he had joked about Hitler as early as 1949, preceding Mel Brooks by over a decade. In an interview with Paul Krassner, Bruce recalled, "If you will look in *Variety*, you'll find that the first review I ever got—in 1949—was for a bit I did about Hitler being an M.C."[84] But after the news of the Eichmann capture and trial, he began to regularly discuss the Nazi mass murderer in his act. Taking the most controversial stance possible, he spoke from the point of view of the accused: "Eichmann really figured, you know, 'The Jews— the most liberal people in the world—they'll give me a fair shake.' Fair? *Certainly.* 'Rabbi' means lawyer. He'll get the best trial in the world, Eichmann. *Ha*! They were shaving his leg while he was giving his appeal! That's the last bit of insanity, man."[85]

Where the first routine in both *The Essential Lenny Bruce* (1967) and *Lenny Bruce: Let the Buyer Beware* (2004) is "Are There Any Niggers Here Tonight?" both collections end with a Thomas Merton poem Bruce would use to close his shows, "My Name Is Adolf Eichmann." Ominously, he would have the stage lights lowered, and then intone:

My name is Adolf Eichmann.
The Jews came every day
to vat they thought vould be
fun in the showers. . . .
I, Adolf Eichmann,
vatched through the portholes.
I saw every Jew burned
und turned into soap.
Do you people think yourselves better
because you burned your enemies
at long distances
with missiles?
Without ever seeing what you'd done to them?
Hiroshima . . . *Auf Wiedersehen*[86]

In November of 1961, just one month after his first arrest for obscenity, Bruce gave a legendary performance at the Curran Theater in San Francisco. In the course of discussing the Eichmann trial of the previous summer—and he was certainly the first to approach that landmark event in Holocaust consciousness from a comedic perspective—he made a revealing remark: "Dig this cat [Eichmann], shlepped out, and they [put him] on trial—and set me back another thousand years, cause *it's in to be Jewish*."[87] Provocative as always, Bruce observed how the trial was being used to raise Jewish consciousness, pitching him backward in his—that is, the Jew's—centuries-long quest to assimilate, and simultaneously observing the advent of a new age of Jewish acceptability in America. The question remains to what degree Bruce served as a catalyst for the historic change he observed.

What is unquestionable is the degree to which Bruce influenced subsequent generations of Jewish comedians. Beyond Larry Gelbart's transvestite corporal, Bruce's assimilatory impersonations foreshadowed other comedic masking/unmaskings, such as Mel Brooks's Yiddish-speaking Indian chief, Andy Kaufman's "foreign-man" Elvis impersonator, and Sacha Baron Cohen's Hebrew-speaking Kazakh antisemite, Borat. Bruce's incisive explorations of Jewishness, especially into the differences between Jews and gentiles, prefigured Philip Roth, Woody Allen, Jackie Mason, and Larry David. And his irreverent attitudes toward sex, religion, politics, and "dirty-words" have lived on in the political, satirical, and scatological humor of George Carlin (though Irish, his signature routine "Seven Words You Can Never Say on Television" is virtually an ode to Bruce), Bill Maher (half-Jewish), Lewis Black, Sarah Silverman, Howard Stern, and many others. Richard Lewis, yet another Jewish comic deeply influenced by Bruce, calls him a "comedic prophet," "the major stimulation to my . . . comedic aspirations," and his own "Hendrix of comedy." Combining all three elements, Bruce's distasteful but fascinating attempts at Holocaust humor are echoed by Mel Brooks's 1967 film (and later hit Broadway musical) *The Producers* and Larry David's frequent references to Holocaust survivors in his series *Curb Your Enthusiasm* (in one episode, David has an elderly Jewish survivor argue with a cast member of the television show *Survivor* as to who is the *real* survivor— appalling, perhaps, but convulsingly funny nonetheless). All in all, Bruce must be seen as a central figure in the history of American Jewish comedy.

Lenny Bruce and the 1960s

Lenny Bruce was also a seminal influence on the "revolutionary consciousness" of the Sixties counterculture. Bob Shayne, editor of the *Los Angeles Free Press*, explained it as early as 1968:

> The word of Lenny Bruce . . . doesn't sound exactly revolutionary today. But the reason it doesn't is that Lenny Bruce said it yesterday. People heard it,

thought about it, repeated it to other people, passed it on to younger people, and it evolved into "Do your thing." He may not have said anything totally new, but he spread concepts that were virtually unheard of a short five-ten years ago, concepts that have become the basis of the "new morality."

"Lenny didn't go looking; the cause found him," says Alan Myerson, director of the Committee and one of the thousands of people in their twenties and thirties who have adopted Lenny's word and spread it to the teens who think they invented it. "Four years ago it was unheard of for students to storm a university. I don't know if those kids at Columbia necessarily ever heard of Lenny, but for the people who directly influence them he was as important as Che Guevara."[88]

Along similar lines, sociologist John Murray Cuddihy wrote in 1974, "As was abundantly clear from its earliest protests, the New York–based Yippies derived a good deal of their inspiration from 'sick' comedian-satirist Lenny Bruce and his 'insider's' criticism of middle-class Jewish gentility."[89] The "missing link" here was Paul Krassner, radical absurdist and founding editor of *The Realist*, and thus, according to Cuddihy, "grandfather of the subsequent underground press."[90] Krassner was also a friend and collaborator of Bruce's (he edited *How to Talk Dirty and Influence People*), and a few years later, in 1967, he co-founded the Yippies (Youth International Party) with Abbie Hoffman and Jerry Rubin. As Krassner recalls, "When I met Abbie Hoffman, I told him that he was the first person who made me laugh since Lenny died (the previous year), and Abbie said, 'Really? He was my god.'"[91] Hoffman, hippie prankster and provocateur extraordinaire, dedicated his book *Woodstock Nation* to Bruce, writing, "This story is for you, Lenny, from all the Yippies."[92] He was once arrested for having the word *fuck* written on his forehead, and though he denied it was inspired by Bruce,[93] the resonance between their rebellious personae is unmistakable. Introducing Abbie Hoffman's memoir, fellow traveler Norman Mailer draws the comparison as well: "Reading this book . . . I began to think of Dustin Hoffman's brilliant portrait of Lenny Bruce where at the end . . . he will try to make the judge believe that under it all, Lenny, too, is a good American."[94]

Indeed, the parallels between the obscenity trials of Bruce and the famous Chicago Seven trial (following the Democratic Convention of 1968) are striking. At his sentencing in his New York trial, Bruce protested: "I am a Jew before this court. I would like to set the record straight, that the Jew is not remorseful."[95] Taking a similar stance, Abbie Hoffman recalled, "When the judge [Julius Hoffman] sent Dave [Dellinger] behind bars in the final days of the trial, I really exploded. 'You're a disgrace to the Jews. You would have served Hitler better,' I screamed. 'You *shtunk*!' And then in the sharpest thrust of all, I called him a '*shanda fur de goyim*' which roughly translated is a Yiddish expression meaning 'frontman for the gentiles.' "[96]

The line of influence from Lenny Bruce to Abbie Hoffman thus indicates a vital Jewish element in the Sixties counterculture. After all, like Bruce and Hoffman, Mailer, Krassner, Rubin, Lee Weiner, Allard Lowenstein, Mark Rudd, Phil Ochs, Bob Dylan, Allen Ginsberg, Richard Alpert (Ram Dass), and others were all radicalized Jews, nice Jewish boys gone bad.[97] Of Rudd, Hoffman confided, "Make no mistake, [he] was a member in good standing of the International Jewish Conspiracy"[98]—implying, humorously of course, that the movement of which he was a leading figure was in some way related to the Jewish experience. If we consider the Jewish irreverence of Bruce to be the critical precedent for the Jewish irreverence of Hoffman, Rubin, Krassner, and the others, then this further implies that the rebellious tenor of the Sixties had its roots in, among other things, the generational and assimilatory tensions of 1950s American Jewry. All of which is to agree with Michael Staub that there was indeed something very "Jewish" about the Sixties.[99]

With all of this expressed Jewishness, one might think that Bruce's impress would be found as well in the Jewish counterculture. With the creation of Shlomo Carlebach's House of Love and Prayer in San Francisco, Arthur Waskow's Farbrengen in Washington, Art Green's Havurat Shalom in Boston, and the New York Havurah, a Jewish religious version of the counterculture—later called Jewish Renewal—was in full swing around the country. The high point of the movement may have been the 1973 publication of *The Jewish Catalog*, edited by Michael Strassfeld, Sharon Strassfeld, and Richard Siegel. In none of this, however, was any explicit reference to Bruce to be found. He had represented a far more secularist and compromised Jewishness, and had little to say to young Jews intent on reconstructing a meaningful Judaic identity. Yet as I've argued, his spirit lived on in the Sixties counterculture overall, and might be seen at least as an indirect influence on the Jewish sub-(counter)culture.

What *was* the response of contemporary Jews to Lenny Bruce? Though few of that generation recall a direct connection—for example, seeing him perform onstage—Bruce nevertheless had struck a chord in the American Jewish consciousness. On one level, he simply aroused the anxieties of many of his contemporaries, as testified by political cartoonist **139**

Jules Feiffer, who recalled being "struck by Bruce's candor about his Jewishness—[he said]: 'It frightened me because when I grew up, you didn't wear your Jewishness on your sleeve, because you were essentially among enemies.'"[100] And in a recent history of Jewish comedians in America, Lawrence Epstein observes that "Bruce and many other Jews of his generation felt caught between an American and a Jewish identity, uncomfortable in either one . . . [He thus] played out in public the anguish of many American Jews, some of whom did not recognize their confusion and many of whom were unable or unwilling to express it openly."[101]

Sometimes this anxiety prompted a public response. When asked in 1961 if he ever felt pressure to tone down his act, Bruce answered, "Yeah, I've had guys telling me what to do—you know, civic pressure, church groups, synagogues. I get letters from rabbis . . ."[102] On the other hand, he also received public support from some other fellow Jews. After Bruce was arrested for obscenity twice in one week while performing at a Greenwich Village coffeehouse in April of 1964, Beat poet Allen Ginsberg (another seminal Jewish figure of the Sixties) organized the "Emergency Committee against the Harassment of Lenny Bruce." In June, Ginsberg issued a press release titled "Arts, Educational Leaders Protest Use of New York Obscenity Law in Harassment of Controversial Satirist Lenny Bruce." In support of Bruce's First Amendment rights, a petition was circulated and signed by eighty-eight prominent personalities; nearly half were Jewish, including Woody Allen, Theodore Bikel, Robert Brustein, Bob Dylan, Harry Golden, Albert Goldman (Bruce's future biographer), Joseph Heller, Lillian Hellman, Nat Hentoff, Irving Howe, Alfred Kazin, Paul Krassner, Irving Kristol, Max Lerner, Norman Mailer, Paul Newman, Norman Podhoretz, Meyer Schapiro, Susan Sontag, Elizabeth Taylor, and Lionel Trilling—quite an extraordinary cross-section of the New York Jewish intelligentsia and entertainment personalities. The petition, sent to newspapers all over, included this bit of hyperbole: "Lenny Bruce is a popular and controversial performer in the field of social satire in the tradition of Swift, Rabelais and Twain." It was later used by the defense in his New York trial.[103] For our purposes, the episode provides evidence both of Bruce's celebrity and perceived social importance, as well as the presence of prominent Jews among his supporters.

The Mythologizing of Lenny Bruce

Even as his legend has grown through the forty-plus years since his death, there has been little serious treatment, whether artistic or academic, of the Jewish element of Bruce's career. During that time, his memory has been shaped by a series of myth-making texts, collectively evoking a Rashomon-like portrait of ever-shifting perspectives. The first such text was written by Bruce himself, a purported memoir titled *How to Talk Dirty and Influence People*. Originally serialized in *Playboy* magazine during his declining years of 1963 to 1964, and published as a book in 1965, it combines some recounting of his actual life experiences with exaggeration and fantasy. In much of it, Bruce rehashes his standup routines, and toward the end, merely reprints the transcriptions of his court cases. Unfortunately for those hoping to better understand the man, the book was written to serve two purposes contrary to the usual self-analytical ends of autobiography: to entertain the readers of Hugh Hefner's "hip" men's magazine, and to defend himself against the onslaught of negative publicity surrounding his arrests for obscenity onstage and drug abuse off.[104]

In either case, the book is itself a performance, and therefore an intriguing record of Bruce's ability to *shpritz*, that is, to free-associate comedic material. Much of his Jewish material shows up, including his best-known Jewish-themed routine, "Jewish and Goyish." Appearing on page 5 of the memoir, the bit is preceded by a discussion of his use of Yiddish: "Perhaps at this point I ought to say something about my vocabulary. My conversation, spoken and written, is usually flavored with the jargon of the hipster, the argot of the underworld, and Yiddish." But according to Bruce, his use of Yiddish—and hence his Jewishness—is idiosyncratic, a purely subjective condition, as he further explains: "To me, if you live in New York or any other big city, you are Jewish. It doesn't matter even if you're Catholic; if you live in New York you're Jewish. If you live in Butte, Montana, you're going to be goyish even if you're Jewish."[105] From the very beginning of his definitive self-portrait, he announces in no certain terms that he is a Jew—but a Jew of a different sort.

The first posthumous contribution to the multivalent myth was a slim volume titled *The Essential Lenny Bruce*, published late in 1967, the year following Bruce's death. An anthology of Bruce's comedic monologues transcribed and edited by John Cohen, the collection sold 250,000 copies in just two years. It quickly made its way onto college campuses and established Bruce as a hero of the blossoming counterculture. Cohen makes this connection patently clear, as he writes in the book's epilogue:

> Lenny Bruce did not die of an O.D.: he was murdered. Murdered by the same people and for the same reasons protesters are getting their heads cracked open in Oakland and New York and Milwaukee and Washington

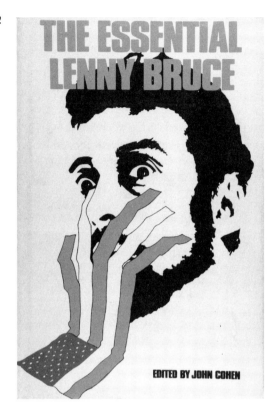

The Essential Lenny Bruce (1967) cover illustration by Frank Gauna, capturing the effective silencing of Bruce by American legal authorities.

D.C. and on college campuses—because Bruce's words and gestures said too clearly just what people are saying now. . . . The only people who really dig Lenny Bruce are the people who are doing the same thing Bruce did—cutting loose, turning on, turning away, trying to turn America around." [106]

Cohen does not comment on the organization of his book, but its table of contents is telling. The chapters are thematic, and the first section covers perhaps his most important theme: racism, the continued oppression of African Americans. Following the chapter titled "Blacks," however, comes what Cohen may have considered Bruce's second most important topic: "Jews." It is that chapter that provides much of the raw material for my discussion here, but its very existence is significant given the broad appeal of the book.

In the summer of 1971, nearly five years after Bruce's death, *Rolling Stone* magazine noted the recent trend toward mythologizing the man:

Because Lenny Bruce's myth and legacy are so rich his resurrection, like his death, was inevitable. In the last few weeks, in fact, New York has seen a frenzy of Lennys come back from the grave. It looked at first to be a festive, down-home Lenny revival; there were two Lenny plays, a dramatic movie Lenny (two kinescope recording Lennys and a TV pilot Lenny on the same bill), an emerging Lenny book, and a whole gaggle of Lenny disciples, all claiming the right of succession going all the way back to the actual Lenny. All was not kosher.[107]

The centerpiece of all this activity was the collaborative effort of Marvin Worth, Bruce's former manager, and writer Julian Barry to produce *The Lenny Bruce Story* as a film. Stalled as a movie project, however, the original script was adapted for the stage by Tom O'Horgan, director of *Hair* (then the big hit musical on Broadway), and the play opened in May at the Brooks Atkinson Theatre (just across the street from *Hair*). Barry and O'Horgan fixed Bruce's legacy firmly within the counterculture, couching his story in the idiom of the psychedelic Sixties, and further burnishing the myth of Bruce as a hero of free speech, free love, and free expression of every kind. Starring Cliff Gorman in the title role, *Lenny* the play highlighted Bruce's riffs on race and religion, incorporating the actual routines into the action onstage.[108] The play thus presented Bruce as a kind of societal "shaman," speaking truth to power and serving as rebel-in-chief of a turbulent time.[109]

The year 1974 was the high point of Lenny Bruce memory making. In that year, Worth at last completed the movie version of *Lenny*. As directed by Bob Fosse and starring Dustin Hoffman in the title role, the film was a smash success, earning six Academy Award nominations; and it has certainly played the major role in creating the popular image of Bruce. Yet by "Hollywoodizing" his life, some notable distortions resulted. Highlighting the character of Hot Honey Harlowe, the burlesque dancer who became Bruce's wife (played memorably by Valerie Perrine), the script was made over as a romantic narrative, framing the film with their love affair, marriage, and divorce, and ultimately casting Honey as the "living memory" of the Bruce legend. The clear implication is that Bruce's biting satiric comedy had its source in his love/hate relationship with the voluptuous redheaded stripper. As his biographer would write, "After being Lenny's wife, Honey became his muse . . . Arousing in Lenny the deepest rage he ever felt, she inspired in him the most brilliant humor he ever created."[110] There is some truth to that, to be sure, but it is by no means the full story. More problematic still, the depiction of Bruce by actor Hoffman is endearing and compelling, but bears little resemblance to the real Lenny Bruce. As one reviewer wrote at the time, **143**

"Bob Fosse's movie is a disappointment [in part] . . . because it will now define and describe Lenny Bruce and his comedy for all those who have no means to know better. What they see is a trendy, liberal, middle-class, gentile translation of a life and art that was perverse, radical, lower-class and unassimilatedly Jewish."[111]

Neither the film nor the play included the "Jewish and Goyish" routine, but both versions of *Lenny* did include two other significant Jewish episodes in his story. First is a scene in which Lenny and Honey (fictionalized as "Rusty" in the play) visit his mother Sally and aunt Mema in Brooklyn. Preceding Dustin Hoffman's turn as a Jewish father in *Meet the Fockers* by thirty years, here Hoffman is the Jewish son taking his *shiksa* girlfriend home to meet the family.[112] Later, in the course of re-creating Bruce's nightclub routines, Hoffman performs the infamous bit "One Who Killed Our Lord." With its stark opening admission, "I am of Semitic background . . . I'm Jewish," the bit builds into a mock confession of the murder of Christ. Its fuller implications were discussed earlier here, but the moment operates in the film as an unequivocal declaration of Jewishness. In the end, however, it is an inconsequential plot point, neither emphasized nor elucidated any further.

The year 1974 also saw the publication of the "definitive biography" of Lenny Bruce, *Ladies and Gentlemen, Lenny Bruce!!* written by Albert Goldman and based on the journalistic research of Lawrence Schiller. Goldman's detailed biographical portrait makes abundantly clear the extent to which Bruce abused drugs, and thus is often derided as sensationalistic and mean-spirited. But despite the "yellow" reputation of its author, the book offers the most comprehensive study of the comedian to date. As *New York Times* reviewer Christopher Lehmann-Haupt writes, "Mr. Goldman has refused to mount a hobbyhorse. Instead, he has given us Lenny Bruce in all his many guises—showman, jazzman, hipster and whore; scam-artist, liar, fink and junkie . . . genius, rebel, artist and hero."[113] The book is a fascinating read. As a contribution to Bruce's image, however, it is decidedly negative—having precisely the opposite effect of the feel-good movie.

Goldman's biography, in its kitchen-sink approach to its subject, does treat certain Jewish aspects of Bruce's life. For example, Goldman titles the chapter on Bruce's family background "Jewboy," and describes a visit to his father, Mickey Schneider:

Seating you at the dining-room table neatly covered with flowered plastic, he plies you with coffee and cakes, reminding you for all the world of an

old Jewish woman who has lost her husband and her children and now is
reduced to holding her world together with the formalities of hospitality.
There is something heavy and lugubrious about this man, even when he
smiles: something that bespeaks a lifetime of *tsuris* that only another Jew
could understand.[114]

Goldman was of course a fellow Jew in this scenario, and later in the
chapter, he adds a bit of pop psychology regarding Jewish families:

> In Jewish families like the Schneiders, you often have a grandmother who
> is an all-powerful matriarch, a domineering old lady who has a weak hus-
> band, or no husband at all, and rules her sons and daughters with unques-
> tioned authority . . . Almost as bad, though, is the lot of the sons, who are
> never allowed to rise to their full masculine stature lest they jeopardize the
> authority of their mother. Brought up in the crossed rays of the most in-
> tense Jewish love, they develop into twisted personalities, loving where they
> should hate and hating where they should love. They attach themselves to
> women who hurt them and treat with contempt the women who offer them
> simple love. They often display great talent in their work, but as men they
> have curiously ineffective characters.[115]

Ostensibly talking about the father, Goldman clearly intends this description to apply to the son as well—and consequently to many Jewish men
of that generation. In a subsequent chapter, "How Sick Humor Came Up
the River from Brooklyn to Manhattan," the author details the mentor-
ing role played by Joe Ancis, who, among other things, taught Lenny
to be Jewish. As discussed earlier, this is an idiosyncratic yet revealing
account of cultural transmission. But overall, in 800 pages of biographic
shpritzing, Lenny's Jewishness remains a relatively minor issue.

Also in 1974, Bruce fan and history professor Frank Kofsky published
Lenny Bruce: The Comedian as Social Critic and Secular Moralist. The
scholarly essay had its origins in a panel devoted to Bruce at the 1971
meeting of the American Historical Association organized by a colleague,
Leon Litwack. Kofsky notes that "Litwack, like myself, had been a follower of Lenny Bruce for over a decade."[116] Referring to the organization
of John Cohen's anthology, Part II of the book is titled "Blacks, Jews, and
Lenny Bruce," and in it Kofsky offers a rare, sustained discussion of
Bruce's Jewishness. Taking off from Bruce's explanation of his preferred
vocabulary—that of the hipster, the underworld, and Yiddish—Kofsky
relates the outsider status of both blacks and Jews to Bruce, claiming
that the so-called sick comedian "was horrified, repulsed, and sickened

146 by the wholesale immorality that he saw being condoned and even actively encouraged by Establishment political, intellectual, and religious spokesmen." Kofsky then theorizes: "He utilized language as a vehicle for symbolically conveying his outrage and disgust at this situation. For what is most significant about Yiddish, the highly charged language of Black musicians, and the argot of the underworld is that each of these functions as the 'mother tongue,' so to speak, *for a group that is beyond the pale by the standards of the dominant culture* . . . Bruce adopted portions of the language of these three tightly knit subcultures to signify his repudiation of the present social and ethical order."[117] The problem with this interpretation is that it treats Bruce ahistorically, seeing the early-1960s figure through the lens of the later counterculture—a history professor perhaps ought to have known better.

Though much was written about him in the 1960s and early 1970s, popular culture all but ignored Bruce through the more conservative years of the Reagan era. Perhaps some felt enough had been said. As Steve Allen mused some fifteen years after his friend's death, "It is difficult and perhaps impossible at this late date to say anything analytical about Lenny Bruce that has not already occurred to others, so extensive is the literature on him."[118] The truth was, by then Bruce's image had been tainted by his association with drugs and social rebellion, and few wanted to touch the subject. Not until the Clintonian 1990s would a series of projects emerge to rehabilitate Bruce's reputation. The first was a 1992 reissue of his memoir, *How to Talk Dirty and Influence People*. The new edition merged with the myth-making trend of later years. In a brand-new introduction, Eric Bogosian reiterates the notion that Bruce was a patron saint of the Sixties generation, going so far as to suggest that "Saint Lenny . . . died for our sins."[119]

In 1992 as well, Fred Baker produced a documentary film about the comedian, *Lenny Bruce Without Tears*. Including clips of Bruce's television performances and interviews with friends and associates, the film is otherwise marred by its use of random stock footage to illustrate Bruce's recorded routines—because unfortunately, Bruce's nightclub and concert performances were never recorded on film (with one late exception). A far more successful film project was the 1998 documentary by Robert Weide, *Lenny Bruce: Swear to Tell the Truth*. Sympathetically narrated by actor Robert De Niro, the film portrays Bruce as a tragic figure, a victim of government persecution. Though the police most often arrested him for public obscenity, the documentary pushes another thesis: Bruce was persecuted (and ultimately hounded to death) for religious blasphemy.

In his standup comedy, he had dared to criticize the church, accusing organized religion of outright hypocrisy, and the largely Catholic police departments of New York and Chicago were out to get him. As evidence, the documentary has his acolyte Paul Krassner relate an anecdote of the Bruce trial in Chicago that took place on Ash Wednesday, when all members of the jury, as well as some of the court officials, entered the courtroom with ash on their foreheads—surreal, but true.[120] Neither documentary, however, dwells very much on the question of Lenny's Jewish identity—it is acknowledged, certainly, but never explored.

In 2002, legal scholars Ronald Collins and David Skover published *The Trials of Lenny Bruce: The Fall and Rise of an American Icon*, a detailed investigation of Bruce's court battles, in particular his campaign to invoke the First Amendment's promise of freedom of speech in defense against the charge of obscenity. In Collins and Skover's view, Bruce is an "American icon" less for his comedic pioneering than for his role in enlarging the sphere of free expression in this country. The book offers a more political take on Bruce's career, and shifts the emphasis from the "crime" of irreligiousness back to his social transgressions of taboo language and forbidden speech. Further, *The Trials of Lenny Bruce* counters the view of Bruce as a depraved drug addict by making the case for his personal heroism and historical significance.

However impassioned their argument may be, Collins and Skover's legalistic perspective has not replaced the idea of Bruce as a comedy legend. The prevailing trend remains an emphasis of the artistic over the sociopolitical contribution of Bruce. In 2004, record producer Hal Willner issued a long-awaited definitive compilation of Bruce's standup routines—many never before publicly available—in a six-CD collection titled *Lenny Bruce: Let the Buyer Beware*. The overall effect, quite intentional, was to establish Bruce's status as a great American artist. Similarly, two recent studies of the comedic efflorescence of post–World War II America—Gerald Nachman's *Seriously Funny: The Rebel Comedians of the 1950s and 1960s* (2003) and Richard Zoglin's *Comedy at the Edge: How Stand-Up in the 1970s Changed America* (2008)—have further solidified Bruce's place in modern standup comedy, marking his singular career as the turning point between the Borscht Belt humor of the 1940s and 1950s and the more subversive, observational comedy of the 1960s and beyond.

Comics themselves acknowledge Bruce's influence regularly. Jon Stewart, current dean of political humor in America, has stated Bruce's iconic stature in no uncertain terms. Introducing a 1997 television tribute to

George Carlin,[121] Stewart recounted the "holy trinity" of comedy for all contemporary comedians: Carlin, Richard Pryor, and Lenny Bruce. Left unstated was the fact that Bruce had preceded the other two and was a principal inspiration for both. Zoglin's book, in particular, argues the central role of Bruce, calling him "the founding father of modern stand-up comedy," further explaining that "for Carlin and a new generation of comics who revered Bruce and learned from him, his death touched off a creative explosion that would echo through the 1970s, move stand-up comedy to the very center of contemporary culture, and define the shape of a distinctly American art form. And it all started with Lenny Bruce."[122]

The Jewhooing of Lenny Bruce

As Collins and Skover outline so well in *The Trials of Lenny Bruce*, his death begat his canonization as a cultural icon. *The Essential Lenny Bruce* led to the Marvin Worth/Julian Barry productions for stage and screen, which led to numerous hagiographic publications, documentaries, and other tributes. In contemporary Jewish culture, on the other hand, celebration of Bruce has been somewhat more subdued. Most of the Jewhooing literature of the 1970s through 1990s either lists him peripherally[123] or else ignores him altogether.[124] The major exception is Darryl Lyman, who profiles Bruce in his *Great Jews in [. . .]* volumes, writing, "Lenny Bruce revolutionized American humor . . . he attacked organized religion and became one of the first entertainers to publicly confront the problem of being Jewish in a gentile world."[125]

If most Jewish publications of the 1960s and 1970s virtually ignored Bruce and downplayed his significance, a major change would come about in the 1980s—oddly, the same years when general treatment of Bruce was on the wane. One turning point, perhaps, came in a scene from the 1979 Woody Allen film *Manhattan* in which the characters debate the greatness of artists such as Gustav Mahler, F. Scott Fitzgerald, and Ingmar Bergman—and Lenny Bruce makes the list of those the Allen character (Isaac) praises as all-time greats. Spurred by the popularity of Allen (whose film *Annie Hall* had won best picture in 1977), the 1980s would see a burst of interest in Jewish humor in academic circles, with newfound attention paid to Bruce. In 1981, scholars Joseph Dorinson and Jack Nusan Porter published articles depicting him as a "Jewish Humorist" and "Jewish Comic," respectively.[126] Tel Aviv University held the First International Conference on Jewish Humor in 1984, and the published proceedings include another piece by Dorinson, titled "The Jew as Comic: Lenny Bruce, Mel Brooks, Woody Allen."[127] And in 1987,

Sarah Blacher Cohen edited *Jewish Wry: Essays on Jewish Humor*, including articles on Bruce by Sanford Pinsker and our old friend Albert Goldman.[128]

In 1972, popular Jewish author Harry Golden had put out *The Golden Book of Jewish Humor* and given short shrift to Bruce, commenting briefly, "The apotheosis of the stand-up comedian was Lenny Bruce, whose drug addiction, politicizing, and scatological language outraged us in the late 1950's. There isn't a disc jockey today, however, who doesn't ape Lenny Bruce although the disc jockeys carefully edit him."[129] Just ten years later, however, a new collection of American Jewish humor appeared that would become the "classic" work in the field for the next generation: William Novak and Moshe Waldoks's *The Big Book of Jewish Humor*. This work would finally give Bruce his due, acknowledging him as "a pioneer in the rediscovery of a publicly articulated Jewish sensibility."[130] In the introduction to their 1981 volume, Novak and Waldoks try to explain the antipathy that many Jews had toward comedians such as Bruce:

> Jewish comedians and writers may be critical of the Jewish community, but as we have said, there is nothing new about that. What may also disturb the official Jewish community is that some of the contemporary humorists, such as Lenny Bruce and Wallace Markfield, taunt not only the Jews but also the *goyim*.
>
> The point, then, is that the real offense of the contemporary humorists is not in their dwelling on Jewish inferiority, but rather their revealing the more or less secret feelings of Jewish superiority. And so, for example, Sam Levenson and Harry Golden, who have stressed the similarity of Jews to other Americans, have been far more readily embraced by a nervous community than, say, Lenny Bruce and Philip Roth, who have made much of the differences.[131]

So according to Novak and Waldoks, official Jewry's distancing from Bruce had less to do with his use of drugs and obscenity than with his unabashed Jewishness—"*shpritzing* the *goyim*" in Pinsker's phrase,[132] a Philip Roth–like exposure of Jewish feelings of superiority, and his insistence on marking the difference between Jews and other Americans. This last point is the most crucial. Bruce's "Jewish and Goyish" routine, more than anything else, has established his cachet in contemporary Jewish culture. Though Novak and Waldoks include some of Bruce's notable religiously irreverent routines—for example, "God Talk," "Christ and Moses," and "One Who Killed Our Lord"—it is clear that "Jewish and

Goyish" weighs most heavily on their minds. Part Two of the book is titled "Jewish & Goyish," and the routine then opens the chapter; it is followed by a related routine ("To a Jew f-u-c-k and s-h-i-t have the same value"), and is finally reprinted, prominently, on the back cover.[133] To Jews of the post-1960s generation, the old distinction between Jews and non-Jews must have seemed archaic, yet as presented by Bruce— self-revealing, ironic, and subversive—it continued to resonate.

It should not surprise us to find that references to Bruce nowadays almost universally cite "Jewish and Goyish." In his 2001 history of American Jewish comedians, Lawrence Epstein calls this "one of Bruce's most famous routines," and claims that by suggesting a new Jewish identity transcending both religion and ethnicity, "Bruce anticipated where the culture was going."[134] Film critic J. Hoberman, in his 2003 volume (co-edited with Jeffrey Shandler) *Entertaining America*, concurs: "In one of his most famous routines, Bruce laid out his definition of Jewishness: "Dig, I'm Jewish. Count Basie's Jewish [and so on]."[135] In the introduction to his 2003 collection *Key Texts in American Jewish Culture*, Jack Kugelmass cites the routine as signifying the present "increasing ambiguity of what once seemed so unambiguous—the distinction between Self and Other, between 'what's Jewish and what's goyish,' as Lenny Bruce's classic and strikingly enduring comedy routine has it."[136]

References to the "Jewish and Goyish" routine pop up in some unexpected places as well. A novel by Zadie Smith, *The Autograph Man*, reprints the routine as its frontispiece.[137] In an article on photography, MacDonald Moore and Deborah Dash Moore explain a comment by William Klein, "I think that there are two kinds of photography—Jewish photography and goyish photography," by comparing it to the iconic routine: "Klein's ethnic binary resembles Lenny Bruce's division of America into Jewish and goyish."[138] Even its inclusion in recent textbooks of Jewish history—for example, *The Jewish Americans: Three Centuries of Jewish Voices in America* (2007) and *The Jews: A History* (2009)[139]— seems somewhat surprising given Bruce's earlier negative reputation. Perhaps the most telling example is Michael Staub's introduction to his 2004 anthology *The Jewish 1960s*, which begins as follows:

> In the early 1960s, the often lewd stand-up comedian Lenny Bruce had begun delivering one of his more famous satirical routines. In this instance, however, the subversive content had little to do with obscenity. Rather, Bruce extemporized in unexpected ways on the multiple meanings of Jewishness. There was a big difference, Bruce said, between Jewish and goyish (that is,

gentile). But it wasn't always what you thought. Not all Jews were Jewish, nor were all non-Jews goyish. It was more complicated. And much simpler. . . . So, you may be wondering, what was Jewish about the 1960s? Why an anthology on the Jewish 1960s? Or let's phrase the question another way: How was this decade different from all other decades? Again, the answer is simple, if also more complicated. If the 1950s were goyish (and they were), then the 1960s were *very* Jewish. Pumpernickel to the white bread that preceded it. Dig?[140]

Indeed, if *Jewish* for Bruce was the equivalent of *hip* and *iconoclastic*, then the 1960s and succeeding decades are far more Jewish than the earlier era. Goldman stated this in more literal terms: "Lenny's obsession with Jewishness proved prophetic of the whole period of the sixties: the Jewish Decade."[141] That is to say, the post-1960s era is one in which America's Jews have left a deep impress on the greater culture, infusing it with their own idiosyncratic point of view and ironic sense of humor— that is, their Jewishness. Of course, the price of their success has been the rejection of ethnic difference and cultural segregation—Jews have by now fully Americanized. Yet the underlying fact of their difference persists nonetheless, an observation continually evidenced by the undying popularity of the Bruce routine "Jewish and Goyish."

Following Bruce's example, limning the difference between Jews and non-Jews has become a staple of American Jewish comedy. Jackie Mason made a career of it, and younger standup comedians from Jon Stewart to Sarah Silverman have made it a rite of passage, often opening their acts with some account of the familiar distinction. Given the high incidence of intermarriage, this distinction often takes the form of a Jewish-gentile romantic relationship: for example, Woody Allen's classic family dinner scene in *Annie Hall*, splitting the screen between the WASP-y Halls and the Jewish Singers; a similar scene highlights the 2000 film *Meet the Parents*, but increases the tension when the Jewish character, played by Ben Stiller, makes a feeble attempt to say grace. Larry David recreates the same sense of excruciating Jewish-gentile awkwardness in numerous episodes of *Curb Your Enthusiasm*; and in her 2006 concert film, Sarah Silverman explains that her [former] boyfriend, Jimmy Kimmel, is Catholic whereas she is Jewish—which poses a problem only if they have children, to whom they'd explain, "Mommy is one of the chosen people, and Daddy believes that Jesus is magic!" This comes in a performance the *Los Angeles Times* has called "as ruthlessly provocative as anything since the heyday of Lenny Bruce," and the comparison is apt.[142]

The "Jewish and Goyish" routine pops up on the Internet as well, on Jewish humor sites such as Jewlarious.com (sponsored by Aish Ha-Torah), Bangitout.com, and MyJewishLearning.com. On the last, both the original routine and an updated version appear. Introducing the original, the website declares, "Lenny Bruce (1925–1966) is something of a patron saint—make that rebbe—to American Jewish comedians . . . In the following piece, he takes humorous aim at the Jewish propensity to see the world as starkly divided, often absurdly, between things that are 'Jewish' and those that are not." The newer version, titled "Bruce was Jewish but his comedy could use a little updating," explains, "Lenny Bruce's 'Jewish and Goyish' skit is a classic of American-Jewish comedy. The following piece updates the skit for a 21st-century audience."[143] It begins: "Dig: I am Jewish, Harrison Ford is Jewish, The Iron Chef is Jewish. Kid Rock is Goyish. Kathie Lee is goyish. Billy Joel is as Jewish as it gets, Elton John is goyish." And so on. None of it is particularly clever or funny, but the very fact that Lenny Bruce is being adapted demonstrates the resonance of his comedic perspective and the renewed relevance of his view of Jewishness.

A more successful (that is, funnier) version can be found in *Heeb* magazine, a satirical journal for today's Jewish youth culture, which bills itself as "the bastard love child of Emma Goldman and Lenny Bruce."[144] *Heeb* has the Jewish/goyish theme running throughout its issues as subtext. In one issue, a chart titled "The Whole Megillah" divides contemporary culture into "kosher" and "*trayf*" (unkosher) categories, such as "intelligence" (kosher) versus "intelligent design" (*trayf*), and "Craig's list" (kosher) versus "*Schindler's List*" (*trayf*).[145] Bruce himself appears in another recent issue, on a page listing "great addicts in Jewish history," along with King Solomon (sex addiction), the Baal Shem Tov (unidentified), Sarah Bernhardt (drugs and alcohol), Sigmund Freud (cocaine), and so on.[146] Apparently, the "new Jews" of today are all too willing to forgive Jewish geniuses their flaws.

With the distance of time, perhaps, we have become more willing to admit the bad-boy element of Bruce as intrinsic to his cultural achievement. Hence, another tribute that makes reference to his drug use is Jon Stewart's 1998 piece, "Lenny Bruce: The Making of a Sitcom."[147] Included in a collection of comic essays clearly inspired by Woody Allen's essay collections of the 1970s, it is Stewart's fantasy of what the discourse might have been had Bruce been approached by a television network to develop a sitcom. The piece was written, note, at a time when Stewart was trying to find his own place on television (he began hosting

The Daily Show in the following year, 1999) and also in the wake of the most successful crossover ever from standup comedy to television sitcom, *Seinfeld* (on air 1989–1998). The conceit is that the sitcom would, à la *Seinfeld*, center on the real life of the comedian—but Bruce's real life was so outlandishly sordid that the television executives blithely attempt to "clean up" the plot scenarios he submits on nightclub napkins. They are continually impressed, however, by how quickly he responds to their notes—a clever joke playing on Bruce's use of "uppers," drugs that would "speed" him up. Besides reflecting on Stewart's own struggles with the media establishment, the essay by the then up-and-coming comedian offers us a fascinating commentary on the divide between the popular appeal of comedians and the not-always-appealing reality of their lives. Throughout his book of essays, Stewart displays the razor-sharp wit and penetrating insight that would soon propel him to become the most important comedic social critic of the 2000s—the Lenny Bruce of our time.

More recent tributes to Bruce include the specialty beer produced by Shmaltz Brewing company in 2006, "Bittersweet Lenny's R.I.P.A." In its press release, Shmaltz noted that it was "the 40th anniversary of the death of prophetic Jewish comedian Lenny Bruce," and marked the occasion with the release of the new beer. The release further explained, "In keeping with Lenny Bruce's comedic style, this rye-based double IPA is brewed with an obscene amount of malts and hops with shocking flavors, far beyond contemporary community standards."[148] Like Stewart's essay, the beer tribute manages to both celebrate Bruce and acknowledge his dark side at the same time.

And in one final indication that a new appreciation for Bruce may be on the rise, the cover of Beth Wenger's companion volume to the 2007 PBS series *The Jewish Americans*[149] (one of the history textbooks noted earlier) features Bruce prominently, together with other notables of American Jewish life such as Rebecca Gratz, Irving Berlin, Gertrude Berg, Albert Einstein, Hank Greenberg, Bess Myerson, Ruth Bader Ginsberg, and Rabbi Sally Priesand—all the usual suspects in the pantheon of American Jewish heroes. Yet here, the cover illustrations also include three less savory and more controversial figures, anti-celebrities really, who did not always arouse pride in their fellow Jews: Julius and Ethel Rosenberg, and Lenny Bruce. Their inclusion reflects no sanitizing of their image as lawbreakers, but rather an acknowledgment of the many American Jews who passionately supported them, and a reassessment of their social and cultural importance—certainly true of the man many once reviled as "Dirty Lenny."

Bruce reached the peak of his career in the winter of 1961, with a legendary midnight concert at Carnegie Hall. Sadly, that year also saw the beginning of his tragic downfall, with the first of dozens of arrests for either obscenity onstage or drugs off. Yet before his sad decline, Bruce had already left a legacy behind—as we have seen, a legacy usually described as a seminal contribution to the blisteringly honest style of standup comedy practiced by George Carlin, Richard Pryor, Robin Williams, and others. Moreover, Bruce modeled a social critique that grew, in just a few years, into the rebellious ethos of the Sixties counterculture. In both these areas, as I have suggested, there was a significant Jewish component. In comedy, Bruce channeled the Jewish experience into routines challenging the status quo of assimilation, contemplating the disintegrative effects of antisemitism and offering a new iteration of Jewish identity—a new American Jewish comedy that was taken up by Woody Allen, Joan Rivers, Jackie Mason, Richard Lewis, David Steinberg, and many others. And in the sociopolitical realm, Bruce's fearless forays into the issues of racism, sex, drugs, freedom of speech, the hypocrisies of liberalism, and so on, were given new life by a generation of Jewish radicals—Paul Krassner, Abbie Hoffman, Jerry Rubin, and others—who saw Lenny Bruce as their "rebbe."

Finally, as I have argued, a new language and public assertion of Jewish identification also ought to be attributed to Bruce—not the simplistic ethnic pride of a few years later embodied by "Kiss Me, I'm Jewish" buttons and the like, but rather a more conflicted, more layered relationship with one's Jewishness. But then, no celebrity of the early 1960s would have a more conflicted and layered Jewish identity than our next figure, Bob Dylan.

Wandering Jew

Dylan is a wandering Jew. He leaves Minnesota for
New York. He leaves the folk world for rock 'n' roll. He
leaves the city for the country. And for the last 15 years,
he's been on tour almost all the time . . . as many readers
of this newspaper [the Forward] know, he's really Robert
Zimmerman, right? A nice Jewish boy from Minnesota.
He can deny it, he can sing songs for Jesus, but he is one
of us, right? It's such an interesting phenomenon—the
tenacity of Jewishness, the paradox, embodied by Dylan
himself, of diasporism and identity. We wander, we wear
masks, we change our names as did Dylan—but there's
always that thrill when we see a landsman.

    JAY MICHAELSON,
    "He Wandered the Earth as an Exiled Man"

Bob Dylan, like Lenny Bruce before him, is an icon of Jewish iconoclasm. Both were pathbreaking artists of the early 1960s who had the *chutzpah* to perform their own words and express their innermost thoughts—until then a rarity in American entertainment—and both became pivotal figures in popular culture, forever changing the nature of their respective art forms. In the words of one historian, Dylan "reclassified the job of pop musician as audaciously as Lenny Bruce was redefining the role of a comedian."[1] Though both were personally absent from the counterculture of the later 1960s, their bodies of work exerted a profound influence on an era of political protest and cultural revolution. Like the controversial comic, the folk/rock singer-songwriter expanded the boundaries of our language and of our very consciousness.

Journalist Nat Hentoff, who knew and interviewed both men, described Dylan's stage presence in 1975 as "that cracking, shaking energy 155

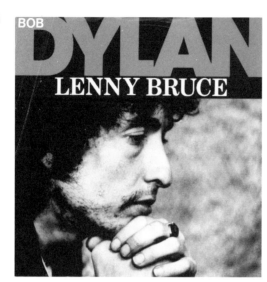

Record jacket for
single "Lenny Bruce,"
by Bob Dylan (1981).

which reminds me of another klezmer on the roof, another Tateh in rag-time, Lenny Bruce."[2] Music critic Robert Shelton similarly compared Dylan's music to Bruce's comedic style: "Like Lenny Bruce, he was riffing, in and out of communication, like a jazzman going in and out of a melody line. It was word music, chin music, symbol music."[3] Dylan himself mentioned his contemporary in several contexts,[4] and in 1981, fifteen years after Bruce's death, recorded a song titled "Lenny Bruce." In paying tribute to the departed comedian, Dylan used the occasion to implicitly measure his own rebellious posture against a kindred soul: "He was an outlaw, that's for sure / More of an outlaw than you [read: Dylan] ever were. . . . Lenny Bruce was bad, he was the brother that you never had."[5] Dylan's real-life brother, David Zimmerman, had stayed close to home and was more the "nice Jewish boy" type; whereas Bruce, fellow iconoclast and provocateur, was anything but.

Despite the two performers' similarities, the nature of their fame diverges considerably. Where Bruce's image has subtly shifted about in the years since his death, Dylan's has gone through radical changes during his lifetime, from early on to the present day. In fact, Dylan did something that no Jewish celebrity or other American pop figure had ever done before. As he became very, very famous, and indeed throughout his career, he continually changed—changed his name, his style, his look, his voice, changed his persona in every way. Before Dylan, the famous tended to establish a persona that resonated with the public, and then stick with it—why mess with a good thing? Dylan, on the other hand, never embodied the conventional type of fame, and did not attempt the construction of a fixed identity—but rather, he pursued its *de*construction, and came to personify the postmodern notions of masking and performance. Famously, he once joked, "I have my Bob Dylan mask on."[6] Later, he played a man named "Alias" in Sam Peckinpah's film *Pat Garrett and Billy the Kid* (1973); and more recently, he made a film with the purposefully enigmatic title *Masked and Anonymous*. In addition to his estimable prowess as a musician and lyricist, Dylan was a seminal figure in American culture for his protean self-invention, for the bafflingly cubistic images he projected in stark contrast to the familiar, recognizable profile of the celebrity.

Although his celebrity image has remained enigmatic throughout his career, Dylan's celebrity status is due primarily to his artistic achievement, an achievement that has made him an American musical icon on the level of Irving Berlin or Elvis Presley. The canonization of Bob Dylan began with his induction into the Rock and Roll Hall of Fame in 1988, followed by a Grammy Lifetime Achievement Award in 1991. He was a Kennedy Center honoree in 1997, and was awarded a Pulitzer Prize special citation in 2008. From 1991 to 2010, his longtime record label, Columbia, raided its vaults to issue nine volumes of *The Bootleg Series* recordings, including some of his famous concerts from the early 1960s. Focused mainly on the same period, the first volume of Dylan's memoir, *Chronicles*, came out in 2004. With the artist's participation, film director Martin Scorcese made a documentary in 2005 about Dylan's rise to fame, *No Direction Home: Bob Dylan*, and a companion volume was issued at the same time, *The Bob Dylan Scrapbook: 1956–1966*. Once again, these looked particularly at his early years, the period of his greatest creativity and of an astonishing personal evolution as well.

In 2006, Michael Gray published *The Bob Dylan Encyclopedia*, a monumental work covering most every aspect of Dylan's life and music.[7] In that same year, choreographer Twyla Tharp mounted a Broadway production based on Dylan's music, called *The Times They Are A-Changin'*. And a museum exhibition, *Bob Dylan's American Journey: 1956–1966*, again focused on his early life and work, was launched in Seattle, later traveling to New York, Minneapolis, and Los Angeles. At its Minneapolis stop in 2007, the exhibition was accompanied by an academic conference with many of the world's leading Dylan scholars in attendance.[8] Also in 2007, Todd Haynes made an unconventional biopic film titled *I'm Not There*, using multiple actors to play the role of Dylan at various stages in his career. All of this activity indicates a growing

157

appreciation for the historical stature of Bob Dylan—though it may seem farfetched to some, an increasing number of students of American culture accept the assessment of Clinton Heylin (whose book jacket calls him "the world's leading Bob Dylan scholar") that "Dylan is the pre-eminent popular artist of the century,"[9] and some say that Dylan will ultimately be recognized as the Shakespeare of our time.

Of course, if they're right, then our contemporary bard will turn out to have been a Jew—for Dylan, as is well known by now, was born and raised Robert Zimmerman, a Jewish kid from Hibbing, Minnesota. Yet in all of Dylan's many incarnations, as indeed throughout the recent burst of adulation, rarely is his ethnic Jewish background acknowledged or his Jewishness represented. Throughout his career, Dylan has por-trayed himself as an orphan, a wanderer, a minstrel, a guitar player, a lover, a poet, an iconoclast, a mystic, a Christian—but almost never as a Jew. Apparently, it is one identity he does not feel comfortable wearing in public. Writing in 1971, John Gordon compared him in this regard to the writer Norman Mailer: "Of all the poses of his life, says Norman Mailer, there is only one which he utterly can't bear—'that of a nice Jewish boy from Brooklyn.' Substitute Hibbing: both Mailer and Dylan are nice Jewish boys who have grown up into virtuosos in the public manipulation of self."[10] Hence in Dylan's memoir, finely detailed and wonderfully written in so many ways, there is hardly a word about being a Jew. Nor does Michael Gray's encyclopedia have much to offer on the subject. While devoting a lengthy entry to Dylan's Christian "Born Again period," Gray adds little on Dylan's relation to Judaism, Jewish identity, or Jewish influences in his music.

Following their lead, filmmaker Todd Haynes barely broached the topic at all. In choosing six actors to represent six different aspects of Bob Dylan, Haynes included one black and one female, but none who are Jewish or who even remotely read as Jews—this, despite the fact that both Haynes and his co-writer on the film, Oren Moverman, are themselves self-identified Jews. When asked to explain the omission of any reference to Dylan's Jewishness in the film, Haynes replied, "That is the most secret and well-preserved of his personae . . . I think Dylan's relationship to his Jewishness is much more private than any of the other roles he has played; it's kept close to his relationship with his family life, and I don't think we're supposed to know more about it than that." Tell-ingly, Haynes adds, "For all his desire to efface himself [as a Jew], he is the natural inheritor of the role of the Jewish performer. It's there in his wit, his politics and his performances—the way he throws himself into them."[11] How, we might ask, could this Jewish writer/director implicitly group Dylan with Al Jolson and Jon Stewart, yet fail to explore such associations in his movie?

To be fair, both the academic conference in Minneapolis and the Skirball Cultural Center in Los Angeles did invite one speaker to address the question of Dylan's Jewishness—this author. I opened my talk at the Skirball, a Jewish-sponsored institution, as follows:

> I have to start by taking note of a rather sharp irony. The Bob Dylan exhibition would not be here at the Skirball Cultural Center if not for the fact that Bob Dylan is, in some sense, a Jew. And yet, ironically enough, there is next to nothing on Dylan's Jewishness in the exhibition; in fact, what little there was originally, had to be excised here at the Skirball for lack of space. So even though we all know that Bob Dylan comes from a Jewish background, the exhibition devoted to his legendary career doesn't say a word about it. And that somewhat odd circumstance accounts for my presence here on the program.[12]

The title of my lecture was "'Einstein Disguised as Robin Hood': The Enigmatic Jewishness of Bob Dylan." Enigmatic indeed. The baffling nature of Dylan's Jewish identity derives from two sharply contrasting facts: On the one hand, in his public life, he has embodied the modern phenomenon of assimilation—the escape from inherited identity. Yet despite his clear attempt to evade such definition, Dylan's Jewish background has aroused an extraordinary amount of comment and interest on the part of others. It is precisely this contradiction that makes the question of his Jewishness so interesting. Again, as self-defined in public statements and throughout a very public career, he is a radical individualist, a member of no ethnic or religious group at all. Asked by interviewer Ron Rosenbaum in 1978, "Did you grow up thinking about the fact that you were Jewish?" Dylan flatly replied, "No, I didn't. I've never felt Jewish. I don't really consider myself Jewish or non-Jewish. I don't have much of a Jewish background. I'm not a patriot to any creed. I believe in all of them and none of them."[13] Dylan's recent image-making media treatments, all informed by his wishes, follow suit and suppress the theme of Jewishness. Yet as noted by his many biographers, he was born and raised a Jew and is at least incidentally Jewish; and then, as claimed by certain of his fellow Jews, he is a more integrally identified Jew deeply engaged in his Judaism.

Some resolution of this stark contradiction might be found in a telling verse from one of Dylan's classic songs, "Desolation Row" (from the **159**

1965 album *Highway 61 Revisited*), in which he describes one character as "Einstein, disguised as Robin Hood." The image makes sense if we imagine it to be an alter ego of Dylan's—in which case his true self behind the scenes is akin to the archetypal Jewish genius, while his public persona is more like the dashing goy played by Errol Flynn in the movies, the pop star as romantic renegade. But then, as the next line continues, "with his memories in a trunk, [he] passed this way an hour ago." In other words, though Zimmerman/Einstein may have become Dylan/ Robin Hood, he still retains memory of his former self. It is not an inner transformation, but merely an outer disguise. The lyric is a perfect evocation of Dylan's particular form of assimilation—while he abandoned all external markers of Jewishness, putting on the mask of a non-Jewish American and thereby hiding his origins, he himself has remained cognizant of those origins, and thus as far as we know, may very well continue to think of himself as a Jew.

The very quality that makes Dylan so fascinating as a celebrity figure—his capacity for constant redefinition and re-creation of self—renders the question of his Jewish identity all the more elusive. The title of Haynes's film, *I'm Not There*, says it all regarding Dylan's Jewishness—on the surface at least, it doesn't seem to be there at all. Below the surface, in the man's own heart and mind, we just don't know; but that has little relevance to the question of Dylan's public image. On that level, Dylan has been consistent from the very beginning of his career. In the construction of his celebrity, he fiercely claimed the individualist's right to define himself outside of categories imposed by others, and thus eschewed his Jewish name and Jewish heritage. With the exception of several unpublicized trips to Israel and a somewhat secretive flirtation with Hasidic Judaism, he has, at least in public, consistently denied or downplayed his own Jewish identity. In the end, the very denial of his Jewishness forms a significant part of Dylan's image. This basic attribute, his commitment to complete assimilation, *or at least the appearance of* assimilation, is a defining feature of the famous person we know as Bob Dylan.

This chapter does not provide a full-length exploration of Dylan's life and art. Nor does it attempt to uncover either the hidden Jewish meaning of his music or the hidden Jewish life of the man. Instead, it examines various aspects of Dylan's career, especially the period of his initial rise to fame from 1961 to 1965, in order to situate him within the history of American Jewish celebrity. General consensus has it that Dylan was one of the most important American artists of the twentieth century, and he is certainly one of its most famous Jews as well. Beginning with some brief discussion of Dylan's reported Jewish origins, this chapter mainly examines the multiple ways in which the Jewishness of Bob Dylan has been perceived and projected by others.

Following the lead of his many biographers, the first section of the chapter recites the facts of his early life, the mundane details of his Jewish family background and upbringing—as documented in the vast corpus of Dylan literature. At the same time, we may observe the persona he offered the world, his iconoclastic self-invention and the images of self he chose to project throughout his career, including the persistent denials of his own Jewishness. In later sections, we discern how others have constructed their own images of him—which, keep in mind, is a form of identity, too. Though Dylan's personal identity may be idiosyncratic to the core, we can see how other people tend to ascribe Jewishness to him, how others, most often other Jews, tend to identify him as a member of the tribe—the Jewhooing of Bob Dylan. In sum, these varying perspectives demonstrate sharply contrasting understandings of Dylan's Jewishness—a set of contrasts projecting an image of him as the archetypal American Jew of the third generation: American insider and Jewish outsider simultaneously. Like Dylan, the third generation would find broad social acceptance while still experiencing a sense of alienation, resonating to both the greater culture and to the insistent demands of self.

"Boy from the North Country": Zimmerman's Escape

The biographical literature on Bob Dylan is voluminous.[14] Following the pioneering portrait by Anthony Scaduto published in 1971, major biographies include Robert Shelton's *No Direction Home* (1986), Bob Spitz's *Dylan: A Biography* (1989), Clinton Heylin's *Bob Dylan: Behind the Shades* (1991), and Howard Sounes's *Down the Highway* (2001).[15] All of these biographical treatments, as well as dozens of anthologies and related studies on Dylan, describe him as being of Jewish origin. In stark contrast to Dylan's own memoir, his numerous biographers give ample weight to his Jewish upbringing, personal connections, and religious experience. After duly reporting his birth in 1941, the biographies all cover his Jewish antecedents and family history. Dylan, they point out in turn, was born Robert Allen Zimmerman and grew up in the small town of Hibbing, on the Mesabi Iron Range of northern Minnesota. To the cosmopolitan ear, such middle-American origins sound like the middle of nowhere—certainly young Zimmerman felt likewise and escaped as soon as he was able. But contrary to the image of geographic isolation and cultural desolation—and contrary to the myth he would later cultivate—his early upbringing and formative milieu were surprisingly Jewish.

Starting with the biographical facts, here's what we know: Bob Dylan was the child of Jews. His parents, Abe (short for Abram) and Beatty (for Beatrice), were both children of Yiddish-speaking immigrants, members of an extended Jewish family that had settled in Minnesota early in the twentieth century. Abe's parents were Zisel (Zigman) Zimmerman and Chana (Anna) Greenstein, both from Odessa. After emigrating to the United States, they settled in Duluth and had six children, Abram being the youngest. Beatty's parents were Lithuanian Jews named Benjamin David Solemovitz (later changed to Stone) and Florence Sara Edelstein. Florence's parents, Bob Dylan's maternal great grandparents, were Boruch Edelstein and Lybba Jaffe, who brought their family to the United States in 1902, arriving at the Great Lakes port city of Sault Ste. Marie, Michigan, and three years later settling in the mining town of Hibbing, Minnesota. In 1934, twenty-two-year-old Abe Zimmerman met eighteen-year-old Beatty Stone at a Zionist club social event, and the couple soon married. They initially settled in Abe's hometown of Duluth, and later moved to Hibbing. Their first child was born on May 24, 1941. The name on the birth certificate was Robert Allen Zimmerman; the name he was given at his *bris* (the Jewish ceremony of circumcision) was Shabtai Zisel ben Avraham.

Despite growing up on the Minnesota Iron Range, far from the Jewish population centers of the eastern seaboard, young Bobby Zimmerman grew up Jewishly—surrounded by Jewish relatives and enjoying a full range of Jewish experience. His parents were, in many ways, typical second-generation American Jews: speaking some Yiddish in their parents' home but English everywhere else, fervent believers in the American dream, not particularly religious but ethnically and culturally Jewish, and prone to investing tremendous energy in their children. Abe, the dutiful Jewish father and husband, worked hard, became president of his B'nai B'rith lodge, and hoped his son would follow him into the family business. Beatty, president of her Hadassah chapter, was a stereotypically doting Jewish mother, described by one biographer as "a bubbly woman . . . headstrong, nervous, volatile, and warm."[16] Upon meeting Beatty in the 1970s, poet Allen Ginsberg was nonplussed to discover that "the 'mysterious' Dylan had a chicken-soup *Yiddishe* mama!"[17]

A beloved firstborn son, Bobby grew up amidst doting grandparents, uncles, aunts, and cousins, and even knew his great grandfather Boruch,

High school graduation photo of Robert Zimmerman, 1959. A Jewish boy from the Minnesota heartland aspiring to be the next Little Richard.

known as B. H. (for Benjamin Harold), who died in January of 1961 — the very moment, it so happened, that the nineteen-year-old Bob Dylan arrived in New York to make himself anew. Just six years earlier, Bobby had celebrated his bar mitzvah, for which he had prepared by studying Hebrew with a visiting rabbi. The lavish affair was attended by 400 invited guests—who in turn lavished their praise on the young man's performance—and Dylan's public singing career had begun. We have to imagine, as well, all the high holiday services, Passover seders and other family *simchas* he attended while growing up in the Jewish subculture of Hibbing. Moreover, for a few years during adolescence, Bobby spent his summers at Camp Herzl—a summer camp popular with Minnesota Jews—forming bonds with other Jewish youngsters, some of whom, such as Larry Kegan and Howard Rutman, became lifelong friends. As fourteen-year-olds, the three camp friends formed a group called "The Jokers" and together made Bobby Zimmerman's earliest known recording at the Terlinde Music Shop in St. Paul, Minnesota, in 1956.[18]

So that's one side of the picture: contrary to our image of the adult artist, Dylan's childhood, the most formative time of one's life, was chock-full of Jewish experience. Of course, it may have been precisely this background that later propelled him in the opposite direction. If Bobby Zimmerman's parents were the stereotypical Jewish couple of their generation, then it follows that Dylan would later recall his up-bringing with all the resentment of the stereotypical Jewish son. As he **163** related to Nat Hentoff, "I kept running because I wasn't free, I was constantly on guard. Somehow, way back then, I already knew that parents do what they do because they're up tight. They're concerned with their kids in relation to *themselves*. I mean, they want their kids to please them, not to embarrass them — so they can be proud of them. They want you to be what *they* want you to be. So I started running . . ."[19]

One early indication of both his Jewish roots and his post-adolescent rejection of them can be found in a startling poem Dylan composed during his college days. Signed "Dylanism," the poem begins by addressing "mothers," and his own in particular, with the familiar Hebrew phrase: "Shalom Alechem, all you mothers / And don't think that your son is so great," and ends, "Look at me, ma, I'm stoned. / Get the hell out of my Life / Before I tell your mother on you."[20] A more famous composition of Dylan's offers a similar rejoinder to his father. The opening lines of "Highway 61 Revisited" — one of the best-known songs from his artistic peak of 1965 — retells the biblical story of the sacrifice of Isaac, casting his father Abe in the role of Abraham, and implicitly comparing his own childhood oppression to the near death of the first Jewish son: "Oh God said to Abraham, 'Kill me a son' / Abe said, 'Man you must be puttin' me on.'"[21] Ironically, the song is often cited as evidence of Dylan's attachment to Judaism, when it seems far more likely to have been written from the opposite point of view, as a fare-thee-well to his Jewish past.

Thus the young adult Dylan would attempt to *escape* from the Jewishness of his youth. Such an attitude of rejection was characteristic of many Jews of his generation for whom their parents' insular Jewish ethnicity and 1950s suburban Judaism was embarrassing, even anathema — in this regard, Dylan was a typical third-generation American Jew. But Dylan, aspiring to fame as a musician, went further then most of his contemporaries. Reimagining himself as an American troubadour in his late teens and early twenties, he self-consciously assumed a new identity that brooked no intrusion of his actual Jewish roots. In the course of re-inventing himself as a folk musician named Bob Dylan, he obliterated all memory of his middle-class Jewish upbringing. Maintaining this public stance throughout his career, Dylan has consistently avoided any overt affirmation of his ethnic origins. He not only created a new public persona for himself — as is characteristic of show business celebrity — but in the process erased all external traces of his Jewish background. Though it is entirely possible that Bob himself continued to feel Jewish within, Dylan the public figure would no longer be seen by others as a Jew, becoming in effect a *non-Jew*. Dylan did not merely acculturate, as was the norm for his generation; his was a case of total social and cultural redefinition, that is, assimilation.

Of course, the key to this Houdini-like escape trick and metamorphosis was the name-change. Much like an aspiring young magician named Erich Weiss, Bob chose a new name in the hope of making it in show business, substituting Dylan for Zimmerman in his first year out of high school. There are myriad explanations for the choice of *Dylan*, but rarely is the import of *Zimmerman* discussed. A typical Jewish family name (of German origin, it means "carpenter"), it could not have been a happy one for an American youngster living in a small town in Minnesota in the 1950s, especially one who idolized Hank Williams and Elvis Presley and aspired to musical stardom himself. Echo Helstrom, his teenage girlfriend in Hibbing, later recalled, "I casually said to Bob, 'Gee, *Zimmerman*, that's a funny name. Is it Jewish?' Well, Bob didn't answer anything at *all*, he just looked straight ahead with his face sort of funny. Later in the week John took me aside at school and said, 'Listen, Echo, don't ever ask Bob about being Jewish again. He doesn't like to talk about it.'"[22]

This apparent discomfort with being a Jewish outsider, combined with the ambition to make it as a popular musician, led inevitably to a change of name. So the teenager known around town as "Zimmy" began to seek a pseudonym and eventually settled on *Dylan*, often thought to be inspired either by the poet Dylan Thomas or the television character Marshall Dillon, but likely chosen just because he liked the way it sounded. In one of his many, often contradictory explanations, Dylan addressed the issue in a 1965 interview with Joseph Haas, for *Panorama* magazine:

HAAS: What about the story that you changed your name from Bob Zimmerman to Bob Dylan because you admired the poetry of Dylan Thomas?

DYLAN: No, God no. I took the Dylan because I have an uncle named Dillon. I changed the spelling but only because it looked better. I've read some of Dylan Thomas' stuff, and it's not the same as mine. We're different.[23]

Neither Robert Zimmerman nor Bob Dylan has an uncle named Dillon. Dylan's change of name was the cornerstone of an elaborate project of self-invention, so he became accustomed to dissembling regarding the name as he did concerning everything else about his past. As Ron Rosenbaum later explained, "Before he came to New York City back in 1961, he calculated that the name Bob Zimmerman would not harmonise [*sic*] well with the ramblin' hillbilly persona he had fabricated for himself."[24]

As in our earlier discussion of Lenny Bruce, such name-changes have been common among entertainers, often minimized as just a convention of show business—as when aspiring actor Emanuel Goldenberg chose the stage name Edward Robinson, but "to remember who he really was,"[25] the newly christened Robinson added the middle initial G. No such nostalgia for Robert Zimmerman. By adopting a new moniker, he took what amounted to an ontological leap, a complete transformation and redefinition of self. As one biographer observes, "The name Dylan signified a formal, if not final, rejection of Bobby's roots . . . Certainly no one would suspect him of being a Jew."[26] Stephen Whitfield adds, "To bestow a new patronymic is to test the possibilities of self-invention . . . The onomastic switch made a point: he affirmed his own right to be anyone from anywhere, emerging from a hazy and partly fabricated past to wriggle out of any fixed identity."[27]

For a brief time Dylan lived a double life. By day, as a freshman at the University of Minnesota in Minneapolis, he lived at the Jewish fraternity as Robert Zimmerman; while at night, in the bohemian district of Dinkytown, he turned into Bob Dylan. But this Jekyll and Hyde existence was short-lived—Bob Dylan would soon take over entirely. Already in high school, he had transformed himself from a middle-class Jewish kid into an aspiring rock 'n' roller; now, over the course of his first year away from home, he transformed himself yet again, from a small-town punk into an urban hipster, substituting folk music for rock, and finalizing the transition from Zimmerman to Dylan. There would be no going back— he became a man possessed, possessed with his own new self.

One story indicating how the change of name reflected a personal transformation is told by Ellen Baker, a friend from Dylan's college days in Minneapolis, who recalls her first meeting with him: "We talked and he said he was from Hibbing, but I didn't find out his name was Zimmerman until later." But then she adds, "He came over a few days later for dinner. He said something like, 'Boy, I really like Jewish food. It's really nice to come to a real Jewish home for a Jewish dinner.'"[28] And moreover, says Baker,

> Some of the people around used to call him "That itinerant Jewish folk singer." He wanted so much to be part of what he was singing about. I used to ask him, "How's the man of the soil today?" And that's what he was. Full of the Jesse Fuller thing, being down to earth, being a man of the soil. When all the time he was the son of a Jewish furniture dealer from up on The [Iron] Range. . . . But Bob would rather have been from some place in

Arkansas. He wanted to be part of another kind of romantic and glorious tradition, part of some sort of folk Dust Bowl tradition. But he couldn't be a man of the soil with a name like "Zimmerman," could he?[29]

Beyond changing his name, therefore, he also rewrote his life story— as Irwin Silber put it to Dylan in 1964, "you've chosen your name and recast your past."[30] Concocting one tall tale after another, Dylan affected the persona of an all-American folkie and "man of the soil." Of course, by inventing a new personal narrative, his intention was not to reject his Jewish heritage, but rather to adopt the heritage of American folk music, attempting to acquire the "authenticity" of the folk tradition. Yet as Morris Dickstein perceptively notes in his history of the Sixties, "One of the paradoxes of 'sincerity' in folksinging is how often it involves the assumption of other people's roots, or imaginary ones, rather than a search for one's own."[31] Hence Dylan would typically claim, falsely, that he spent much of his childhood outside of Hibbing. As he told one interviewer, "he ran away from home seven times: at ten, at twelve, at thirteen, at fifteen, at fifteen and a half, at seventeen, and at eighteen. His travels included South Dakota, New Mexico, Kansas, and California."[32]

Even more emphatically, Dylan conjured himself up as an orphan with no family at all—in fact, the degree to which he attempted to deracinate himself as he became famous cannot be emphasized enough. He would habitually obscure his true background, even lying to his first great love, Suze Rotolo, who recalls, "When I first met him, he told me incredible tales—about being an orphan and that he had run away from his foster parents in Fargo, North Dakota."[33] In his rise to fame, Dylan presented himself as the man with no past, a Woody Guthrie–like wanderer without roots, without a home.[34] He thereby disassociated himself as best as he could from his parents, his hometown, his origins.

"In New York Town": Dylan's Early Days in Greenwich Village

As Bob Dylan made his rapid ascent to celebrity, from 1961 to 1963, his Jewish identity remained a secret, even to some of his closest friends.[35] Certainly the general public did not know at first that he was a Jew— and why would they? So the question arises, when *did* the public catch on? At what point did the Jewishness of Dylan become part of his public persona? Two points should be noted: first, some of his early associates in Minnesota knew that Dylan was Zimmerman all along—for example, Jon Pankake and Paul Nelson, editors of the *Little Sandy Review*, wrote in 1962 that they "first met Bob in the summer of 1960, while he was still a student at the University of Minnesota [and] was listed in official university enrolment [*sic*] records as Robert Zimmerman."[36] Second, it must be added that to the present day, many remain unaware of Dylan's Jewish background. In general, however, the news got out at one particular moment: Dylan's "true" identity was first publicly revealed when *Newsweek* magazine, in its issue of November 4, 1963, outed him as a Jew named Zimmerman. Prior to that date, he had spent nearly three years in the closet, so to speak.

A young but determined Bob Dylan arrived in New York City on January 24, 1961, coincident with the start of John F. Kennedy's presidency. After spending most of the year sleeping on friends' couches and playing music in whichever clubs would have him, his big break came in the fall. *New York Times* music critic Robert Shelton had begun to notice Dylan playing around Greenwich Village, and after attending his opening night performance at one of the better-known venues, Gerde's Folk City, promptly interviewed him and rushed home to write the first major newspaper review of the still unknown folksinger. Published in the *Times* on September 29, 1961, the review simply *kvells* over the newcomer: "A bright new face in folk music is appearing at Gerde's Folk City. Although only 20 years old, Bob Dylan is one of the most distinctive stylists to play in a Manhattan cabaret in months. . . . Mr. Dylan's highly personalized approach toward folk song is still evolving. He has been sopping up influences like a sponge . . . But if not for every taste, his music-making has the mark of originality and inspiration, all the more noteworthy for his youth." Commenting on Dylan's appearance, Shelton writes, "Resembling a cross between a choir boy and a beatnik, Mr. Dylan has a cherubic look and a mop of tousled hair . . . His clothes may need a bit of tailoring, but . . . there is no doubt that he is bursting at the seams with talent."[37] Intentionally or not, Shelton chose the Christian-tinged "choir boy" and "cherubic" to describe the young Jew; of course, no mention is made of Dylan's Jewish background.

Ironically, the milieu described in Shelton's review was quite Jewish —for as his column revealed, the Greenwich Village folk scene was full of Jews. The review was not of Dylan alone—as it turned out, he was playing at Gerde's on a bill behind the Greenbriar Boys, a bluegrass group whose members included Ralph Rinzler and Bob Yellin, two Jews in cowboy hats.[38] Other Jewish folk and bluegrass revivalists then playing in the Village included John Cohen and Tom Paley of the New Lost City Ramblers, Bob Cohen of the New World Singers, Dick Weissman of the Journeymen, and Eric Weissberg of the Tarriers (formerly

Hootenanny magazine (March 1964) cover photo of Dylan and Joan Baez taken at the 1963 Newport Folk Festival by Ken Kay.

of the Greenbriar Boys). So many urban Jews were playing American roots music during the 1960s that a term was coined to describe the phenomenon: *Jew-grass.*[39] Some other Jewish folk performers of Dylan's milieu included Theodore Bikel, David Blue (born Cohen), Oscar Brand, Ramblin' Jack Elliott, Ronnie Gilbert and Fred Hellerman (of the Weavers), Barry Kornfeld, Jo Mapes, Phil Ochs, Happy Traum, and Peter Yarrow (of Peter, Paul and Mary). Yet another, Shel Silverstein, "the noted Greenwich Village artist, musician, and song writer," even wrote a song satirizing the trend. In his 1962 composition "Folk Singer Blues," Silverstein writes about wanting to "sing a song about the chain gang" and "go walkin' up the highway," but then hilariously douses the illusion of folk authenticity with the chorus, "But wha-da-ya do if you're young and white and Jewish."[40] The song was published in the March 1964 edition of *Hootenanny* magazine, which featured a young Bob Dylan on the cover, and one can only imagine who Silverstein had in mind.

No wonder, then, that Dylan's new Greenwich Village friends—fellow folkies such as Dave Van Ronk and Ramblin' Jack Elliott—would good-naturedly humor him when he spun his yarns about being descended from Native Americans or being an orphan from New Mexico. They all intuited Dylan's "secret identity" and accepted the ruse. As Van

Ronk remarked, "Nobody held it against him. Reinventing yourself has always been part of show business."[41] Dylan was certainly not the only one on MacDougal Street to have remade himself. Ramblin' Jack, the premier Woody Guthrie imitator and another key influence on the young Dylan, was born Elliot Adnopoz, the son of a Jewish doctor in Brooklyn, New York. When Dylan first heard the truth about his mentor's background, sitting in the Gaslight café sometime around March of 1961, he is said to have doubled over in laughter—here was someone who had done a better job of obscuring his origins than even he. Van Ronk later recalled, "We had all suspected Bobby was Jewish, and that proved it."[42] In a much later retelling of the incident, Van Ronk adds yet another salient detail: "Bobby nearly fell off his chair laughing. It seemed to strike him much funnier than it did us, because we always assumed that Jack had been a cowboy. Then, two years before *Newsweek* revealed Bob's own background, I knew that Bobby too was an actor. He never said anything, he just laughed till I thought he would burst."[43]

Dylan himself avoided all explicit references to being Jewish, with a few curious exceptions. In several of his early folk compositions, he interpolated issues of Jewish concern—surprisingly so, given his apparent eagerness to hide his own Jewishness. Nevertheless, in "With God on Our Side," he originally included this verse: "When the Second World War / Came to an end / We forgave the Germans / And we were friends. Though they murdered six million / In the ovens they fried / The Germans now too / Have God on their side." In "Talkin' John Birch Paranoid Blues," a scathing satire of right-wing red-baiters, he again references the Holocaust: "Now we all agree with Hitler's views / Although he killed six million Jews / It don't matter too much that he was a Fascist / At least you can't say he was a Communist!" And, in a later verse of the same song, he refers to the recent Hollywood film about Israel: "Now Eisenhower, he's a Russian spy / Lincoln, Jefferson and that Roosevelt guy / To my knowledge there's just one man / That's really a true American: George Lincoln Rockwell / I know for a fact he hates Commies cus he picketed the movie Exodus."[44] Though indicating Dylan's awareness of the Holocaust and of antisemitism, none of these lines is exactly a ringing announcement of his identity as a Jew.

Nor do the lines compare in blatant ethnic identification to another song he often sang for comic relief. Something like Mel Brooks's Yiddish-speaking Indian chief in the 1974 film *Blazing Saddles*, Dylan signaled both his true roots and his remove from them when he slipped into his number "Talkin' Havah Nagilah Blues," a staple of his early coffeehouse performances.[45] Introducing his send-up of "Havah Nagilah" with the sly "Here's a foreign song I learned in Utah," he would launch into a ridiculously distorted and truncated version of the familiar Hebrew refrain. Critics tend to overlook the Jewish significance of this; for example, Gil Turner notes, "Dylan's flare for the comic is usually put to use in the talking blues form . . . 'Talkin' Havah Nagilah' was made up especially for members of the audience that shout out requests for songs way out of his line."[46]

Israeli folk songs such as "Havah Nagilah" were a staple of 1950s folk music, led by the Weavers ("Tzena, Tzena"), Theodore Bikel, and Harry Belafonte. Belafonte was one of those who popularized "Havah Nagilah" and had been an early influence on the young Dylan—who was thrilled to play harmonica on the established star's latest album in June of 1961. Further, the early 1960s Greenwich Village scene included a number of Israeli folksingers, all part of the same folk music milieu as Dylan. For instance, in early November 1961, Dylan performed in New York on the same night as Shoshana Damari, Uri Ziffroni, and Yaffa Yarkoni; and five months later, he appeared on the same bill as Varda Karni at Folk City—this, at the very time he was spoofing "Havah Nagilah."[47] In his *New York Times* review, Shelton interprets "Talking Havah Nagilah" as "burlesque[ing] the folk-music craze and *the singer himself*." Nevertheless, he concludes by honoring the young folksinger's obfuscations and protecting his true identity: "Mr. Dylan is vague about his antecedents and birthplace, but it matters less where he has been than where he is going, and that would seem to be straight up."[48] Though he doesn't confess it in his 1986 biography of Dylan, Shelton almost certainly knew of his subject's Jewish background but nonetheless chose to respect the privacy of his new discovery. His probable inside knowledge is suggested by the "singer himself" comment, but even more compellingly by the fact that Shelton's original name was Shapiro.[49]

The success of the Folk City club date, and Shelton's review, led to Dylan's "discovery" by John Hammond and his subsequent signing with Columbia Records. Made in late 1961, Dylan's first record album was released on March 19, 1962. Though the record was not commercially successful, the taste of public notice only spurred Dylan onward in his quest for fame. The first album had contained just two original compositions, "Talkin' New York" and "Song to Woody," and it was during that winter that Dylan first began writing songs in earnest. In the spring of 1962, he wrote what became perhaps his most famous song, "Blowin' in the Wind," and soon began recording a second album that would consist   **171** of original material. He spent the next several months busily composing new songs and honing his performance style. On April 12, 1963, he gave a concert at the Town Hall in New York that would establish him "as *the* major new voice in folk music."[50] His new status was confirmed a few weeks later, as Peter, Paul and Mary's harmonized version of "Blowin' in the Wind" became a popular hit. On May 27, Columbia released the new album, *The Freewheelin' Bob Dylan*.[51] In addition to "Blowin' in the Wind," it includes Dylan classics "A Hard Rain's A-Gonna Fall," written against the background of the Cuban missile crisis, and "Don't Think Twice, It's All Right," written against the background of a Dylan romantic crisis.

During that auspicious summer of 1963, Dylan was quickly becoming the darling of the folk music world, and a hero to its close ally, the civil rights movement. In early July, he accompanied Pete Seeger and Theodore Bikel on a SNCC-sponsored (Student Nonviolent Coordinating Committee) voter registration drive in Mississippi. Later that month, the rising young star was invited to headline the Newport Folk Festival together with Seeger; Bikel; Peter, Paul and Mary; and Joan Baez. In August he performed at the March on Washington and stood by as Martin Luther King Jr. delivered his famous "I Have a Dream" speech. Dylan became a fully confirmed star with his next major concert, on October 12 at New York's most prestigious venue, Carnegie Hall (clearly, he had been practicing). And all the while, he kept silent regarding his true name and background.

During that same period, 1962–1963, another "folksinger" took the country by storm—and in stark contrast to Dylan, he did so in an unabashedly Jewish vein. As I discussed in Chapter 1, this was none other than Allan Sherman, who, like his contemporary Dylan, had also chosen to parody "Havah Nagilah." In fact, Sherman's recording of "Harvey and Sheila" was made in November of 1962, just a few months after Dylan's recording of "Talkin' Havah Nagilah Blues," recorded during the *Freewheelin'* sessions in March 1962. When "Blowin' in the Wind" became a hit in the summer of the following year, one of its chief rivals for radio airplay was Sherman's new smash hit, "Hello Muddah, Hello Fadduh" (". . . Here I am at Camp Grenada"). Obviously, Sherman and Dylan represent two very different types of music. The parallel is only worth making due to the disparity between Sherman's popularly accepted Jewishness and Dylan's persistent reluctance to identify. At the very moment that Jewish was first becoming "in" in America, the soon-to-be most famous young Jew in America was still trying desperately hard to "pass."

Though clearly averse to being seen as a Jew, the young Dylan nevertheless tended to gravitate to other Jews—marking him, from our perspective, as an "associational" Jew.[52] We've seen this already with his lifelong loyalty to Jewish summer camp friends such as Larry Kegan, Louis Kemp, Judy Rubin, and Howard Rutman.[53] It continued in college with friends Ellen Baker, Gretel Hoffman, and David Whitaker, all Jewish. It was Whitaker, a few years older and wise in the ways of the counterculture, who introduced him to Woody Guthrie, who, in turn, became a principal influence on Dylan. The non-Jewish Guthrie (though he married a Jewish woman and raised his children as Jews) became a kind of spiritual father to the young Dylan, serving as both musical role model and his most cherished personal hero. As he did with his own father, Dylan would later break with paternal tradition, moving beyond the acoustic folk style he had embraced under Guthrie's influence. The fact that both his real father and Guthrie suffered from debilitating diseases (Abe Zimmerman had polio; Guthrie, Huntington's disease) makes the parallel all the more poignant. Nevertheless, Guthrie could not himself serve as a surrogate *Jewish* father. For that purpose, Dylan found a new mentor in the person of Ramblin' Jack Elliott, Guthrie's premier interpreter and a Brooklyn-born Jew. When Dylan arrived in Greenwich Village, he sometimes was called the "son" of Ramblin' Jack, who in turn would later introduce Dylan's songs with these words: "Here's a song from my son, Bob Dylan."

Beyond Guthrie and Elliott, there would soon arise two other father figures in Dylan's life—two Jewish gurus who each played a key role in the development of the Dylan myth, both fifteen years his senior: Allen Ginsberg, the Beat poet who showed him the manipulations of word, and Albert Grossman, the road manager who showed him the manipulations of image. Dylan himself became some freakish cross between the mystic Ginsberg and the materialist Grossman, capturing the liberating qualities of the one as well as the beat-the-system cleverness of the other, conflating the Jewish genius of both. Moreover, when he made his celebrated switch from a solo folk act to an electric rock 'n' roll band in 1965, prominent among the backup musicians he chose were fellow Jews Al Kooper, Mike Bloomfield, Barry Goldberg, Harvey Goldstein, and (the part Jewish) Robbie Robertson. Other Jewish associates during those early days included Al Aronowitz, David "Blue" Cohen, Nat Hentoff, Barry Kornfeld, Robert Shelton, Paul Rothchild, and Israel "Izzy" Young. And last but not least, his first wife and the mother of his children was former model Sara Lownds—born Shirley Noznisky. Like both his father Abe Zimmerman *and* his idol Woody Guthrie, Dylan married a "nice Jewish girl." As much as he may have wanted to leave the fold, it seems he was just more comfortable with members of his own tribe.

In this regard we see the *Newsweek* magazine article in a somewhat different light. As Dylan's star began to rise through 1963, curiosity about his background began to grow as well. In advance of his breakout Carnegie Hall concert, reporters from *Newsweek* contacted his managers to arrange an in-depth interview. The resulting story, written by fellow Jew Dick Schaap (who later became well known as a sports reporter) and titled "I Am My Words," called his very identity into question. Adding insult to injury, the accompanying photo is captioned, "Bob Dylan: What's in a name?" The article castigates Dylan for his "hip talk, punctuated with obscenities," and continues, "His singing voice scratches and shouts so jarringly that his success, at first, seems incredible . . . [yet] his knack for stirring audiences is unmistakable." In fact, the reporter admits, "Dylan is practically a religion."[54] Despite such grudging acknowledgment of his success, the thrust of the article is its direct challenge to Dylan's veracity and its sensationalized exposure of his great secret. Noting first that "his audiences share his pain, and seem jealous because they grew up in conventional homes," Schaap then writes,

> The ironic thing is that Bob Dylan, too, grew up in a conventional home, and went to conventional schools. He shrouds his past in contradictions, but he is the elder son of a Hibbing, Minn., appliance dealer named Abe Zimmerman, and, as Bobby Zimmerman, he attended Hibbing High School, then briefly the University of Minnesota. Dylan admits he was born in Duluth and raised in Hibbing, but . . . he denied that Bob Dylan was ever Bobby Zimmerman. "Dig my draft card, man," he said. "Bob Dylan." (He changed his name legally on August 9, 1962.) His parents? "I don't know my parents," he said. "They don't know me. I've lost contact with them for years."[55]

In a national magazine, Dylan's folkie persona was exposed as false, his original Jewish name revealed, and moreover, he was caught in a lie. At the very moment he spoke the words, "I don't know my parents," Abe and Beatty Zimmerman were ensconced in a New York City hotel awaiting the Carnegie Hall concert he had flown them out to see. Professing puzzlement concerning Dylan's motives for obfuscating, Schaap further writes, "Why Dylan . . . should bother to deny his past is a mystery. Perhaps he feels it would spoil the image he works so hard to cultivate. . . . Dylan says he is writing a book that will explain everything. But, he insists, the explanations are irrelevant. 'I am my words,' he says. . . ."[56]

But the press was of another opinion, refusing to accept that an artist can be defined by his or her art alone, insisting instead that the facts of one's life matter; in Dylan's case, the truth behind the image was that of a middle-class Jewish boy made good. In no uncertain terms, the *Newsweek* article called him on his deception, and, somewhat more subtly, criticized him for his apparent assimilation. In any event, the cat was now out of the bag.

"No Place to Run": Dylan's Christian Phase and Other Evasions of Jewishness

Outed as a Jew in the midst of his rise to fame, Dylan nonetheless continued to evade any public embrace or even acknowledgment of his Jewish background—even while the image of him as a Jew continued to grow apace in the minds of his fans.[57] His attempt to escape his roots reached a high point in the late 1970s, when, reeling from the failure of his marriage and what must have felt like the end of an era (that is, the end of the Sixties, but also the demoralizing conclusion of the Rolling Thunder Revue tour—as documented by the 1978 film *Renaldo and Clara*, a failed venture itself), he was searching for answers and apparently found them in Christianity. Joining a church community in Los Angeles called the Vineyard Fellowship, he soon became "born again" as a Christian believer. Though there is no reason to doubt the sincerity of his conversion, the effect—whether intentional or not—was to divorce him from Judaism, cut him off from other Jews, and call his own Jewishness into question.

During this phase of Dylan's career, he recorded three albums of gospel-influenced Christian music: *Slow Train Coming* (1979), *Saved* (1980), and *Shot of Love* (1981). The music was generally acknowledged to be of high quality, the song "Gotta Serve Somebody" from the 1979 album winning him his first Grammy Award. The reaction of many fans, especially Jewish fans, was exemplified by Harold Leventhal, the beloved "folk music impresario" who managed the Weavers and many others. Attending the Grammy ceremony at which Dylan was honored for his Christian music, Leventhal "went over to Dylan's table, put out his hand and loudly proclaimed, '*Mazel Tov!*' "[58] Similarly, while reuniting with his friend and fellow Jewish musician Michael Bloomfield in late 1980, Bloomfield kidded him, "So I hear you're a Christian now. *Oy gevalt!*"[59] These sarcastic comments captured the bemusement of some Jews by what they considered Dylan's irrational departure from his senses, the loss of his *yiddishe kop* (Jewish head). A particularly measured response was given by Ron Rosenbaum, who had interviewed Dylan for *Playboy* magazine just prior to his religious conversion. Rosenbaum offers four theories to explain the mystifying turn of events, number two being that "Dylan is trying to erase once and for all his Jewish identity." And Rosenbaum comments, "When I heard the born-again Bob album, I felt a sense of loss as a Jew. But on the other hand it could have been worse . . . I, for one, would counsel tolerance for this conversion, because throughout his career Dylan has had a habit of undergoing conversions . . ."[60]

Others in the Jewish community saw Dylan's conversion as an act of ethnic and religious betrayal, and were subject to deep disappointment and dismay. In an "unauthorized spiritual biography," Nadine Epstein and Rebecca Frankel go so far as to claim, "Not since Shabbatai Tzvi's 17th century about-face [in converting to Islam] did an exit from Judaism shock the tribe like Dylan's Christian period."[61] Laurence Schlesinger, who went on to become a Reform rabbi, recalls that he watched Dylan's 1979 television appearance "in utter disbelief, stunned by his" performance of an explicitly Christian song; and could only surmise that "something very strange, indeed, had occurred in Bob Dylan's life and mind; something rather bizarre that I could neither explain nor believe."[62] Similarly, Cantor Jeff Klepper recalls, "When Dylan released the Christian themed *Slow Train Coming* and sang selections on Saturday Night Live the event had a strong negative effect on me. I didn't purchase any of Dylan's new material until well into the 1990s. After seeing him in 1974 and 1975, I didn't attend his concerts for over 20 years."[63]

To be sure, many Jews deeply lamented Dylan's conversion to Christianity, likely the same who rejoiced at his flirtation with Hasidism. According to J. J. Goldberg, "Jewish Dylanophiles raged when he publicly dabbled in Christianity around 1980, then exulted when he flirted with Lubavitch chasidism a few years later."[64] But most Dylan fans simply rationalized the problem away, claiming that he was beyond all that, as Klepper further explains: "While there are many who want very much to see Dylan as a Jew, Bob Dylan as a cultural figure transcends religion."[65] Indeed, Bob Dylan represents something greater than religious fealty—he was, from the beginning, intent on breaking free of the past, his career an ongoing project of liberation and self-creation that would ultimately subvert whatever the past had to offer. Certainly Dylan himself never felt any sense of transgression—spending three years as essentially an evangelical preacher was simply "part of [his varied] experience."[66] Still, one has to wonder what subconscious role might have been played by his own religious background—if becoming a born again Christian is not the ultimate act of rebellion of a Jewish boy, what is?

Dylan's resistance to being seen as a Jew has become even more evident in recent years. In his 2004 memoir, *Chronicles: Volume One*, he writes eloquently of his youth in Minnesota, his family, friends, and early days in New York City—but not a word about the Jewish experience inherent in all of it. Though the memoir was by no means intended as a comprehensive autobiography, the near-total absence of Jewish references still jumps out (at least to the Jewishly attuned reader) and begs for explanation. One of the pleasures of the book is Dylan's gusto for recalling and depicting the various characters he met in the early days of his career. He also loves to relate arcana of American history. Thus, when introducing noteworthy figures in his life, such as John Hammond, Pete Seeger, Ray Gooch, Paul Clayton, Woody Guthrie, and Dave Van Ronk, he is quick to point out their purebred American heritage: for example, "[Hammond] was legendary, pure American aristocracy." "Pete's ancestors had come over on the *Mayflower*, . . . his relatives had fought the Battle of Bunker Hill, for Christsake." "Ray . . . came from a long line of ancestry made up of bishops, generals, even a colonial governor." "Clayton . . . was from New Bedford, Mass., the whaling town—he sang a lot of sea shanties, had a Puritan ancestry, but some of his relatives had been from the early Virginia families."[67]

Yet when Dylan chronicles other important contacts in the New York folk music scene, such as Lou Levy, Israel "Izzy" Young, Moses Asch, Irwin Silber, Clive Davis, Harold Leventhal, and Albert Grossman, not a word is uttered about their historical backgrounds and ethnic origins (all Jewish). The effect of this silence is a kind of studied disinterest in the Jewish past, and, when combined with his apparent adulation of Americana, reveals a clear bias for one over the other. Dylan scholar Nina Goss expands on this observation, writing, "It assumes they are mutually exclusive [in Dylan's mind]—to be Jewish is less than, other than, even incompatible with being iconically, normatively American—an assumption consistent with the suppression of his Jewishness for most of his career."[68]

Explicitly Jewish subject matter does intrude from time to time, but Dylan shows little interest in exploring it in any personalized way. At one juncture in the memoir he relates the story of sitting in Johnny Cash's living room with a group of other musicians, when the country music great Joe Carter asked him out of the blue, "You don't eat pork, do you?" His only response was "Uh, no sir, I don't" and a cryptic reference to Malcolm X.[69] He notes that Cash and Kris Kristofferson were taken aback, but offers no further explanation or reaction to the implied anti-semitism of Carter's comment. Similarly, in reminiscing about the early Greenwich Village days, Dylan recalls once being asked, "You ever heard of Auschwitz?" Dylan's reply: "Sure I had, who hadn't?"[70] The comment is followed by a descriptive paragraph on the Holocaust, but no sense of personal connection intrudes.

Throughout his narrative, Dylan is simply allergic to the words *Jew* or *Jewish*. A third of the way through the book, he offers a nicely descriptive portrait of his Jewish grandmother, but in completely de-Judaized terms: "My grandmother had only one leg and had been a seamstress . . . She was a dark lady, smoked a pipe . . . My grandmother's voice possessed a haunting accent—face always set in a half-despairing expression . . . She'd come to America from Odessa, a seaport town in southern Russia . . . Originally, she'd come from Turkey . . . Her family was from Kagizman, a town in Turkey near the Armenian border, and the family name had been Kirghiz . . . My grandmother's ancestors had been from Constantinople."[71] All this is fine, but he is describing (without naming) his paternal grandmother Anna Zimmerman (born Greenstein), a Yiddish-speaking Jewish immigrant. Another memoirist might have evinced some interest in his Hebraic origins, and may very well have mused over his apparent Sephardic roots. But Dylan prefers to imagine his antecedents as not Jewish at all—and he concludes, "As a teenager, I used to sing the Ritchie Valens song 'In a Turkish Town' . . . and it seemed to suit me."[72]

Most blatant of all such aversions, Dylan disavows his own family name of Zimmerman and all that it implies, and even the very existence of his former self. In discussing the sources of the invented name Bob Dylan, he writes, "What I was going to do as soon as I left home was just call myself Robert Allen. As far as I was concerned, that was who I was—that's what my parents named me . . . There was little of my identity that wasn't in it."[73] And then he goes even further: "As far as Bobby Zimmerman goes, I'm going to give it to you right straight and you can check it out. One of the early presidents of the San Bernardino Angels was Bobby Zimmerman, and he was killed in 1964 . . . That person is gone. That was the end of him."[74] A similar study could be made of Martin Scorsese's 2005 documentary on the early years of Dylan's career, *No Direction Home*, whose centerpiece is an extensive interview with the famously taciturn singer, conducted by his manager, Jeff Rosen.

Again, the subject of Dylan's Jewishness is all but ignored, and seems to be studiously avoided.

One might object that it is the man's right—first, to define himself as he pleases, and second, to relate his story according to his own self-definition. Yet the willful avoidance of Jewishness in Dylan's self-narrative becomes evident when measured against the enormous significance he attained among many Jews and others as a "Jewish poet," "Jewish mystic," and even "Jewish prophet." Moreover, if Dylan as a pop cultural symbol and musical influence played such an important role in the revolutionary trends of the day, then it is fair to ask, how and in what measure did his perceived Jewishness add to the message? As we have seen, his Jewish identity was revealed at the very moment he reached the peak of his fame and influence—surely, the public perception of Bob Dylan now included this not inconsequential fact—so it is legitimate to ask, what role did it play? More specifically, we might pose two related sets of questions:

1. What did Dylan's Jewish identity mean to the general public, and how, if at all, was his Jewishness reflective of the revolutionary youth culture?
2. What did his countercultural persona mean to Jews, and how, if at all, has it contributed to the evolution of American Jewish identity?

"Call me Zimmy": The Jewhooing of Bob Dylan

The answer to such questions may be found in the popular responses to Dylan that speak directly to the theme of his Jewishness—the Jewhooing of Bob Dylan.[75] Like all Jewhooing, it points out the Jewish background of the celebrity in question, and then projects certain aspects of Jewishness onto that person as well. The Jewhooing of Dylan is especially acute as it plays off the sharp tension between his consistent evasion of Jewish definition and the extensive Jewish content of his life. It thereby fulfills one basic motive of Jewhooing, the countering of the celebrity's assimilation, and comes in response to specific elements of his life.

The first stage of Dylan Jewhooing came in the wake of Dylan's own dabbling in Jewish identification following the death of his father in 1968, and as he approached his thirtieth birthday in 1971. The timing also corresponds to the renewed burst of Jewish consciousness amongst American Jews following the Six Day War of 1967. Rumors about Dylan's reengagement with his Jewishness began to circulate, as cataloged by Jonathan Braun in a 1971 article first published in the Jewish students' journal of the City College of New York, and later reprinted in *Rolling Stone* magazine under the title "Is Bob Zimmerman Really

Jewish?" Braun notes how the latest rumor to circulate about Dylan "concerns something which has been fairly well-known to the youth community for quite a while: Dylan's Jewish identity" and continues:

> The news-making ingredient, however, is Dylan's alleged newfound Jewish pride . . . Stripped of its sensationalist fantasy, the possibility that Bob Dylan may be examining his Jewish heritage is actually quite plausible. Dylan, after all, is Jewish; and at a time when increasing numbers of Americans, particularly young Americans, are experiencing an intense rebirth of ethnic consciousness, it is more than likely that an artist critic of society—even if he has become a silent critic—like Dylan, would find himself taking a fresh look at the past. As one City College Dylanologist said, "It would be just like him to keep us guessing about his Jewishness."[76]

In the same year, Anthony Scaduto concluded the first significant biography of Bob Dylan as follows: "At this writing, Dylan's search for personal salvation seems to be coming around full circle, back to the religion of his fathers. Bob has started to study Judaism, and Hebrew. Dylan, who gets so Gemini-enthusiastic about everything, has made several trips to Israel in the last year or so to 'sniff the breeze,' as a friend puts it . . . Dylan refuses to discuss it. But it is obvious that his search for his past has led him back to the heritage he was denying since Minneapolis."[77] Expanding on his comments in the revised edition of 1973, Scaduto adds that "ever since his motorcycle accident Dylan has gone through what some have called a metamorphosis. In working through the chaos that fame made of his life, he has returned to Judaism, a heritage he had always denied."[78] Scaduto further explains Dylan's rumored involvement with the Jewish Defense League, and notes his loss of enthusiasm for both the militant Jewish group and for Israel itself. As for his religious interests, Scaduto quotes him saying, "I get twenty or thirty letters a day asking me to speak on Judaism at some temple or other. I don't have anything to say about it. Those people have nothing to do with me. I feel that far away from it."[79] Scaduto immediately adds that "none of these feelings, Dylan made it clear, detract from the reality of his return to his roots: the Judaism of the individual," and goes on to assert Dylan's adherence to a more personal and individualized form of religion:

> Dylan has been and is today a man seeking *personal* salvation. That search has led Dylan to religion. Not institutional religion, but the religion of the inner being, the unknown inside us all. God is "I"—before He becomes so-

cialized. In attempting to reconcile the conflict between the inner being and the outer world—a conflict Dylan has felt since his childhood—he has embraced Judaism, a religion that makes a great deal of sense, for Dylan. Not because it is the religion of his fathers, but because Judaism is an existential way of being in the world, a religion in which man may come face to face with his Creator and continue to maintain his own identity.[80]

Scaduto thus provides fodder to the Jewhooing trend, portraying Dylan as a Jew in no uncertain terms.

Though always about pointing out Dylan's Jewishness, the Jewhooing of Dylan comes in several distinct forms. First, and perhaps most common, is the claim of Jewish influence in his songwriting—that well before his explicitly Christian phase, his lyrics contained the religious themes and biblical references indicative of a "Judeo-Christian" orientation. One reviewer of Dylan's memoir comments, "You won't find much about Dylan's religiosity in *Chronicles: Volume One*—unless, of course, you're one of those Dylanologists who notices that the title itself may be a biblical reference. It you're one of them—okay, one of us—you've been noticing these coincidences for a long time."[81]

Examples of such Jewish readings of Dylan's music abound, as in Alan Rinzler's encomium to the most iconic Dylan song of all, "Blowin' in the Wind." Calling it "an immortal spiritual anthem," he elaborates: "It's universal—the melody, the words, the experience of singing it . . . is so spiritually cathartic, it's like chanting from Ecclesiastes. It's biblical. Specifically it's Old Testament and traditionally Jewish, particularly with Dylan's device of answering questions with yet more questions. And the answer? Is it blowing *away*? Or . . . Is it like the *ein sof*, the Judaic unknowable divine deity beyond all human comprehension?"[82] It is a lovely and compelling interpretation of Dylan's poetry, and likewise, Rinzler applies a Jewish lens to Dylan's music in his description of the song "One More Cup of Coffee" (co-authored with Jacques Levy): "It sounds like a cross between a cantor singing Kol Nidre and a gypsy singing to his horse high in the mountains."[83] Again, a nice bit of music criticism; as with any great artist, Dylan's art is open to interpretation. However, it is just that—interpretation—a subjective reading shedding no light on the artist's intent. The interpretive act of the listener may be a Jewish expression itself, but offers no insight on the actual Jewishness of the artist or of his art—Jewhooing, plain and simple.

Although most Jewhooing will come from other Jews, the Jewish question in Dylan's music has piqued the interest of non-Jews as well.

In the same year as Scaduto's biography, Australian Dylan critic Craig McGregor noted the Jewishness of Dylan's work, writing, "No one can come from a Jewish background without being profoundly influenced by it, whether the process is one of acceptance, compromise or rejection. Dylan is no exception, and one doesn't need to know much about his change of name or his contradictory, carefully disguised relationship with his parents to realize it. . . . Recently Dylan seems to have been rediscovering his Jewishness all over again, coming to terms with it."[84] McGregor goes on to emphasize the religious imagery in the music, implying its Jewish roots—it is a particularly Christian perspective, equating Jewish identity with religious affiliation.

Similarly, Dylan's late 1970s bout of religious revivalism—his born-again phase—has occasioned much comment on the part of Christian observers who, like McGregor, see in it the return of the prodigal Jew. The main text in this regard is the 2002 book *Restless Pilgrim: The Spiritual Journey of Bob Dylan* by Scott Marshall with Marcia Ford. Though primarily about Dylan's Christian phase, the book casts a wider net by asserting the religious nature of Dylan's entire career. To do so, however, it had to treat his Jewish background and Jewish seeking as integral parts of his overall spiritual quest. Thus, ironically enough, a book on Dylan's Christianity becomes yet another example of Jewhooing. As its back cover proclaims,

> As a young Jewish musician, Bob Dylan faithfully explored the roots of modern American music—the spirituals and gospel songs. It is not surprising then, Dylan's words, both in his songs and in his interviews, have often touched upon biblical themes. . . . A curious icon of popular culture, yet distinct in his Judeo-Christian expressions, Bob Dylan doesn't fit neatly into the typical rock 'n' roll mold. Who else would have the chutzpah to publicly contribute to Orthodox Jewish communities while publicly singing songs about Jesus' crucifixion, resurrection, and eventual return? *Restless Pilgrim: The Spiritual Journey of Bob Dylan* wrestles with the seemingly contradictory facts of Dylan's preoccupation with Jesus and his own Jewish heritage, by looking through the lens of this reluctant legend's four-decade career.[85]

Scaduto, McGregor, and Marshall and Ford notwithstanding, Dylan's Jewishness would leave its impress most of all on young Jews. Jewish journalist J. J. Goldberg recalls how Dylan

> fled, Jonah-like, from the role of prophet—the very thing that had brought him to the world's attention. Nowhere was that flight more apparent than

in his relationship with his Jewish fans. From the first, the meteoric rise of Dylan, ne Zimmerman, touched off rhapsodies of expectation among Jewish baby-boomers. After all, his words had helped millions worldwide to make sense of the turmoil around them and within them. Young Jews wanted him to take the next step and help them sort out the confusion of their Jewish souls. But he couldn't. The fact was, he was as lost as they were.[86]

Though Dylan would not lead the way, many took the matter into their own hands. Thus some of the most fervent religious interpreters of Dylan's oeuvre were Jewish hippies, who began to treat his work "midrashically" in the countercultural 1960s. As Goldberg further recalls, "Over the years, a cottage industry grew up to ferret out Judaic content—some genuine, some merely imagined—in his lyrics. Fans stalked him on his spiritual journeys the way other performers might be staked out during restaurant outings."[87] Beyond reading deeper meanings into every line of his songs, they saw the man himself as a religious symbol of transcendence and salvation. Mel Howard, producer of the 1975 tour film *Renaldo and Clara* (released in 1978), explained it as follows: "And, incidentally, Dylan's Jewish . . . and I'm heavily Jewish, I speak Yiddish, so there's that, the mythology of Dylan as a latter-day Hassid as a Cabalistic kind of poet, all that, and as a kind of extension of the whole idea of the wandering Jew, wandering poet, the person who is inspired and goes amongst the community to carry the message of inspiration and renewed faith and renewed hope."[88]

The principal example of this phenomenon was one Stephen Pickering, who, according to Scaduto, was one of the few writers to "have recognized that . . . in all his songs since he waved farewell to protest almost ten years ago, Bob Dylan has been creating a body of work that is rooted in the Jewish mystical tradition."[89] Michael Gray, in his *Bob Dylan Encyclopedia*, notes that "Pickering was the first to assert, not always convincingly but with an aggressive torrent of opaque argument, the centrality of the Jewish faith and Jewish teachings to Dylan's work—a stance he had already developed by the time of *Praxis: One*. He wrote from what he called the Center for the Study of Bob Dylan & Torah Judaism."[90] Pickering, an obsessed Dylan fan since 1962, devoted a decade of his life to what might be called *Jewish Dylanology*. He expressed his basic perspective in one of his many interpretive reviews of Dylan albums, in which he notes "the brilliant religiosity that pervades Dylan's present work. This religious intensity is, of course, traceable to Dylan's Jewish background, and, in turns, extends and pervades through

TWO DOLLARS: FIFTY CENTS

PRAXIS: ONE

Existence, Men and Realities

Praxis: One by Stephen Pickering (1971). The photo depicts Dylan visiting Israel in June 1971.

everything he has ever written."[91] This is as succinct a statement of Dylan Jewhooing as one will find in Pickering's voluminous writings.

But Pickering went much further. In the preface to his first publication, *Dylan: A Commemoration*, he asserts that through his music, "Dylan has created, in a real sense, an 'ideology' of Hasidic consciousness," and further explains, "Our discussion of Dylan in this volume and in future ones is rooted in our belief that Dylan's embracing of a Martin Buber–like Hasidism (compare *New Morning* to *I and Thou*, for example) can prove a path to self-dialogue . . . Dylan is, if you will, a 'holy man.' His archetypes, rooted in the Kabbalah and other sources, are not relics."[92] He then shifts into high Jewhooing mode with his next publication, *Praxis: One: Existence, Men and Realities*.[93] Its cover photograph is the now-famous June 1971 UPI photo of Dylan, recently turned thirty, visiting the Wailing Wall in Jerusalem, holding a cardboard *kippah* on his head. Scaduto had included the photo in his book as well, but here it is highlighted on the cover of a book (actually an oversized magazine format) that includes articles such as "Bob Dylan incognito (in Israel)" by Catherine Rosenheimer; "On a Jewish Revolution" by Baruch Ballin and David Biale; "A Mischnah Gas for SP; BZ:BD:BZ, JaH, Aba" by David Meltzer; and Pickering's own "Bob Dylan and The Book of Splendor [the *Zohar*]."

In his introduction to *Praxis*, on a page adorned with Hebrew letters, Pickering repeats his earlier contention that "Dylan is, however unconsciously, a participant in the Hasidic (or Kabbalist) tradition," having "created an 'ideology' of Hasidic consciousness."[94] Going well beyond Steven Goldberg's earlier contentions that "Bob Dylan is a mystic" and his music is the "poetry of salvation,"[95] Pickering sees in Dylan the mystical embodiment of the Jewish tradition. For example, in his article on Dylan and the *Zohar* (the foundational text of *Kabbalah*—Jewish mysticism), he relates the ten divine emanations, or *Sephirot*, to Dylan's first ten record albums: *Malkuth* (God's kingdom on earth) is paralleled by *Bob Dylan*; *Yesod* (foundation) by *The Freewheelin' Bob Dylan*; *Hod* (majesty) by *The Times They Are A-Changin'*, and so on. In lengthy reviews of more recent Dylan albums, Pickering extrapolates on this basic premise—of "the interrelationships between the archetypal motifs of Dylan's work and those of Judaic mysticism."[96] Moreover, he faults most rock critics for being "unable (or unwilling) to discuss Dylan's Jewish consciousness," and even accuses some of antisemitism.[97] Besides articles by Pickering and others on Dylan's work, the book is littered with quotations by Martin Buber, Will Herberg, Elie Wiesel, Rabbi Adin Steinsaltz, Nachman of Bratslav, and other rabbis. It is, in sum, a nexus of contemporary trends—a dovetailing of Dylanology, the Jewish counterculture, and the Jewhooing of Bob Dylan.

But Pickering was still not done. In a small volume ostensibly intended to prepare the way for Dylan's return to concert touring in 1974, he returned to his own "investigation into Kabbalah's rearticulation, however intuitively, in Dylan's poetry."[98] Now adding his own Hebrew name, Chofetz Chaim Ben-Avraham, Pickering begins his text with a telling author's note: "This book [is] written by a religious Jew . . ."[99] Advancing the notion of the poet-as-mystic, he states, "Poetry . . . is the Ineffable's search for man. The response the light reflected and bent into prismatic rainbow of hope and dream, is to be found in a Bob Dylan/Robert Zimmerman, a son of Imagination."[100] And playing on the hidden meaning of words and names, a Kabbalistic motif, Pickering observes,

> In Aramaic, the language of the Talmud and of the *Zohar* (*the* vast text of Jewish mysticism, first published in 1190), Dylan is *di-lan*, "ours." To quote Jewish poet Joel Rosenberg (from whom I received these provocative plays-on-words), "Bob (in Aramaic, *baba*, 'gate') Dylan is the gateway to the Presence." Dylan is a gateway, not a prophet; he shows us what is in *his* soul, not, directly, our own souls. His songs are messages to himself, and we

are allowed to listen to this mythopoetic self-dialogue, this gateway to his soul's dialogue with the divine.[101]

Pickering/Ben-Avraham would also publish titles such as *Aggadah: Studies in Bob Dylan and Torah Judaism*; *Kavannah: Mystic Steps and Dylaneutics*; and *"Knockin' on Heaven's Door" and "Billy": A Jewish Speculation*. But his magnum opus was *Bob Dylan Approximately: A Portrait of the Jewish Poet in Search of God—A Midrash* (1975). Now packaging his ideas in a glossy volume illustrated by color photographs, he makes his most elaborate case yet for the Jewishness of Dylan, opening his introduction this way:

> Bob Dylan is a post-Holocaust Jewish voice, searching for and rediscovering the manifestations of God. He has told me: "I have never forgotten my roots. I am a Jew." . . . Bob Dylan is one of a succession of Jewish mystics—Yitzhak Luria, Avraham ben Samuel Abulafia, Moses Cordovero, Rav Avraham Yitzhak Kuk, [and so on] . . . This book is a midrash, a searching out, through description and commentary, of Bob Dylan's 1974, North American tour. This book presents an authentic perspective of Dylan—as a Jew.[102]

Thus, in addition to portraying Dylan's music as an expression of Jewish mysticism—for example, "By singing his prayers Bob Dylan conjures the currents of the soul. Bob Dylan's prayer/poems reflect exile and the promise of teshuvah (redemption)"[103]—Pickering/Ben-Avraham now indulges in outright Jewhooing, projecting ever more Jewishness onto the image of Dylan:

> Today: Bob Dylan prays and shares his prayers . . . he has studied with Rav Shlomo Friefeld of Far Rockaway, New York (a most learned man) . . . he does not eat pork . . . as did Dylan, his children have gone to a *religious* Jewish summer camp . . . he has contributed to Israel . . . with his wife, in 1971 he visited the Mount Zion Yeshiva in Israel . . . at one time (according to Rabbi Richard Rocklin of Charlotte, North Carolina) he contemplated renting an apartment in Jerusalem . . . and, after several visits to Israel, he applied for membership on a kibbutz (according to the kibbutz's secretary, they delayed in answering his application and never heard from him again).[104]

All this Judaizing of Dylan had to have some effect on Jewish fans. For example, in reviewing Pickering's *Bob Dylan Approximately* for the fanzine TBZB (see next section) in March 1976, Mike Metzger wrote that it "was the book I had been waiting for," further explaining,

Like the average Jewish teenager growing up in the sixties, my judaistic feelings were null. In the past few years, however, I have become more aware of my Jewishness. Though it's not really enough to become religious, at least when someone asks me if I am a Jew, I no longer reply, "No, but my parents are." And here was a book that said Bob Dylan—perhaps the greatest influence in my life—wrote his songs in search of the Jewish God. Undoubtedly this book could settle my confused state of Jewishness.[105]

In 1978, a graduate student named Daniel Matt went so far as to send a copy of *Bob Dylan Approximately* to his academic mentor, the great scholar of Jewish mysticism Gershom Scholem. Matt's hope, as he explained, was to give Scholem "a hippie's perspective on Robert Zimmerman (Dylan's real name)."[106] Now a professor of Jewish mysticism himself, Matt has recently written, "For many years I worshiped Dylan. I occasionally referred to him as *Baba Dilan*, Aramaic for 'our gateway.' For some reason I always wanted him to be very deeply Jewish, whether or not he was."[107] What reason might that be? We can only surmise, but it seems reasonable to describe fans such as Metzger and Matt as young Jewish hippies in search of some resolution between their Jewish and countercultural selves, looking for a way to blend their worship of Dylan with their commitment to Judaism. The "real" Dylan offered no such resolution, but it could be found in the imaginative process of Jewhooing.

The degree of Pickering/Ben-Avraham's investment in Dylan's Jewishness has never been surpassed, but as we shall see, it set a pattern that would be repeated many times over. One can only imagine the terrible disillusionment such a *hasid* (pious follower) of "Rebbe" Dylan must have experienced when, just a few years after the publication of *Bob Dylan Approximately*, the reborn Jewish mystic became a born-again Christian. In fact, Dylan had elicited such a feeling of betrayal in some of his fans before, when in 1965 he switched from acoustic folk to electrified rock 'n' roll. The peak moment came at a now famous 1966 concert in Manchester, England, when one disgruntled fan called out, "Judas!" The incident was widely reported, though somehow is never described as an antisemitic expression of Jewhooing. By calling out as he did, the audience member accused Dylan of being a traitor, certainly, but the expression chosen was an implicit denunciation of Dylan as a traitorous *Jew*. In fact, as Ron Rosenbaum points out, it can even be seen as a case of double Jewhooing: "When you think about it, it was an accusation that he was being Judas to his own Jesus."[108]

Another early Jewish fan who combined the general feeling of betrayal with Pickering's meticulous interpretation of Dylan's every word was A. J. Weberman. Certainly the most colorful of such Dylan-obsessed fans, it was Weberman who coined the term *Dylanologist.* In Scaduto's description, Weberman is "the self-styled 'Dylanologist' who has made a career of interpreting Dylan's lyrics and going through his garbage to learn all he can of the man he both idolizes and hates."[109] In a later biography, Howard Sounes adds,

> Born Alan Jules Weberman in Brooklyn in 1945, he became obsessed with Bob's music when he was at Michigan State University in the early sixties. Listening to the albums while stoned on marijuana or LSD he made what seemed to him a major discovery. "I realized it was poetry and required interpretation," he explains. "I developed the Dylanological Method, which is looking at each word in the context in which it appears and looking for words that have a similar theme that cluster around it (concordance). I started to devote a lot of time to just sitting around interpreting Dylan's poetry."[110]

Of all the Dylan biographers, Robert Shelton devotes the most attention to this clown prince of Dylan followers: "The Scavenger was a would-be anarchist star, a wheeler-dealer of the freaked-out New Left, a garbage groupie, a self-promoting, speedy-talking hustler named Alan Jules Weberman. He proclaimed himself 'the world's greatest authority on Dylan,' 'the father of Dylanology.'"[111]

But sometime in the late 1960s, Weberman turned against his idol, accusing Dylan of betraying his earlier idealism and selling out for fame and fortune. When not searching through Dylan's garbage for "dirt" on his erstwhile hero, he appointed himself "Minister of Defense, Dylan Liberation Front" and held demonstrations in front of his home—all, ostensibly, to rescue the reclusive pop star from his perfidy. A central part of Weberman's critique seemed to concern Jewish politics. As late as 1974, he was still leveling the accusation that Dylan was a right-wing Zionist. Heralding Dylan's return to the concert circuit in that year, *Newsweek* magazine reported that "Super-Dylanologist A. J. Weberman, who became famous by going through Dylan's garbage cans for relics of Saint Bob, now thinks the tour smells suspiciously like a Zionist plot." Weberman is quoted accusing Dylan as follows: "He's doing it now because of the war in the Middle East . . . He is an ultra Zionist. He is doing the tour to raise money for Israel. He has given large sums of money to Israel in the name of Abraham Zimmerman [Dylan's father's name]. He's very ethno-oriented." *Newsweek* then gives Dylan the last word: "I got blue eyes . . . I don't know how Jewish that is."[112]

In January of 1971, Weberman took a group on a field trip to Dylan's home in Greenwich Village, and confronted his nemesis directly—he was confronted in turn by Dylan himself. Characterizing Dylan as "a cross between someone in his 'current bag' and a Talmudic scholar," Weberman recreated their meeting in the *East Village Other*:

> Then D said, "Al, why'd ye bring all these people around my house for?" "It's a field trip for my Dylan class, man . . . but actually it's a demonstration against you and all you've come to represent in rock music . . ." "Al, did you ever write anything about my Karate? Ever write anything about my race & stuff it in my mailbox?" "I knew you took Karate but I never wrote anything about it . . . your race . . . ?" "What race are you, Alan?" "The human race." "And what race were yer parents?" "Well, they considered themselves Jewish, I guess." "You sure you never wrote anything about my race?" "No, man, it ain't yer race I object to, it's yer politics and lifestyle." "Well, I didn't think ya would, Al." "Hey Bob, what do you do with all your money?" "It all goes to Kibbutzim in Israel and Far Rockaway." "But you were one of the first Jews to put down Israel." "Where?" "In the liner notes to ANOTHER SIDE OF D." "Don't remember!"[113]

Weberman subsequently managed to talk to Dylan on the phone, and recorded their conversations. Though produced by a man many see as a lunatic, the document is nonetheless a rare instance of a direct encounter between a superstar and a hardcore fan. It is also a dialogue between two Jews, as Weberman comments, "You know, if I lived in another age I might have been a Talmudic scholar," to which Dylan replies, "So would I."[114] Several years later, in 1977, Weberman would somehow persuade Folkways Records to release the recorded "interview" as an album titled *Bob Dylan vs. A. J. Weberman: The Historic Confrontation*. On it, Dylan can be heard once again asking Weberman, "You sure you didn't write any letters about my race?" And Weberman attempts to explain: "He may have been referring to part of my EVO [*East Village Other*] 'garbage article,' where, after finding cards and thank-you notes from D's family, I wrote—'Good to see Dylan is still a Zimmerman.' What I meant by that was, 'Good to see D still associates with middle class, lames like his straight relatives.' It was a riff in the Lenny Bruce LIMA OHIO & John Lennon 'don't believe in Zimmerman' tradition & not antisemitic."[115]

Beyond the Jewhooing of Bob Dylan's songwriting, there are at least three other varieties of Dylan Jewhooing. As indicated by both Stephen Pickering and A. J. Weberman, one is simply reference to his original Jewish name, Zimmerman. Dylan is probably the only major celebrity whose birth name is constantly evoked by his fans and commentators—with the possible exception of Marilyn Monroe, memorialized by Elton John as *Norma Jean*. In Dylan's case, the citing and reciting of *Zimmerman* in myriad contexts suggests that something other than nostalgia is afoot. That is to say, the pointed use of his "real" name has to serve some purpose; it must communicate some message—but what?

One of the first instances of the phenomenon came in 1970, when former Beatle John Lennon recorded a song titled "God," in which he proclaimed the end of 1960s idealism ("The dream is over") and offered a litany of newly rejected beliefs. After a chorus denying the existence of God ("God is a concept / By which we measure our pain"), he lists the other authorities in which he doesn't believe: "I don't believe in Bible . . . Tarot . . . Hitler . . . Jesus . . . Kennedy . . . Buddha . . . Mantra . . . Gita . . . Yoga . . . Kings . . . Elvis . . . I don't believe in Zimmerman."[116] Similar to the album cover of *Sgt. Pepper's Lonely Hearts Club Band* (1967), Lennon was here listing the deities of contemporary culture in order to burst their inflated celebrity—and his own. (Though he had not succeeded in including Hitler and Jesus on the 1967 album cover, Elvis and Dylan were there, along with Lenny Bruce.) Like Lennon himself, Dylan was an icon of the Sixties counterculture, and in debunking him along with other sacred cows, Lennon resorted to using his real name. Look, the song points out, he's not really who he claims to be—he's a fake. As Weberman warned Dylan, "[E]veryone in rock with a political consciousness is gonna come down on you. Lennon has started already by calling you Zimmerman."[117]

In the same year as Lennon's "God," an early bootleg album of Dylan concerts from the early 1960s (including the epochal 1966 Royal Albert Hall concert in Manchester, England, later issued officially as *The Bootleg Series, Vol. 4*, and further immortalized by Martin Scorcese in *No Direction Home*) was issued with the title "Looking Back," but more prominently printed in block letters on the cover is the artist's name, Zimmerman. According to Bobsboots, a website devoted to Dylan bootlegs, "Looking Back" was "the first LP of the RAH show to be released in the United States. The cover on this piece leaves lots to be desired. The front cover loose line sketch looks very little if any like Bob. As the L.P.

is credited to Zimmerman with no mention of Dylan anywhere, perhaps the Zerocks Label was going for complete anonymity even down to the drawing."[118]

More likely, the use of the name Zimmerman was an indication of the growing interest in Dylan's "true" identity. The significance of the name as a marker of Jewish identity was clearly demonstrated when, following his much-publicized trip to Israel in 1971, a rumor developed that he planned to change his name back to Zimmerman. Interviewing Dylan on an Israeli beach, *Jerusalem Post* reporter Catherine Rosenheimer informed him of the *Time* magazine article that "said, among other things . . . that he was 'thinking about' changing his name back to the one he grew up with: Robert Allen Zimmerman; that, having become Dylan (out of his admiration for the poet Dylan Thomas) about nine years ago because 'I had a lot to run away from. Now I've got a lot to return to'—he was 'returning to his Jewishness.'"[119] Dylan denied the rumor, of course, but the very fact that some believed it might happen reveals their longing for him to publicly assert his Jewishness, and thus revert to his "authentic self" as a Jew.

Because he was having none of it, others would do it for him—and the Jewhooing of Dylan proceeded apace. In October of 1972, *National Lampoon* magazine published a comic strip titled "The Ventures of Zimmerman"[120] in which Dylan was depicted as a Jewish superhero—his secret identity, à la Clark Kent, was Robert Zimmerman. Whether intentional or not, the depiction gave a nod to the longtime association of Jews with comic book superheroes,[121] and nicely evoked the subtext of Jewish dual identities. Unfortunately, the humorists of *National Lampoon*—Tony Hendra and Sean Kelly co-authored the strip, and Neil Adams drew it—allowed antisemitic stereotypes to infect their work. The cover portrays Dylan as a *kippah*-wearing fighter pilot standing next to his jet plane adorned with Jewish stars and called "Master of War" (a reference to Dylan's antiwar song "Masters of War"). As if a donation of Jewish philanthropy, the plane is marked "Gift of Mr. Robt. Zimmerman." The cover also offers the lame jokes "semitized for your protection" and "Approved by the Elders of Zion," and is purported to be published by "IJC—International Jewish Comics" (IJC could also be read as "International Jewish Conspiracy"—get it?). Even the price listed on the upper right-hand corner contains a "Jewish" joke: "For You, $1.95." The contents only grow worse, depicting both Dylan and his father as conniving, money-hungry Jews. It is, in sum, a grossly distasteful and insulting publication—but for our purposes, it helps to

191

explain some of the motives behind the use of the name Zimmerman. In the end, calling Dylan "Zimmerman" is calling him a Jew.

In even poorer taste, *National Lampoon* repeated the exercise in its May 1974 issue with a sequel strip titled "Son-O'-God Meets Zimmerman," in which the resurrected Jesus appears in Israel, only to be captured by the Israeli army—this is offensive enough, as one soldier exclaims, "Hava Negila! We got the bastard again!" The strip really goes off the rails, however, when Jesus escapes and begins to convert the Jews of Israel and thereby dissolve the Jewish state—but then, to the rescue comes Dylan, who happens to be visiting Israel at the time. Riding off on his motorcycle, Dylan promptly dies in an accident (crashing into the Wailing Wall) and is himself resurrected as "the eternal spirit of crass chutzpah, heir apparent to George E. Jessel, mister commercial kitsch himself . . . ZIMMERMAN!"[122] None of it makes much sense, but the apparent intention is to link Dylan and Israel, smearing both as materialist, militarist, and corrupt. Dylan, as Zimmerman, is the embodiment of Jewish self-interest and paranoia. It is, in short, another example of antisemitic Jewhooing.

Another telling use of Zimmerman as an accusation of sorts came during the Rolling Thunder Revue tour of 1975. Playwright Sam Shepard had been invited along to provide dialogue and direction for a film to be made of the tour (later titled *Renaldo and Clara*), and would later describe his experience in a book. In one memorable passage, Shepard reenacts an ad-libbed scene between Dylan and Joan Baez. Journalist Larry "Ratso" Sloman later suggested that the provocative scene "almost became a psychodrama about their old relationship."[123] Meeting Dylan in a bar, Baez needles him with questions about his identity, including the following bit of dialogue:

> BAEZ: Didn't you used to play the guitar?
> DYLAN: No, that was that other guy.
> BAEZ: What other guy, Bob?
> DYLAN: That little short guy. I forget his name.
> BAEZ: Oh, you mean that little Jewish brat from Minnesota? His name was Zimmerman.
> DYLAN: Yeah.[124]

Even Baez, Dylan's former girlfriend and fellow folk icon, could stoop to using Dylan's Jewish name as a teasing put-down. A more benign example is the first Dylan fan magazine in America, launched in 1975 by Brian Stibal. At first Stibal called it TBZB: *Talkin' Bob Zimmerman Blues*, and

Record cover of *Robert Zimmerman vs. A. J. Weberman—Grudge Match!* (1988).

then from 1976 to 1979 he shortened the title to *Zimmerman Blues.* A similar title would later be used by Dave Engel in his book about Dylan's origins, *Just Like Bob Zimmerman's Blues: Dylan in Minnesota.*[125] In sum, these all use the name Zimmerman as a way to contravene Dylan's assimilatory gesture of changing his name.

Ironically, Dylan would cite it himself: in his Grammy-winning song "Gotta Serve Somebody," on the 1979 album *Slow Train Coming,* he sings, "You may call me Bobby, you may call me Zimmy." The fact that this bit of self-exposure came during his Christian phase may be pure coincidence, but the subsequent response of his fans was not. Indicating their awareness of his "true identity," the makers of bootleg recordings of Dylan's music began to use Zimmerman quite frequently in their offerings: for example, *The Zim's Picnic* (1979), *Zimmerman's Joy* (1983), *Zimmerman: Ten of Swords* (1985), *Young Zimmerman* (1986), *Robert Zimmerman vs. A. J. Weberman—Grudge Match!* (1988), *Zim Zim Zabob* (1988), *Dr. Zimmerman's Original Oldtime Hootenanny* (1989), *You May Call Me Zimmy* (1997), and *It Ain't Me Babe—Zimmerman Framed—The Songs of Bob Dylan* (2001).

The 1988 record *Robert Zimmerman vs. A. J. Weberman—Grudge Match!* was a reissue of the earlier *Bob Dylan vs. A. J. Weberman,* which had been pulled from production after the threat of legal action by Dylan's people; so the new release likely replaced the name Dylan with Zimmerman as a way to avoid such censure. But at the same time, the new version was packaged with some telling cover art: caricatures of **193**

Dylan and Weberman (the latter made to look like a pig) on either side of a prominent Star of David, with smaller Jewish stars bordering the top and bottom. Despite the legal issues, therefore, this renamed record was a clear example of Jewhooing. *Dr. Zimmerman's Original Oldtime Hootenanny* had no such ambiguity; its alternate title, as printed inside on the disc, was *Who You Really Are*. Likewise, Bob Spitz's 1989 biography titled its opening section simply, "Zimmy."

Jewhooing Dylan's Body

Besides the use of Bob Dylan's name as a form of Jewhooing, others would assert his Jewishness through the visual representation of his physical appearance. At least four physical characteristics can be cited to mark Dylan as a Jew. First, he has been said to have a "Jewish nose"—a stereotypical attribute all too often seen as negative. As historian Sander Gilman writes, "In popular and medical imagery, the nose came to be the sign of the pathological Jewish character. . . . But how could one eliminate the symptom of the 'nostrility' of the Jew, that sign which everyone at the close of the nineteenth century associated with the Jew's visibility?"[126] The association of a certain shape of nose with Jewishness has not diminished in the more recent past, and Dylan's profile has been implicated.

Second, Dylan's famously unruly and curly hair may be read as a particularly Jewish look, and in fact he has been credited as the inspiration for the "Jewfro" hairstyle. These first two Jewish-associated traits were often linked in the antisemitic context of nineteenth-century Europe, as noted by the proto-Zionist writer Moses Hess: "The Germans hate less the religion of the Jews than their race, less their peculiar beliefs than their peculiar noses. . . . Jewish noses cannot be reformed, nor black, curly, Jewish hair be turned through baptism or combing into smooth hair. . . . The Jewish type is indestructible."[127]

Third, Dylan is fairly thin and of small stature, a physical characteristic of many male Jews—who are consequently seen in emasculated or even feminized terms. Fourth, his rough, scratchy singing voice—often cited by those who don't care for his music—can be understood as a "Jewish" trait as well. Early in his career, Dylan's singing was often contrasted unfavorably with more mellifluous—and non-Jewish—crooners such as Andy Williams and Johnny Mathis. All of these traits are referenced in the phenomenon of Jewhooing, that is, in the popular artistic representation of Dylan's physical image, because to those who want to see him as being Jewish, Dylan looks (and sounds) the part.

Dylan must be one of the most photographed popular musicians of all time, so feverish was the scramble to take his picture, both onstage and off. Like so many others in his personal circle, the preponderance of photographers to whom he gave access were fellow Jews—but like him, they tended to be reticent about their own Jewishness. Elliott Landy, for example, responded to a correspondence on this question as follows: "I really have none other [response] than he may have felt comfortable with people whose background was in some way close to his. We never talked about being Jewish, nor did I think about me being Jewish nor Him being Jewish. It never came up at all, even in casual conversations or observations of other people. For our relationship, the concept of being Jewish or religion just did not exist."[128] Yet for the cover of *Nashville Skyline* (1969), Landy photographed Dylan in a black hat looking for all the world like an Orthodox Jewish *yeshiva bocher* (religious student).[129]

Of course, an artist need not be aware of the allusive qualities of his or her own work. The same is true for other Dylan photographers, such as John Cohen, Don Hunstein, Barry Feinstein, Daniel Kramer, Jerry Schatzberg, and Sandy Speiser.[130] The best known of their photographic images of Dylan are those that became the iconic covers of his record albums: Hunstein is responsible for the covers of *Bob Dylan* (1962) and *The Freewheelin' Bob Dylan* (1963); Feinstein for *The Times They Are A-Changin'* (1964); Speiser for *Another Side of Bob Dylan* (1964); Kramer for *Bringing It All Back Home* (1965) and *Highway 61 Revisited* (1965); Schatzberg for *Blonde on Blonde* (1966); and Landy for *Nashville Skyline* (1969).[131] Each of these chroniclers took many hundreds more images of Dylan, and each brought his own style to bear.

What these image makers all had in common was the desire to show the "real" Dylan, photographing him not only onstage, but in the dressing room, in the recording studio, on the road, in cafés, and most of all, relaxing at home. These candid depictions have the intention of removing the mask of celebrity, of stripping away the falsity of the public persona to reveal the authentic person behind it. In Dylan's case, this meant portraying him as an ordinary guy rather than a pop star; a reader and a chess player rather than a jet-setting millionaire; and a family man and a friend rather than a solitary recluse. It is also worth noting that Dylan himself had a hand in creating his image. As Kramer relates,

> He is quick to respond to a joke or funny situation, but he is just as quick to fight the smile on his face, as if he did not want to be seen that way. This carried over into the way he saw himself in his pictures. When making

selections, he usually chose the photographs in which he was serious or non-committal. Through his publicity pictures he could have created any kind of Dylan he wanted to. He chose to present a serious one, feeling intuitively that this was the best image for him at that time.[132]

Interestingly, Dylan censored any images depicting him as jokey or playful, though he is often said to be quite funny. While his intention may have been to create an image of himself as a serious artist, the effect was to negate any intimation of humor—a trait often identified with Jews and Jewish culture. Whether serious or humorous, the one image he apparently did not want projected was that of Jewishness. (The only photographic image of the period that does this in explicit fashion is the often-published photo of him at the Wailing Wall, in Jerusalem, as described earlier.) The Jewish photographers who helped him shape his image colluded with him toward that end.

On the other hand, visual artists, working independently and with greater creative leeway, felt no such compunctions. Two key examples are the iconic posters of Dylan created by fellow folk musician Eric von Schmidt in 1965 and graphic artist Milton Glaser in 1966. As David Hajdu describes it, Schmidt was commissioned by Joan Baez's manager Manny Greenhill "to do a painting of Baez and Dylan for a tour poster." The result was "lovely and ingenious, a Lautrec-influenced watercolor designed for silk-screening." The poster has since become one of the best-known items of early 1960s Dylan memorabilia. But according to Hajdu, Dylan rejected the image at the time, reportedly because he "thought Joan's face was too big and too much in the foreground, and he thought Eric had made his nose look too big."[133] Although it's possible that this was only an aesthetic judgment on Dylan's part, it seems more likely that he was reacting to the implied Jewishness of his profile as portrayed by his friend Schmidt.

As the founder of Push Pin Studios, Glaser is one of the most influential figures in contemporary graphic design. His Dylan poster, widely distributed as an insert in *Bob Dylan's Greatest Hits* (1967), is perhaps his second most recognizable graphic image (after the ubiquitous "I Love NY" logo). It was later added to the collection of the Museum of Modern Art and has graced the covers of numerous books, including Glaser's own collected works. Said to be inspired by a self-portrait of Marcel Duchamp and also by Islamic painting, Dylan is drawn in black silhouette. But boldly framing the blackened profile is a shock of wavy psychedelic hair, and it is the hair that one first sees. The multicolored tangle jumps out in stark contrast to the black silhouette of Dylan's face. As Glaser intended, the image captured the Sixties in all its countercultural glory.

The motif would continue to characterize artistic representations of Dylan, as for example, 1960s-era graphic art by Cathy Endfield, Martin Sharp, Michael Foreman, and Peter Max. In general, Dylan artwork of that period tends to highlight his frizzy mop of unruly hair, a style that later came to be known as a Jewfro. Although the Beatles are usually credited for introducing long hair as the reigning style of the youth culture, Bob Dylan deserves credit as well. In his case, however, hair also has ethnic associations (much like its parallel in black culture, the Afro), so its use as a visual symbol of the counterculture might be understood to reflect the inherent Jewishness of the 1960s in addition to a general sense of liberation.

Though the psychedelic hair is most noticeable, the other half of Glaser's image has the more resonant intonation of Dylan's Jewish identity. Portraying Dylan's face in black silhouette meant, first of all, that the most personal aspect of his identity would be enshrouded in mystery. Glaser's graphic conception thus splits Dylan's celebrity image into public and private halves, the former externalized through his magical music and performances, the latter internalized in the inscrutability of his words and thoughts. At the same time, the view in profile also highlights the shape of Dylan's nose, by all accounts the "hooked" nose associated with Jewish physiognomy. That is, by all accounts but Dylan's—in 1961 he made the following statement: "Did I ever tell ya I got my nose from the Indian blood in my veins? Well, that's the truth, hey. Got an uncle who's a Sioux."[134] But to most observers, the ethnic import of Dylan's nose is clear. As noted by Nora Ephron and Susan Edmiston in 1965, "He looked like an underfed angel with a nose from the land of the Chosen People."[135] When asked if he had meant to inscribe Jewishness into his image of Dylan, Glaser replied, "[N]ot intentionally, but you never know what lies in the subconscious."[136] This is made plausible by the simple fact that Glaser is Jewish himself.

The significance of the nose becomes further apparent upon review of Dylan art and graphic representation. In March of 1972, caricaturist Robert Grossman was commissioned to illustrate the cover of *Rolling Stone* magazine for a feature on Dylan. He created a dual portrait of Dylan, in which his earlier incarnation as a Greenwich Village folkie stares dolefully from the background at the more recent version of Dylan in the foreground, looking equally melancholy. In addition to the mournful eyes, both images are notable for their oversized noses, the one on

Dage i Dylan (Denmark, 2001). The 1997 cover illustration by Per Marquard Otzen is a prime example of caricatured portrayals of Dylan verging on antisemitism.

DAGE I DYLAN

Genhør med Mr. Tambourine Man - Redigeret af Torben Bille

Informations Forlag

the contemporary Dylan especially prominent and distended. If the artist were not named Grossman, and the journal not a loyal chronicler of Dylan, the image might be read as a demeaning caricature of antisemitic intent. Other images emphasizing Dylan's nose may be found on the March 1976 issue of *Zigzag* magazine, and on the cover of the 1976 bootleg album *Passed Over and Rolling Thunder*. And again, in both cases the exaggerated nose brands him a Jew. The Jewish overtones of these images attain a more unsettlingly antisemitic tone with a series of European bootleg illustrations beginning in the 1980s: *Holy Soul and Jelly Roll* (1986), *Dollar Snack* (1986), *Dreams* (1987), *The Real Voice of America* (1994), as well as a 1997 Danish book illustration all depict an uglified, big-nosed version of Dylan in the antisemitic tradition of *Der Sturmer*.[137] However disturbing these images may be, they nonetheless reveal the commonplace perception of Dylan as a Jew.

One plan for a more positive and celebratory Jewish representation of Dylan turned out to be an opportunity lost. In the late 1970s, art dealer Ronald Feldman commissioned Andy Warhol to create a series of images of famous Jews, the collection known as *Ten Portraits of Jews in the Twentieth Century*. Warhol referred to them as his "Jewish geniuses," and the list initially included Dylan, who he knew personally and thought a good choice to represent Jews in music, but alas, the 1960s figure was dropped in favor of fellow Jewish composer George Gershwin. As Warhol explained in August 1979, "I think they were considering Bob Dylan but I read that he turned born-again Christian."[138] But contrary to Warhol's recollection, Christian conversion was not in itself a disqualifying factor, as Feldman recalled it differently: "Dylan had become a born-again Christian, and [his] and Warhol's research had turned up the fact that Sarah Bernhardt, whom they had already settled on, had converted to Catholicism—'so we already had that.'"[139] In either event, the canonization of Dylan by Warhol was not to be.

By the mid-1990s, however, the art world was ready for a Jewish image of Dylan, as seen in Kenneth Goldsmith's 1995 work titled *Bob Dylan*. At its center is a graphic reproduction of an early photographic image of a pensive-looking Dylan—borrowed from the cover of his fourth album, *Another Side of Bob Dylan* (1964)—surrounded by upended Hebrew letters and smaller portraits of fellow 1960s icons and fellow Jews Allen Ginsberg and Abbie Hoffman. As a youth in suburban New York, Goldsmith had "experienced anti-Semitic assaults which intensified his feeling of otherness. Looking for ethnically specific role models, he became enthralled with the counterculture [of the 1960s], whose ranks included numerous Jews." In this painting, as in a series he created along similar lines, "he honors Jewish heroes of this epoch in American history such as Abbie Hoffman and Bob Dylan, *seeking to identify with the ethnic aspect of their highly public personas*."[140] In 1996, the work was included in the Jewish Museum of New York exhibition *Too Jewish? Challenging Traditional Identities*. To be further explored in the final chapter, the exhibition was a high-water mark of Jewhooing. Clearly, the times were a-changin' for public Jewish identification, when Bob Dylan could be Jewhoo-ed by a highbrow art museum.

Jewhooing Dylan through Performance

All of the sources just mentioned exemplify the Jewhooing of Bob Dylan either by reading Jewishness into his words and music, or by simply seeing the man himself (whether by his name or by his looks) in Jewish terms, defining him as a Jew. Yet another type would take a significant

step farther—a form of Jewhooing in which the observer becomes a
participant, not just seeing the man in Jewish terms, but now taking a
direct part in the performance of Dylan's (supposed) Jewish identity. The
phenomenon may have had its start in Israel, where, in the wake of the
1973 Yom Kippur War—Israel's Vietnam—young Israelis created their
own version of the American counterculture, and in so doing, often appropriated the image of the most famous Jew of the 1960s, Bob Dylan.
One example was the Argentinian-born folksinger Shlomo Ydov, who,
curly-haired and bearded, resembled Dylan in appearance as well as musical intent. His 1973 hit "Yaldei ha-Yareach" (Children of the Moon)
was an ode to the culture of youthful rebellion. It begins, "They left their
parents, as had Donovan and Dylan," and adds, "They learned the truth
from Lenny Bruce, [Allen] Ginsberg, and the writings on the subway
walls [a reference to Simon and Garfunkel]."[141]

The title of "the Israeli Bob Dylan" best refers to Yonatan Geffen, who
looked even more like Dylan than did Ydov, with a mop of curly hair
and prominent nose. Geffen is an Israeli icon—the nephew of Moshe
Dayan and father of pop star Aviv Geffen—whose rise to fame in the
1970s echoed Dylan's in many ways, especially in his multiple roles of
poet, musician, and muse of the counterculture. Following the Yom Kippur War, Geffen and fellow musician Dani Litani created a show titled
Zeh haKol Beintayim, Beintayim zeh haKol (That's all for now, For now
that's all), which was intended to be a one-time performance, but given
the enthusiastic public response, ran for over 600 nights. The program
they put together, "inspired by the protest songs of the Sixties," included
several Dylan classics translated into Hebrew by Geffen: "Blowin' in the
Wind," "Girl from the North Country," "Masters of War," and "A Hard
Rain's A-Gonna Fall."[142] Thus, through the medium of Yonatan Geffen,
Dylan's music and persona were transposed into the Jewish culture of
Israel. And like Ydov, Geffen also drew a connection between Dylan and
Lenny Bruce—by interspersing his Dylan songs with monologues based
on famous Bruce routines such as "To is a Preposition; Come is a Verb,"
"Jewish and Goyish," and "Jews Killed Christ." Somewhat like Bruce's
Bavarian mimic routine and like Dylan's appropriation of Woody Guth-
rie, this demonstrates the form of Jewhooing in which one performer
channels another.

One of the first to do this in America was comedian Richard Belzer,
who, in the late 1970s, began to incorporate a "tribute" to Dylan in his
standup routine. He later described it in a radio interview with Terry
Gross:

[W]hen I was a *teenager*, and was first getting into Bob Dylan, then we found out his real name is *Zimmerman*, and he's a *Jew*, from *Minne*soht*aa*, and this was like a *revelation*, to have a hero that's a *Jew*—So I said, if his name's Zimmerman, he must have had a bar mitzvah. So I fantasized what Bob Dylan's bar mitzvah must have been like. [In a clogged nasal voice] "Ah, Baruh Atah Ado*noi* Elohenu Meleh ha*olam*, asher kidshanu b'mitzvo-*tah*—" And then he gets *older*: "Oy! Oy!" [In an especially cranky, clogged nasal voice] "Vonce upon a tame, ya dreshed so fine, ya t'rew da bums a dime in ya prime—[and then in a triumphantly I-told-you-so clogged nasal voice] DIDN'T YA! People call, shed b'ware doll ya bound ta fall, you t'ought dey was all, KIDDIN' YA!"¹⁴³

The routine, amusing on the page but blisteringly funny in performance, can be viewed in a 1978 clip preserved on the YouTube website. Belzer's comic conceit of imagining Dylan as both a bar mitzvah boy and a crotchety old Jewish man—à la Mel Brooks's 2,000-year-old man—not only is hilarious, but also presents a new twist on the Jewhooing tradition. Beyond pointing out Dylan's Jewish background, and in addition to subtly criticizing his apparent assimilation, the routine further transports Dylan into a past and future of Jewish possibility—making him appear more Jewish than he ever would or could be.

Belzer included the routine in his act for years, and later wrote a comedic song for Dylan as well. As performed in his 1997 HBO special *Another Lone Nut*, Belzer introduces "The Ballad of Bob Dylan" by lauding the creative output of the songwriter, adding, "but there isn't one song to explain the mystery of Bob Dylan, and I would like to nominate this song for that very purpose." Sung from Dylan's point of view, in a Dylan-esque voice, the chorus is, "Well, I'm a skinny Jew, one of the few, from Minnesota, they had a quota." Clever rhyme, and it cleverly makes the point that Dylan was an anomaly, a Jew from the heartland. Belzer, a Jew from Connecticut, turned *himself* into the joke, anomalously performing as Dylan.

"And played it pretendin' ": Contemporary Dylan Jewhooing
The most recent phase in the Jewhooing of Bob Dylan began in the late 1980s.¹⁴⁴ The canonization process was about to ensue (as mentioned earlier, with his induction into the Rock and Roll Hall of Fame in 1988), and in 1987, he had once again visited Israel; this time, to perform publicly and with great fanfare. In a 1989 biography—itself an example of Jewhooing, and thus poorly regarded by most Dylan scholars—Bob

Spitz frames his study with vivid accounts of Dylan's concert appearances in Israel. Here he is portrayed as a Jewish returnee, representing to the Jewish people nothing less than their long-awaited messiah:

> Was this any way for the Chosen People to live? Especially after waiting all this time for the Messiah? For twenty-five years they'd expected Him— *twenty-five years*! And all the time they remained faithful, undoubting, singing his praise. . . . Dylan had never played in Israel before, although his popularity there was enormous. In Israel, he was a true folk hero, a living legend celebrated under two different names: *Dylan*, the elusive superstar, and *Zimmerman*, the elusive Jew. "Robert Zimmerman—" one of the newspapers gushed with anticipation, "the people of Israel, your countrymen, welcome you!"

Spitz adds that "Israel hadn't witnessed such an extravaganza since . . . well, since Barbra Streisand's visit in the early 1970s."[145] So much for the question of ethnic pride—like Streisand, Dylan has become an exemplar of Jewish fame and success. But then we are led to ask, how has this impacted the Jewish identity of those so willing to idolize him? Given that he does not present any sort of normative model of Jewish behavior, what does our knowledge of his Jewish background communicate, and how does it further resonate? While Israelis responded to the sheer ethnicity of a world-conquering "Jewish hero" (though Spitz also notes the context of the late-1980s peace movement in Israel, in which many looked to Dylan as a symbol of antiwar activism), Jews living in the American diaspora may have had a more complex relationship to their own Jewishness, and hence, to Dylan's.

The 1990s ushered in a new era in Dylan Jewhooing as Dylan's iconic status continued to grow. In 1991, Larry Yudelson published an article in the *Washington Jewish Week* titled "Bob Dylan: Tangled Up In Jews," and subsequently posted the piece on the Internet—the website became the first fan site devoted entirely to Dylan's Jewishness.[146] Yudelson, who describes himself as "both a Dylanologist and a Jew," is a contemporary version of Stephen Pickering. His web page, as he writes, "is devoted to studying and collecting trivia relating to the Jewish religious/cultural odyssey of Shabtai Zisel ben Avraham v'Rachel Riva, a.k.a Bob Dylan." Yudelson lists "highlights of Dylan's Judaic journeys" by decade:

> Changing his name from Zimmerman in the early '60s
> Considering moving to a kibbutz in the early '70s.

Converting to born-again Christianity in the late '70s.
Studying with Lubavitch Hasidim in the early '80s.[147]

By the turn of the twenty-first century, a series of new books would locate Dylan in a Jewish context. The first was a biographical treatment of his formative years in Minnesota, Dave Engel's *Just Like Bob Zimmerman's Blues: Dylan in Minnesota* (1997). Dylan turned sixty in 2001, and as the process of canonization accelerated, the Jewhooing trend exploded as well. Several books of the period established the genre of Rock 'n' Roll Jewhooing, all of which highlighted Dylan as a matter of course: Michael Billig's *Rock 'n' roll Jews* (2000), Guy Oseary's *Jews Who Rock* (2001), Scott Benarde's *Stars of David: Rock 'n' Roll's Jewish Stories* (2003), and Janet Macoska's *Jews Rock! A Celebration of Rock and Roll's Jewish Heritage* (2008).[148] Regarding Dylan, Billig writes, "In his musical and spiritual quest, Dylan also seems to have been something of a Wandering Jew. He did not remain locked within born-again Christianity. He went through a Jewish phase . . . [and] was later photographed at the Western Wall in Jerusalem, wearing tallit (prayer shawl) and tefillin (phylacteries) on the occasion of his son's Bar Mitzvah."[149]

The current period has also seen a resurgence of Jewhooing performance art. Like Richard Belzer, other Jewish comedians such as Gilbert Gottfried and Sandra Bernhard have also made reference to Dylan in their routines, but the most significant performer of Dylan's Jewishness was not a comedian but a cantor—Jeff Klepper. Growing up listening to folk music, Klepper became a musician early, especially entranced by Pete Seeger. It was only natural that he took on the role of song leader in Reform Jewish summer camp, where he "helped to create a new style of song-leading and composition in Jewish camps and youth groups beginning in the late 1960s."[150] Klepper subsequently became a leading figure in the creation of contemporary Jewish liturgical music. He is also a huge Dylan fan, writing, "We have been blessed to live at the same time as Bob Dylan, who turned 60 in 2001, ('ad meiah v'esrim,' Bob, may you live to 120, staying forever young!) and to derive meaning and insight from his boundless creativity."[151]

Around 1974, inspired by the *Planet Waves* album and Dylan's return to concert touring, Klepper began giving informal classes at camp called Jewish Dylanology. He played (what was then) a rare bootleg recording of "Talkin' Hava Nagilah Blues," and "discussed Dylan's Jewish background and pointed out Jewish and Biblical references in songs such as 'Highway 61' and 'Forever Young.'" In a thoughtful and wide-ranging response to an interview query, Klepper elaborates on the process by which he came to write Jewish-themed parodies of Dylan songs:

> Along with (or maybe because of) so much serious commentary on Dylan's work, has come an extraordinary amount of satire and caricature, much of it focusing on Dylan's idiosyncratic singing voice and vocal phrasing. Many of his songs have been parodied (with varied results) in order to express a political opinion, or simply for fun. Parodies of popular songs have been around for centuries, so my own attempt to write several Dylan parodies beginning in the late 1980s was hardly noteworthy. But, as a cantor, I wrote my parodies from a Jewish perspective . . . My initial attempt with Dylan material began as an idea that I would impersonate Bob Dylan for my synagogue's Purim shpiel. I called a friend who had written his own Purim parodies in years past, and he agreed to work with me on the Dylan project. When the idea for "Just Like a Chazn" to the tune of "Just Like a Woman" popped into my head, I realized that I could comment on Dylan's own Jewish identity by imagining how Yiddish and Hebrew phrases would sound in his voice. What's more, in the guise of Dylan as "protest" singer, I could spoof aspects of Jewish life that were ripe for satire.[152]

As a Jewish musician, Klepper clearly has been inspired by Dylan's example—but more than that, he is a Jewish Dylan impersonator, with a little Allan Sherman mixed in. He adds, "From the initial batch I kept the two or three best ones, and kept working on them for several years until I had ten or so. Then I did a whole concert as Dylan, with guitar and harmonica, which was recorded."[153] He called his one-man show *Like A Rolling Cohen*—after the title of his takeoff of Dylan's 1965 classic "Like a Rolling Stone." The show also included parodies of "Tangled Up in Blue" ("Tangled Up in Jews"), "Knockin' on Heaven's Door" ("Hockin' Me Til I'm Sore"), "Ballad of a Thin Man" ("Do you, Dr. Cohen?"), and "Rainy Day Women #12 & 35" ("Rainy Day Shabbes #1836").

Several more of Klepper's Jewish rewrites of classic Dylan songs can be heard on a 2002 album of his live performances, *Jewish Music For The Masses*: for example, "Stuck Inside of Monsey with the Brooklyn Blues Again" (takeoff of "Stuck Inside of Mobile with the Memphis Blues Again"), "Cantillation Row" ("Desolation Row"), "High Holy Day Blues" ("It Takes a Lot To Laugh, It Takes a Train to Cry"), and "Just Like a Chazzn" ("Just Like a Woman"). Klepper even includes his own version of "Talkin' Havah Nagilah Blues," which he explains as follows: "Since this is the only 'Hebrew song' Bob has ever recorded I had to cover it here. His publisher told me I am the first person besides Bob to sing it on a record. Back in 1961 (when hardly anybody suspected Bob was Jewish) it seems to have been a satire on the prevalence of poorly sung ethnic songs performed by coffee house singers in Greenwich Village." Equally telling are the liner notes explaining the inspiration for each song. For example, regarding "Cantillation Row," Klepper writes, "Bob Dylan's 'Desolation Row' is one of the greatest songs ever written. It peels away layers of reality to reveal the absurdity lurking beneath the surface of our consciousness. I've tried to do the same thing here with the inner workings of a modern day synagogue. I hope I'm not telling secrets out of shul. When I sing this, it's rabbis and cantors who laugh the hardest, and I think I know why."[154]

Demonstrating the high degree of identification that Jewish fans feel with their idol, Klepper also describes the nature of his own attachment to Dylan: "Personally I feel a kinship with Bob Dylan, the Jewish kid with a guitar who had a vision and stayed true to it in spite of hardship, self-doubt, and the pitfalls of showbiz and fame." But at the same time, he remains aware of Dylan's more elusive nature: "I couldn't ask for a better comic foil for my parodies, knowing that the reason they are funny is that Dylan himself is so private and enigmatic."[155] Perhaps the best example of Klepper's combination of fan-like attachment and critical detachment is his spoken introduction to "Just Like a Chazzn." Imitating Dylan's voice, and thus speaking as Dylan, he relates, "I can tell you now a little secret. I always wanted to be a cantor . . . and they wouldn't let me. Joined a little shul in, uh, Los Angeles, and they wouldn't let me be the cantor . . . I asked if I could blow the shofar . . . and they said, 'you know how to do that?' I said, well, I'd have to do it on the harmonica [blows sh'varim on the harmonica] . . . they turned me down. So I, I just like to sing with the cantor, whenever I can."[156] The effect is hilarious, nicely displaying Klepper's ability to both "channel" Dylan and project Jewishness onto him; to both honor his hero and, in a kind of tongue-in-cheek wish fulfillment, gently mock Dylan's lack of overt Jewish religiosity, all at the same time.

Another Jewish super-fan who "plays" Dylan is musician Joel Gilbert. Founder of "Highway 61 Revisited—the world's only Bob Dylan Tribute Band," Gilbert is the world's foremost Dylan impersonator—or, as he prefers to call it, "a *recreator* of Dylan's great stage shows and music." Discovering a love for Dylan while studying at the University of London, Gilbert recalls,

I was so transfixed with the power and majesty of his performances in *Don't Look Back*, that I was driven to feel it within myself by recreating it. I also noticed that Dylan's speaking voice was similar to mine—so I thought "if I talked like Dylan, maybe I could sing like him too?" So back I went to the Camden Lock Market, now purchasing every Dylan bootleg tape I could find. As I learned song after song, I realized I could experience the same magic I felt watching Dylan. This joyous feeling still exists for me, even some 500 shows later of performing with my Dylan tribute band, Highway 61 Revisited.[157]

But Gilbert is more than a Dylan imitator—he is a Dylanologist. He first published a music instruction book titled *The Acoustic Bob Dylan, His Music Styles and Guitar Techniques*. Then, as a documentary filmmaker, he has produced and directed five documentaries on various aspects of Dylan's career, including *Bob Dylan World Tours, 1966–1974: Through The Camera Of Barry Feinstein* (2004), *Bob Dylan 1975–1981: Rolling Thunder and The Gospel Years* (2006), and *Inside Bob Dylan's Jesus Years: Busy Being Born . . . Again!* (2008). In each, Gilbert tracks his own search for the truth of Bob Dylan by visiting sites of Dylan's life and interviewing figures associated with Dylan's early years, such as Ramblin' Jack Elliott, Izzy Young, Barry Feinstein, Jerry Wexler, and, of all people, A. J. Weberman. That the last two films just cited concerned Dylan's Christian phase might seem at odds with yet another interest of Gilbert's—the Jewish experience. Yet as he describes the films, both "go very deep into the theme of Jews, Jews for Jesus, and Dylan's Jewish roots, how he reconciled that with evangelical Christianity and then his subsequent return to Judaism."[158]

In my interview with him, Gilbert expanded on the theme of his personal affinity with Dylan. Just like Dylan, he had a bar mitzvah, attended Jewish summer camp, and spent time in Israel. Moreover, he notes that "there is certainly some coincidental physical resemblance. Both Dylan and I have unique and similar Jewish backgrounds—Ashkenazi on our father's sides and Sephardic on our mother's side." Echoing Belzer's comedic impersonation of Dylan, Gilbert adds that "the older he gets, the more he looks and sounds like an old Jewish grandpa type. A. J. Weberman put it best when he said 'Dylan was a folk rocka, but now he's an Alta Cocka.'" He further recalls how "Dylan's songs seemed comfortable and familiar as he was from a similar background as myself—Hibbing Minnesota is a small population town in the Midwest, with one synagogue and a few Jewish kids in each grade. Oak Ridge, Tennessee where I'm from is identical, except it is in the South. I identified many themes in his early material that I felt were influenced by a Jewish, small town upbringing." Due to their shared Jewishness, Gilbert asserts that he "can understand many themes in his music that are not readily understood by non-Jews," and adds, "Though I don't really believe in such things, someone told me once that Dylan and I were 'channeling from the same cosmic source.'" Yet he's careful to state that "everyone sees Dylan through their own mirror or life experience. Very simply, he is whatever Dylan you want him to be." Nonetheless, Gilbert admits that "Dylan's Jewish fans seem to identify with him even more so because of his faith."[159] Certainly, Gilbert is a key example of this phenomenon.

Yet another contemporary Jewish fan and interpreter of Dylan is Seth Rogovoy. Rogovoy is a self-described "writer, award-winning critic, book author, lecturer, teacher, musician, and radio commentator," who "frequently writes about Jewish music and culture for publications including *Forward*, *Hadassah* Magazine, and the *Berkshire Jewish Voice*." As the author of *The Essential Klezmer: A Music Lover's Guide to Jewish Roots and Soul Music* (2000), Rogovoy is a leading expert on the Klezmer revival of the past two decades. His other area of expertise is the music of Dylan, having "taught a variety of college-level and adult-ed courses on klezmer, Jewish music, and Bob Dylan, about whom he has written extensively" and as "a singer-guitarist and leader of several bands, including the Rolling Rogovoy Revue and Seth Rogovoy and the Grove Street Band. He frequently performs at . . . Bob Dylan tribute concerts throughout the Northeast United States."[160]

Rogovoy has now drawn on his experience as a Jewish musicologist and rock critic to write a full-length study of Dylan as a Jew. In my correspondence with him, Rogovoy explained that he had first discovered Dylan in the early 1970s as an adolescent on suburban Long Island. Interestingly, he recalls that he "knew he was Jewish, I assume, from the very beginning, as that just would have been known in my home, plus Dylan made that explicit in the liner notes to [his 1974 album] *Planet Waves* ('Hebrew letters in the wall,' 'Jacob's ladder,' etc.)." When Dylan adopted Christianity at the end of the decade, Rogovoy "was very upset, [and] felt personally betrayed, when he 'became a Christian,' as we all assumed when *Slow Train Coming* was released." But then, in 1983, Dylan released a song with a clear pro-Israel message, and Rogovoy "felt we'd got him back on our side definitely with *Infidels*, with 'Neighborhood Bully.'" Note the phrase "our side"—Rogovoy, like so many Jews of the time, saw the conversion as a defection, from one "team" to another. But in the years since, his view of the matter has evolved: "Now of course I have a totally different understanding of his 'born-again' period, and see it as part of a continuum of Dylan writing and performing in the Jewish prophetic tradition."[161] As for his own motivations for writing a book on the Jewish Dylan, he writes,

> As I studied Jewish scripture in my 30s and 40s, I was constantly coming across passages and stories and lines and themes that I recognized from Dylan songs. (I knew the Torah of Bob Dylan better than the Torah of Moses at that point.)
>
> The more I learned about the Jewish prophetic tradition, the more I could identify that Dylan not only drew from the Prophets extensively, but that his work could best be appreciated seen as part of that tradition (if not necessarily divinely inspired, certainly inspired).
>
> With a solid command of Dylan and Judaism, as well as [being] a previously published music historian, I realized I was uniquely qualified to write this book, which has never been written.
>
> In the process of writing it I simply discovered that Dylan's depth of familiarity with the most intricate details of Biblical stories and prophecy knows no bounds, and his artistry in putting these stories and themes and quotations through his own midrashic process and reinventing them as Bob Dylan songs is astonishing.[162]

It is Stephen Pickering redux, yet another intensive and obsessive reading of Dylan's words through the prism of Jewish Scripture. And yet, even in this time of relatively unembarrassed Jewishness, the editors of Rogovoy's book have demonstrated some hesitance over the Jewish emphasis of the work. The book's title is *Bob Dylan: Prophet, Mystic, Poet*; yet Rogovoy and his publisher had at one point considered the far more telling subtitle *Prophet, Mystic, Jew*. The author would not venture a guess as to why this change was made, but apparently someone is still concerned, at this point in time, with sounding "too Jewish." The book, published in 2009, is the most sustained exploration of the Jewish element of Dylan's work to date.[163]

Klepper, Gilbert, and Rogovoy are all singular examples of the kind of Dylan Jewhooing in which identification is taken to an extreme—but as Jewish fans of a Jewish Dylan, they are merely the tip of the iceberg. Dylan's fan base has always had more than its fair share of Jews, and an especially common type of Dylan fan is the Jewish male baby boomer. This cohort of Jewish men generally discovered Dylan in high school or college and followed his lead (ironic, given Dylan's admonition not to follow leaders in "Subterranean Homesick Blues") into the 1960s youth culture. They were active participants in the counterculture, and today they are the cream of the crop of Dylan fans, still attending Dylan concerts well into middle age (Dylan, having passed his seventieth birthday, continues to tour). And much like their idol, many have succeeded in American culture while struggling all the while with their Jewish identity. Some remain unreconstructed assimilationists, while others have found their way to a more engaged Jewish life; but all continue to see in Dylan their generation's ideal of an identifiable Jew being accepted as fully American.

In the early twenty-first century, therefore, the Jewishness of Bob Dylan has become apparent to most. Perhaps the Jewish association most often cited by Jewhooing Dylan fans is his son-in-law since 1988, Peter Himmelman, also a singer-songwriter, but unlike Dylan, an Orthodox Jew. Of course, we can only imagine the effect that having an observant member of the family may have had on Dylan—but we can more easily ascertain the salience of this particular Jewish connection to many Jewish fans. When the subject of Dylan's Jewishness comes up, as often as not, the name Peter Himmelman is cited to demonstrate that yes indeed, Dylan has some Judaism in his life.

Another common citing of such "proof" takes place when people share stories of Dylan's various Jewish activities. He bought a synagogue building. He studied at a yeshiva. He showed up at high holiday services. Larry Yudelson relates, "Evidence of his Jewish involvement continues to mount. One friend of mine saw him at a Minneapolis bris [circumcision ceremony]. Another heard he davens at the UCLA Hillel. One writer tells the story of how Dylan attended synagogue in jeans, scruffy beard and a battered hat and was recognized by the rabbi and invited to open the ark. The congregation was abuzz: Why was this apparent bum being honored?"[164] One of the most circulated such stories concerns a Passover seder Dylan attended at Temple Israel of Hollywood in Los Angeles. Asking if he could bring a friend, he showed up with Marlon Brando—who, in turn, brought another guest, Indian activist Dennis Banks, who came in full Native American regalia. Asked by the rabbi to play a song, Dylan complied with "Blowin' in the Wind."[165]

"And the last part": Conclusion

From the moment he was outed as a Jewish boy named Robert Allen Zimmerman—by *Newsweek* magazine in November of 1963—Bob Dylan has been identified in the public eye as a Jew.[166] That is, despite his own protestations, he became a very famous American Jew. Given the extraordinary level of his fame, and the cultural influence of celebrity in general, there is bound to be meaning in that; and the Jewish historian has to wonder whether Dylan will eventually come to be seen as a "great Jew of the twentieth century" despite his own likely aversion to such an ascription.

Indeed, some of the most famous Jews in history have had deeply ambivalent relationships to their own Jewishness, sometimes rejecting it outright. Thus a recent book on the Enlightenment philosopher Benedict Spinoza has the provocative subtitle, "The Renegade Jew Who Gave Us Modernity."[167] It joins a tradition of historical studies of highly assimilated Jews who, the authors maintain, can be understood only in the context of their Jewish backgrounds.[168] However suppressed or mitigated in later life, the Jewish identities of such figures as Karl Marx, Sigmund Freud, Franz Kafka and Albert Einstein are, they suggest, determinative. Hence, the figure of genius—of Jewish birth—is claimed by Jewish history. Like Spinoza, Dylan changed his original Jewish name (Baruch to Benedict and Zimmerman to Dylan) and then, as he rose to fame, thoroughly disassociated himself from the Jewish community and its concerns. Like Spinoza, he was a seminal figure in Western cultural history whose role in the creation of a new consciousness derives, in some measure at least, from the initial distancing from his Jewish heritage. And like the recent book on Spinoza, a study of Dylan might very well have as its subtitle, "The Renegade Jew Who Gave Us the Sixties."

The assimilatory impulse, the attempt to escape from Jewishness, is evident in Dylan's celebrity (if not in the man himself), and our understanding of American Jews' reaction to him begins and ends with that basic fact. In the end, might it be that Dylan's assimilation *is* the Jewish behavior of his with which so many have identified? But if so, there was something different about his assimilatory path, something that gave Jews of that generation a clue as to the path they might take. Even as he rebelled against his Jewish past, Dylan also rejected the conventional alternative, the goal of joining the American majority and entering the cultural mainstream. He broke the mold on either end, carving out a third path by refusing to capitulate to either Jewish expectations or American norms. Dylan made no direct contribution to the Jewish revival of the post–Six Day War era, yet his contribution may have been substantial nonetheless. For in so definitively rejecting the old American dream of "joining the club," he showed Jews—and other outsiders—a way off the treadmill of assimilation.

Bob Dylan was hardly the first Jewish intellectual in modern history to proclaim his total liberation from his roots while refusing to join the established culture; nor was he the first to whom a generation of Jewish souls hearkened—Heine, Marx, and Freud come to mind, for example. But Dylan was the first to do so in a way that both rejected the culture and celebrated it at once. He did so in his view of America: dismissive of its limitations, but glorying in its liberating potential. A similar duality can be seen in his connection to Jewishness, simultaneously rejecting and relating to it—the latter often oblique and perhaps even unintentional on his part, but there is a relationship nonetheless. For his was a *Jewish* success story—in the eyes, anyway, of his fellow Jews—and in the context of this study of Jewish celebrity, that's what counts. Despite his own denials, Dylan is undeniably a famous Jew—one who became famous while singing "Havah Nagilah" to other Jews in New York City—and, at a time when fellow Jewish artists like Barbra Streisand were hitting it big as well. It is precisely this context—his cohort of fellow famous Jews—that gives Bob Dylan an implicit Jewishness, despite his own protestations to the contrary.

Thus, Dylan makes an intriguing comparison with Sandy Koufax and Lenny Bruce. Whereas Koufax is a Jewish hero with no real Jewish content, and Bruce has an ambivalent celebrity image among Jews despite his significant Jewish content, Dylan seems to be a far more elusive figure on both counts: Is he a Jewish hero, or not? Does his work and life contain meaningful Jewishness, or not? In the final analysis, the answer must remain inconclusive. In this chapter, I have attempted to demonstrate the extreme nature of both characteristics of Jewish celebrity in Dylan—his extraordinary urge to escape from Jewishness, on the one hand, and the extraordinary urge of others to see him as a Jew, on the other.

Our fourth case study, of Barbra Streisand, will offer yet another type of Jewish celebrity. Like Koufax, she is an unequivocal Jewish hero; like Bruce, her creative output is filled with Jewish content; and like Dylan, she evokes all the ironies and ambiguities of a skinny Jewish nerd attaining superstardom. Yet unlike them all, Streisand consciously and purposefully exploited her Jewishness in the construction of her celebrity. She is also the only woman in the group—might there be some connection between her gender and her explicit ethnic identification? That is a question for our next chapter to answer.

Hollywood Jew

Woody Allen, Barbra Streisand, and Bette Midler are something more than celebrities; they are demi-mythic figures, heroes and heroines of mass culture; . . . they have acquired these stations not by underplaying Jewish looks, manners, and backgrounds, and not in spite of them, but precisely by exaggerating these characteristics almost to the point of iconic abstraction. They have become majority heroes by italicizing minority profiles and now reside on the "inside" without seeming to have ever left the "outside."

ALAN SPIEGEL, "The Vanishing Act"

Barbra Streisand's meteoric rise to fame during the early 1960s directly paralleled Dylan's and took place in the very same setting—New York City's Greenwich Village. Just one year younger than Dylan, the eighteen-year-old Streisand had been living in the city for well over a year, struggling for success as a stage actress, by the time Dylan arrived in early 1961. Streisand first came to public attention singing in downtown clubs in the summer and fall of 1960, gained further notice over the next year appearing on television talk shows, and was cast for her first role in a Broadway show in November of 1961. Like Dylan, she succeeded beyond all expectations, becoming a major star in just a few short years.

Dylan and Streisand were both musical prodigies with prodigious talents and ambitions, and their remarkable careers have lasted for half a century—but that's where the similarities end. For one thing, their Jewish trajectories have been radically different, as we shall see. Further, the first several years of Dylan's performing life have remained the most iconic of his career—he is remembered, that's to say, *by* his rise to fame.

213

Streisand, on the other hand, has had a more varied career overall, and her early years in New York City tend to be obscured by her second and third acts in Hollywood and Malibu. Hence controversial feminist critic Camille Paglia could exclaim in 2007: "Oh, Streisand! I'm such a fan of her early work. Today you cannot imagine what it was like when Streisand burst on the scene in the 1960s. There was nothing like her. . . . Barbra Streisand broke the mold, she revolutionized gender roles. How has this been forgotten?"[1]

We begin therefore with a consideration of Streisand's early years, always keeping in mind how the image of the star was conditioned by multiple contexts of the early 1960s: the ethnic revival of Kennedy era America; changes in the nature of fame and celebrity; a marked generational shift in contemporary Jewish life; and perhaps most important, contemporary stereotypes of Jewish women and the emergent feminist movement. Streisand reflected many of these trends in the construction of her own persona, and American Jews responded accordingly, awarding her a unique status as an icon of American Jewish fame, an exemplary blend of Jewish *chutzpah* and American success.

Her most ardent fans—Jewish women and gay men—saw her as the embodiment of the ugly duckling made good, the outsider who conquered the heights of Hollywood stardom and musical superstardom through sheer talent and drive. At the same time, they responded to the dualism of her aesthetic: both *shlemiel* and diva, self-consciously unattractive and glamorously chic, Brooklyn Jewish-whiny and the most beautiful voice in the world—moving from one extreme to the other at will. Many of her film roles highlighted this Jekyll-and-Hyde quality, exemplified most famously—and most Jewishly—by the 1983 film *Yentl*. In life, Streisand neither changed her name nor fixed her nose, and in turn, her singular image as an American Jewish celebrity was sealed. As the "kooky kid" from Brooklyn who became a major Hollywood player, Streisand represents the triumph of the underdog and as such, became heroine to legions of fans. As a major *Jewish* celebrity, she represents something more: American integration without assimilation, the persistence of Jewish identity in the open society. This chapter concludes with a look at how the Streisand image has continued to evolve in recent years, again reflecting changes in American Jewish culture overall.

In considering Streisand's rise to fame, it is worth recalling that the woman said to be "the greatest female singer of the twentieth century"[2] began her career intending to become a stage actress and ultimately a movie star. She had harbored such ambition since childhood, and, after

High school graduation photo of Barbara Streisand, 1959. A look of determination in her eyes, she would move to Manhattan to pursue an acting career just a few months later.

STREISAND, BARBARA
Freshman Chorus, 1, 2; Choral Club, 2-4.

graduating from high school six months early in January of 1959, she moved from Brooklyn to Manhattan to pursue her dream. Taking acting lessons and auditioning for theatrical parts, she met with one rejection after another until stumbling into an alternative path to fame. In the summer of 1960, friends convinced her to enter a talent competition at the Lion, a Greenwich Village gay bar—as a singer. Immediately hailed as a sensation, Streisand was soon booked for multiple appearances at a better-known venue, the Bon Soir. On one long-forgotten occasion, the up-and-comer was performing at the Bon Soir on the same night that a well-known comedian named Lenny Bruce was appearing at the Village Vanguard just a few blocks away.[3]

In the following year, Streisand won a part in an off-Broadway musical comedy revue, *Another Evening with Harry Stoones*, in which she appeared with the young Dom DeLuise. The show closed after one performance (on October 21, 1961), but Streisand continued to find gainful employment as a nightclub singer. While performing uptown at the more upscale Blue Angel, she was discovered by Arthur Laurents, who was about to direct a musical version of Jerome Weidman's *I Can Get It for You Wholesale*. Laurents arranged for Streisand to audition for a small part, and she made her Broadway debut on March 22, 1962. **215**

Following the show's close, she continued her climb to national fame through nightclub and television appearances, and released her first two records, *The Barbra Streisand Album* and *The Second Barbra Streisand Album* (on the same label as Bob Dylan, Columbia Records) in February and August of 1963, respectively. She was invited to the White House to sing for JFK on May 23 of that year, cheekily telling the president, "You're a doll." According to a cover story in *Time* magazine, "[W]hen he inquired politely how long she had been singing, she said: 'As long as you've been President.'"[4]

Even as she took the nation by storm as a chanteuse, Streisand continued in her quest for success as an actress. Finally, at the ripe old age of twenty-one, she found her first starring role in a Broadway show when she won the part of Fanny Brice in *Funny Girl*. The musical opened on March 26, 1964—just six months before the opening of *Fiddler on the Roof*—and seemingly overnight, a star was born. As one biographer puts it,

> Barbra Streisand was now a bona fide star. A day seldom passed without Barbra's name appearing in the press—what she said, what she wore, where she went. The spotlight had caught Streisand in a blaze of stardom. She was "the Face"; she was everywhere—the covers of five major magazines, the pages of *Vogue*, the jackets of three bestselling albums, the theater pages of the nation's leading newspapers. She could also have been called "the Voice" since her records were played so frequently on radio and over Muzak in elevators and throughout restaurants.[5]

In subsequent years Streisand only burnished her stellar reputation. Beyond the first two albums, she recorded and released nine more from February 1964 to October 1967, of which seven, like the first two, went gold. She won a Grammy Award three years in a row, from 1963 to 1965. In 1965, she also made her first television special, *My Name Is Barbra*, broadcast on April 28—it was a huge success, winning five Emmys; and a second special, *Color Me Barbra*, was broadcast on March 30, 1966, to similar acclaim. In June of 1967, she gave a historic outdoor concert in New York's Central Park, drawing a record-breaking 135,000 people to hear her perform live. And all of this took place before her first film, the screen version of *Funny Girl*, opened in September 1968. For her superstar-making performance in that film, she won the Oscar for best actress (in a tie with Katherine Hepburn), thus completing the grand slam of entertainment awards at the remarkably youthful age of twenty-six.

And all the while, as she burst into public consciousness, Streisand did so as a recognizably Jewish figure. Diametrically opposite the midwestern Dylan, the Brooklyn-born and -bred Streisand appeared on the scene as a Jew, explicitly and unapologetically. She did so in three distinct ways: first, her looks announced her ethnicity in no uncertain terms; second, her personality—or at least the persona she affected— was Brooklyn Jewish to the core; and third, from the start she embodied Jewish characters in her comedic roles onstage and in film. Streisand, like Sandy Koufax, is a Jewish icon, a hero to the Jews. Like Lenny Bruce, she employed a Brooklyn-inflected humor to effectively subvert American cultural norms. And like Bob Dylan, she was an alienated child who transformed herself while still in her teens and took the musical world by storm. But unlike any of the others, she has consistently projected a Jewish image, infusing it into both her public persona and her popular art. Streisand, unlike Koufax, Bruce, or especially Dylan, seems to be a Jewish star untroubled by her Jewishness.

Barbara Joan: Looking Jewish

Though "Jewish looks" may be a contested category, in Streisand's case there is no contest—no one has ever said of her, "Funny, she doesn't look Jewish!" Her apparent-to-all Jewish appearance is an essential aspect of her celebrity persona, and the visibility of her Jewish body has been the subject of extensive comment, as for example Liora Moriel's declaration of its historical import: "Before Streisand, conventional wisdom stated that looking Jewish, for an actress, meant being relegated to supporting roles. Now, thirty years after Streisand, looking Jewish, ethnic, or in any way different has become chic."[6] The first aspect of Streisand's Jewishness to be addressed, therefore, concerns her looks, both in terms of her general level of attractiveness and the more particular ethnic aesthetics of "looking Jewish."

In the first instance, as a female star, her physical appearance has always been of great concern both to her public and to the performer herself. A key element of the Streisand myth and persona is the notion that she had been an unattractive child and teenager; but then, somewhat miraculously, the homely child had turned into a beautiful woman. Streisand said it herself in a 1964 interview: "Brooklyn's ugly duckling [became] Broadway's beautiful swan."[7] As if to demonstrate the transformation, she chose a childhood photo as the opening image for her first television special, *My Name Is Barbra*, and used it as well for the cover of the record album (*My Name Is Barbra*, released in May 1965).

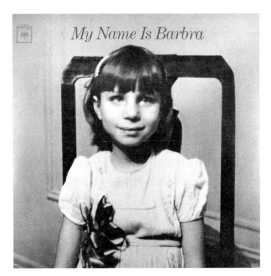

My Name Is Barbra

Record cover of *My Name Is Barbra* (1965). Streisand chose a childhood photo of herself at age seven to adorn her fifth solo album.

The photograph shows a seven-year-old Barbara Joan Streisand, smiling angelically, but still the funny-looking child she was purported to be. Her doe-like eyes, peering out from beneath brown bangs, are slightly crossed and a bit narrowly set, especially in proportion to her already bulbous nose and outsized mouth. As a child she is adorable—easy to imagine her Jewish *bubbe* calling her *shayne punim* (Yiddish for "pretty face") but at the same time, one might also imagine a less charitable relative calling her a *meeskeit* (an "ugly girl" or woman). The backside of the album, however, is another story: a photo montage of contemporary Streisand poses, looking just like a *Vogue* model. The contrast between child and adult, and hence the implicit transformation, is striking.

The young Barbara appeared much the same throughout her adolescence, only growing more angular and long-faced. Her own mother dissuaded her from an acting career, claiming, "I didn't think she was pretty enough," to which Streisand responds, "The more she said I'd never make it, that I was too skinny [read: unattractive], the more determined I got."[8] As she attempted to enter show business, Streisand faced constant criticism for her looks and encountered tremendous resistance. According to biographer James Spada, "With her strange looks, personality, and clothes, few people would give her a hearing . . . Most of the people she went to see told her to change herself—fix her nose, discard the outlandish outfits, subdue her Brooklyn accent. Barbara would have none of it."[9]

Early devotee Rene Jordan describes Streisand's appearance at her first nightclub performance in June 1960: "[She] looked like nothing they'd ever seen before at the Lion. Her lank hair was half mousy brown, half navel orange. Her face, suffused by a layer of white makeup, was early Dracula's daughter. On both sides of an aggressively prominent nose were two piercing, close-set, slightly crossed eyes, emphasized by heavy rims of Cleopatraesque black paste."[10] Similarly, photographer Bob Deutsch relates, "She was an ugly kid with a terrific voice. The first picture I ever took of her is when she's coming from Erasmus High School, to go to work in *Wholesale*. School books in her arms, her hair is stringy and long and falling all into her face. She was a real unattractive girl. I never thought she'd be a movie star; I only thought she had an incredible voice. Even when she did *Funny Girl*, she wasn't pretty. But she was unique."[11] And the critique dogged her throughout her career, as when she "appeared in *The Way We Were* (1973) with Robert Redford, [and] people cattily commented on how much prettier the male star was than the female."[12]

Streisand openly acknowledged her unattractiveness in an early interview in *Coronet* magazine, titled "I Was an Ugly Duckling." In it, she coyly admits that she doesn't meet the current Hollywood standard of beauty, stating, "I'm no Suzanne Pleshette." Yet at the same time, she suggests that somehow she had found a way to transcend her supposed "handicap":

> In an age and an art that worships beauty, I'm managing pretty well so far in show business. . . . You know, maybe not being a beauty explains my success. Maybe being the girl that guys never look at twice, and when I sing about that—about being like an invisible woman—people feel like protecting me. . . . When I'm good, when I'm pleased with my performance, I feel powerful. I forget about being an ugly duckling. I feel—well, why not—I feel like a swan. Maybe that's it—Brooklyn's ugly duckling and Broadway's beautiful swan.[13]

Of course, the physical feature most often commented on was her prominent nose—certainly the most commonly stereotyped "Jewish" feature.[14] This raises a question: are we dealing here with physical unattractiveness per se, or is the issue really one of ethnic difference, of "looking Jewish"? Or perhaps some overlaying of the two—Jewishness as a form of ugliness—whereby Jewish looks are seen as unattractive because their characteristic features do not meet the universally recognized standards for beauty. What is unconventional is deemed unattractive, and because Jewish looks both depart from the norm and represent

Photo taken by Craig Simpson during Streisand's singing engagement at the Bon Soir nightclub in September 1960.

"Jewishness," they come to be seen as ugly. This socially constructed bias against Ashkenazic Jewish features—and Streisand epitomizes the type—thus represents a subtle form of antisemitism in our culture, or better, a Jewish *othering*. In fact, when her nose is commented on, the usual intent is to describe her unattractiveness; yet the subtext, just as surely, is to label her a Jew, an ethnic outsider. Hence, *Newsweek* magazine described Streisand as "a Brooklyn girl with small, sad eyes and an absurd nose."[15]

In the wake of her smash success in *Funny Girl*, *Time* magazine featured Streisand on its cover, and commissioned artist Henry Koerner for the cover portrait. Although he downplayed Streisand's nose in his oil painting, the text within shows no such compunction: "This nose is a shrine. It starts at the summit of her hive-piled hair and ends where a trombone hits the D below middle C. The face it divides is long and sad, and the look in repose is the essence of hound." And, captioning a photograph in profile: "To some, her profile is Nefertiti's; to others, purebred Brooklyn."[16] More positively, *Life* magazine's feature story on Streisand—its cover photograph depicting her frontally, not in profile—reports the new popularity of her "look," even stating that "it may be only a matter of time before plastic surgeons begin getting requests for

the Streisand nose (long, Semitic and—most of all—like Everest, There). Like the nose, the girl is unique."[17] The nose of course, was not unique in the sense that it had associations with a certain group. Others would obliquely indicate its Jewish association, treading lightly around a delicate issue. In 1968, for example, journalist Pete Hamill noted "her sculptured, Semitic nose; everybody has written about it and talked about it."[18] Similarly, Camille Paglia writes, "What was so amazing about Streisand was her aggressive ethnicity. The Nose, which she refused to have changed, was so defiantly ethnic. It was a truly revolutionary persona."[19]

Beyond the nose itself, therefore, is the legendary decision not to have it fixed, sometimes grouped with Streisand's decision to keep her Jewish last name. Film historian Lester Friedman even suggests that "Streisand's name and nose in their unaltered state represents a turning point in the cinematic portrayal of Jews, one that shows Jewishness as something to be proud of, to exploit, and to celebrate."[20] For Streisand, it is the equivalent of Koufax's decision not to pitch on Yom Kippur, the touchstone of her reputation for ethnic loyalty and enduring Jewish identity. As early as 1964, she recalls facing the question:

> I've got pretty eyes, though, and long lashes. But who notices, with my nose? . . . But I haven't worried too much about my nose since the opening of "Wholesale." I really had a good case of first-night jitters. I was so nervous I asked one of the show's backers if he thought I should do something about my nose. "If you do," he answered, "you won't be Barbra Streisand anymore." That clinched it. No nose job. Because most of all I want to be true to myself. Really, people should be left to be themselves, instead of everyone trying to change everyone else. For what?[21]

Thus Streisand defied the odds by becoming a star despite her lack of conventional female beauty, despite her nose, and despite "looking Jewish." Her achievement extended beyond this, however, as she not only succeeded without the benefit of normative beauty, she ultimately turned her looks to her advantage—as Hamill adds, "instead of hurting her, Barbra Streisand's nose was now part of her beauty, turning her into an exotic. The looks and the voice made her an *original*."[22] Streisand, in just a few years and through sheer force of will—aided by makeup, hairstyling, and high fashion—pulled off the trick of changing our perception of her, from pitiable *meeskeit* to glamour queen. Noting the extraordinary change he saw in her appearance, critic Rex Reed proclaimed, "No more cracks about Barbra Streisand's nose. After *Funny Girl*, they'll be as obsolete as Harold Teen Comics. It took the combined efforts of God knows how many people to do it, but I'll be damned if they haven't made her beautiful. In the most remarkable screen debut I will probably ever see in my lifetime, the toadstool from Erasmus High School has been turned into a truffle, and I, for one, couldn't be happier about the transformation . . ."[23]

And similarly, biographer James Spada would later write, "By the time she made her first film, *Funny Girl*, the homely and awkward young girl was being called beautiful and graceful, and she *was*. It wasn't the beauty which left-handed compliments had called 'the beauty of her talent,' it was true beauty, and while certainly not in the classic Hollywood mold, it was nonetheless real."[24] Recalling Streisand's first Broadway role, Arthur Laurents adds the notion that her appearance changed in relation to her perception of herself, writing that "it wasn't until New York [after previewing in Boston] that she found her audience. That was when she began to stop thinking of herself as homely." On the relationship between self-confidence and beauty, Laurents further comments,

> Changing fashion wasn't all that made her more attractive; what she thought of her face played an equal part. Her opinion of her looks has been the measure of her dissatisfaction far more than the accepted chilly mother who actually brought her homemade chicken soup to *Wholesale* rehearsals and very good it was. The key to that opinion was the way Barbra dressed. As her opinion of herself climbed, her outrageously outlandish clothes disappeared. These days she tends to dress with a simplicity that is stylish.[25]

That Streisand somehow managed to re-create herself as a beauty is, as I will discuss further, key to her appeal to gay men. But it is also central to her Jewish celebrity. In redefining her "ugly Jewish looks" as beautiful, she made it possible for Jewish women to feel more desirable, more feminine, and more sexually confident than before. One observer, Henry Bial, attributes Streisand's remarkable transformation into a sex symbol to the beginning of her film career in the late 1960s, culminating in her appearance on the cover of *Playboy* magazine in October of 1977. Her photo is accompanied by the caption "What's a nice Jewish girl like me doing on the cover of *Playboy*?" Bial explains it as follows:

> Her *Playboy* cover represents the apotheosis of an evolution in the way the Jewish body is perceived by an American audience. That is, the very characteristics of Streisand's stage and screen persona that marked her as a "homely frump" in 1962 mark her as a cover girl in 1977. Hence, the presence of the label "Jewish" on the magazine's cover carries a dual sig-

nificance: on one hand, it suggests that Streisand has become a sex symbol *in spite* of her Jewishness; on the other hand, it suggests that Streisand's Jewishness somehow contributes to her sex appeal.[26]

As argued here, however, the shift in perceptions of Streisand's looks occurred much earlier; and it was her own doing. How she accomplished it is further explored in this chapter, but what remains clear is that Streisand, almost singlehandedly, challenged the idea that Jewish looks are ugly; and by providing a new model of "Jewish beauty" herself, she helped make Jewishness aesthetically attractive and romantically appealing in 1960s America. Like Marilyn Monroe, she had become an icon of female sexuality. At first look it may seem farfetched to compare Streisand to the sex symbol of the twentieth century. But where Monroe had transformed herself from a pretty factory girl named Norma Jean into the gorgeous goddess named Marilyn, Streisand one-upped her, turning a Brooklyn *meeskeit* named Barbara Joan into the glamorous diva named Barbra. "Hullo, Gawgeous!" would never had been the same triumphant boast with Monroe that it became with Streisand. And in the process of making ugly beautiful, she made Jewish *goyish* —that is to say, mainstream, accepted, as American as Marilyn Monroe.

Barbra: Acting Jewish

But how did she do it? How did Barbra Streisand convince us that she was beautiful after all? In a provocative study of Jewish ethnicity and American show business, Henry Bial offers a possible answer when he surmises that "*Funny Girl* demonstrates that the woman who looks Jewish can gain acceptance not by erasing, hiding, or avoiding her Jewish looks but by *acting Jewish*."[27] In this view, the secret of Streisand's transformation from ugly to beautiful lay in her performance of Jewish ethnicity. But that performance was twofold: it is most often related, as in Bial's account, to her choice of roles in both her theatrical and film careers (as discussed in the next section); but first, it applies to her initial creation of a public image and celebrity persona. As is well known, Streisand had grown up in the urban Jewish environment of post–World War II Brooklyn, and she would later develop a comedic film persona derived from this rich background. Less often observed is the intermediate stage, when college-aged Streisand established an image as a wacky, offbeat Brooklyn girl, a funny Jew from across the river.

We first have to ask, what does it mean to "act Jewish"? Just as we think of "Jewish looks" as a reductive stereotype that nonetheless affects how we perceive the Jewishness of others, we might also speak of a stereotypical Jewish personality. So we may legitimately ask, what behaviors are believed to be characteristic of Jews? Or, put another way, how might one's personal presentation project Jewishness? Again, the first impression we receive is visual, and thus one can project Jewishness through physical appearance, by fitting the stereotype in some way, as we've suggested regarding Sandy Koufax, Lenny Bruce, Bob Dylan, and most especially, Barbra Streisand. But the three previously discussed Jewish celebrities also give us some clues as to the question of acting Jewish. Koufax was portrayed by biographer Jane Leavy as the ultimate *mensch*, the quintessential "nice Jewish boy," and there is something in this description of warmth and likeability that is often associated with Jews—and the Streisand persona, projecting the affability of a "nice Jewish girl," has it too. Whereas Bruce and Dylan exuded a certain Jewish charm as well, they better represent the opposite archetype, the "wicked son" as it were, because both epitomize the social rebel and cultural iconoclast—again, a stereotypically Jewish category to which early Streisand belongs as well.

In terms of a recognizably Jewish persona, however, Bruce comes closest to being a precedent for Streisand—both were fast-talking and funny, clever and charismatic "New York Jews." The New York Jew is sometimes labeled as pushy and over-aggressive, but a more favorable assessment would emphasize his or her quick wit and verbal agility. It is a cultural type readily identified by its distinctive accent and sense of humor; and as such, the New York Jew has become a familiar figure in our culture, as much positive archetype as negative stereotype, as described by David Samuels: "A New York Jew is a kind of universally acknowledged wizard, like a Swiss banker, an English tailor, or a Parisian couturier. Fast-talking, funny, obnoxious, able to conjure some shimmering, tantalizing brilliance on the fly while complaining about the stale Danish and bad coffee and waving a folded copy of the *New York Times* at the oncoming traffic, with one foot planted firmly on the cracked sidewalk and the other tapping on the curb."[28]

Though not all Jews are New Yorkers, of course, the popular image of the New York Jew nevertheless encapsulates the characteristic traits and behaviors that have come to be read as "acting Jewish." Through the early 1960s, therefore, well before her film career of the post-1968 period, Streisand constructed a persona drawn from the ethnic culture of her youth, and she came to embody a cultural type—the New York Jew, or more precisely, the Brooklyn Jew. Coming from Brooklyn in a literal sense, the actress drew upon her background to create a more figurative invented self, which only seemed "authentic" due to its real-life referent. Building on her "natural" Brooklyn Jewishness, with all its idiosyncratic intonations and mannerisms, Streisand established an engagingly "real" public image. At least one film critic would later mistake her film persona for the real thing, falsely accusing her of not having to act because she was merely being true to self onscreen: "A born superstar, she has had only to be herself, to be the kind of thick-skinned but nice Jewish girl who grows in Brooklyn."[29]

Indeed, from the very start, Streisand projected a persona that was patently ethnic, urban, nonconformist, quirky, and irreverent—both legacy and invention, it was, in short, her distillation of Brooklyn Jewish culture. Yet few relate her early outlandish behavior to either Brooklyn or Jewishness. Instead, the descriptive word that stuck to her from the start was *kooky*—she was called this so often, in fact, that it seems to have served two purposes: by labeling her a kook, observers could explain away her oddball persona without touching on the more sensitive question of its cultural origins; and moreover, it served to other her, to keep her at a safe distance from the conservative mainstream. Might it be that, in early 1960s America, the term *kook* was code for *Jew* and *kooky* stood in for *Jewish*?

Kook, a now outmoded term for eccentric or oddball derived from *cuckoo*, entered the language sometime around 1960, and fortuitously Streisand appeared just then to illustrate the type. In her first year as a budding celebrity, she built her kooky image through numerous appearances on television variety and talk shows. Camille Paglia reminds us that "those early appearances of hers on TV shows, variety shows and her early records—they were welled up with emotions and style and camp and wit. She was funny, funny!"[30] Streisand quickly became popular as a guest on television talk and variety shows, first appearing on the *Jack Paar Show* on April 5, 1961, and later on the *Tonight Show* and the *Joe Franklin Show*. In 1963 alone, she was booked as guest on the television specials of Bob Hope, Dinah Shore, Judy Garland, and Garry Moore. In one of those early appearances, on October 4, 1962, brand-new *Tonight Show* host Johnny Carson introduced her as "a most unusual girl" and asked about the "kooky" reputation in his interview:

CARSON: D'you think you're kooky yourself? I mean, people refer to you, have, haven't they, as kind of kooky?

STREISAND: Yeah, I don't understand it, I really don't.

CARSON: I don't know the terminology of the word, what it means.

STREISAND: Well I tell you, this is very interesting, because, um, when I decided, not decided, I always knew I wanted to be in the theater, but I never made rounds or anything like that. It was very depressing. But I did, I did for two days, and it was during the winter, it was very cold, I wore a big coat and big hat, because I can't stand the cold, but, um, so I walked into offices and they really thought I was nuts . . . like one woman said to me, when you go make rounds, when you meet people you should wear stockings and high heeled shoes and so forth. I said it's freezing out, lady, y'know? It's so cold, what difference does it make if . . . if I'm an actress and if I'm talented or not talented, what difference does it make if I wear tights or not? So, kooky, kooky, people said I was kooky, but now they sort of look at me and say I'm a style-setter or something . . .[31]

Despite her own disavowal, the "kooky" tag had become key to her early image. In 1963, *Newsweek* magazine already describes her in the past tense as a "Young Kook" with "a weakness for the offbeat. As a teenager, she colored her hair to suit her mood . . . As a show-stopper in *Wholesale*, she divorced herself from the play, reading *Mad* magazine between her numbers. . . . [but] now a star, at least in nightclubs and on Columbia Records, she . . . does not quite have the old call to nuttiness."[32] Tellingly, the term was first applied by her fans. Her earliest biographer, Rene Jordan, recalls the excitement surrounding her initial appearance at a downtown club: "Word of mouth had turned the Lion cubs into a platoon of amateur press agents, glorying in the fact that they were the first on their blocks to witness the phenomenon. 'Hey, there's this kook at the Lion. Fabulous, *not* to be believed.' . . . The word had spread like wildfire and they were lining up Ninth Street, around the corner to Sixth Avenue, to see 'that kooky kid, what's her name?' "[33]

If anything sealed Streisand's reputation as the "kookie kid from Brooklyn,"[34] it was a series of local television appearances in 1961 on Mike Wallace's *PM East* and the *David Susskind Show*. Appearing on *PM East* no fewer than fifteen times, she cultivated an image as a "colorful and controversial" character. James Spada recounts: "On one of Wallace's shows, she launched into a blistering tirade against milk, on another she administered a psychological test to the other guests to determine if they were schizophrenic. Once, she said to David Susskind, 'I scare you, don't I? I'm so far out I'm in.' "[35] She had just reminded the television producer that he had once rejected her for a job. But she may have threat-

Press photo of a vampy Streisand, the "kookie kid from Brooklyn," circa 1961.

ened Susskind for another reason as well—for he, like Mike Wallace, was an assimilated Jew. Markedly distinct from them, Streisand's ethnically identifiable looks, accent, and attitude announced that here was a new kind of Jewish celebrity. Her blatant ethnicity must have been unsettling to Susskind and Wallace, much in the way the unmediated Jewish otherness of East European immigrants earlier in the century threatened the settled Americanness of uptown Jews. In the assimilated eyes of Susskind and Wallace, Streisand seemed "too Jewish";[36] yet she was bursting with talent, and moreover was good for ratings, so they kept inviting her back. **227**

The "kooky" label also provides a clue to its cultural source. Jordan recalls the origin of the term, attributing it to the influence of a beatnik classmate of Streisand's in high school: "Susan was not good-looking by any means, but she received a lot of hard-earned attention at school by being outrageously different . . . In England she would have been labeled an eccentric, but in Brooklyn she was claimant to a newly minted term. She was a kook . . . Barbara admired her courage, and Susan is the one person she has ever admitted to having copied. . . . [yet] she outdistanced Susan by several light-years and won her special niche as the superkook."[37]

Note that the term is associated with Brooklyn. This seems logical insofar as World War II–era Brooklyn was ground zero for outsider humor, a reputation attributable to two circumstances. First is the cultural geography of the borough: as an integral part of New York City, Brooklyn embraces all the bravado and brashness associated with the great metropolis; yet at the same time, Brooklyn lies outside of and apart from the urban center of Manhattan, and so embodies the outsider and the underdog as well. Brooklynites are thus a people divided, split between an inflated sense of their own importance and a pained sense of their second-class status. In other words, Brooklyn is a perfect breeding ground for a sharp sense of irony and has long been associated with a comic outlook on life.

This particularly Brooklyn attitude was personified by a stock character of American popular culture in the 1930s and 1940s—the urban wiseguy, speaking a mile a minute in a strange dialect called "Brooklynese." The film actor John Garfield is perhaps the best-known exemplar of the type (born Jacob Julius Garfinkle, he grew up in both Brooklyn and the Bronx), yet it is even better exemplified by three memorable figures from pop culture: the animated characters Betty Boop and Bugs Bunny, and the Cowardly Lion character in the 1939 film *The Wizard of Oz*. None of these beloved fictional creations is usually associated with either Brooklyn or Jewishness, yet all were vocalized by Jewish actors (Mae Questel,[38] Mel Blanc, and Bert Lahr respectively) and all were modeled on the urban, ethnic, Brooklyn type that populated the cultural milieu of Streisand's youth. It wasn't coincidental, therefore, when Bugs Bunny's street-lingo catchphrase "What's up, Doc?" later became the title of a Streisand screwball comedy film.[39]

The second circumstance accounting for the comedic outlook of Brooklyn was its dense population of Jews—by midcentury, Brooklyn was home to the largest urban Jewish community in history, with nearly one million Jewish inhabitants.[40] Together with their Irish and Italian neighbors, they made Brooklyn an intensely ethnic enclave, as Streisand biographer Anne Edwards notes: "Brooklynites are a people unto themselves. Those raised there speak their own dialect. At the time of Barbara Joan Streisand's birth, the tremendous number of foreign-born, over 900,000, and the ethnic majority of the 2.8 million population . . . made it quite different from any of New York City's other boroughs and uniquely set it apart from other cities in America."[41] In the interwar period, Brooklyn's Jews made up fully one-third of Brooklyn's population and nearly one-half of the Jewish population of New York City.

This level of residential density, combined with the relative segregation of ethnic neighborhoods in World War II–era New York City, made for a modern American version of the East European *shtetl*—a community dominated by its Jewish population, and at least seemingly, an all-Jewish world. As Linda Nochlin recalls, "Growing up in Brooklyn, Crown Heights to be specific, in the 1930s and '40s, meant living in a world where almost everyone was Jewish. Not for me the depressing experience of 'otherness' or marginalization or alienation described by so many who have written on growing up Jewish. In my basically secular, culturally ambitious, secure middle-class neighborhood, being a Jew was considered a good thing, when it was considered at all."[42]

In such a homogeneous environment, Jews felt free to be themselves and created an informal, even familial ambience, as well as a communal culture of secular Jewishness; and as in its East European precedent, a central element of this culture was its humor. Like the borough they lived in, Brooklyn Jews also tended to exhibit the neurotic conflict between grandiosity and inferiority, a dynamic often cited as a principal source of Jewish humor.[43] No longer impoverished immigrants, and not yet affluent professionals, most Brooklyn Jews of the World War II era were squarely middle class—and occupying the transitional state between poverty and affluence, middle-class Jews often relied on humor to express their indeterminate status. Given this confluence of culture, class, and community, the fact that Brooklyn has produced such a preponderance of comedians and entertainers ought not surprise. To wit, the stellar list of Brooklyn-born or -raised Jewish comedians includes Joey Adams, Woody Allen, Mel Brooks, Jack Carter, Larry David, Buddy Hackett, Gabe Kaplan, Danny Kaye, Alan King, Zero Mostel, Joan Rivers, Jerry Seinfeld, Adam Sandler, Phil Silvers, Jerry Stiller, Henny Youngman, two of the Three Stooges, and of course, Barbra Streisand.[44]

Indeed, early Streisand personified the ethnic "wiseguy" spirit of Jewish Brooklyn. Certainly, other ethnic communities of Brooklyn had their
own brand of urban moxie, producing their own share of show business personalities—the Italian Jimmy Durante and Joy Behar, the Irish
Jackie Gleason and Jimmy Fallon, the African American Eddie Murphy
and Chris Rock, and the Hispanic Rosie Perez and Jimmy Smits are all
from Brooklyn. But the postwar Jewish culture of Brooklyn had its own
particular flavor, as defined by a hyper-articulate, nervous patter (think
Woody Allen) and a tendency toward cosmopolitanism, an orientation
to the greater world and its concerns (think Carl Sagan—also a Jewish
boy from Brooklyn).

In addition to the comedians just listed, Jewish Brooklyn has produced
big talkers with broad vision, such as sportscasters and newscasters
Marv Albert, Howard Cosell, and Larry King; politicians Barbara Boxer,
Bernie Sanders, and Chuck Schumer; lawyers Alan Dershowitz, Ruth
Bader Ginsburg, and "Judge Judy" Judith Scheindlin; entertainment mo-
guls and impresarios Clive Davis, David Geffen, and Joseph Papp; musicians Neil Diamond, Kinky Friedman, Lainie Kazan, Carole King, Steve
Lawrence, Barry Manilow, Lou Reed, Neil Sedaka, and Beverly Sills; actors Richard Dreyfuss, Harvey Fierstein, Paul Mazursky, Debra Messing,
Eli Wallach, and Shelley Winters; and writers Paul Auster, Joseph Heller,
Roger Kahn, Alfred Kazin, Norman Mailer, Arthur Miller, Norman Podhoretz, and Neil Simon. Imagine all of these figures together, talking, and
you'll get some idea of the Jewish voice of Brooklyn.

Of course, just as Bert Lahr and Mel Blanc did not speak like their
characters in ordinary conversation, neither did Streisand retain her
Brooklyn Jewish accent at all times. In fact, it is remarkable how quickly
and effortlessly she would switch from one to the other, from the Jewish
inflections of Brooklyn to the assimilated intonations of the American
mainstream. One early illustration of this unusual ability can be heard
in a nightclub performance of November 1962, as she introduces a song
from the comedy revue in which she had costarred a year earlier. In the
measured tones of the New York arts world, she recalls the show as
"Another Evening with Harry . . ." but then hits the last word in the title,
"Stoones," in her "kooky" (that is, Brooklyn Jewish) voice—a startling
shift used to hilarious effect.[45]

Streisand's use of this comic device is on full display in her 1965 television special *My Name Is Barbra*. Sitting alone onstage, atop a timpani
drum, she introduces the second segment (a medley of poverty songs
opening with "Second Hand Rose," performed on location in Bergdorf-

Goodman's upscale department store) by replicating a bit she did in her nightclub act, torch-singing "I've got the blues" in a lower register, over and over. Between each overdramatized chorus of "I've got the blues," however, she tosses off a spoken line in a higher-pitched, Jewish-y voice:

Low-octave singing: "I've got the blues"
High-pitched speaking: "Oh, wow"
Singing: "Have I got the blues"
Speaking: "I'm not kidding round"
Singing: "I've got the blues"
Speaking: "Ai-yai-yai-yai-yai-yai"
Singing: "I got the blues" [eight times, now more stylized and mellifluous]
Speaking: "Now I feel betta"[46]

Once again, the rapid switching is extremely funny, and she then proceeds into a monologue in which the device is used repeatedly; the effect is a comedic tour de force.

Not surprising, then, that Streisand later applied this trick to a full-length film, *On a Clear Day You Can See Forever* (1970), in which she played a dual role: Daisy Gamble (not explicitly Jewish, though easily imagined as such—more on that follows) and Melinda Winifred Waine-Tentrees. The latter character was itself a dual role; in a nod to *My Fair Lady*, Streisand switched between the character's original Cockney accent and her acquired upper-crust British accent. Critic Arthur Knight raved: "She is marvelous in [*On a Clear Day*]—deft with her lines as she switches effortlessly from a glamorous British beauty of the nineteenth century to a drab little New York college girl of today, equally authoritative in her movements and gestures to make both roles convincing."[47] *Newsweek* magazine was also impressed with Streisand's acting ability, adding that "she flashes lightning-like between Melinda's airs and Daisy's earthiness."[48] But *Time* was less enthusiastic, calling her "clumsy American" character "Jerry Lewis in drag."[49] Jerry Lewis, let us recall, was known for his antic (read: kooky), high-pitched (read: Jewish-whiny) Melvin character, an Americanized *shlemiel*—like Streisand's character, one with roots in Jewish Brooklyn.

Note that what I am describing as Streisand's Jewish accent should not be confused with the more Yiddish-inflected accent of Myron Cohen or Jackie Mason, or even Mel Brooks's 2,000-year-old man; all of these comedic voices echoed the interwar speech of Jewish New Yorkers. Streisand's speech pattern was more characteristic of the postwar third generation, dropping the recognizably Yiddish pronunciation while retaining its ethnic flavor—more Woody Allen's Jewish whine than Jackie Mason's Yiddish brogue. (Later, it would reappear in the voice of Fran Drescher's Nanny character—Drescher's autobiography is titled *Enter Whining*.) But neither Allen nor Mason ever pulled the trick of switching back and forth, as would Streisand. This now-you-see-it-now-you-don't routine of hers should not be misconstrued as an attempt to simultaneously play to two audiences, Jewish and gentile—what Henry Bial refers to as "double coding."[50] True, Streisand's "Jewish" persona was double coded in the sense that her ethnic act was more easily identifiable to Jews than to non-Jews (and to non-Brooklynites, for that matter). But the rapid switching back and forth, from Jewish to non-Jewish persona, had another purpose and was used to different effect.

First, it revealed the extent of her own cultural assimilation. Whereas Streisand started out in life as the provincial Jewish girl from Brooklyn, she had quickly become a sophisticated Manhattan adult. Having successfully acculturated, she had not erased her former self, but rather kept it intact as a fixed element of her personality. Here was a new solution to the problem described by sociologist John Murray Cuddihy as "the ordeal of civility"—the trauma experienced by modernizing Jews in so rapidly moving from the comfort of the informal Jewish community to the more formal behavioral demands of gentile society.[51] In Streisand's stage and film performances, she persistently called upon her original, "authentic" Jewish voice and ethnic persona as a comic device—thus recalling "who she *really* was"—but at the same time, she demonstrated its nonessentialism, its *inauthenticity*, by switching in and out of it at will. Jewishness, in this unique-to-Streisand performance, is an *essential* part of self, intrinsic and permanent, and at the same time, is a *constructed* identity that can be deconstructed, a mask that can be taken off, an identity that one may escape. Streisand, alone among American Jewish entertainers, had it both ways.

So we begin to get a better sense of how Streisand borrowed from her ethnic background—the urban Jewish subculture of Brooklyn—to create her public image. Pete Hamill, Brooklyn Irish himself, recalls the Streisand persona of 1963: "I had followed Barbra around for a few days, writing about her for the first time. She was a charming, funny girl then, with a zany stream of talk, *a fine tough Brooklyn sense of the absurd*, and, of course, the hard core of that beautiful talent."[52] Commenting on how she took from her own past to construct a marketable persona, *Newsweek* magazine wrote in 1970, "She was purely her own invention, nothing prefabricated, no resemblance to starlets living or dead. She was a regular person with a genuine past from a real place that happened to be Brooklyn, which made people laugh. She really was pure, but pure what, exactly? Her first starring role, Fanny Brice in the Broadway production of *Funny Girl*, supplied one answer—pure oddball. It was such a persuasive answer that it seemed for a time to be the only one."[53]

A good illustration of Streisand's early project of self-creation can be found in the habit she developed of disavowing her Brooklyn origins in favor of more exotic locales such as Turkey and Madagascar. As Rene Jordan points out, however, this was entirely tongue in cheek. When Streisand moved to the Bon Soir, "she updated the tales about her origins, scouring the map from A to Z. Now it turned out she was born in Aruba, raised in Zanzibar. When she told these transparently fabricated stories in the nasal clamor of pure Brooklynese, she was having fun. She knew she was fooling no one, least of all herself."[54] Later, when asked to submit a biographical blurb for the program of *I Can Get It for You Wholesale*, Streisand began, "Barbra Streisand is nineteen, was born in Madagascar and reared in Rangoon, educated at Erasmus Hall High School in Brooklyn . . ."[55]

But such tomfoolery is a long way from, say, Bob Dylan's attempts to obfuscate his true origins. Streisand was strongly identified with her Brooklyn roots, and despite having plenty of negative things to say— she once quipped that Brooklyn was all "boredom, baseball, and bad breath"[56]—she was also savvy enough to capitalize on her ethnic origins, claiming Brooklyn as her own. Jerome Weidman, author of *Wholesale*, recalling the playbill joke about Madagascar, elaborates:

"Get a load of this," the press agent said. "I asked the cast to give me some stuff for the biographical notes in the program. Look at what this dame gives me." He thrust Miss Streisand's composition at me. I read: "Not a member of the Actor's Studio, Miss Streisand is nineteen and this is her first Broadway show. Born in Madagascar and reared in Rangoon, she attended Erasmus Hall High School in Brooklyn . . ."

I looked up and said, "Was it hot in Madagascar?"

"How the hell should I know?" said Miss Streisand. "I never been to the damn place."

"That's my point," the press agent said. It's a phony. Nobody reading that will believe you."

"What the hell do I care?" said Miss Streisand. "It's me I'm worrying about, not anybody reads the program. I'm so sick and tired of being born in Brooklyn, I could plotz. Whad I do? Sign a contract I gotta be born in Brooklyn? Who asked for it?"

"Don't you like Brooklyn?" I said.

"What's that got to do with it?" she demanded. "I hapna *love* Brooklyn, but it's like the name Barbara. Every day with the third 'a' in the middle, you could go out of your mind. I mean, what are we here for? Every day the same thing! No change? No variety? Why get born? Every day the same thing, you might as well be dead. I've got nineteen years Barbara with three 'a's' and all my life born in Brooklyn. Enough is enough. Don't you understand that?"

I certainly did. I had been nineteen myself once.[57]

Finally, a word should be said about her change of name, from *Barbara* with three *a*s to *Barbra* with two. She made the change in advance of her first nightclub engagement, anticipating seeing her name on the marquee. As in Weidman's recollection, she compared her original name to Brooklyn: both were anathema to her insofar as they were boring, old hat. That is, the change of name was like the move from Brooklyn to Manhattan—it signified a new life, a new self. But again, it was not a total rejection of her past; unlike her contemporary Bob Dylan, Streisand did not unrecognizably alter her Jewish surname. Rather, the one-letter alteration of her first name was merely a symbolic change and represented no attempt to obscure her origins. By changing her name, she would announce her personal transformation while *at the same time* embracing her roots and the ethnic culture of her youth.

Streisand: Stage Jew

Throughout her career, and key to her fame, Barbra Streisand has played a succession of explicitly and implicitly Jewish roles both onstage and on film. In most every case, she has imbued the character with the ethnic sensibility and mannerisms already described, that of the Brooklyn Jew. Her onscreen persona has been so consistent that it is fair to say that Streisand is the type of movie star who establishes a familiar character and then plays essentially the same role over and over—always recognizable as herself, she is more Marilyn Monroe than Meryl Streep. Her characters, therefore, are almost always recognizable as Jews. Joyce Antler, a leading historian of American Jewish women, writes,

> Streisand has appeared in a large number of movies with heroines who are explicitly or implicitly Jewish: *Funny Girl* (1968) and *Funny Lady* (1975), the story of Fanny Brice; *The Way We Were* (1973), about Katie Morosky, a

politically ardent Jewish coed in the late 1930s; *Hello, Dolly!* (1969), about the widowed matchmaker Dolly Levi; *A Star is Born* (1976), the story of a struggling singer named Esther Hoffman; *The Main Event* (1979), about a Beverly Hills business executive; *Yentl* (1983), the story of the passionate Yeshiva student; and *The Prince of Tides* (1991), in which Streisand plays a psychoanalyst, Dr. Susan Lowenstein.[58]

Beyond these explicitly marked Jewish roles, there is a series of implicitly Jewish roles in which Streisand's ethnic persona is even more pronounced—and it must be stressed that *any* Streisand role will be read as Jewish, given the extraordinary level of Jewishness inscribed in the actor herself. These non-explicit but still clearly Jewish roles include *On a Clear Day You Can See Forever* (1970) and her nonmusical, screwball comedies of the early 1970s: *The Owl and the Pussycat* (1970), in which she plays a prostitute named Doris; *What's Up, Doc?* (1972), playing a character named Judy Maxwell; and *For Pete's Sake* (1974), as Henrietta "Henry" Robbins. All these roles allowed her to flex her comedic muscles as the wisecracking, fast-talking New York Jewish type she had by then perfected.

As argued earlier, Streisand's personal background was the source material for the public persona she crafted, which then became the foundation of her stage and screen characterizations. But the onscreen persona of a kooky New York Jewish girl had another source as well. Streisand, while relying on her own life experience in the creation of her character, was also channeling a broader history of Jewish actors and entertainers, and their "Jewish" characterizations. As would Streisand, many of her predecessors had chosen to adopt a recognizably Jewish demeanor for the characters they played. Though they were fully acculturated Jews in life, eschewing stereotypical behavior and relatively unmarked as Jewish in appearance, their stage characterizations were intentionally more ethnically identifiable than they were themselves. Playing "Jewish" in this way—similar to the phenomenon described by Henry Bial as "acting Jewish" and by Harley Erdman as "staging the Jew"[59]—is somewhat analogous to the minstrel tradition of blackface, and might best be termed *Jewface*. Streisand is only the latest in a long line of Jewish performers to adopt the convention.

Her fascination with Jewish actors and Jewish characters—and Jewish actors *playing* Jewish characters—may be traced back to her fourteenth birthday, when she was taken to her first Broadway play. In April 1956, the adolescent Barbara attended a performance of *The*   **235**

Diary of Anne Frank with Susan Strasberg in the title role. The award-winning play also included comic actors Jack Gilford and Lou Jacobi in its cast, and was directed by Garson Kanin—who would later direct Streisand in *Funny Girl*. According to Rene Jordan, "that night, over dinner, she announced she would become a stage actress."[60] And Jordan elaborates:

> As her first theatergoing experience *The Diary of Anne Frank* had been a crucial choice. She could identify with all that had happened on the stage: the rituals and the pain, the bickering and the martyrdom. . . . Anne Frank, her father, her sister, even the grasping neighbor Mrs. Van Daan—those people she could identify with. Strangely enough, audiences were paying good money to see their plight onstage. She, too, was Jewish and had suffered. She was sure she could persuade audiences, in time, to clamor for her drama.[61]

Young Barbara began to envision herself as not only following in the footsteps of Jewish theater legends, but playing them onstage, embodying them. Early on, she announced her intention to someday play the role of Sarah Bernhardt; and most critically, she took on the role of Fanny Brice, originally in the Broadway show *Funny Girl* (1964) and then in the film version (1968) and its sequel, *Funny Lady* (1975). But first, she experienced it herself—a Jewish actress playing a Jewish role: in one early instance, a comedy number she sang in the short-lived revue *Another Evening with Harry Stoones*; and then again when cast as Miss Marmelstein in *I Can Get It for You Wholesale*. In fact, it was the solo number from *Stoones* with which she auditioned for *Wholesale*. The song was "Value," "in which she weighs the advantages of one rich boyfriend against the other, [and which] stopped the show on opening night."[62] The comedic song begins, "Call me a boob, call me a *shlemiel* . . . ," thus generating humor through the use of Yiddish, reminiscent of Lenny Bruce. But it's more the scenario described by the song than the words themselves that renders the performance so "Jewish." As the story unfolds, the singer reveals that she is only interested in Harold (Heshie) Mengert and Arnie Fleischer for their money—it is a parody of middle-class Jewish life, more like a Mike Nichols and Elaine May routine than a typical Broadway number. In any event, it worked for Streisand, and she added the song to her nightclub act, later featuring it in her concert in Central Park.

As for winning her first Broadway role, director Arthur Laurents recalls,

I had jump-started her career by casting her in her first Broadway show, *I Can Get It For You Wholesale*. When she came in to audition for me—I was directing—there was no part for her. One role was still open—Miss Marmelstein, the secretary to the dress company's boss. But Miss M. was a fifty-year-old spinster and Barbra was nineteen. True, with her bird's nest of scraggly hair and her gawky, disorganized body, she was a poster girl for Spinster Incarnate. Equally true was the debit side: thrift shop clothes which proclaimed eccentricity, behavior which was calculated spontaneity.[63]

Barbra won the part with the extraordinary power of her singing: "when she sang, she was moving, funny, mesmerizing, anything she wanted to be."[64] And because she opened the audition by singing "Value," her kooky Jewish persona must have moved the auditioners as well, for they were all New York Jews. Jerome Weidman recalls of that opening song that it "may not actually be the funniest song ever written, but it certainly came out that way when filtered through Miss Streisand's squint, fur coat, gestures and vocal cords [*sic*]," also noting the resulting "laughter of the theatre professionals around me."[65] The play's authors quickly realized they would have to beef up her part, so composer Harold Rome gave Streisand a number of her own, a song simply titled "Miss Marmelstein," and with it the nineteen-year-old ingenue stole the show. The song was tailor-made for Barbra, giving her ample opportunity to put on her Brooklyn accent and Jewish expressions as she belted out "Oh, why is it always Miss Marmelstein? / . . .Even my first name would be preferable / Though it's terrible, it might be better: it's Yetta."

Though the theatrical stage of that era had its share of Jewish subject matter, the repetition of the obviously Jewish name in a Broadway theater must still have struck a chord in 1962. With Streisand infusing her performance with all the ethnic humor she could muster, the effect was all the more bracing, especially for a largely Jewish audience. Critics singled her out for praise, though some still reverted to criticizing her appearance: John McLain of the *New York Journal-American* wrote that she "resembles an amiable anteater." But more typical was John Simon's review for *Theatre Arts*: "Miss Streisand possesses nothing short of a Chekhovian brand of heartbreaking merriment [is it Chekhovian, or *Jewish* humor?]. Gifted with a face that shuttles between those of a tremulous young borzoi and a fatigued Talmudic scholar . . ."[66] Unlike her nightclub act, therefore, Streisand's first signature number on the Broadway stage was an unabashed display of Jewishness—fully two years before anyone had heard a fiddler on the roof, and some forty years before

Mel Brooks's similarly overtly ethnic revival of *The Producers*. It was the role that launched her toward stardom, and moreover, it established a pattern she would repeat throughout her career—acting Jewish.

As suggested earlier, Streisand was not the first to employ this strategy. Jewish stars earlier in the century—most notably Irving Berlin, Fanny Brice, Eddie Cantor, and Groucho Marx—had similarly exploited the device of Jewface to build their careers. Like Streisand, entertainers of the immigrant era had consciously adopted a Jewish voice in their stage performance (or in Berlin's case, compositions) despite the fact that they themselves no longer spoke with a Jewish accent, or, as in the case of Brice, could even speak Yiddish at all. Famously, Berlin had encouraged Brice to learn some of the *mameloshen* as he introduced her to the possibility of playing Jewish.[67] When Streisand later inhabited the role of Fanny Brice, she was doubling up on the Jewface strategy—playing a Jewish performer who was herself performing Jewishness. Of course, she wasn't entirely alone in this, as Milton Berle had begun his career imitating Eddie Cantor; Eddie Fisher similarly modeled himself on Al Jolson; and, more in the vein of Streisand and Brice, Bette Midler began her career impersonating Sophie Tucker. But Streisand's appropriation cut deeper—both in dependence and in transcendence—than any of these.

At the same time, Streisand was also building on a greater tradition of Jewish "funny girls," most notably Molly Picon, Sophie Tucker, and Belle Barth. Recent studies of Jewish women in comedy[68] have identified distinct trends, as in Sarah Blacher Cohen's survey of "unkosher comediennes"—bawdy, sexually risqué female comics such as Tucker and Barth; this is a trend more recently represented by Joan Rivers, Bette Midler, Sandra Bernhard, and Sarah Silverman.[69] Yet another archetype of women's comedy, one likewise associated with Jewish comediennes, is the wacky, klutzy (yet endearing) clown—the smart girl playing dumb, epitomized by Judy Holliday. This tradition of lovable kooks extends to non-Jewish comediennes such as Carole Lombard, Lucille Ball, Phyllis Diller, and Carol Burnett, but associates to Jews nonetheless (Diller and Burnett, for example, are sometimes mistaken for being Jewish[70]). The trend would later continue with Totie Fields, Elaine May, Madeline Kahn, Goldie Hawn, Gilda Radner, Laraine Newman, Fran Drescher, Lisa Kudrow and Deborah Messing—all kooky Jewish women. The fact that Brice belongs to both categories—both a Jewface performer and a kooky comedienne—made it inevitable that Streisand would see her as a model. That the opportunity to play Brice came her way was nothing short of *bashert* (Yiddish for "meant to be").

Certainly the most significant film role of Streisand's career was her first, Fanny Brice in *Funny Girl*, for the simple reason that so much in Brice's career and persona foreshadowed her own. Barry Dennen, Streisand's first boyfriend and early mentor, introduced her to the legacy of her predecessor, recalling, "I played Barbra almost all the original Brice recordings, including 'Second Hand Rose.'" He continues, "The record of Fanny singing 'I'd Rather Be Blue' was still playing on the phonograph. Barbra slammed down the phone and gesticulated at the hi-fi speakers. '*Listen* to her!' Barbra exclaimed. 'How can she get *away* with that? Singing in a Yiddish accent!' She got up, wandered over to the window, looked down at the cool autumnal cityscape and muttered, 'Hey, I guess when you're a star, you can get away with anything.'"[71]

Later, perhaps to defend the originality of her performance, Streisand claimed that she was not imitating Brice in any way—and was even quoted as saying, "I've never seen her or heard her."[72] Yet the parallels between the two were striking, and she could not help but be aware of the uncanny resonance of their lives. In an accounting of *The 50 Greatest Jewish Movies*, film historian Kathryn Bernheimer draws the comparison:

> Ostensibly the story of famed singer and comedienne Fanny Brice, *Funny Girl* just so happens to be an equally accurate portrait of Barbra Streisand, the unconventional actress who made her screen debut in the hit musical. In fact, Streisand soon became an even more influential multimedia artist than Brice, who was known as the greatest female entertainer of the day . . . Like Streisand, Brice enjoyed unexpected public acclaim for her broad physical comedy and became an icon of Jewish womanhood.

Bernheimer also notes that "Brice and Streisand were both born in New York City, in 1891 and 1942 respectively," and that "Like Brice, Streisand retained her New York accent. Unlike Brice, however, Streisand refused to surgically alter her prominent, proudly Jewish nose. She was among the first Hollywood stars to gain recognition because of her ethnicity rather than in spite of it. The first modern Jewish superstar."[73] Further, Bernheimer claims *Funny Girl* to be "one of the cinema's premier show-biz bios and a brilliant showcase for the most influential female Jewish entertainer of the century, which accounts for its ranking among the top ten Jewish films of all time."[74] (She ranks it number 7, between *Annie Hall* [6] and *Gentleman's Agreement* [8].) But aside from the comments about Streisand's New York accent and Jewish nose, Bernheimer does not explore other aspects of her Jewish characterizations.

Another film historian, Lester Friedman, takes us a step farther as he captures the particularly Jewish element of the persona: "[In *Funny Girl*] Streisand revels in the role of the Henry Street comedienne, making her face and body a constantly changing collage of characteristic ethnic expressions and movements. Her phrasing and accent highlight her actions. Here, for once, is the Jewish performer being Jewish, instead of hiding behind a neutral name or twisting his/her features out of shape to conform to a standard of WASP beauty."[75] Similarly, regarding Streisand's performance in *Hello, Dolly!* Friedman writes, "Without mentioning a word about background or religion, Streisand infuses the film with what we have come to recognize as 'Jewish' elements: expressions, humor, facial shrugs, bodily movements, hand gestures. Though certainly not a great musical, *Hello, Dolly!* clearly demonstrates the fusion of Streisand and Jewishness that, even in her non-Jewish roles, she seems powerless to separate."[76] He makes it clear, therefore, that Streisand's stage Jewishness extends to behavior, "expressions and movements," as he put it.

Others would go further, linking the Jewish identity of the character to character traits associated with Jews. In her discussion of cinematic stereotypes of Jewish women, feminist writer Letty Cottin Pogrebin cites Streisand's characterization in *Funny Girl* as emblematic of the "Jewish Big Mouth." She notes, "While the Princess demands her privileges, the Big Mouth demands her rights. Often an Ugly Duckling, she is so bright, funny, accomplished, and confident that people forget her looks. But she has one major problem: she acts like a person. She lets everyone, especially the men in her life, know who she is and what she thinks. If she wants something, she goes for it. A nonconformist, she won't play her assigned role—either as a Jew or as a Woman."[77] Pogrebin provocatively adds that "the progenitor of the Jewish Big Mouth character was none other than thirteen-year-old Anne Frank."[78] Describing the most famous victim of the Holocaust as "headstrong" and "rambunctious," Pogrebin implies a direct parallel between Frank and Streisand, noting that the stereotype of a strong-willed, outspoken Jewish girl "is best exemplified in Barbra Streisand's Jewish trilogy, *Funny Girl*, *The Way We Were*, and *Yentl*."

Not surprisingly, Pogrebin identifies with this stereotype herself (especially as compared to more negative images of Jewish women such as the JAP stereotype), but still notes the Big Mouth's "curse": "she is not allowed to have it all. She has to pay a price for her independence, and the price is love."[79] It follows that "in *Funny Girl*, Fanny Brice loses Nicky Arnstein because her success unmans him . . . In *The Way We Were*,

Katie (Streisand) loses Hubbell (Robert Redford) because her passion and commitment disturb the calm of WASP stability and confidence."[80] In this view, Streisand's stock Jewish character encapsulates the dilemma of modern feminism, echoing its *cri de coeur*, "Can the modern women have it all?"

Although *Funny Girl* enabled Streisand to channel the Jewish stage persona of Brice, the quintessential Barbra-as-Jew role is Katie Morosky in *The Way We Were*. A fictional character based on a college acquaintance of the author's, Katie is drawn to encompass several aspects of Jewishness. The screenplay's original author, Arthur Laurents, recalls,

> [I named the character] Katie because like Becky or Jenny, it was Jewish but less pointedly. She had to be a Jew; Barbra herself had arrived as one. Not flaunting, not defying, just simply declaring at Hollywood Customs: Here is a Jewish movie star. And Katie could only be a Jew because of her insistence on speaking out, her outrage at injustice, her passion, her values, and because I was a Jew. Besides, it was fresher and high time that the movies, the only industry founded by Jews, had a Jewish heroine.[81]

Note how the character was created a Jew both to reflect the actual Jewishness of author and actor, and to represent stereotypical Jewish qualities of personal outspokenness and political liberalism. Moreover, it allowed Laurents to employ one of the enduring themes of American stage and screen: interfaith (or inter-ethnic) romance.

From the Broadway hit *Abie's Irish Rose* and the classic film *The Jazz Singer* to *Bridget Loves Bernie* and *Thirtysomething* on television, the scenario of a Jewish-gentile love relationship has served to express a key tension of American life—the often sharp conflict between the particularisms of family, faith, and community, and the universalism inherent in modern society, especially so in pluralistic and democratic America. In Streisand's case, in which the conventional genders of male Jew and female gentile are reversed, the theme of inter-ethnic love has another purpose as well: it serves to further highlight her Jewishness, thereby restoring Jewish women to public view. Katie Morosky in *The Way We Were*, both as written and in Streisand's memorable characterization, is a recognizably ethnic Jew. Katie's romance with Hubbell Gardner, as played by Robert Redford, is emblematic of Jews' desire to be accepted and even loved by America. Pogrebin amplifies the point: "In *The Way We Were* . . . the love theme contains an important difference: the object of the woman's affections is a Gentile and the theme is Jewish Big Mouth Wins Gorgeous Goy by Being Her Intense Natural Self. Since we know by now that stereotypes symbolize much more than themselves, we could translate that to read The Jewish People Finally Make Good in America."[82] But, Pogrebin adds, we are at the same time meant to understand that Jews are different, in some ways superior, and therefore ought to remain apart. In this sense the Jewish character played by Streisand serves as a contrasting foil to the non-Jewish love interest. Her choice in the end to reject him and remain alone is tragic in the context of romance, but also, and perhaps more critically, heroic from the perspective of ethnic pride and survival. Pogrebin concludes by comparing *The Way We Were* to another film about Jewish-gentile romance:

> To me, these movies are warning Jews not to sell our souls for a piece of the American dream. Ultimately, I took *The Way We Were* and *Dirty Dancing* not as antiassimilation stories but as subtle films of Jewish pride in which the ethical standard is upheld by a female . . . Jewish women *kvell* (beam with pride) watching Barbra Streisand and Jennifer Gray, with their frizzy hair and non-pug noses, win the love of Robert Redford and Patrick Swayze . . . At the same time, we understand that neither union can last because each woman is a cut above her man—and in this culture, that's not allowed; the masculine rules of the hegemony hold fast.
>
> Katie Morosky, a working-class woman who fights to save the world from fascism, red-baiting, and nuclear war, is the moral superior of Hubbell Gardner, the Beekman Place Adonis, star athlete, and dashing naval officer, who wrote about himself, "He was like his country; everything came easy to him." *The Way We Were* is about *not* doing it the easy way, not compromising, not selling out your principles, not laughing at Eleanor Roosevelt jokes or ironing your kinky hair, or naming names for the red-baiters.[83]

The third major film to establish the Jewish persona of Streisand was *Yentl*. If *Funny Girl* enabled Streisand to play the real-life Jewish role of Fanny Brice, and *The Way We Were* offered her the chance to inhabit the life of a representative American Jewish character, then *Yentl*, her most explicitly Jewish film (and her first as producer, director, and star), saw her explore the links, overlaps, and echoes between her own life and a fictional character; between "authentic" Judaism and play-acted Jewishness; and between the ambiguities of ethnicity and the ambiguities of gender. Published in 1962, Isaac Bashevis Singer's short story "Yentl the Yeshiva Boy" entranced Streisand when she first read it in 1968. Wanting from the start to make it into a feature-length film, she did not succeed until 1983, but as an expression of her own Jewish identity, the project may be seen as a product of the Streisand of the 1960s.

Yentl should also be seen as yet another example of Streisand's habit of attaching herself to the legacy of a female performer of the past, channeling her talent and persona, and in the end, making it her own. The most obvious example is Fanny Brice, but Streisand did this as well with Judy Garland—first when she appeared on Garland's television special in October 1963, in which she was literally anointed successor to both Garland and Ethel Merman (who also made a guest appearance); and later, in casting herself in the Garland role in the 1976 remake of *A Star is Born*. She similarly stepped into Carol Channing's shoes in the film version of *Hello, Dolly!* (having lost out to Channing for the Tony Award for best actress in 1964); and her French album, *Je m'appelle Barbra*, was her turn as Edith Piaf. The screwball comedies of the 1970s likewise cast her in the mode of earlier film comediennes, such as Katherine Hepburn in *Bringing Up Baby* and Judy Holliday in *Born Yesterday*. Much in the same vein, *Yentl* had her echo the Yiddish film star Molly Picon and replicate her signature role in the 1936 film *Yidl mitn Fidl*. In both cases, the central character was a Jewish girl in prewar Poland who dressed up as a boy.[84]

Playing the part of a cross-dressing *yeshiva bocher* (yeshiva boy) in a mainstream Hollywood film was a remarkable choice for Streisand, both for its explicit evocation of traditional Jewish life and for its gender-bending portrayal of transvestism—both subversive moves in American popular culture, and in the end, bold theatrical devices that ought to be understood in combination. The teasing description of *Yentl* as "*Tootsie* on the Roof" made this same point humorously.[85] As in our discussion of Lenny Bruce, cross-dressing can be read as a metaphor for Jewish assimilation: the Jew passing as a gentile; the male or female passing as his or her opposite. *Yentl* builds on a tradition of such cinematic cross-dressing— *Yidl mitn Fidl* (1936), *Some Like it Hot* (1959), *Tootsie* (1982)—but then renders the metaphor literal by making the false "boy" a yeshiva boy. And just as the usual genders are reversed, the story also reverses the direction of the "assimilation." Here, the acculturated Jewish movie star (Streisand) plays an Orthodox Jewish woman (Yentl) who dresses herself up and passes herself off as a male Talmudic scholar (Anshel)— black hat and *payis* (sidecurls) as drag. Refracted by the dramatic device of cross-dressing, it is a brilliant overlapping of multiple dualities: male/female, secular/traditional Jewish life, actor/role, and celebrity image/reality. Marjorie Garber, in her incisive discussion of *Yentl*, further explains:

> Streisand's own cultural identity as a Jewish musical star, with unWASPy looks, a big nose, and a reputation in the business for shrewdness (read, in

the ethnic stereotype, "pushy"), redoubles this already doubled story. As a Jewish woman in a star category usually occupied by gentiles (despite— or because of—the fact that many male movie moguls were Jews) she is Yentl/Anshel in another sense as well, "masquerading" as a regular movie star when in fact she differs from them in an important way. . . . In fact, that transvestism here should be not only a sign of itself, and its attendant anxieties . . . but also of other contingent and contiguous category crises (oppression of Jews in Eastern Europe, and the need or desire to emigrate; oppression or at least a certain "attitude" about female Jewish artists in Hollywood, and about women in the producer's role—the role so often occupied by Jewish *men*) is a compelling illustration of what I take to be the power of the transvestite in literature and culture. Streisand, who displaces both WASP women and Jewish men in her dual roles as star and producer, lobbied long and hard to get this particular property to work as a film.[86]

In the end, *Yentl*'s contribution to the Jewish image of Barbra Streisand was twofold. First, on the surface, it confirmed her explicit Jewishness and positive Jewish identity. As the producer and director of the film as well as its star, Streisand's making of *Yentl* demonstrated her own, real-life Jewishness—thereby linking the image with the reality, and proving beyond a shadow of a doubt that here was a Jewish movie star with a Jewish heart, that "Streisand's Jewishness is not a role, but a lifestyle."[87] Second, it also confirmed the dualism of her Jewish aesthetic, that her Jewishness was indeed a role as well as being the reality beneath the mask. Jewishness, as embodied by Streisand, is both an inherent state and a fungible identity, both true nature and nurtured image. Is it any wonder that Jewishness has been projected onto her more than any other figure in the history of American entertainment?

Streisand as Cultural Symbol

To better understand how Barbra Streisand became a symbolic figure for American Jews, it proves instructive to examine her equally iconic stature among gay men, women (though not necessarily feminists), and liberals—all groups with strong overlaps, affinities, and parallels with Jews.

We'll start with her widely acknowledged "gay appeal." Streisand's popularity in the male homosexual community has been apparent since her initial success in a Greenwich Village nightclub, as Liora Moriel notes in her entry for the encyclopedia *Jewish Women in America*:

> The underground [read: gay] bar scene fostered a sense of self and a sense of humor that readily warmed to Streisand: The kooky outsider finally found

a place where her persona was appreciated and applauded . . . Hired for a one-week engagement, Streisand stayed at the Lion Club for three, building an idiosyncratic songbook and perfecting a wacky delivery style of impromptu one-liners. By word of mouth alone, the Lion Club was mobbed every evening to hear Streisand. She had become a gay icon overnight, and has remained so ever since.[88]

Yet the reason for this popularity is not quite so clear, as observers have offered varying explanations. In the first case, there is simply the basic analogy between Jewishness and "queerness"—gays and Jews are both outsiders, at times marginalized and maligned by mainstream society, but also critical contributors to its culture. As one scholar puts it, "In another sense her queerness is located in her Jewishness, which is part of what produces Streisand's popularity within a queerly inflected homosexual culture. Queers can identify with her so much, not simply because she has a huge voice and star quality—so does Julie Andrews—but because she's different. She isn't simply white and Christian. Barbra doesn't quite fit."[89]

For others, Streisand's gay appeal lies more specifically in her transformation from ugly duckling to sex symbol, her move from "unattractive" to "beautiful." For example, designer Isaac Mizrahi recalls that in his youth, Streisand was "one of my icons. She was kind of a misfit, and yet she convinced everyone she was beautiful, including me. She *is* beautiful, but she's not the prototypical ideal of female beauty."[90] Arthur Laurents, like Mizrahi both gay and Jewish, expands on this notion by emphasizing Streisand's persistent self-image as an unattractive girl. He hypothesizes that despite her glamorous public image, "each morning she must look in her unrelenting mirror over the bathroom sink: Have a good day. Her gay audience identifies with her stormy self-rejection and empathizes."[91] Such self-loathing is the psychological consequence of being a despised minority, forced to suppress one's true identity in order to "pass" in the majority culture—a form of victimization common to both gays and Jews.

Another perspective highlights Streisand's transgression of gender boundaries and what was perceived by some as an androgynous quality. For instance, her costar in *The Way We Were*, Robert Redford, has observed, "Her femininity brings out the masculinity in a man, and her masculinity brings out a man's femininity, vulnerability, romanticism, whatever you want to call it." Camille Paglia picked up on this aspect of the star's sexual persona, especially as she herself so strongly identified with Streisand. In her estimation, "Early Streisand remains for me the best Streisand. She visibly seethed with emotion. When drag queens imitate her, it's always from that period, with that smooth, sleek helmet hair, when she was still singing in cabarets."[92] But Paglia's identification stems more from Streisand's perceived "male" quality of empowerment than from her "female" emotionalism:

> There has always been a conflict in Barbra Streisand, as in Oscar Wilde, between her populist politics and her aristocratic and tyrannical persona. In early pictures, with her hair swept back, she looks so grand, like a Russian duchess. This is what gay guys liked about her—the arrogant, monarchical divahood, which is definitely not democratic. Streisand has always been a kind of drag queen herself. That's true of Sandra Bernhard too, and it's true of me and of a lot of women who didn't feel particularly feminine when they were growing up. For women like that, by the time you figure out what femininity is, you've become a female impersonator.[93]

In this analysis, gay men respond to Streisand for her qualities of ego and self-aggrandizement, qualities more traditionally associated with stereotypes of powerful and dominant men than with images of self-effacing and genteel women. As the quintessential diva, self-made star, and major Hollywood player, Streisand upends the norm. Paglia further draws a parallel between the unattractive (and thus unfeminine) girl who learns to become an attractive woman and the female impersonator, the drag queen. Gay men identify with this masquerade to the degree they feel their "true" self to be female—they are, in a sense, male impersonators.

Together, the points made by Paglia engender a view of Streisand as the empowered victim—the formerly oppressed victim who finds personal liberation and achieves power—and it is this image of empowerment that I think best explains her gay appeal. Although gay men had idolized female performers before, most notably Judy Garland, their worship of Streisand reached a new height with the 1996 opening of a museum/store devoted to all things Barbra. Located in the predominantly gay Castro neighborhood of San Francisco, the "shrine" to Streisand was called *Hello, Gorgeous!!* Its creator, Ken Joachim, claimed that "he felt inspired by the notion that his life, especially his oppression as a gay man, was 'very parallel' to Streisand's."[94]

It is important to remember in this context that Streisand's rise coincided with the rise of the gay liberation movement in the 1960s and 1970s, and so, unlike Judy Garland, Streisand would serve gay men as a political as well as psychosexual symbol. Moreover, a series of Jewish comediennes arising in Streisand's wake also developed a strong gay following—most notably Joan Rivers, Bette Midler, and, as noted by Paglia, Sandra Bernhard. All were talented though aggrieved women who "made it" by getting up onstage and "knocking them dead"—"killing" the audience, and, in a sense, their male predecessors. June Sochen explains of such aggressive Jewish women entertainers: "An acerbic, fast-talking woman is seen as dangerous . . . A performing Jewish woman is a force to be reckoned with—and possibly feared."[95] This further suggests that it is the representation of empowerment, of the formerly oppressed acquiring power and displacing the oppressor—as embodied by the female performer, the stage comedian, and not least, the American Jew—that truly underlay the iconic stature of Streisand.

Given all of this, it may seem puzzling that Streisand is not more of a feminist icon. Beyond their failure to embrace her, some feminist writers have gone so far as to criticize the star for being outright sexist, while only purporting to be supportive of women's equality—a critique exemplified by Felicia Herman's article "The Way She *Really* Is." While admitting that "Streisand's films are intended to serve as criticisms of society's mistreatment of women," Herman argues that "the films also subvert their own feminist messages," continuing,

> They portray Streisand's characters as pure, long-suffering women with whom the audience cannot help but sympathize, thus oversimplifying sexist oppression and denying women their individuality and human complexity. And these are women who simply want to "make it in a man's world"; they do not call for the overthrow of the status quo but rather argue that women can exhibit the qualities that society most values and that it traditionally attributes to men . . . in each film, the Streisand character's feminism ultimately yields to the more important power of the traditional romance. Her characters suppress their own needs for those of their men and willingly trade in their independence and individuality to "get the guy." . . . Rather than celebrating feminism, these films first dilute it and then condemn it.[96]

While rightly observing that Streisand was no radical feminist, Herman misses the point that she may have been an important feminist symbol nonetheless. For one thing, Herman's argument depends on too circumscribed a view of the star's influence as conveyed only by her films of the 1970s. It ignores the celebrity persona established by Streisand in the 1960s, and further, it privileges the art over the artist; but this is misconceived when the celebrity is as big as Barbra Streisand. Herman also misconstrues when she writes, "Streisand's ability to be unapologetically

Jewish and wildly famous at the same time is due, in large part, to the effects of the countercultural movements of the 1960s and 1970s, which sanctioned overt ethnicity as a form of revolt against the white, male, Anglo-Saxon Protestant ruling elite."[97] More accurately, Streisand's rebellion (and the fame that came with it) predates the countercultural revolution of the later 1960s, and, much like her contemporaries Lenny Bruce and Bob Dylan, may have inspired and influenced it—not the other way around. For this perspective we turn once again to Paglia:

> When she first exploded upon the world in the early 1960s in *Funny Girl*, what Streisand represented was an electrifying new individualism that looked forward to the Sixties counterculture. The nonconformism of her sexual persona was so radical compared to what we had been raised with for the prior fifteen years, with all those cheerful, sanitized blondes, such as Doris Day and Debbie Reynolds. There was a whole series of blond nymphettes, such as Carol Lynley and Sandra Dee, prefiguring the Barbie doll. They were sweet, docile, winsome, harmless, very attentive and deferential to men.
>
> What was so amazing about Streisand was her aggressive ethnicity. The Nose, which she refused to have changed, was so defiantly ethnic. It was a truly revolutionary persona. She was a brilliant new icon of modern womanhood.[98]

In this view Streisand was not an ideological feminist so much as a new model of womanhood. She was, Paglia asserts, "a unique combination of earthiness and elegance, sensitivity and assertion, [and] she remains one of the great symbols of modern woman, independent, self-directed, always in process."[99] Which is to say, Streisand's celebrity persona was doing the work of feminism, rather than the star herself pushing a political program through her art. If Betty Friedan (whose feminist manifesto, *The Feminine Mystique*, was published in 1963) was the W. E. B. Dubois of second-wave American feminism, then Streisand was its Jackie Robinson[100]—the one who actually "broke the mold" and "revolutionized gender roles."[101] According to Paglia, Streisand foreshadowed the counterculture through her individualism and nonconformism, and heralded the feminist revolution through both her "aggressive ethnicity" and her "radical sexual persona." On the latter point, Paglia embellishes: "In terms of twentieth-century popular culture, Streisand is a unique sexual persona. Fanny Brice, whom she was playing in *Funny Girl*, was a superb stage comedian, but she never had the status of a sexual being . . . Streisand's greatness is that she was able to inject the madcap Fanny Brice persona with all the sensuality and glamour of the great stars."[102]

Streisand was indeed unique in combining comedic appeal with sex appeal. As described earlier, she had traded on her kooky New York Jewish persona to build her fame; but unlike her fellow Jewish comic entertainers, male or female, her celebrity would also encompass the far more glamorous roles of movie starlet, pop diva, and even sex symbol— Marilyn Monroe meets Groucho Marx. Paglia further relates Streisand's feminist attitude to her ethnic background, noting that "matriarchal Jewish culture, from which Streisand sprang, never needed feminism to liberate its raucously outspoken women."[103] Though this is a somewhat exaggerated statement, Paglia is nonetheless correct in attributing some measure of the women's liberation movement to a history of strong women in Jewish culture—how else to explain the preponderance of Jewish women in the leading positions of second-wave feminism? As an uninhibited Jew, therefore, Streisand was also a liberated woman; and as a liberated woman in the early 1960s, she was a feminist before the feminist movement of the late 1960s and 1970s.

A similar parallel can be drawn between Streisand's Jewish background and her enduring commitment to liberal political causes. A central aspect of her celebrity image is her leftward-leaning politics, or as Sochen notes, "Her liberal sympathies have become part of the public definition of her."[104] Her biographers unfailingly list her liberal credentials: for example, "Barbra used her free time not only to read political journals, but to participate actively in political campaigns. She had previously campaigned for Senator Eugene McCarthy and New York Mayor John Lindsay. During 1970 she worked for Congresswoman Bella Abzug, who became a close friend. In November, she performed at a 'Broadway for Bella' benefit at Madison Square Garden, made appearances at two fund-raising parties, and did street campaigning for the Congresswoman."[105] And more recently, her Jewish women's encyclopedia entry includes the following information:

She champions environmental projects and is a dedicated Democratic fundraiser; she raised so much money for Bill Clinton's 1992 election campaign that she was invited to attend the inauguration. She later spearheaded a boycott of Colorado ski resorts when that state passed Proposition 2 to deny gay men and lesbians any legal recourse against even the most blatant homophobia . . . Speaking at Harvard University's J.F.K. School of Government in 1995, she explained her philosophy: "I know that I can speak more eloquently through my work than through any speech I might give. So, as an artist, I've chosen to make films about subjects and social issues I care about, whether it's dealing with the inequality of women in *Yentl*, or producing a film about Colonel Grethe Cammermeyer, who was discharged from the army for telling the truth about her sexuality."[106]

Whether it's Democratic politics or environmentalism or gay rights or women's equality, Streisand has established herself in the public mind as a crusader for the liberal cause. Yet despite the common association of Jews with progressive politics—both by stereotype and in reality— rarely is Streisand's liberalism linked to her Jewishness. The one glaring exception—no surprise—is Camille Paglia:

> [I]n point of fact, her political commitment long predates the rise of Clin- ton. She is an authentic heir of leftist politics in America. Her beliefs can be traced to her origins in ethnic, working-class Brooklyn. She came out of the crucible of Jewish political activism. Streisand's radical politics go back to the passionate Jewish liberalism that pervaded 1950s avant-garde circles and descended in turn from labor-union agitation in the 1930s. Greenwich Village in the late 1950s and early 1960s was seething with folk singers, and many of the populist songs being performed in coffee houses were labor protest songs of the 1930s. In a sense, Streisand is coming out of that. Even her crisp, emphatic diction is immediately recognizable as the old voice of Jewish political activism.[107]

Though Paglia clearly overstates the degree of radicalism both in Strei- sand's middle-class Brooklyn youth and in her brief Greenwich Village experience, the notion that her identity as a Jew has informed her liber- alism is on the mark. For many American Jews of the 1950s and 1960s, liberalism became a surrogate religion, either redefining their Judaism or replacing it altogether.

The Jewish embrace of liberal politics has been interpreted by some as religiously or culturally determined, and by others as a form of com- munal self-interest or reaction to the Holocaust, but no one will deny its basic historical reality.[108] Streisand's liberal orientation can be un- derstood therefore as a characteristic trait of her generation of young Jews. Though she came to it as a young adult, under the influence of Bella Abzug and others, her own Jewishness should be seen as a source of her liberalism. Her liberalism, consequently, then became a sign of her Jewishness—and the same may be said of her status as a gay icon and as a feminist symbol. In each case, a cultural orientation or political commitment derives, to some degree at least, from a Jewish background; and the resulting cultural or political stance may then be read as "Jewish" in itself. This syllogism helps explain the unusual degree of negative comment and even outright hostility directed toward Streisand over the years—though couched as homophobia or sexism or anti-liberalism, the common denominator is antisemitism.

Anti-Streisandism

Almost from the very start of her career, Barbra Streisand was subject to harsh criticism as well as adulation—and to this day, she is denigrated nearly as often as she is celebrated. The extreme degree of such Barbra-bashing alerts us to the extraordinary nature of her celebrity: not merely a famous singer and successful actor/director, Streisand had become an icon, a living symbol. As argued earlier, her iconic status extended from the Jewish to the gay, feminist, and liberal categories as well; and as an extra-vulnerable double minority, a Jewish woman, she became a lightning rod for anti-liberal, sexist, homophobic, and antisemitic sentiment in post-1960s America.

In the introduction to her 1996 book *Diva: Barbra Streisand and the Making of a Superstar*, Ethlie Ann Vare writes, "She's unabashedly Jewish, unabashedly female and unabashedly liberal in a national climate that isn't particularly friendly to any of the above." And Vare further recalls her own mother's reaction to Streisand: "My mother always said Barbra was 'too delicatessen for me . . .' a line only another Jew could get away with. Streisand's 'too,' all right. Too strong, too opinionated, too talented, too picky, too damn certain about everything she does. Love her for it or hate her for it."[109] The quote, especially the "delicatessen" comment, reveals the common denominator of the widespread dislike of Streisand—for many Jews and non-Jews alike, she is simply "too Jewish." For example, it's not hard to read between the lines of this 1965 newspaper review (of her first television special) to discover the sentiment:

> Barbra comes on too strong for my taste. . . . It is no secret by now that the Trojan War was not fought on her behalf, and that she looks and talks like somebody's unmarried sister on the loose in the Borscht Belt. Some of her admirers have gone so far as to claim that Barbra is going to put plastic surgeons out of business, which reminds me of the time not so long ago when Audrey Hepburn was going to put bosoms out of business. There is the matter of Barbra's nose, you see, and how much integrity it took for her

to keep it as it is. I don't mind her keeping it; it's her flaunting it as the latest Paris style that I find peculiar.[110]

"Barbra comes on too strong" is a criticism Streisand heard from the very beginning of her career; and because she presented herself as unequivocally Jewish from the start as well, it requires little imagination to hear in this comment intimations of the "pushy Jew" stereotype. Following several national magazine covers of Streisand in 1964 to 1965, *Gentlemen's Quarterly* put her on the cover of its winter issue of 1965–1966, but with a difference. In this photo, her mouth is wrapped up with a ribbon, with a tag reading, "Do Not Open Until Christmas." The provocative image manages to both muffle her voice, essentially calling her a "loud mouth," and also to subtly brand her a Jew, insofar as the Christmas reference reads as a dig. But in no uncertain terms, the image portrays her as a pushy Jewish woman. The critique would haunt Streisand throughout her career, and she would later summarize the invective leveled against her in a 1992 speech given at a women's film awards event. Though meant to lament the double standards of sexism, it can just as easily be read as a cataloging of all the anti-Streisand sentiments she had heard throughout the years—simply substitute "Barbra Streisand" for "woman":

> A man is commanding—a woman is demanding.
> A man is forceful—a woman is pushy.
> A man is uncompromising—a woman is a ballbreaker.
> A man is a perfectionist—a woman's a pain in the ass.
> He's assertive—she's aggressive.
> He strategizes—she manipulates.
> He shows leadership—she's controlling.
> He's committed—she's obsessed.
> He's persevering—she's relentless.
> He sticks to his guns—she's stubborn.
> If a man wants to get it right, he's looked up to and respected.
> If a woman wants to get it right, she's difficult and demanding.
> If he acts, produces, and directs, he's called multi-talented. If she does the same thing, she's called vain and egotistical.[111]

A similar substitution game could be played by replacing "man" and "woman" with "gentile" and "Jew."

The conflation of Streisand's reputation for pushiness with her Jewishness is on full display in two early examples of Barbra-bashing in popular culture. In 1971, two popular humor magazines devoted feature articles to the ridiculing of Streisand: *National Lampoon* put "Barbra Streisand on Trial" in its March issue; and in June, *Mad* magazine devoted one of its movie parodies to *all* of Streisand's films to that date—all three were lavish movie musicals, which invited criticism for the anachronism of the form itself. As advertised on the cover, the parody was titled, "On A Clear Day You Can See A Funny Girl Singing 'Hello Dolly' Forever."[112] Though not a bad joke in itself, it makes the pointed accusation that "when you've seen one Barbra Streisand movie, you've seen them all!"—that all of her films were essentially the same, and that in them she had recycled the same persona over and again. The cover illustration is even more damning: it has the magazine's perennial cover boy, Alfred E. Neuman, dressed up as Barbra in *Hello Dolly*, and worse, conspicuously wearing a fake nose.

The satirical piece inside, authored by Frank Jacobs and illustrated by Mort Drucker, is more of the same—funny material, but nonetheless reflecting anti-Streisand sentiment. Streisand is renamed "Bubby Strident," a perfect illustration of the conflation of pushiness ("strident") and Jewishness ("bubby"). The piece also makes fun of her Brooklyn Jewish accent. One movie audience member is quoted as saying, "I've seen this picture 31 times . . . The first time for the plot, the second time for the camera-work, and the other 29 times to decipher the lyrics when Bubby sings!" To which her friend responds, "Why didn't you do what I did? I brought along an interpreter from Brooklyn!" Taking off from the reincarnation theme of *On a Clear Day*, the parody has Bubby confess:

> In real life I'm Bubby Strident! But in my first two *movie incarnations*, I was Bubby Borscht in "Bubby Girl" and Bubby Liver in "Hello, Bubby!" Except that when I was *them*, it was the same as being *me*, because no matter *what part* I'm playing I'm *always* the same zany, freaky girl from Brooklyn![113]

In sum, the *Mad* parody depicts Streisand as a money-grubbing, self-aggrandizing, power-mad harridan—again, the antisemitic subtext isn't hard to locate. One might object that *Mad* magazine's editors and writers were Jewish themselves, so the accusation of antisemitism doesn't wash. But as the parody demonstrates, Jews are quite capable of echoing the anti-Jewish sentiments that may exist in the greater culture. And, keeping in mind that the "too Jewish" complaint was most often leveled by Jewish producers and film/television executives, such a subtle brand of antisemitism may certainly be evinced by fellow Jews.

Hence, a more recent example of anti-Streisand discourse in popular

Taurus the Bull, painting by Aron Kincaid, 1977. An especially mean-spirited example of "Anti-Streisandism" portraying a horned Barbra as a "bull in a china shop" and evoking antisemitic stereotypes of both *nouveaux riche* barbarism and Jewish female monstrousness.

culture was authored by a Jewish writer, Matt Stone, co-creator (with Trey Parker) of the animated series *South Park*. Airing on February 18, 1998, the twelfth episode of the show's first season was titled "Mecha-Streisand," and depicts Barbra Streisand as a power-mad villain who arrives in South Park, is transformed into a Godzilla-like giant monster, and goes on a rampage, destroying the town. Portraying Streisand as a monster is an overblown yet fairly straightforward condemnation of the mega-star; but the even worse calumny of the episode lies in the first half, before she is transformed. As herself, Streisand is depicted as a demented and horribly ugly woman—a monster in human form. In a sense, this is a reversal of Streisand's self-invention as a beauty, and a denial that she should be beloved at all—as if Stone and Parker are pleading the case that she is a mistaken celebrity, a false idol.

Such uglified graphic portrayals of Streisand crop up repeatedly in caricature: for example, two caricatured portraits in 2009 by Russ Cook and Paul Moyse; and a particularly nasty depiction in a 1977 painting by Aron Kincaid, who grotesquely depicts Streisand as "a bull in a china shop," complete with bull's horns—the antisemitic intimation is unmistakable. In fact, these examples are all comparable in their antisemitic overtones to the European caricatures of Bob Dylan; but then, these are American. Such intense dislike of Streisand is a homegrown phenomenon, again reflecting her status in American culture as an icon of Hollywood success, female empowerment, liberalism, and Jewishness combined.

Negative sentiments have even appeared in recent Hollywood films, as in *Bedazzled* (2000), in which the devil, played by Elizabeth Hurley, calls herself "the Barbra Streisand of Evil," playing on Streisand's status as a diva and reputation as a megalomaniac. And more chillingly, in *The Believer* (2001), a group of neo-Nazis discuss which prominent Jews to target for murder—the glib answer: Barbra Streisand. Yet another example of such Barbra-bashing appeared during the presidential campaign of 2008, when Streisand was backing Hillary Clinton in the Democratic primary. Fast losing ground to Barack Obama, Clinton hung in until the last minute, a situation that inspired a campaign button whose caption read, "It ain't over 'til the fat lady sings," and which depicted a grossly overweight Barbra Streisand as Clinton's last supporter. Finally, on the Internet, amid the many sites for Streisand fans, there is one devoted to all the negative press she receives: The Irreverent Guide to Barbra Streisand.[114]

Conclusion: The Iconic Jewish Celebrity of Barbra Streisand

Though derogatory views of Barbra Streisand persist, her image today has settled into a mostly positive combination of musical diva, movie star (and sometime director), liberal crusader, wife and mother, and, above all, celebrity icon. She is now famous for being famous, and for having inspired legions of adoring fans. As with other cultural icons, her career unfolded in three acts: (1) the early, meteoric rise to fame; (2) the star's struggle with celebrity and continued attempts to remake her image; and (3) the achievement of iconic status.

This progression corresponds to her creative output: fifteen albums made from 1962 to 1968, marking the phase of her emergence; and then, from 1968 to 1991, the second phase, in which she focused on her film career, making some fifteen feature films. This was also the period in which Streisand most publicly grappled with her celebrity—as when she gave an interview to *Life* magazine in 1970 titled, "Who Am I, Anyway?"[115] And not coincidentally, it was soon thereafter that the first biographies appeared, beginning with James Spada's *Barbra: The First*

Decade (1974) and Rene Jordan's *The Greatest Star: The Barbra Streisand Story* (1975). Subsequent years would see publication of Spada's *Streisand: The Woman and the Legend* (1981), Shaun Considine's *Barbra Streisand: The Woman, the Myth, the Music* (1985), and Randall Riese's *Her Name is Barbra* (1993).[116] From the evidence of their names, Spada, Jordan, Considine, and Riese (as well as more recent biographers Christopher Andersen and Tom Santopietro) all seem to be non-Jewish men; and if at least some can be assumed to be gay men as well, they represent her most hardcore fans. Falling within phase two of Streisand's career, it is as if, together with their idol, these authors were working out the anomalies of her celebrity through the writing of biography. Indeed, Streisand's own "biographical" exercise came in 1983 with the making of *Yentl*.

The third career phase, of iconic stature, was heralded by a Grammy Legend Award in 1992 and a Grammy Lifetime Achievement Award in 1994—followed by the opening of the *Hello, Gorgeous!!* museum/store in 1996. Intriguingly, the turning point of the mid-1990s would also be marked by the publication of four new biographies, all written by Jewish women: Nellie Bly (Sarah Gallick), *Barbra Streisand: The Untold Story* (1994); Allison Waldman, *The Barbra Streisand Scrapbook* (1995); Ethlie Ann Vare, ed., *Diva: Barbra Streisand and the Making of a Superstar* (1996); and Anne Edwards, *Streisand* (1996).[117] In each, the identification of biographer with subject is patently clear, as one reviewer notes: "Edwards says she was drawn to Streisand as a subject because they're both strong Jewish women who are involved in Hollywood, musically inclined and politically involved."[118] This latter set of biographies coincided with the attainment of Streisand's new status as an American icon; insofar as they were all written by Jewish fans, there again appears to be some integral connection between Streisand's celebrity and her identification as a Jew.

Three examples from the popular culture of the 1990s further demonstrate the point. America in that decade, under a new Democratic president and enjoying a time of prosperity, also saw a period of ethnic revival in which Jewish images pervaded the culture—one of which was the image of Streisand as both an American and a Jewish icon. As her image continually popped up in the media, these two sides of her celebrity would be inextricably bound together.

The first appearance of Streisand-worship in this vein occurred on the television comedy revue *Saturday Night Live*. On its broadcast of October 12, 1991, cast member Mike Myers introduced a new recurring character: Linda Richman, host of the fictional talk show *Coffee Talk*. The character was an instant hit. Besides cross-dressing as a woman to play the part, the non-Jewish Myers also crossed the Jewish-gentile divide, as the character was based on (and named after) his Jewish mother-in-law from Queens. A stereotypical New York Jew, Myers's Richman was prone to using obscure Yiddish expressions such as *shpilkes* and *verklempt*—the latter became a national catchphrase. Another marker of her Jewishness was her worshipful devotion to Streisand. On that very first appearance, Richman announced, "This week's show is dedicated to the best entertainer in the history of show business. Barbra Streisand." And after some initial pleasantries, she continued discussing the topic with her best friend Sheila (played by Kirstie Alley):

LINDA RICHMAN: Okay, back to Babs. She's coming out with a new movie, *Prince of Tides*.

SHEILA: And by the by that Babs and I are exactly the same age.

LINDA RICHMAN: Me too. (holds up *Vanity Fair*). But I ask you, is this the body of a 50 year old lady?

SHEILA: You know, I would die for [her] hands.

LINDA RICHMAN: They're like buttah. . . . Now let's talk. Why do we love Barbra Streisand so much. Is it because she's so vaulty [?] and brash?

SHEILA: No it isn't. The reason is, she got out. Now when I was a little girl, I wanted to be a ballerina, and my mother told me, "Sheila, you're a poor mescite [*sic*] from Brooklyn with a hook nose. You will never, ever be a ballerina." And like a schmuck, I listened. Barbra, no, she got out. Excuse me I'm a little emotional about this right now.

LINDA RICHMAN: Listening to your story, I'm a little verklempt myself. Give me a second. Talk amongst yourselves (holds it all in). There I feel better. You're right she got out.[119]

Clearly, Linda Richman and Sheila identify strongly with their idol, noting their similar age and, more important, their common roots in the Jewish culture of the New York City boroughs. But Streisand "got out," that is, she found success in the greater world of American show business—their fantasy fulfilled. Later in the sketch, the two discuss the upcoming film *Prince of Tides*, with Sheila expressing skepticism over Streisand's choice of leading man, Nick Nolte. Nevertheless, Richman insists, "Barbra must know what she's doing." Sheila quickly agrees, "She must," to which Richman responds, "She's god." Such hyperbole captures the degree to which Streisand is worshipped, literally, by her Jewish fans.

Linda Richman's obsession with Streisand yielded the segment's most memorable moment when, on the *Saturday Night Live* broadcast of February 22, 1992, she invited her friend Liz Rosenberg (played by Madonna, and named after the pop singer's real-life spokeswoman) and Liz's mother (played by Roseanne Barr) to join her on *Coffee Talk.* Madonna playing a Jewish girl from Queens was riotous enough—she even used the occasion to poke fun at her own celebrity image—but another shocker was in store. As in the transcript quoted earlier, Richman's favorite expression of approval was "like buttah," and upon using it as she often did to describe Streisand, an unexpected guest joined the scene—Barbra Streisand in the flesh. Caught by surprise on live television, Myers, Madonna, and Barr somehow managed to stay in character, as Myers/Richman exclaimed, "I can die now! Excuse me, I have to go die now!" The overlay of fictional characters with real life was later extended when Streisand had "Linda Richman" join her onstage for a bit of comic relief during her 1993/1994 New Year's Eve concert.

Beyond *Saturday Night Live,* television situation comedy in the 1990s yielded a host of Jewish characters and subject matter in hit shows such as *Seinfeld* (1989–1998), *Northern Exposure* (1990–1995), *Friends* (1994–2004), and *The Nanny* (1993–1999).[120] The last was the star-making vehicle for Fran Drescher, who created the show and played the title role of Nanny Fran Fine, a caricatured version of herself as a whiny but winning Jewish girl from Flushing, Queens (not Brooklyn, but close). Not surprisingly, Drescher had grown up idolizing Streisand, later describing her as "God's gift to all little Jewish girls in need of a leader."[121] Her Nanny character was described by one television critic as "Streisand-does-Mae West,"[122] and indeed, Drescher had clearly emulated her idol. Both were New York Jewish "funny girls" who created comedic characters based on the stereotypical behavior of their native culture, and both, therefore, were Jewface performers. Unlike Streisand, however, Drescher was a pretty brunette with a button nose. As if to compensate for her good looks, she exaggerated her shrill voice and Queens accent, exhibited outlandish fashion sense, and played her character as ditzy, vain, and manipulative (though always upbeat and quite charming). In sum, the character was a mass of stereotypes, and the show elicited much negative comment from Jewish viewers.

But like Streisand's earlier incarnation of Brooklyn Jewishness, Drescher's ethnic caricature entertained more viewers than it offended. Perhaps to honor this legacy, and as one of the chief indicators of her character's Jewish identity, the Nanny character (together with her mother Sylvia and grandmother Yetta) was depicted as an obsessive Streisand fan. A running joke throughout the series, the Streisand theme reached its apogee in an episode titled "Ode to Barbra Joan," which aired on April 13, 1994. In it, Mother Fine (played by Renée Taylor, who years earlier had appeared with Streisand on the same bill of a Greenwich Village club) asks (regarding Streisand), "Don't you love her anymore?" to which the Nanny responds, "Ma, She's our leader." Settling into a Streisand-induced swoon, they continue:

MOTHER FINE: I just love her.
NANNY: I love her more.
MOTHER FINE: I loved her first.
NANNY: I'll love her last.

The scene simultaneously parodies and celebrates the Streisand-worship common to Jewish women of a certain age (Streisand's cohort). In this case, the Nanny's one-upping her mother signifies the passing of the torch to a new generation. *The Nanny* would later deepen its observation of the phenomenon when it had its three Jewish woman characters—Fran, Sylvia, and Yetta—sitting on a couch watching the *Saturday Night Live* sketch with its own three stereotypical Jewish women (played by Myers, Madonna, and Barr) sitting on a couch discussing their love of Streisand. The adulation of Streisand existed in that moment on the real-life television program within the sitcom, within the fictional world of the sitcom itself, and in its reflection of the real world—all in one gloriously postmodern intertextual scenario.

The stereotype of Jewish women enamored of Barbra Streisand emerged in popular culture at the same moment that she became a cultural icon—again suggesting a relationship between her fame and her Jewishness. Yet another illustration of this appears in a key scene of a 1993 comedy film starring Robin Williams: *Mrs. Doubtfire*. Williams plays a divorced father who, upon losing his custody battle with his ex-wife, disguises himself as a woman (a nanny, no less) in order to spend time with his children. Enlisting the aid of his gay brother (played by Harvey Fierstein) who just happens to be a makeup artist, Williams's character tries on several possible female disguises. The first, a Latina sexpot, is deemed too scary for the children. The second errs in the opposite way—a kerchief-wearing Jewish grandmother, judged too old (but allowing Williams's character to reveal his Jewish background, telling his brother, "No, no, I feel like *Bubbe*, this is not working," after which they

259

break into a song from *Fiddler on the Roof*). Their third try is something in between: a Jewish diva, none other than Barbra Streisand.

As Streisand, Williams sings the opening lines from *Funny Girl's* "Don't Rain on my Parade," in a standard rendition of the Streisand persona of drag shows—but in this context, she also represents an archetypal figure of American Jewish womanhood. Coming on the heels of the Jewish grandmother, the Streisand image reads as a more Americanized and sexualized version of a Jewish woman. Though rejected (before the brothers settle on the dowdy but randy Mrs. Doubtfire character), the use of Streisand here is quite telling: in his attempt to become a woman, Williams's character conflates femininity with Jewishness—just as the celebrity image of Streisand had done. As the scene suggests, Streisand had become an iconic image in popular culture, uniquely combining the gay appeal of a drag queen with the Jewish appeal of an ethnic hero with the overall appeal of a larger-than-life American celebrity.

The pop cultural phenomenon of Streisand's Jewish celebrity reached a culmination of sorts in a venue of higher culture, New York's Jewish Museum. In 1996, curator Norman Kleeblatt mounted the exhibition titled *Too Jewish? Challenging Traditional Identities*, in which the image of Streisand took center stage. The exhibition brought together works by contemporary Jewish artists on the subject of Jewishness—artworks that were "for the most part confrontational and often embarrassing"[123]—in a far more critical examination of the subject than anything the Jewish Museum had ever offered before. As Kleeblatt noted, until then, the Fifth Avenue institution itself had been guilty of the assimilationist avoidance of anything "too Jewish."

As both the embodiment of "too Jewish" and its transcendence, Streisand was the perfect symbol for the museum's newfound comfort with overt Jewishness. Artist Deborah Kass contributed two Barbra-based pieces to the exhibition, both made in 1992. The first is a group of identical panels titled *Four Barbras* (the Jewish Jackie Series), a reference to Andy Warhol's *Jackie [Kennedy] Series*; it was intended "to call attention to the one major female Jewish superstar whom Warhol omitted from his cosmopolitan Hollywood register."[124] Like the Warhol original, the effect of creating a wallpaper-like multiple image of Streisand was to render her both iconic and ordinary, both celebrating her American celebrity and questioning her Jewish representativeness. Kleeblatt interprets the question of Jewish representation rather straightforwardly: "Through Barbra Streisand, Kass proudly presents the physical stereotype of Jewish female ethnicity."[125]

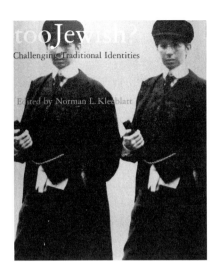

Exhibition catalogue for *Too Jewish? Challenging Traditional Identities* (1996), with cover illustration taken from artist Deborah Kass's 1992 work, *Triple Silver Yentl (My Elvis)*. The image reversed the usual relationship between star and role, turning Streisand's most explicitly Jewish character, Yentl the yeshiva "boy," into a bona fide American celebrity.

That Kass saw her subject in somewhat more complex terms is demonstrated by another work of the same year, *Triple Silver Yentl (My Elvis)*. Stylized from a movie still, rendered in monumental scale, and most critically, refracted into a triple image, Kass's portrayal of Barbra-as-Yentl is a powerful statement of the power of the woman artist. Included in the exhibition and also used for the cover of the *Too Jewish?* catalogue, the artist's treatment of Streisand's most overtly Jewish character flipped the Barbra/Yentl coin around. Like the star who played her, the character herself was now a celebrity figure to be idolized, the artist's personal Elvis Presley—the very epitome of cool. Noting the close identification between artist and subject, Kleeblatt writes, "The 1962 story by Isaac Bashevis Singer on which the Yentl tale is based can, for Kass, be read from a homosexual vantage point. This sexually deceptive image of Yentl adds a third, now lesbian element to Kass's earlier exploration of her feminist and Jewish identities. The image of Barbra Streisand, Kass's hero from her teenage years, acts as the surrogate for the artist's Jewish identity."[126] But as she shared with me, the artist prefers to emphasize Streisand's meaning as a role model of female empowerment, and primarily employed the Yentl image as a metaphor for being a woman artist. Kass herself is in fact both a woman and an artist; both a liberal and a lesbian; both a New Yorker and a Jew; and also, a big, big Streisand fan from an early age. As she recalls,

For me there's the ethnic aspect of how, when Barbra hit the scene, people like my parents disliked her because she was "too Jewish." Why doesn't she **261** fix her nose? Why doesn't she change her name? But to be an adolescent coming across Barbra Streisand was the most exhilarating moment of identification. I'm sure it's how a lot of gay boys felt about her at my age, 13 or 14. It was an identification with powerfulness, talent, with being yourself and being different at the same time.[127]

Today, Kass's Brooklyn studio is adorned not only with her own artistic images of Streisand, but also with several earthy quotations of Streisand's hung around the room to remind her of her idol's take-no-crap attitude. Kass is, moreover, an aficionado of Streisand's music, an avid concertgoer, and a devotee of the television show she claims is inspired by Streisand, *Glee* (see discussion in Chapter 6).[128] Her portrayals of Streisand are, on one level, the extreme identification of a serious fan. But Kass combines popular fandom with the thoughtfulness of an artist. The triple image of Yentl reflects this beautifully, as it captures her own multiplications of identity and all the potential cross-fertilization therein. So once again, the celebrity image of Streisand serves as a mirror in which the female Jewish fan comes to see herself. Recycling the Yentl image of Streisand's 1983 film, Kass's 1992 artwork (and its inclusion in a 1996 museum exhibition) thus turned the notion of a cross-dressed yeshiva student into a metaphor for American Jewish identity overall.

Yet another provocative use of Streisand's image in the *Too Jewish?* show was created by performance artist Rhonda Lieberman. Her piece, *Barbra Bush* (1992), is an ironic take on the "Chanukah bush"—a Jewish version of the Christmas tree, "replete with images of Barbra Streisand emblazoned on six-pointed 'Jewish' stars."[129] Originally made as a Christmas display for the New York clothier Barney's, Lieberman managed to take a swipe at the then first lady, as well as at the shallowness of Jews who so envy their Christian neighbors that they have to have a holiday tree. But her use of Streisand as the very symbol of American Jewishness, a kind of Jewish archangel, brings the piece to a different level. Besides commenting on American Jews' proclivity to assimilate American culture, Lieberman also reflected their need to be represented by exemplary Jews, that is, the Jewhooing tendency.

Lieberman also contributed an essay to the exhibition volume, titled "Jewish Barbie," in which she imagines a Jewish version of the popular Barbie doll. Barbie was introduced in March of 1959 by a Jewish toymaker, Ruth Handler—but like so many other cultural products of Jews, it was stripped of any recognizably Jewish characteristics. Lieberman's fantasy restored the inherent Jewishness of the iconic doll, including, of course, adulation of Streisand. She writes, "As a young diva, Jewish Barbie looks to Barbra as a beaconness of Jewish glamour in a world hostile to multitalented strong women who should be worshipped."[130] Lieberman's fantasy would later turn into reality when, in 2010, the maker of Barbie dolls, Mattel, introduced the "Barbie (Pink Label Collection) Barbra Streisand Doll." Streisand fans greeted the new product with enthusiasm, as reflected in the following online review:

> I recall the sixties. Barbra Streisand was considered the "ugly duckling" while Barbie was the all-American idea of what beauty and perfection were. And now Barbra Streisand is a Barbie doll!
>
> Isn't it wonderful that today Ms. Streisand's unique looks have not only garnished her the well deserved accolade of being a "Barbie As" doll but her perserverence [sic] not to alter herself or her looks to suit the supposed time-honored ways helps millions of people to accept their looks (and themselves).
>
> So, if you're counting, Barbra can: sing, dance, act, direct, write, influence people positively . . . and you wonder why she's my favorite?[131]

Streisand fans and doll collectors alike are apt to respond to the Barbra Barbie, not least for the way it conflates two immediately recognizable icons of 1960s pop culture. Moreover, as the quote attests, it reconciles the two diametrically opposed icons, the ugly-duckling Barbra and the glamorous Barbie. Of course, that is precisely the synthesis achieved by Streisand herself. For fans, the essence of Streisand's appeal lies in just this reconciliation of opposites, the outsider as insider, the outcast's fantasy of finding acceptance. For Jewish fans, this is further magnified by the Jewishness associated with both Streisand's and their own outsider status, as well as the Jewishness associated with "making it." That is, both sides of the equation, both ugly Barbra and beautiful Barbie, can be read as Jewish. The creation of the Barbra Barbie doll merely renders this abstraction concrete.

The quote also hints at one other reason for the contemporary adulation of Barbra Streisand—the critical factor of nostalgia—as the reviewer begins, "I recall the sixties." Like Sandy Koufax, Lenny Bruce, and Bob Dylan before her, Streisand has become an iconic figure representing an iconic time. For baby boomers especially, but not only, Koufax, Bruce, Dylan, and Streisand are echoes of the Sixties, capturing its revolutionary spirit as well as our contemporary longing for a more innocent time. They also represent Jewishness—both our own, and the Jewishness associated with the Sixties. Encapsulating the modern Jewish condition, the 1960s was a time of boundary crossing and of paradigm shift; it was a time of identity confusion and identity clarification; it was a time when American Jews began to feel more Jewish, but it was also a time when they more fully entered their identities as Americans. Our four celebrities embody and reflect this tension all too well.

Jewhooing into the
Twenty-first Century

EPILOGUE
6

When you feel like the only kid in town without a
   Christmas tree,
Here's a list of people who are Jewish, just like you
   and me . . .
   ADAM SANDLER, "The Chanukah Song"

Jewish celebrity begets Jewhooing.[1] Hence each of
the preceding chapters began with a brief history of
the early 1960s rise of our four famous American
Jews—Sandy Koufax, Lenny Bruce, Bob Dylan, and
Barbra Streisand—and then concluded by surveying
the Jewhooing of their celebrity personae over the
subsequent half-century. That the phenomenon is
alive and well in the early twenty-first century may
be illustrated by two concurrent events of late 2010,
which together encapsulate the state of Jewhooing in
the new millennium. The first was the opening of the
National Museum of American Jewish History in Philadelphia, and the
second was a promotional film made for a philanthropic organization,
the American Jewish World Service. In the first case, Jewish celebrity was
highlighted as an intrinsic element of the American Jewish experience. In
the second, Jewish celebrity consciousness was gently mocked, and in the
process unpacked and deconstructed. In both cases, celebrity was put to
the good use of raising funds for Jewish causes—and in both cases, Jewhooing came into play. Before looking more closely at these two simultaneous though contrasting expressions of Jewhooing, it behooves us to
take a retrospective view of the phenomenon overall—a phenomenon,
as it turns out, that has only gained in momentum in the new century. **265**

A Brief History of Jewhooing

Historian Susan Glenn first adopted the term *Jewhooing* in a 2002 article, defining it as "the social mechanism for both private and public naming and claiming of Jews by other Jews." She illustrates the concept by recalling "what parents and grandparents like mine did when, while reading the newspaper or watching television, they wondered out loud if this or that public figure or celebrity—perhaps with their Christian-sounding name and all-American looks—was or wasn't a member of the tribe."[2] Having defined the term, Glenn traces its history from the *Jewish Encyclopedia* of 1901–1905 through several midcentury Who's Who–type listings to the fin-de-siècle examples of Adam Sandler's 1994 "The Chanukah Song" and the 1997 outing of Madeleine Albright as a Jew.

Glenn describes "The Chanukah Song" and its sequels as "gleeful and irreverent send-ups [that] poke fun at the private and public rituals of Jewhooing, even as they participate in them."[3] With its key line, "When you feel like the only kid in town without a Christmas tree, here's a list of people who are Jewish, just like you and me," the song has become the major touchstone of the Jewhooing trend, generating numerous sequels, tributes, and parodies—all succinctly surveyed by Eric Goldstein in his 2006 history of American Jewish identity, in which he writes, "Both the success of the recording and the admiration Sandler drew from Jewish listeners around the country suggested that the song had hit on some of the most important issues of identity confronting American Jews at the turn of the twenty-first century."[4] That the song belongs to a longer tradition of Jewhooing is demonstrated by its lesser-known predecessor, Steve Kurland's 1984 comedy song "Famous Jews."[5] Kurland's repeated chorus, "There are so many famous Jews," frames lengthy lists of well-known Jews both in show business and other areas of popular culture, and includes the occasional humorous verse such as this:

Come next high holiday
don't be surprised if, say
you're sitting in a shul somewhere
and Dylan comes in to pray![6]

Given this comical aspect of Jewhooing, Glenn's brief history of Jewhooing places too great an emphasis on serious reference works such as encyclopedias and biographical dictionaries. The spirit of Jewhooing is both more lighthearted and more celebratory than that, better evidenced by local Jewish newspapers and popular publications such as Mac Davis's *They Are All Jews* (1937) and *Jews at a Glance* (1956). Such book-length listings of "great Jews" were expressly intended to build Jewish pride by "reveal[ing] the possibilities to which Jews may aspire,"[7] so naturally they became common as bar mitzvah presents (certainly a motive for their publication in the first place). Especially appealing to adolescent boys, a subgenre of such Jewhooing literature is the Jewish athletes collection, beginning with Harold Ribalow's much reprinted *The Jew in American Sports* (1948), and later followed by Robert Slater's *Great Jews in Sports* (1983) and Buddy Silverman's *The Jewish Athletes' Hall of Fame* (1989).[8]

Slater's contribution was published by the New York–based Jonathan David Publishers, specializing in what it calls "popular Judaica." Following its initial publication of *Great Jews in Sports* in 1983, Jonathan David issued a series of "great Jews" volumes, including Darryl Lyman's *Great Jews on Stage and Screen* (1987); *The Jewish Comedy Catalog* (1989); *Great Jews in the Performing Arts* (1999); *Great Jews in Entertainment* (2005); as well as Elinor Slater and Robert Slater's *Great Jewish Men* (1996) and *Great Jewish Women* (2006). Such publications have multiplied in recent decades: for example, Martin Greenberg's *The Jewish Lists* (1979); Tim Boxer's *The Jewish Celebrity Hall of Fame* (1987); Seymour Brody's *Jewish Heroes & Heroines of America* (1996); Philip Brooks' *Extraordinary Jewish Americans* (1998); and Steven Pease's *The Golden Age of Jewish Achievement: The Compendium of a Culture, a People, and Their Stunning Performance* (2009). And most recently (at this writing), a four-volume encyclopedia, *Jewish Americans* (2011), part of Salem Press's Great Lives from History series, contains essays on 654 figures, including, need it be said, Sandy Koufax, Lenny Bruce, Bob Dylan, and Barbra Streisand—though of the four, only Koufax makes the cover, together with Henry Kissinger, Paul Newman, Lauren Bacall, Woody Allen, and Sammy Davis Jr. Many more such collections could be cited, all having the same polemical purpose: to celebrate Jewish achievement and thereby instill group pride—a common ethnic practice. But what other ethnic group has so many shelves in the bookstore devoted to its popular heroes? What other group, for that matter, has a term like Jewhooing?

By way of explanation, allow me to cite three especially evocative examples of the Jewhooing phenomenon. One is a 1975 short story by Ralph Schoenstein, "Let Us Now Claim Famous Men."[9] Recalling his childhood experience as a Jewish boy whose grandfather commissions him to seek out "hidden Jews" in the greater culture, Schoenstein writes, **267**

I collected many things as a boy, from trolley transfers to baseball cards, but nothing was more fun than helping my grandfather build his collection of surprising Jews, that tinseled Hebraic underground whose infiltration of the establishment allowed him to poke a passing Methodist and proudly say, "You know that Leslie Howard? The blond movie star with the fancy accent and the ruler for a nose? Well, he couldn't care less about Bethlehem." . . . It was the secretly kindred celebrities that he loved to use for oneupsmanship against the Christian foe . . . And it became my job to find for my grandfather the most surprising Jews. I was, in short, the only boy in America who shared a mission with the Third Reich.

I can still remember the first great find that I brought to him: Jake Pitler, a Brooklyn Dodger coach. The entire world, of course, knew where Sandy Koufax went to pray, but Pitler was a Hebrew in the hole.[10]

The grandfather was engaged in a form of "oneupsmanship," as Schoenstein suggests—but what motive had the grandson for telling the story in the 1970s? Surely no longer a defensive measure against the Christian majority, the humorous story should be read instead as a baby boomer's nostalgia for a simpler time—when one could still tell the difference between "us" and "them"—as well as a subtle critique of his fellow third-generation Jews, who, despite their social integration and supposed sophistication, were still indulging in the old habit of Jewhooing.

As a second example, toward the end of the 1970s, New York art dealer Ronald Feldman commissioned pop artist Andy Warhol to create a series of images of famous Jews, the collection later titled *Ten Portraits of Jews in the Twentieth Century*. Feldman originally gave Warhol a long list of possibilities, including notable European-born Jews such as David Ben-Gurion, Marc Chagall, Anne Frank, Gustav Mahler, Karl Marx, Amedeo Modigliani, Arthur Rubinstein, and Leon Trotsky; and American Jewish celebrities such as Woody Allen, Saul Bellow, Jack Benny, Milton Berle, Eddie Cantor, Sammy Davis Jr., Bob Dylan, Al Jolson, Norman Mailer, Louis B. Mayer, Arthur Miller, Jonas Salk, Paul Simon, Barbra Streisand, and an unnamed "baseball player." (Amusingly, the list mistakenly included several non-Jews: for example, Albert Camus, George M. Cohan, Charlie Chaplin, Henry Miller, Mary Pickford, Albert Schweitzer, John Steinbeck, and Igor Stravinsky.)[11]

After winnowing the list down to ten (in part by eliminating living figures from contention), Warhol portrayed the following "Jewish geniuses": George Gershwin, Sarah Bernhardt, Albert Einstein, Franz Kafka, Gertrude Stein, Martin Buber, Louis Brandeis, the Marx Brothers,

Golda Meir, and Sigmund Freud. The idea was to represent various fields by highlighting their most famous and significant Jewish practitioners (music—Gershwin, acting—Bernhardt, science—Einstein, and so on), thereby asserting the significant contribution of Jews to modern culture and society.[12] Not surprisingly, Feldman and Warhol were criticized for crass commercialism, for pandering to the basest instincts of the Jewish public. It was in fact a case of Jewhooing, yet in this case, the practice was upgraded from a lowbrow ethnic behavior to a higher-brow art form (somewhat like turning a Campbell's soup can into a work of art). With the celebrity imprimatur of Andy Warhol, the pop art images have found their way into the hallowed halls of American elite culture, touring Jewish art museums and galleries in 1980 to 1981, and later showing in retrospective at New York's Jewish Museum in 2008 under the title *Warhol's Jews*.[13]

A third example of Jewhooing occurred on network television. Airing on October 8, 1988, the popular comedy program *Saturday Night Live* included a satirical sketch about a television game show provocatively called *Jew, Not a Jew*. Written by Al Franken (currently US Senator from Minnesota), Tom Davis, and Jim Downey, the spoof had Tom Hanks (that evening's guest host) playing the emcee of *Jew, Not a Jew*, a fictional game show revolving around the question of Jewish identity. Hanks began by explaining the rules: "According to Jewish law, anyone whose mother is a Jew, is a Jew . . . But for the purposes of our game, anyone with any Jewish lineage at all will be considered a Jew." The audience laughed uproariously at the absurdly out-of-context reference to the *halacha* of Jewish identity, and perhaps also due to the unfamiliarity of hearing the word *Jew* spoken repeatedly and unabashedly on live television (tweaking the "too Jewish" anxiety and subverting the taboo against explicit Jewish subject matter on television).

The game then commenced, with two gentile couples vying to identify public figures as Jews, or not. The first celebrity image displayed was that of Penny Marshall, a comedic actress and director often mistaken for being Jewish (she is of Italian descent). The second was of Michael Landon, well-known actor whose Jewish identity is less well known. And the third image was of former New York City mayor Ed Koch, a somewhat obvious exemplar of ethnic Jewishness. In the first two cases, the couples' debates over the Jewish identities of the celebrities drew laughter from the studio audience. In response to the image of Koch, one of the contestants (played by Kevin Nealon) exclaimed, "He's a Jew, Bob, a Jew," eliciting the biggest laugh of all. The humor lay in the exaggerated depiction and discomfiting exposure of a familiar though largely unacknowledged phenomenon—Jewhooing—and the ambiguities of Jewish identity it represented. On the day after its airing, relates media scholar David Zurawik, the "Jew, Not a Jew" sketch drew much negative response, primarily from Jewish executives such as Brandon Tartikoff, who felt the piece was antisemitic, uncomfortably reminiscent of Jew-baiting. What they really meant, Zurawik suggests, was that it was "too Jewish," which is to say, embarrassingly close to the Jewish reality of Jewhooing.[14]

Theories of Jewhooing

Given these examples, we now have some better insight into the root cause of Jewhooing. It is clearly more than simple ethnic pride. As implied by Susan Glenn's example of Madeleine Albright, Ralph Schoenstein's example of Leslie Howard, and Al Franken's example of Michael Landon, the activity of Jewhooing is often related to the perceived assimilation of the Jewish celebrity at hand. Because the great majority of Jews who succeed in the general culture—especially in popular culture—tend to downplay their Jewishness in the process and sometimes seek to "pass" altogether, it becomes the special vocation of their fellow Jews to reclaim them, to out them as co-religionists and members of the tribe.

Underlying this reflexive habit are several other motives particular to Jews, so numerous theories have been advanced to explain the Jewhooing urge. Glenn argues that Jewhooing represents a reassertion of the biological basis of Jewish identity—that is, the first usage of "Jewish identity" discussed in Chapter 1 of this book. At a time when religious tradition and ethnic culture are the more commonly preferred modes of identification, "Jewish by descent" is denigrated as racial and regressive—it was Hitler's criterion, after all—and is often suppressed. Moreover, since intermarriage between Jews and non-Jews is today far more acceptable and commonplace, the numbers of converts to Judaism— "Jews by choice"—as well as children of intermarriage have risen dramatically. Jewish identity defined solely by descent has been called into question as never before. Nevertheless, such "blood logic" lies deep in the subconscious of many Jews and is not so easily erased. The Jewhooing of public personalities such as Albright provides a socially acceptable means of marking as Jewish a figure of Jewish descent who does not herself identify as a Jew—it is an implicit rejection of the individual's right to determine her own identity.

More often, however, Jewhooing relates to and derives from one of the other two iterations of Jewish identity—as an assessment of "who is a good Jew" on the one hand, and as an expression of Jewish identity confusion and the search for the meaning of Jewishness on the other. In this view, Jewhooing is most often employed not to reassert the trope of Jewish descent (Glenn's reading), but to clarify the nature of Jewishness, and to work out some understanding of what it means to be a Jew at a time when Jews no longer seem very distinctive at all. For example, as upwardly mobile beneficiaries of a success-oriented culture, American Jews may also evince interest in celebrities as symbols and measures of their own success. Discussing Adam Sandler's "The Chanukah Song," Eric Goldstein notes that "even as Sandler 'outs' much of Hollywood as Jewish, he also takes pride in his cast of characters *precisely because* they have achieved such success in entering the inner circle of white American society."[15]

At the same time, Jews have been longtime objects of antisemitic imagery and discrimination, and also exhibit a pressing desire to counter negative stereotypes of Jews. Jewhooing, by emphasizing more positive and admirable images of Jews, of Jews who entertain the public and elevate the culture, thereby becomes a weapon in the fight against antisemitism, a pro-Jewish message to counter the anti-Jewish accusation. Schoenstein's grandfather certainly represents this attitude, and another, somewhat sardonic example is the lyric by singer-songwriter Dan Bern in "Lithuania," his song of Holocaust remembrance: "I sometimes want to dance on Hitler's grave, and shout out: Groucho Marx, Lenny Bruce, Leonard Cohen, Philip Roth, Bob Dylan, Albert Einstein, Woody Allen, Abby Hoffman, Leonard Bernstein, Harry Houdini, Sandy Koufax!"[16] Jewhooing captures both the pride in Jewish success and the defensive posture against antisemitism, related phenomena to begin with.

In the companion volume to their museum exhibition *Entertaining America*, J. Hoberman and Jeffrey Shandler suggest yet another explanation for Jewhooing. Noting how "the Jewishness of the Jewish star often becomes part of [the] relationship between star and audience," and reminding us of the history of the early part of the twentieth century when "most Jewish stars would do whatever necessary to obscure their origins," they conclude that often, "talking about a star's Jewishness constitutes an act of cultural subversion, not only undoing the efforts of [the entertainment] industry to conceal or transform it, but also transgressing conventional boundaries of what is deemed appropriate for public consideration in the American mainstream."[17] And similarly, in his discussion of Sandler's "The Chanukah Song," Goldstein explains its appeal as "undermining the assimilationist paradigm of American Jewish popular culture."[18] Jewhooing, in this view, is seen as a subversive move by the Jewish public to counter the assimilatory pressures of popular culture, and by extension, of American society on the whole. Evidenced by the widespread popularity of "The Chanukah Song," the sentiment is often expressed simply by the mischievous pleasure Jews take in outing celebrities as fellow Jews. Some Hollywood stars and other celebrities had changed their names and attempted to hide their Jewishness? "Well, they're not going to get away with it," this thinking goes; "We'll tell the world who they *really* are."

Later in their conversation, Hoberman and Shandler add yet another layer to their analysis of Jewhooing. Hoberman notes that "in the case of Jewish fandom, people are invested in identifying personalities . . . to connect their own consumption of popular culture with a collective Jewish experience." To which Shandler responds,

> This is what I find most intriguing about the Jewish practice of inventorying Jews [that is, Jewhooing]—not only in the entertainment media, where it's most extensive, but also in the arts, politics, academia, etc. Grandparents, parents, and children may have different names in their inventories and collect them in different ways (grandparents in private conversations, their grandchildren on Web sites), but all express a common desire to map Jewish presence and Jewish continuity, two constantly contested issues in the modern age, in terms of celebrity.[19]

All these theories are helpful in explaining the enduring popularity of Jewhooing, but so far, none has zeroed in on the question of what makes Jewhooing particular to Jews. If all minority groups engage in similar behavior, what is it about Jewhooing that is unique to the Jewish experience? Like the celebrity consciousness of other minorities, Jewhooing is a means to magnify the seeming size and importance of an otherwise small and marginal group. But for Jews, minority status and social marginality have been long-standing norms of a lengthy diasporic history. As the result, certain compensatory strategies have evolved to become characteristic of Jewish culture. For example, in Ashkenazic culture, the ideals of *yichus* (Yiddish term for the prestige derived from being related to someone of importance) and *naches* (Yiddish term for the pleasure one derives from the success of others, especially one's children) emerged as forms of status enhancement—made all the more urgent by an environment of social degradation. Though the American Jewish experience has not replicated the repressive conditions of the European ghetto, such a "ghetto" mentality has nonetheless persisted among many Jews and has continued to influence Jewish culture. Both *yichus* and *naches* can be seen as precedents of Jewhooing. Which is to say, Jewish historical experience plays a major role in the shaping of Jewish consciousness; and thus we must turn to history for a fuller explanation of a cultural habit such as Jewhooing.

Perhaps the most important specifically Jewish source of the Jewhooing urge, percolating throughout Jewish history, is the religious concept of *chosenness*. Having sustained the Jews for most of their history, the traditional belief that they are God's chosen people has come under sharp attack in an era committed to universalism and human equality. Most modern Jews no longer espouse the belief in its literal sense, and one Jewish religious movement, Reconstructionism, has repudiated it altogether.[20] Nevertheless, contemporary Jewish culture persists in assigning some element of exceptionalism to Jewish existence—indeed it must, if only as communal *raison d'être*, a rationale for group survival. Thus, while no longer subscribing to the notion of divine chosenness, many Jews today continue to believe, if only subconsciously, that they are a unique people exhibiting special qualities such as high intelligence and a talent for survival.

Though such stereotypical notions of Jewish uniqueness and superiority distort reality, they are a commonly held bias. What Jew today is not susceptible to the pride evoked by citing the impressive number of Jewish Nobel Prize winners or the disproportionate number of Jews in Congress and on the US Supreme Court? On the strength of such "evidence," many Jews continue to see themselves as chosen—though no longer by God, but by history. Jewhooing, in this regard, may be seen as a none-too-subtle suggestion of Jewish distinctiveness in a secular age. A letter to the *New York Times* demonstrates how Jewhooing functions as the secularization of chosenness:

> We secular Jews do not derive the view that Jews are more intelligent or creative than non-Jews from the religious theory of a people chosen by God, or from the endurance and survival throughout history of the Jewish people against all odds. Instead, we note the number and proportion of the Jewish population who have achieved brilliance and excellence in science and in the arts, as compared with the number and proportion of non-Jews who have done the same—a comparison that is factually indisputable.[21]

273

And similarly, in the course of arguing for the advantage of Diaspora Jewish life over Israel as the Jewish homeland, Tony Karon makes the common claim that "all of the great Jewish intellectual, philosophical, moral and cultural contributions to humanity I can think of were products not of Jews living apart, but of our dispersal among the cultures of the world. Maimonides or Spinoza, Marx, Freud, Einstein or Derrida; Kafka, Proust or Primo Levi; Serge Gainsbourg or Daniel Barenboim; Lenny Bruce or Bob Dylan—I could go on ad nauseum—all are products of our interaction with diverse influences in the Diaspora."[22] In this way, Jewhooing may be used to support the diasporist contention that the Jews are, and always have been, an integral part of Western civilization.[23]

Beyond chosenness, there is yet another source of the Jewhooing phenomenon that has run throughout the Jewish historical experience. For almost 2,000 years, Jews have been in the habit of Jewhooing one of the biggest names of all time—Jesus Christ (original Hebrew name: Yehoshua ben-Yosef)—and out of this "tradition" may have grown the tendency to point out the Jewishness of other famous figures as well. The Christian son of God and messianic savior is certainly the most famous person in the history of Western civilization, and hence the ultimate celebrity figure; and like many celebrities today, the question of his Jewish identity is of abiding interest. Historically, Jesus's Jewish identity was observed by non-Jewish figures as diverse as Martin Luther and Rembrandt van Rijn, but it has been affirmed most often in the modern era, by Christians and Jews alike.[24] In fact, Jesus' Jewishness has been noted more and more of late, with book-titles such as *Jesus was a Jew* and *The Jewish Jesus* abounding.

When offered by Jews, such statements are often made from a defensive posture, as a form of Jewish-Christian polemic. By invoking Jesus the Jew, leading nineteenth-century Reform rabbis Abraham Geiger, Isaac Mayer Wise, and Kaufmann Kohler fought back against Christian anti-Judaism.[25] In twentieth-century scholarship, a significant literature emerged on the historical Jesus, portraying him as a Jew of the first century and situating him within a Jewish milieu—a trend begun by the non-Jewish Albert Schweitzer,[26] but one that includes noteworthy works by Jewish historians, such as Joseph Klausner's *Jesus of Nazareth* (1925), Solomon Zeitlin's *Who Crucified Jesus?* (1964), Samuel Sandmel's *We Jews and Jesus* (1965), David Flusser's *Jesus* (1969), and Geza Vermes's *Jesus the Jew* (1973).[27] All of these works share the manifest intention of historicizing Jesus; yet they also serve the latent function of reclaiming him for the Jews. This latter sentiment, close in nature to Jewhooing, underlies the tendency of contemporary Jews to observe that Jesus was Jewish.

In popular culture, as we have seen, comedian Lenny Bruce turned the observation into a famous routine. The perceptive reader will also note that both Sandy Koufax and Bob Dylan were at times compared to Jesus, thereby Jewhooing both the religious icon and the contemporary celebrity at once. Implicit in the comparison, as always, is the notion that Jesus was a Jew. The sentiment can also be found in Texas singer-songwriter Kinky Friedman's song "They Ain't Makin' Jews Like Jesus Anymore,"[28] in Neil Diamond's 2009 cover version of "The Chanukah Song" (in which the original lyric "Tom Cruise isn't [Jewish] but I heard his agent is" is changed to "Tom Cruise isn't, but Jesus Christ is"), and in countless jokes, perhaps the best known being:

How do we know Jesus was Jewish?
Four reasons:
1. He was thirty, unmarried, and still living with his mother.
2. He went into his father's business.
3. He thought his mother was a virgin.
4. And his mother thought he was God.[29]

Such comedic texts do more than bring Jesus down to earth. They appeal to the popular Jewish imagination as a bald exposure of his Jewish identity, an implicit denial of his divinity, and may even serve as some small form of comeuppance after centuries of Christian persecution of Jews. At the same time, these texts function as declaration of the extraordinary Jewish contribution to Western civilization; and in this regard, it is but a short step from such "Jesus Jewhooing" to the oft-made observation that many of the giants of modern thought and culture are Jews: for example, Karl Marx, Sigmund Freud, Franz Kafka, and Albert Einstein. The long-standing tendency to cite the Jewishness of Jesus, Marx, Einstein, and other luminaries of world history can be seen therefore as a precedent and underlying source of the Jewhooing habit. Beyond such historical considerations, the main motive of Jewhooing today remains the construction of Jewish identity and the related countering of assimilation—an unconscious attempt to reverse the very processes of social integration and de-Judaization that touch most every Jew in the modern world. Henry Bial suggests that, in an age when neither religion nor nationalism provide *raison d'être* for most American Jews, Jewhooing (he calls it "reading Jewish") functions as a vestigial motive for group survival.[30] By pointing to Jewish celebrities, the mass of Jewish individuals connect to one another, creating a sort of virtual community and building a framework for their own Jewish identity. Again, there is a paradox at the heart of this. While feeling the need to counter assimilation and build structures of identity, modern Jews have also rooted for the successful integration of famous Jewish figures, thus condemning and applauding assimilation at the same time.

In the end, the Jewish habit of Jewhooing reflects both impulses—both the need for identity and community, and the desire for success and integration. Goldstein concludes his discussion of Sandler's musical contribution to Jewhooing by pointing to the ambivalence it represents: "The song, therefore, embodies a host of mixed emotions about the place of Jews as insiders and outsiders, as white and as distinct in American culture. Given its tremendous popularity, one can safely conclude that this ambivalence is shared by its Jewish listeners, who are tickled by their ability to successfully 'pass' in white America, but at the same time harbor a burning desire to show that they are different."[31] In the final analysis, Jewhooing must be seen as exemplifying—and perhaps in some way resolving—the defining tension of Jewish modernity: the tension between integration/assimilation and identity/survival.

Jewhooing Today

In the present era, the Jewhooing tendency shows little sign of abating. The surprising tenacity of Jewish celebrity consciousness may be attributed to three interrelated factors. First, the turn of the twenty-first century has witnessed yet another generational shift in the nature of Jewish identity, whose catalyst was yet another perceived crisis of continuity. As in the early 1960s, the current period of revival owes much of its impetus to the anxiety arising in response to a newly reported rate of intermarriage. Following the National Jewish Population Survey of 1990, the Jewish community was alarmed—to put it mildly—by a rate nearing 50 percent, and responded with new philanthropic and educational initiatives to, once again, bolster Jewish identity and stem the tide of assimilation.

In the late 1990s, therefore, American Jews launched a nationwide movement of "synagogue transformation," and philanthropists poured millions into "Jewish continuity" efforts, including one especially popular initiative, "Birthright Israel," a fully sponsored trip to Israel for Jewish college students. The children of the baby boom generation—Generations X, Y, and Z—have thus grown up in a period of both great uncertainty and great promise for Jews in America. Again reminiscent of the 1960s, many young Jews—a growing number of whom are now the children of intermarriage—have become further alienated from Jewish life, while a significant minority have looked to reinvigorate Jewish life with their own creativity and innovation. Today's "new Jews" may be seen in the ranks of the writers and editors of *Heeb* magazine, in the thousands of young people who flock to Jewish cultural events and "Limmud" conferences, and in the founders and members of "emergent" Jewish communities such as *Ikar* in Los Angeles and *Hadar* in New York. Born of the tension between such Jewish activism and the inactivity of many other young Jews, we see a new questioning about Jewishness emerging—a questioning that may be addressed, however insufficiently, by Jewhooing. But it is Jewhooing with a difference. For example, the following dialogue was reported in a 1995 Jewish publication:

> In the coffee room of Powell's bookstore [in Portland, Oregon], three teenage boys with spiky hair and skateboards were reading *Interview* magazine and discussing the current music scene. The conversation turned to Robert Zimmerman, a.k.a. Bob Dylan.
>
> Said one: "I don't get why he changed his name from Zimmerman. All the coolest guys I know are named Zimmerman."
>
> His friend: "Yeah, when I grow up I'm gonna change my name to Zimmerman." [32]

From this example alone, it seems that today's generation of young Jews has quite a different take on being Jewish, and therefore evinces a new attitude toward public Jewish identification. What was clear in 1960—that a name like Zimmerman precluded one from pop stardom—can no longer be assumed today. The current generation is also quite media savvy, and has grown up with a keen sense of the Jewish role in popular culture. To them, Jewhooing is second nature, as reflected once again by Sandler's hit song of the 1990s, and by the following statement made in 2008 by two young Jewish culture vultures, Roger Bennett and Josh Kun:

> In our childhood homes, Jewish music meant pop icons of the 1970s and 80s like Barbra Streisand, Neil Diamond, and Barry Manilow, and maybe a version of "Hava Nagilah" or "Tzena, Tzena, Tzena" sung by the Weavers thrown in for good measure. As we were growing up, there seemed to be only two kinds of music made by Jews. On the one hand, there was Barbra singing "People" or Barry belting "Mandy" or Neil rocking through "Sweet Caroline," that holy triumvirate of Brooklyn-born Jews who managed to

spin their roots into massive showbiz windfalls—Jewish enough to fill their people with pride but not so Jewish that they couldn't fill stadiums full of Irish Catholics who knew every word to "I Write the Songs." We knew they were Jews, but more important, we knew they were American icons.[33]

Had Bennett and Kun been writing earlier, pre-1990 let's say, they may very well have betrayed some discomfort with the kitsch of such "Jewish music" and been less eager to celebrate the Jewishness of such pop celebrity figures. But as they say without a trace of self-consciousness, "we knew they were Jews," whose celebrity Jewishness now resides comfortably within their status as "American icons." By the 2000s, with the rise of a new generation, a new comfort level with Jewhooing was apparent.

The generational shift may also be seen by comparing two subsequent museum exhibitions, both mounted by the Jewish Museum of New York (and both discussed in earlier chapters): Norman Kleeblatt's *Too Jewish?* of 1996 and Jeffrey Shandler's (with J. Hoberman) *Entertaining America* of 2003.[34] Though the first was essentially an art exhibition and the second an exploration of pop culture history, both addressed the intersecting themes of American Jewish identity and American Jewish celebrity. But only the former felt the need to acknowledge the taboo against illuminating such subject matter—an anxiety clearly expressed by the exhibition title chosen by the curator, a longtime director of the museum. By 2003, however, and under the direction of a younger scholar (an expert in the fields of modern Yiddish culture and Jewish media studies), the second exhibition had fewer inhibitions to confront. *Entertaining America* was a sophisticated analysis of both celebrity and identity, but it had no qualms about being perceived as an expression of Jewhooing. Among other explanations, the attitudinal shift can be attributed to a generational change, as evidenced by the move from Kleeblatt to Shandler.

A second factor in the Jewhooing revival at the turn of the twenty-first century is simply the exponential growth of Jewish celebrity itself. As in the early 1960s, the 1990s and 2000s have seen the appearance of a new generation of Jewish celebrities, and Jews have therefore reached ever-greater heights of visibility in American popular culture. The new era of Jewish celebrity was signaled by the prominence of two very famous Jews in the 1990s: film director Steven Spielberg—who won the Academy Award for best director in 1993 (for *Schindler's List*) and again in 1998 (for *Saving Private Ryan*)—and standup comedian Jerry Seinfeld—whose eponymously named sitcom was the highest rated television show of the decade (airing on NBC from 1989 to 1998). Their phenomenal success coincided with the arrival of a Kennedy-esque president, Bill Clinton, who, like JFK, stocked his cabinet with Jews, including William Cohen, Dan Glickman, Mickey Kantor, Robert Reich, Robert Rubin, and Larry Summers. In 1997, it came to light that the new secretary of state, Madeleine Albright, was of Jewish descent; and a year later, it also came to light that the president had had an affair with a young Jewish intern named Monica Lewinsky—and Jewish celebrity consciousness had reached yet another apex by century's end.

Mention of William Cohen (whose mother was Irish protestant) reminds us of the growing presence of so-called "half-Jews" in American Jewish life. We've already treated some prominent examples, such as Paul Newman and Peter Sellers, but after four decades of rapid growth in intermarriage between Jews and non-Jews, the current period has seen a steep rise in their numbers and visibility. Though this is not the place to rehearse the parallel growth in commentary and analysis of the effects of intermarriage, we can note how the appearance of more people of partial Jewish descent has changed the nature of Jewhooing.[35] Given that some such individuals choose to identify unambiguously as Jews, while others choose not to be Jewish at all, we may safely assume that the majority of children of one Jewish parent and one non-Jewish parent experience some degree of identity questioning and confusion.

Jewhooing, as we've seen, is sometimes used to address such identity confusion, and a chief example is to be found on the website of InterfaithFamily, an organization promoting the inclusion of such families within the established Jewish community. One popular feature of the website is Nate Bloom's biweekly column "Interfaith Celebrities," which covers any and all "celebrities with interfaith connections." Bloom profiles half-Jewish celebrities such as Matthew Broderick, Jennifer Connelly, Katie Couric, Daniel Day-Lewis, Jon Favreau, Harrison Ford, James Franco, Jake and Maggie Gyllenhaal, Scarlett Johansson, Kevin Kline, Gwyneth Paltrow, Sean Penn, Joaquin Phoenix, Daniel Radcliffe (of Harry Potter fame), Kyra Sedgwick, Jason Segel, and Rachel Weisz, among many others. The column also covers the frequent interfaith couplings and marriages of celebrities, focusing on the children of the rich and famous: for example, John F. and Jackie Kennedy's daughter Caroline, Bill and Hillary Clinton's daughter Chelsea, and Donald and Ivana Trump's daughter Ivanka—all of whom married Jewish men in highly publicized matrimonials.

Anywhere else, such listings would attest to the astounding social success that Jews have found in America; but on the InterfaithFamily

website, the intent is more to validate the growing acceptance and normalcy of interfaith marriage. Insofar as the Jewhooing of such celebrities
serves to cast intermarriage in a positive light, the growth of intermarriage may in fact be spurring Jewhooing; and at the same time, it has
given renewed attention to "Jewish by descent," by denoting celebrities
as Jews who have some Jewish ancestry. An unintended consequence of
this is an increased pool of "Jewish celebrities," as we are now all the
more likely to count those with only partial Jewish backgrounds.

The new century has also seen a remarkable surge in Jewish celebrity
in the political realm. In the summer of 2000, Democratic presidential
candidate Al Gore stunned the Jewish world by choosing Senator Joe
Lieberman as his running mate. Lieberman, who would run for president
four years later, is a modern Orthodox Jew—and perhaps if not for the
poor voting-booth skills of some Jewish retirees in Florida, he would
have become the forty-sixth vice president of the United States. Though
he later fell out of favor for his support of the Iraq war, Lieberman's
ascension to political celebrity was a landmark event both in American
politics and in American Jewish history. Perhaps even more remarkable,
when Lieberman ran for the Democratic nomination in 2004, no fewer
than three of his competitors had their own Jewish ties: John Kerry, the
eventual nominee, had paternal grandparents who were Jewish converts
to Catholicism; Wesley Clark's paternal grandfather was Jewish; and
Howard Dean is married to a Jewish doctor named Judy Steinberg, and
they have raised their children as Jews.

As might be imagined, this coincidence of Jewishness aroused much
Jewhooing-style comment in the Jewish press. Likewise, when President
Bush surrounded himself with a group of Jewish advisors—neocons
and foreign policy hawks such as Elliott Abrams, Douglas Feith, Ari
Fleischer, David Frum, Lewis "Scooter" Libby, Richard Perle, and Paul
Wolfowitz—notice was taken as well (or, in the case of antisemitic Jew-
hooers seeking evidence of Jewish conspiracy, alarms went off). President Obama, too, elevated Jews to highly visible positions, notably his
most senior advisor, David Axelrod, and both his first and third chiefs of
staff, Rahm Emanuel and Jacob Lew. Soon after Lew's promotion was
announced in January 2012, a young man named Andrew Lustig posted
a spoken-word rant on YouTube titled "I Am Jewish." Its opening words:
"I am the collective pride and excitement that is felt, when we find out
that that new actor, that great athlete, *his chief of staff*, is Jewish [em-
phasis mine]." Seemingly inspired by Lew's selection, Lustig's piece was a
case of instant Jewhooing, made possible by the medium of the Internet.

In 2010, Obama supplied another first in Jewhooing history by successfully nominating his solicitor general, Elena Kagan, to become a third sitting Jewish member of the Supreme Court (together with Ruth Bader Ginsburg and Stephen Breyer). Other newly prominent Jewish women in politics included Congresswoman Debbie Wasserman Schultz, chair of the Democratic National Committee; and Congresswoman Gabby Giffords, who attained a tragic fame when she was shot and wounded in early 2011. Perhaps the most stunning development in political Jewhooing occurred when former comedian and *Saturday Night Live* writer/performer Al Franken was elected senator from Minnesota in the 2008 election. The man who had written the "Jew, Not a Jew" sketch was now a prime object of Jewhooing himself—as he became one of twelve Jewish members of the US Senate (only 12 percent as opposed to the 33 percent on the bench).

Franken brings us back to a more traditional arena of Jewish celebrity: comedy. After the initial boom of Jewish comedians during the 1950s and 1960s, many assumed that the peak had passed, and that other minority groups would supersede Jews over time. Yet today, with major comedic figures in film and television such as Jack Black, Sacha Baron Cohen, Larry David, Deborah Messing, Andy Samberg, Adam Sandler, and Ben Stiller, the Jewish role in American comedy remains rather conspicuous. The leading figure in comedy filmmaking today is producer/writer Judd Apatow, who started out working with Stiller in the early 1990s and then enjoyed his first breakthrough success with Garry Shandler later in the decade (as co-producer of the *Larry Sanders Show*). In the 2000s, Apatow made hit film after film with a stable of Jewish comic actors: Jay Baruchel, Jonah Hill, Seth Rogen, Paul Rudd, and Jason Segel. On television, the most-watched comedy program on cable was Jon Stewart's *The Daily Show*, a brilliantly written and performed political satire—Stewart, like his frequent guest commentator, Lewis Black, portrayed himself as a Jew with frequency. And in addition to Black, heirs to the legacy of Lenny Bruce in standup comedy include Dave Attell, Sandra Bernhard, Richard Lewis, Bill Maher, Marc Maron, and Sarah Silverman. In the twenty-first century, the association of Jews with comedy is as strong as ever.

More surprisingly, turn-of-the-twenty-first-century Hollywood experienced a burst of Jewish celebrity. Whereas Barbra Streisand's early 1960s breakthrough had opened the door for a number of recognizably Jewish actors in the later 1960s and 1970s—notably Dustin Hoffman, Elliott Gould, George Segal, and Richard Benjamin[36]—the 1990s and

2000s have seen a veritable explosion of Jewish film and television stars, and the trend is especially notable among women. In addition to Jennifer Connelly, Maggie Gyllenhaal, Scarlett Johansson, Gwyneth Paltrow, Kyra Sedgwick and Rachel Weisz, all mentioned earlier, the new screen Jewesses include Dianna Agron, Rachel Bilson, Selma Blair, Emmanuelle Chriqui, Kat Dennings, Julia-Louis Dreyfus, Lisa Edelstein, Sarah Michelle Gellar, Lisa Kudrow, Mila Kunis, Natasha Lyonne, Julianna Margulies, Idina Menzel, Deborah Messing, Lea Michelle, Amanda Peet, Natalie Portman, Jamie-Lynn Sigler, Alicia Silverstone, and Rena Sofer. In one of the top films of 2010, Darren Aronofsky's psychological thriller *The Black Swan*, every major female role is played by a Jewish actress: the two leads are Natalie Portman (who won an Oscar for the role) and Mila Kunis; and secondary characters are played by Winona Ryder and Barbara Hershey. It's almost as if Aronofsky was engaging in Jewhooing through casting. As all of these figures are Jewish actresses in the spotlight of celebrity (though with varying degrees of acknowledged Jewishness), they may be thought of as the "descendants" of Barbra Streisand.

We may similarly cite other 1960s figures as models and precedents for contemporary Jewish celebrity. For example, Streisand's contemporary Barbara Walters has her own spiritual offspring: Jewish women who are prominent television journalists today include Dana Bash, Andrea Mitchell, Lesley Stahl, and Jessica Yellin. Likewise, Mike Wallace has given us Wolf Blitzer, Richard Engel, Jeff Greenfield, Matt Lauer, and Geraldo Rivera. Of those making news, the most infamous Jew of the early 1960s was not Lenny Bruce but Jack Ruby, murderer of Lee Harvey Oswald—a man who became universally despised and gave his fellow Jews immeasurable anxiety for fear of being linked to him. Paralleling Ruby's infamy today, no survey of contemporary Jewish celebrity would be complete without mention of Bernie Madoff, perpetrator of the biggest Ponzi scheme in history, and unquestionably the most reviled and infamous Jew of the twenty-first century (so far). In a similar vein, Supreme Court justice Abe Fortas's fall from grace in 1968 foreshadowed other political downfalls of prominent Jews, such as Washington lobbyist Jack Abramoff's indictment for corruption in 2006, New York governor Eliot Spitzer's prostitution scandal in 2008, and Brooklyn congressman Anthony Weiner's online sexting exposure in 2011—the first two scandals were even memorialized in feature films.

On a more positive note, Allen Funt, the New York Jew who originated reality TV in his ever-popular show *Candid Camera* (aired on CBS from 1960 to 1967), and an archetypal affable, congenial television personality, has been reincarnated in the person of contemporary television impresario Andy Cohen (producer of numerous reality TV programs, and host of *Watch What Happens Live*). Partly under Cohen's influence, reality TV came to dominate television programming in the first decade of the century, and like him, its stars were often Jews—personalities such as Paula Abdul (*American Idol*), Roseanne Barr (*Roseanne's Nuts*), Nate Berkus (*Nate Berkus Show*), Heidi Fleiss (*Prostitutes to Parrots*), Bethenny Frankel (*Real Housewives of New York City*), Harvey Levin (TMZ), Stacey London (*What Not to Wear*), Dr. Drew Pinsky (*Celebrity Rehab*), Judy Scheindlin (*Judge Judy*), Gail Simmons (*Top Chef*), Gene Simmons (*Family Jewels*), and Patty Stanger (*Millionaire Matchmaker*). Although few appear as identified Jews (one exception is Gene Simmons, who in one episode traveled to Israel to meet his long-lost family), they are all Jewish celebrities subject to Jewhooing (as in this paragraph) because, despite their purported invisibility as Jews, they tend to "read" Jewish. By their very visible celebrity, therefore, they contribute to the ongoing shaping of the Jewish image in American popular culture.

Though contemporary Jewhooing does include extensive listings of modern-day Jewish athletes and musicians, no one of the stature of either Sandy Koufax or Bob Dylan has yet emerged. Still, notice must be taken of the startling rise of three new celebrities in sports and music, all of whom are observant Jews: boxers Yuri Foreman and Dmitriy Salita; and Matisyahu, Lubavitcher reggae star. Though born elsewhere, they each attained their stardom in Brooklyn, and together represent a kind of throwback to forms of Jewish identity rarely identified with American celebrity—Russian immigrant in the case of Foreman and Salita, and ultra-Orthodox in the case of Matisyahu. None, however, seems destined to prefigure a larger trend. Although contemporary pop music contains a number of prominent Jews—for example, the Beastie Boys, Beck, and the late Amy Winehouse—no one of Dylan's seminal accomplishment and impact has arisen (nor is it likely, given the balkanized nature of popular music today). Professional baseball has seen some modest growth in the number of Jewish ballplayers in the 2000s, several of whom are above-average talents (a record three Jewish players were selected for the All-Star Games in the summers of 2008 and 2009: Ryan Braun and Kevin Youkilis in 2008 and 2009, Ian Kinsler in 2008, and Jason Marquis in 2009). Still, no one remotely comparable to Koufax has appeared on the scene. But even without a new Koufax or Dylan, the early twenty-first century has been a boom time for Jewish celebrity and therefore for Jewhooing—a trend further accelerated by the information revolution of the Internet, the third, and perhaps most critical factor.

Whereas both the generational shift and the general increase in Jewish celebrities had echoed the early 1960s, the new medium of the Internet is entirely unprecedented and has had an incalculable effect on all the variables we've discussed: American celebrity, Jewish identity, and Jewhooing. In the first case, celebrities and their public now have less fettered and more immediate connection to one another. Fans can now find information on their idols' past and present almost instantly, and can also find each other through blogs and fan websites. The information resource given us by the Internet has made it possible to uncover every detail of a celebrity's life and work, and then, in turn, grants us access to that information. Celebrities, too, have the ability to contact their fan base directly, as many do through Twitter and other forms of instant messaging.[37] The effect of all this is to further reduce the distance between celebrity figure and fan, ultimately diminishing the larger-than-life monumentality of celebrity in general. Yet at the same time, it can be argued, the power of celebrity has only increased—by virtue of the immediacy and instant access provided by the new medium of the Internet.

Similarly, the Internet seems to have had contradictory effects on Jewish identity. On the one hand, the information technology revolution has created a mass, undifferentiated community of Internet users, all with equal access and neutral standing in the world of cyberspace. For Jews and other small affinity groups, such "Internet individualism" has only further contributed to the erosion of the identity structures of the past, such as family, community, organization, and so on. At the same time, however, the Internet is being used by a growing number of Jews to create new forms of community, and it offers new opportunities for identification with other Jews.

New web-based forms of Jewish community have only recently begun to emerge and are not yet fully understood—but what is clear is that the combination of the technological revolution and the "ever-dying" quality of Jewishness has given rise to a new era in Jewhooing. The best example, of course, is the Jewhoo! website itself, founded in 1997 by Chris Williams and Michael Page (the latter Jewish, the former not). As Susan Glenn describes it, Jewhoo! served as "a portal of entry where the curious philo- or antisemite can learn whether their favorite politicians, sports figures, theatrical and Hollywood stars, or scientists qualify for inclusion in the Jewish hall of fame."[38] Though the original Jewhoo! website is no longer online, several successor sites have filled the void, including Jew Or Not Jew, Heebz, and Guess Who's the Jew! The popularity of such sites attests to the persistent urge to Jewhoo, and further testifies to the enabling role of the Internet.

Jewish celebrity, it should be noted, was not at first a significant part of the information technology revolution, with pioneers such as Bill Gates, Steve Jobs, and Steve Wozniak all non-Jews. More recently however, Internet culture has yielded a number of Jewish figures, most notably Sergey Brin and Larry Page, founders of Google, and Mark Zuckerberg, founder of Facebook. In 2010, the double-sided nature of Jewish celebrity was dramatically represented in the portrayal of Zuckerberg by actor Jesse Eisenberg in Aaron Sorkin's film *The Social Network*; and at the same time, by *Time* magazine's anointment of Zuckerberg as its Person of the Year (making it two Jews in a row—the year before, the title was awarded to Federal Reserve chief Ben Bernanke). The film, however entertaining and intellectually stimulating, is nothing less than a character assassination of a twenty-six-year-old Jewish kid, a portrait of a computer geek as Machiavellian and amoral. The magazine profile, however compelling and socially relevant, is a huge exaggeration of his importance, an undue inflation of his celebrity. Zuckerberg is a perfect illustration of the dichotomous nature of Jewish celebrity. He is, in our collective image of him, both hero and villain, both brilliant billionaire and soulless sycophant. Not surprisingly, Zuckerberg made some attempt to improve his image in the wake of the success of *The Social Network*. On the January 29, 2011, airing of *Saturday Night Live*, he made a guest appearance to surprise guest host Jesse Eisenberg, who had just starred as Zuckerberg in the film. Together with cast member Andy Samberg—playing Zuckerberg as well—the sketch treated the audience to the spectacle of three Jewish celebrity "Zuckerbergs" standing shoulder to shoulder onstage.

Koufax, Bruce, Dylan and Streisand

We now return to our four profiled figures: Sandy Koufax, Lenny Bruce, Bob Dylan, and Barbra Streisand. In the era of postmodern Jewishness and cyber-Jewhooing, their Jewish celebrity has reached a new level, as we've seen in each of the preceding chapters. Koufax at the White House, Bruce given his own variety of He'Brew beer (the Shmaltz label's "Bittersweet Lenny's R.I.P.A."), Dylan's image in a Jewish museum, and Streisand's Barbie doll all nicely illustrate the durability of their Jewish celebrity. That the Jewhooing of the four figures has reached its apogee is demonstrated by the sundry appearances of their names and images in Jewish contexts, and most critically, by their grouping with other famous

Jews. Reporting on the new edition of the *Encyclopedia Judaica* in 2007, Larry Gordon writes, "The first edition, [editor Michael] Berenbaum noted, had some glaring omissions, often reflecting an Israeli and European emphasis and an arm's length approach to popular culture. For example, songwriter Bob Dylan (the Jewish-born Robert Zimmerman) was not there. Sandy Koufax, the Dodger, was not listed even though he had become a great sports hero of American Jewry for not pitching a 1965 World Series game scheduled for Yom Kippur. Dylan and Koufax have hefty entries in the new one."[39]

As in the elite, high-culture venue of the authoritative encyclopedia, so too in the sphere of Jewish youth culture. Its chief organ, *Heeb* magazine, has celebrated both Dylan and Streisand, among others, in its line of Jewish hero T-shirts. British journalist Jonathan Freedland describes the phenomenon:

> I suspect this discomfort is the point of Heeb. It's to take Jewishness out of the realm of bagels-and-Billy-Crystal cosiness and locate it somewhere more dangerous and forbidden. Closer, in other words, to the edge. That a new generation of American Jews feels able to enter this discomfort zone says something paradoxical about them: that they clearly feel truly comfortable. Only a Jewish woman with a Jennifer Lopez figure and no fear of anti-semitism would want to wear a T-shirt whose slogan is Jew-Lo. Only a Jewish man with tremendous tribal confidence would feel relaxed in a Jews Kick Ass shirt (available in Albert Einstein, Bob Dylan, Sammy Davis Jr. and Jesus versions).[40]

What do Einstein, Dylan, Davis, and Jesus have in common? They are all extraordinarily famous, highly talented, and somewhat subversive Jewish figures standing outside the Jewish mainstream—and so collectively represent the new Jewish "cool." And, in a similar group canonization—plural Jewhooing, as it were—the image of Dylan was spotted in the summer of 2005 by this author while visiting the Auschwitz Jewish Center, a museum housed in the old synagogue of the town of Oswiecim, Poland. In its upstairs gallery, exhibited amid drawings of Jewish subject matter by local schoolchildren, is a poster montage of famous Jewish faces, including Einstein, Karl Marx, Steven Spielberg, and Dylan. The title, in Polish, translates as, "And what do you think about these Jews?" What can one think, standing a few miles from the site of history's most heinous mass murder of Jews? Nevertheless, the image of Dylan jumped out, and demonstrated beyond any doubt that he has arrived as a symbolic exemplar of the Jewish people.

At the current moment, a decade into the twenty-first century, three of
the four Jewish celebrity figures profiled in this book are still alive and
well and going strong. As suggested in each of the chapters devoted to
the celebrity culture inspired by them, the Jewhooing of Koufax, Dylan,
and Streisand has reached a peak, and we can only wonder how, if at all,
they have responded to this aspect of their celebrity. Koufax, as earlier
discussed, has attained a uniquely iconic status and has become a symbol of Jewish famousness. On the May 4, 2011, broadcast of *The Daily
Show*, for example, Jon Stewart interviewed David Barton, a Christian
conservative and nonacademic historian. In describing his revisionist
approach to the history of the American Revolution, Barton made the
point that "most Jewish people can't name the Jewish founding fathers,"
to which Jewish comedian Stewart instantly replied, "No, I can . . . um
. . . Sandy Koufax . . . um . . . yeah, you're right, Sandy Koufax, that's
all I got."[41] Stewart's joke, playing on the general ignorance of historical
figures such as Gershom Mendes Seixas and Rebecca Gratz, recast the
American Jewish history timeline with just one name—the greatest hero
of them all, Sandy Koufax. And, as repeated ad nauseum, Koufax's main
claim to Jewish fame is his inactivity on the Yom Kippur of 1965.

Yet another contemporary Jewish comedian and mainstay of cable
television, Larry David, has given us the ultimate tribute to this moment in American Jewish history. In a very funny episode titled "Palestinian Chicken," David's *Curb Your Enthusiasm* had his newly observant
friend, Marty Funkhouser (played by Bob Einstein), cancel a golf ap-
pointment due to the Sabbath. David's exasperated response: "You're
Koufaxing me?!"[42] Like *Houdini* a century before, *Koufax* has become
part of the language. Whether Koufax himself has been amused by such
pop cultural references is unknown. What we do know is that he seems
to have broken out of his shell of late, making an unprecedented series of
public appearances, such as his extensive interview in the documentary
Jews and Baseball, his enthusiastic participation in a public forum in Los
Angeles, and of course, his quite moving visit to the White House. Now
in his late seventies, he seems finally at peace with his Jewish celebrity.

As for Bob Dylan, he is still performing across America and around
the world—and regarding his Jewish celebrity, he still seems to be up to
old tricks, confounding his fans with ever-shifting identities and mixed
messages. In 2009, he released his thirty-fourth studio album and his
first Christmas record, *Christmas in the Heart*, a collection of both religious and secular holiday songs. He claimed it to be an expression of
his affinity for a classic genre in American music, no religious preference

intended. Many Jewish commentators were quick to point out that other Jewish stars such as Barbra Streisand and Neil Diamond have also released Christmas albums; and moreover, some of the most familiar Christmas tunes were written by Jews, such as Irving Berlin's "White Christmas" and Johnny Marks's "Rudolph the Red-Nosed Reindeer." But Dylan's heartfelt delivery of the songs, as well as his titling the album *Christmas "in the Heart,"* suggest the depth of his yuletide feelings.[43]

A year-and-a-half later, while on international tour, Dylan flew to Israel to give a concert (for the third time—the first two were in 1987 and 1993). With his stalwart band behind him, he performed in Ramat Gan stadium on June 20, 2011, before an enthusiastic and mostly Jewish Israeli audience. Yet Dylan, ever the provocateur, chose to open the show with "Gonna Change My Way of Thinking," a song from *Slow Train Coming*, the 1979 album that heralded his Christian period. Though it's possible that nothing was intended by his choice of opening song—after all, this was the very same set list as the preceding concert in London—it was puzzling, to say the least. With its twice repeated gospel lyric, "Jesus is calling, He's coming back to gather up his jewels," the song announces its Christian sentiment in no uncertain terms—an odd way to begin a concert in Tel Aviv, the world's first Jewish city. Intriguingly, though, the first time Dylan sang the line he slurred the words, spitting it out as "Jeez-is coming," and then dropped the phrase altogether in the repetition.[44] Whether this indicates some ambivalence on his part is unclear, but it would be hard to deny that he enjoys the subversive quality of his Christian songs, or that he is unaware of their effects on a Jewish audience. Many Israeli fans were enthralled by his performance nonetheless. One such fan, Bradley Burston, wrote in defense of his hero following a negative review of the concert. In good Dylan Jewhooing tradition, Burston first compares Dylan to the great Hasidic masters, and concludes,

> The reviewer wrote that Dylan, who was last here in 1993, is unlikely ever to visit again. And he may be right. But the crowd in Ramat Gan showed something else. Dylan lives here. He lives in the culture of Israel. He lives in the thought processes of many of the nation's artists and intellectuals and activists, and, of course, its musicians and songwriters and poets.
>
> He has influenced Israel for the better more than any other American Jew . . . Like any true rebbe, certainly like Shlomo Carlebach, Bob Dylan is spectacularly flawed. But like any true rebbe, he has worlds to teach us about ourselves and this life, and we know this much: we are simply not going to get this stuff from anyone else.[45]

Dylan's appearance in Israel provides an instructive comparison with a special concert given by Barbra Streisand on September 26, 2009, at a specially selected location—the Village Vanguard, one of the last remaining nightclubs from Streisand's Greenwich Village heyday.[46] With celebrity fans such as Bill Clinton and Sarah Jessica Parker in attendance, and with her husband James Brolin and her favorite songwriters Alan and Marilyn Bergman sitting close by the stage, Streisand delivered a rare concert in such an intimate setting; and despite the cameras, was visibly comfortable performing before "her people." Unlike Dylan, she opened with a crowd-pleaser, the lushly sentimental "Here's to Life" from the album of jazz standards she would release a few days later, *Love Is the Answer*, and predictably ended the rendition by raising her glass and toasting all with a hearty "*L'Chayim!*" (Hebrew, "To life!"). At the same concert, Streisand also reminisced about the "good old days" in the Village when greats such as Lenny Bruce and Bob Dylan played there as well—she is well aware of the history of which she is a part. We may legitimately wonder whether Streisand is a fan of the most recent popular shrine to her celebrity, the hit television series *Glee*. As artist Deborah Kass pointed out to me, "the entire show is structured around Barbra Streisand," and she is its "organizing principal."[47] The show is about a group of misfits in a high school glee club dreaming of stardom while singing, dancing, and acting their way into everyone's heart—sound familiar? More pointedly, the most diva-esque of the leads, Rachel, is an explicitly Jewish character played by a Jewish actress (Lea Michele). In numerous episodes she expresses her idolization of Barbra, and sings Streisand classics such as "Don't Rain on My Parade" and "Get Happy/ Happy Days are Here Again." Finally, in the episode "Born This Way," Rachel is convinced not to get a nose job through a "Barbra-vention" of her friends, in which the ensemble dances to the hit club song "Barbra Streisand" by Duck Sauce. When *Glee* won a Golden Globe for best television series in 2010, series creator Ryan Murphy accepted the award by saying, "Thank you to the Hollywood Foreign Press and Miss Barbra Streisand." Kass also told me a story which, though a bit gossipy, bears repeating in this context. When, at a Democratic fundraiser, a wealthy owner of one of Kass's portrayals of Streisand (see Chapter 5) got to chat with the real Streisand, she told her that she looks at her image every day in her living room. Streisand replied, "Oh, do you have one of those paintings? I have one too, but if I hang it people will think I'm an egomaniac."[48] So no self-Jewhooing there, but I'll bet she watches *Glee* with glee.

Fifty years since their initial burst on the scene, Koufax, Bruce, Dylan, and Streisand have all become mainstays of contemporary American Jewish culture. In varied ways, their celebrity can be said to have contributed to the construction of American Jewish identity. The point is made especially clear whenever they are grouped or listed together— that is, *group Jewhooing.*

Conclusion

Group Jewhooing has found its major expression in the world of the identity museum. Insofar as they have become arbiters of Jewish identity, contemporary Jewish museums have begun to incorporate exhibits enumerating the many Jews in popular culture. Often, they are among the most popular exhibits with museumgoers, occupying a central position in the overall scheme of the museum; examples include those at the Skirball Cultural Center in Los Angeles and the Museum of Jewish Heritage in New York. The Skirball has a special room dedicated to this purpose situated at the conclusion of its permanent exhibition on the American Jewish experience. One sits in the small, octagonal room surrounded by sound recordings and kaleidoscopic images of the many Jews who contributed to American popular culture. It is a multimedia shrine to Jewish celebrity. Similarly, as described earlier, the Jewish Museum of New York mounted a major exhibition in 2003 titled *Entertaining America: Jews, Movies, and Broadcasting.* Although curated by two noted scholars of popular culture, J. Hoberman and Jeffrey Shandler, and thus rising above a mere listing of celebrities through their incisive interpretation, the exhibition nonetheless functioned as an exercise in Jewhooing.

Then, in 2010, the trend peaked with the opening of a major new museum in Philadelphia, the National Museum of American Jewish History (NMAJH). Even before its opening, the new institution leaned heavily on the legacy of famous Jews in its fund-raising campaign. Its president and CEO, Michael Rosenzweig, writes in his promotional letter, "Because your story is our story. It's the story of Emma Lazarus and Albert Einstein. Of Sandy Koufax and Estee Lauder. Of Leonard Bernstein and Ruth Bader Ginsburg. It's a story of opportunity. Of hope. Of freedom." But as much as opportunity, hope, and freedom, celebrity seems to be a principal motive of the museum too, as the letter continues: "The National Museum of American Jewish History will . . . tell the stories of Jews in America, the stories of Louis Kahn and Barbra Streisand. Of Henrietta Szold, Irving Berlin, Levi Strauss, Diane Von Furstenberg, Benny Goodman, Rebecca Gratz, George Burns, Betty Friedan, Louis Brandeis, Golda Meir,

Jerry Seinfeld, Saul Bellow . . . and in so doing, it will tell your story too."[49] As completed, the museum exhibition contains not one, but two entire walls filled with images of people—both well-known and ordinary American Jews. The probable purpose of this is, à la Rosenzweig, to suggest how the famous American Jew mirrors the experience of all Jewish Americans. But the effect is to reflect a certain ambivalence instead—ambivalence over what constitutes the proper subject for a museum of the American Jewish experience: everyday life, or extraordinary lives?

Together with its main exhibition, the museum also includes an exhibit specifically devoted to famous Jews, prominently located on the ground floor. Called *Only in America*, it is essentially a hall of fame honoring eighteen noteworthy American Jews. Added to the museum on the insistence of a major donor (against the better judgment of the academic historians who planned the main exhibition), the eighteen figures were chosen by polling the general public on the Internet—an excellent illustration of the populist impulse that is Jewhooing. The official website of the museum provides a link to an "Only in America" page, which proclaims, "The results are in! The first eighteen distinguished Jewish Americans to be featured in the Museum's *Only in America* Gallery/Hall of Fame have been chosen. The Gallery will include Irving Berlin, Leonard Bernstein, Louis Brandeis, Albert Einstein, Mordecai Kaplan, Sandy Koufax, Estée Lauder, Emma Lazarus, Isaac Leeser, Golda Meir, Jonas Salk, Menachem Mendel Schneerson, Rose Schneiderman, Isaac Bashevis Singer, Steven Spielberg, Barbra Streisand, Henrietta Szold, and Isaac Mayer Wise."[50] As the text further explains,

> The extraordinary accomplishments of these individuals illustrate that a hallmark of the American experience has been an unparalleled opportunity to aspire, achieve, and possibly change the world. All 218 individuals included in the public vote will be included in an interactive database that will be available to all Museum visitors as well as on its website.
>
> During the summer of 2009, the public voted on the eighteen to be included in the *Only in America* Gallery/Hall of Fame from a list of 218 possible candidates. More than 209,000 votes were cast from 56 countries on the Museum's *Only in America* website. The Museum selected for inclusion in the Gallery the person who received the most votes in each category. In addition to the public's recommendations, the Museum's historians and curators worked to ensure that the group reflected Jews' 350 years of history in the United States, the important achievements of American Jewish women and men, and the diverse fields in which Jews have been involved.[51]

Not surprisingly, the polling process for the *Only in America* exhibit included all four of the celebrity figures profiled in this book. Koufax, Bruce, Dylan, and Streisand were among the 218 famous American Jews run as candidates in the vote. Yet of the four, only Koufax and Streisand made the final eighteen—and for good reason. Despite the inclusion of four eminent religious figures on the final list[52] (added by the supervising historians), the chosen figures mostly represent the idea of secular Jewish contribution to America—a theme in consonance with the chief purpose of the museum, as Rosenzweig phrases it: "Our Museum illustrates how freedom and its choices, challenges and responsibilities, fostered an environment in which American Jews were able to accomplish truly extraordinary things."[53] The "extraordinary things" he had in mind were certainly not the theological writings and religious initiatives of great rabbis, but rather the more worldly achievements and contributions of Jews such as Koufax and Streisand.

Quite purposefully located on Independence Mall directly across from the Liberty Bell, NMAJH represents the synthesis of Americanism and Judaism, and celebrates the comfortable fit between Jews and America—how could it have been otherwise? Hence, its core exhibition emphasizes the very American theme of freedom. Spread between three floors, its three thematic sections are "Foundations of Freedom, 1654–1880," "Dreams of Freedom, 1880–1945," and "Choices and Challenges of Freedom, 1945–Today." The highlighting of both Koufax and Streisand (Streisand's image alone appears in the main exhibition no less than four times) conforms to this rather positive view of American acceptance of Jews and Jewish success in America. Both Koufax and Streisand are unequivocal Jewish heroes because they confirm, rather than challenge, American Jews' idea of themselves.

A very different expression of Jewish celebrity consciousness appeared at the same time, also in late 2010, when the American Jewish World Service (AJWS)—the antipoverty and human rights organization directed by Ruth Messinger—celebrated the twenty-fifth anniversary of its founding and commissioned a special promotional film for the occasion. The five-minute public service announcement, made by comedy mogul Judd Apatow (with writer Jordan Rubin), was not the usual Jewish philanthropic fare. It offered, instead, "a medley of Hollywood stars, Jew and gentile, making light of Jewish stereotypes . . . and generally having more fun at a religious group's expense than their grandparents might think proper." According to a review in the December 11, 2010, issue of the *New York Times*, it was "different from the standard nonprofit propaganda, different enough to have been watched nearly a million times since it made its debut a month and a half ago."[54] The humorous piece (which still may be viewed on YouTube) consists of a series of film and television celebrities speaking directly to the camera. Upending the expectation of a lineup of Jewish stars, Apatow has the first few introduce themselves, "I'm _____, and I'm not Jewish." Such declarations by figures as diverse as Don Johnson, Tracy Morgan, Patrick Stewart, Brian Williams, and Lindsay Lohan turns Jewhooing on its head.

Cleverly, Apatow did not simply "make light of Jewish stereotypes," he subverted them by having a series of celebrities play verbal hopscotch on the dividing line between Jews and non-Jews. On one level, this was appropriate to the occasion, as AJWS is a Jewish-sponsored organization that directs its charity primarily to non-Jews in need. But on a somewhat deeper level, Apatow was exploiting the familiar complexities and contradictions of American Jewish identity for the sake of humor. The *Times* article compared the "Jew/not-a-Jew classification" of Apatow's film to Adam Sandler's "The Chanukah Song," but following our discussion, the film is more resonant of Lenny Bruce's "Jewish and Goyish" routine. Like Bruce, Apatow (who also happens to be married to a beautiful red-headed non-Jewish woman, actress Leslie Mann) was questioning the very boundaries that define Jewish life. As in the comedy of Bruce—and in the celebrity of Dylan for that matter—Apatow's film betrays a profound discomfort with particularistic labels and essentializing categorizations. Though he resolves the dilemma ("Is AJWS a parochial Jewish organization or not?") with good-natured humor, a satirical critique of Jewish identity comes through at the same time.

The AJWS film is therefore the diametric opposite of the NMAJH hall of fame exhibit. Where the Philadelphia museum resides primarily in a comforting worldview of American-Jewish harmony, the Hollywood promo deals in a more unsettling view of American-Jewish dissonance. Where the museum exhibit provides a fitting home to the American Jewish celebrity of Koufax and Streisand, the promotional film is animated by the more subversive spirit of Bruce and Dylan, two Jewish celebrities who challenged the very notion of Jewish identity. Both points of view reflect American Jewish reality; and both, ultimately, are necessary to the understanding of American Jews.

When all is said and done, Jewhooing remains obnoxious in the eyes of many. Why, for instance, is such a fuss made over Koufax's decision to sit out a game for Yom Kippur? Because without the cover provided by the myth, Jewish fans would have to admit the truth of their adulation for Koufax—it has little to do with his religious behavior, and everything to do with his being a great Jewish athlete, a Jew who excelled in an arena where there were few other Jews. But such raw ethnic pride on its own is embarrassing and unseemly. The unseemly life and death of Bruce was also an embarrassment to some. His Jewish celebrity is assured, however, by the legacy of one especially memorable comedy routine, a routine that was anything but. "Jewish and Goyish" was Bruce's midrash on American Jewishness, an incisively revealing deconstruction of Jewish identity. Dylan, a latter-day Irving Berlin who reached heights of fame comparable to Einstein, Robin Hood, and Elvis, deconstructed identity in general. His Jewish celebrity remains annoyingly enigmatic to this day—yet the enduring question of his Jewishness ("Is Bob Dylan a Jew?") will be *his* legacy to the history of both American celebrity and Jewish identity. And finally there is Streisand, whose Jewishness helped create her celebrity, and whose celebrity continues to reflect the state of Jewish identity in America. All four Jewish celebrities emerged during the early 1960s, both their Jewishness and their celebrity reflecting that critical era. The Jewish celebrity of all four has stayed with us to the current day, their transitional "early60s-ishness" foreshadowing our own time, and their Jewish celebrity, once again, setting the precedent for today's.

Together, they demonstrate how Jewish celebrity reflects both the diversity and the complexity of American Jewish identity. In their public lives and popular images, all four figures betrayed the characteristic duality of both Jews and celebrities. As a pitcher, Sandy Koufax was powerful and fearsome, yet as a man, gentle and a *mensch*; he was, paradoxically, an American baseball player who became a religious symbol for the Jews. Lenny Bruce was both a show business hack and an iconoclastic artist; he was, paradoxically, a free spirit who spoke "Jewish" for all to hear. Bob Dylan was both a nice Jewish boy from the Midwest and a born-again Christian living in Malibu; he was, paradoxically, an apostle of authenticity who has never been willing to say, "I am a Jew"— and so let others do it for him. Barbra Streisand was the most gorgeous ugly duckling ever to come out of Brooklyn ("You can take the girl out of Brooklyn, but . . ."); she was, paradoxically, both beloved and reviled, both a Jewish icon and a Hollywood/liberal/feminist/gay-friendly monster.

In every case, the apparent contradictions were blended in the persona of the celebrity; so our consciousness of their celebrity begins to resolve the tensions we experience parallel to theirs. In sum, Koufax,

Bruce, Dylan, and Streisand represent the two sides (at least) of the American Jewish equation: one, the remarkable record of Jewish inclusion and success in America (as represented by the NMAJH exhibit); and two, the challenge America poses for Jews, the dilemma they experience in staying committed to a self-image of exceptionalism (as represented by the AJWS promo) and hence to their own survival. Jewish celebrity consciousness—Jewhooing—uniquely addresses these opposing tendencies and helps maintain a balance between them. Celebrity, as observed throughout this work, has long been an integral element of the American Jewish experience. If the parallels between the early 1960s and today are any indication, the nexus of American celebrity and Jewish identity is bound to continue well into the future.

Notes

1. Introduction

1. Susan A. Glenn, "In the Blood? Consent, Descent, and the Ironies of Jewish Identity," *Jewish Social Studies* 8:2/3 (Winter/Spring 2002), 139–152. The term is derived from the now-defunct Internet website Jewhoo! (itself a takeoff on Yahoo), which functioned as a search engine for famous Jews, enabling visitors to determine whether any given celebrity is, in fact, Jewish.

2. Adam Sandler first performed "The Chanukah Song" on *Saturday Night Live* on Oct. 15, 1994, and recorded it in 1995 for the CD *What the Hell Happened to Me?* (Warner Bros. Records, 1996).

3. Rob Eshman, "What's In a Name?" (editorial), *Jewish Journal* (Oct. 4, 2002).

4. The term *Jewish identity* will be discussed later in this chapter. *Assimilation* is a more problematic term because it has fallen out of fashion in social scientific discourse, largely due to its colloquial usage as a pejorative. As Jonathan Sarna further notes, "Through the years, 'assimilation' has become so freighted with different meanings, modifiers, and cultural associations that for analytical purposes it has become virtually meaningless." *American Judaism: A History* (Yale Univ. Press, 2004), xix. Nevertheless, I will use it in this narrative to denote the various forms of resistance to Jewish identification that were common in pre-1960s America. That the dialectic of Jewish identity and assimilation has been fundamentally altered in the decades since the 1960s is the thesis of this book.

5. Jonathan Sarna, ed., *The American Jewish Experience* (Holmes & Meier, 1986), xvi.

6. Though Jews reside all over the United States (total Jewish population: approximately 5–6 million), at least one out of three live in either New York City or Los Angeles (with Jewish populations of approximately 1.5 and .5 million, respectively).

7. Norman Mailer, from *Cannibals and Christians* (Pinnacle, 1981); quoted on frontispiece of David Desser and Lester Friedman, *American-Jewish Filmmakers: Traditions and Trends* (Univ. of Illinois Press, 1993).

8. Sandy Koufax (with Ed Linn), *Koufax* (Viking Press, 1966), 158. Koufax was referring to a turning point in his baseball career.

9. Woody Allen, *Celebrity* (Magnolia Productions, 1998). Of course, Allen himself is a prime example of American Jewish celebrity, exemplifying both American renown and Jewish representation.

10. Daniel Boorstin, *The Image: A Guide to Pseudo-Events in America* (Atheneum, 1961), 57.

11. Chris Rojek, "Celebrity and Religion," in Redmond and Holmes, eds., *Stardom and Celebrity: A Reader* (Sage Pub., 2007), 171–80.

12. For a lengthier consideration of the term, see P. David Marshall, *Celebrity and Power: Fame in Contemporary Culture* (Univ. of Minnesota Press, 1997), 4–7.

13. In "A Letter From Bob Dylan" (a prose poem written for Sis and Gordon Cunningham), *Broadside* (1965); reprinted in *The Bob Dylan Scrapbook: 1956–1966* (Simon & Schuster, 2005), 37.

14. The three principal American investigators of American celebrity are Leo Braudy (historian), Richard Schickel (film critic), and Joshua Gamson (sociologist). Most scholarly study of the phenomenon is centered in England, where popular culture is better established as an academic subject: for example, Richard Dyer, *Stars* (British Film Institute [BFI], 1979) and *Heavenly Bodies: Film Stars and Society* (BFI, 1987); Christine Gledhill, ed., *Stardom: Industry of Desire* (Routledge, 1991); Chris Rojek, *Celebrity* (Reaktion Books, 2001); Jessica Evans and David Hesmondhalgh, eds., *Understanding Media: Inside Celebrity* (Open Univ. Press, 2005); Paul Willis, ed., *Stardom: Hollywood and Beyond* (Manchester Univ. Press, 2005); P. David Marshall, ed., *The Celebrity Culture Reader* (Routledge, 2006); Su Holmes and Sean Redmond, eds., *Framing Celebrity: New Directions in Celebrity Culture* (Routledge, 2006); and *Stardom and Celebrity: A Reader* (Sage Pub., 2007).

15. This topic is more fully explored by Joshua Gamson in Claims to Fame: Celebrity in Contemporary America (Univ. of California Press, 1994).

16. Quoted in Richard Schickel, *Intimate Strangers: The Culture of Celebrity in America* (Ivan R. Dee, 1985), 109.

17. Leo Braudy, *The Frenzy of Renown: Fame and its History* (Oxford Univ. Press, 1986), 17.

18. June Sochen, "From Sophie Tucker to Barbra Streisand: Jewish Women Entertainers as Reformers," in Joyce Antler, ed., *Talking Back: Images of Jewish Women in American Popular Culture* (Brandeis Univ. Press, 1998), 81.

19. J. Hoberman and Jeffrey Shandler, eds., *Entertaining America: Jews, Movies, and Broadcasting* (Princeton Univ. Press and Jewish Museum, 2003), 151.

20. Schickel, *Intimate Strangers*, x–xi.

21. Schickel, *Intimate Strangers*, 548.

22. Kenneth Silverman, *Houdini!!! The Career of Ehrich Weiss* (Harper-Collins, 1996), 202.

23. Ibid., 203–204.

24. On Houdini's Jewishness, see John Kasson, "The Manly Art of Escape: The Metamorphoses of Ehrich Weiss," in Kasson, *Houdini, Tarzan, and the Perfect Man: The White Male Body and the Challenge of Modernity in America* (Hill and Wang, 2001), 77–155. On Chaplin's "virtual" Jewishness, see J. Hoberman, "The First 'Jewish' Superstar: Charlie Chaplin," in Hoberman and Shandler, eds., *Entertaining America*, 34–43.

25. Schickel, *Intimate Strangers*, 132.

26. Sean Redmond and Su Holmes, eds., *Stars and Celebrity: A Reader* (Sage Pub., 2007), 4.

27. Jonathan Sarna, *The American Jewish Experience* (Holmes & Meier, 1986), xv.

28. Though a case could be made for nineteenth-century celebrity figures such as Adah Isaacs Menken and Emma Lazarus, I prefer the turn-of-the-century immigrant period as a starting point for American Jewish celebrity, both for its mass culture of Jews and for the advent of mass media in the twentieth century.

29. Lulla Adler Rosenfeld, *The Yiddish Theatre and Jacob P. Adler* (Shapolsky Pub., 1988), xiv.

30. Dan Miron, introduction to *Sholem Aleichem: Tevye the Dairyman and Motl the Cantor's Son* (Penguin Books, 2009), xi.

31. See Josh Kun, "Abie the Fishman: On Masks, Birthmarks, and Hunchbacks," in Eric Weisbard, ed., *Listen Again: A Momentary History of Pop Music*, (Duke Univ. Press, 2007), 50–68.

32. Henry Bial, *Acting Jewish: Negotiating Ethnicity on the American Stage and Screen* (Univ. of Michigan Press, 2005).

33. Ample evidence of this is provided in Aviva Kempner's 1999 documentary film *The Life and Times of Hank Greenberg*.

34. See Todd Gitlin, *The Sixties: Years of Hope, Days of Rage* (Bantam Books, 1987), 21: "Nor was it lost on my family and friends that Dr. Salk, as well as Einstein and many atomic scientists, were Jews like us."

35. David Hollinger, "Jewish Intellectuals and the De-Christianization of American Public Culture in the Twentieth Century," Chapter 2 in Hollinger, *Science, Jews, and Secular Culture* (Princeton Univ. Press, 1998). Also see the special issue of *American Jewish History* 95:1 (March 2009), containing a scholars' forum in response to a more recent lecture by Hollinger.

36. From "I'm the Greatest Star" and "If a Girl Isn't Pretty" in the Broadway musical *Funny Girl* (1964), lyrics by Bob Merrill.

37. See, for example, Geoffrey Ward, *Unforgivable Blackness: The Rise and Fall of Jack Johnson* (Vintage, 2006); Chris Mead, *Joe Louis: Black Champion in White America* (Dover, 2010); Robert Rosenberg, *Bill Cosby: The Changing Black Image* (Houghton Mifflin, 1992); and Michael Eric Dyson, ed., *Reflecting Black: African-American Cultural Criticism* (Univ. of Minnesota, 1993), with articles on Michael Jackson, Michael Jordan, Jesse Jackson, Martin Luther King Jr., Toni Morrison, Bill Cosby, Spike Lee, and others.

38. Examples of this burgeoning literature include Jack Kugelmass, ed., *Key Texts in American Jewish Culture* (Rutgers Univ. Press, 2003); Paul Buhle, *From the Lower East Side to Hollywood: Jews in American Popular Culture* (Verso, 2004); Donald Weber, *Haunted in the New World: Jewish American Culture from Cahan to The Goldbergs* (Indiana Univ. Press, 2005); Vincent Brook, ed., *You Should See Yourself: Jewish Identity in Postmodern American Culture* (Rutgers Univ. Press, 2006); and Paul Buhle, ed., *Jews and American Popular Culture* (three volumes; Praeger Perspectives, 2006).

39. Michael Alexander, *Jazz Age Jews* (Princeton Univ. Press, 2001); and Hoberman and Shandler, eds., *Entertaining America*. Relevant articles include Carol Ockman, "When Is a Jewish Star Just a Star? Interpreting Images of

Sarah Bernhardt," in Linda Nochlin and Tamar Garb, eds., *The Jew In The Text: Modernity and the Construction of Identity* (Thames & Hudson, 1995), 121–139; Donald Weber, "Taking Jewish American Popular Culture Seriously: The Yinglish Worlds of Gertrude Berg, Milton Berle, and Mickey Katz," in *Jewish Social Studies* 5:1–2 (Fall 1998/Winter 1999), 124–153; and Holly Pearse, "As *Goyish* as Lime Jello-O? Jack Benny and the Construction of Jewishness," in Simon Bronner, ed., *Jewishness: Expression, Identity, and Representation*, Jewish Cultural Studies Vol. 1 (Littman Library of Jewish Civilization, 2008), 272–290.

40. There is a growing trend in contemporary Jewish studies to draw a parallel between Jewish and "queer" identity. See, for example, Daniel Boyarin, Daniel Itzkovitz, and Ann Pellegrini, eds., *Queer Theory and the Jewish Question* (Columbia Univ. Press, 2003).

41. Quoted in Mary Anne Staniszewski, "First Person Plural: The Paintings of Deborah Kass" in Michael Plante, ed., *Deborah Kass: The Warhol Project* (Distributed Art Pub., 1999), 30.

42. On Jews in musical theater, see Andrea Most, *Making Americans: Jews and the Broadway Musical* (Harvard Univ. Press, 2004); in comedy, see Lawrence Epstein, *The Haunted Smile: The Story of Jewish Comedians in America* (Public-Affairs, 2001); in popular music, see Jeffrey Melnick, *A Right to Sing the Blues: African Americans, Jews, and American Popular Song* (Harvard Univ. Press, 1999); and in Hollywood, see Neil Gabler, *An Empire of Their Own: How the Jews Invented Hollywood* (Anchor Books, 1988). Note: I have kept these representative lists to groups of three, but in each case they could be easily expanded.

43. See Shaye Cohen, *The Beginnings of Jewishness: Boundaries, Varieties, Uncertainties* (Univ. of California Press, 1999).

44. Glenn, "In the Blood?" 139–152. On the recent interest in Jewish genetics, Kenneth Marcus writes, "Public reception of Jewish genomic research also suggests that racial conceptions of Jewish identity persist . . . Regardless of the validity of the recent genomic studies, the intense media interest and Jewish communal fascination with this research suggest that both Jews and non-Jews continue to understand Jewish identity to be in part a matter of bloodlines." *Jewish Identity and Civil Rights in America* (Cambridge Univ. Press, 2010), 133. Also see Susan Martha Kahn, "Are Genes Jewish? Conceptual Ambiguities in the New Genetic Age," in Susan Glenn and Naomi Sokoloff, eds., *Boundaries of Jewish Identity* (Univ. of Washington Press, 2010), 12–26.

45. Due to the 1950 Law of Return, guaranteeing all Jews the right to Israeli citizenship, determination of Jewish identity became a legal necessity. See Gad Barzilai, "Who Is a Jew? Categories, Boundaries, Communities, and Citizenship in Israel," in Glenn and Sokoloff, eds., *Boundaries of Jewish Identity*, 27–42.

46. Barzilai, "Who Is a Jew?" 28.

47. Baruch Litvin, and Sidney Hoenig, ed., *Jewish Identity: Modern Responsa and Opinions on the Registration of Children of Mixed Marriages; David Ben-Gurion's Query to Leaders of World Jewry: A Documentary Compilation* (Philipp Feldheim, 1965).

48. On the phenomenon of "virtual Jews," see Hoberman and Shandler, eds., *Entertaining America*, 40–43.

49. For a particularly sharp critique of the stereotype of Jewish looks, see Daniel Segal, "Can you tell a Jew when you see one? Or thoughts on meeting Barbra/Barbie at the museum," *Judaism* (April 1999). And for a more balanced view, see Susan Glenn, " 'Funny, You Don't Look Jewish': Visual Stereotypes and the Making of Modern Jewish Identity," in Glenn and Sokoloff, eds., *Boundaries of Jewish Identity*, 64–90.

50. However, some use precisely these two rubrics to differentiate between varying conceptions: for example, Harold Himmelfarb, "Research on American Jewish Identity and Identification: Progress, Pitfalls, and Prospects," in Marshall Sklare, ed., *Understanding American Jewry* (Brandeis Univ., 1982), 56–95.

51. Max Arzt, "Jewish Identity in the Modern World," *The Reconstructionist* 10:10 (June 23, 1944), 9.

52. Marianne Sanua, *Let Us Prove Strong: The American Jewish Committee, 1945–2006* (Brandeis Univ. Press, 2007). Sanua's Chapter 4 is titled "The First Jewish Continuity Crisis and the Triumph of Vatican II (1960–1965)."

53. Erich Rosenthal, "Studies of Jewish Intermarriage in the United States," *American Jewish Year Book* (1963); Rosenthal had participated in the 1960 Conference on Intermarriage and Jewish Life, whose proceedings were later published as *Intermarriage and Jewish Life: A Symposium*, Werner Cahnman, ed. (Herzl Press and Jewish Reconstructionist Press, 1963). Marshall Sklare, "Intermarriage and the Jewish Future," *Commentary* (April 1964); reprinted in *Observing America's Jews* (Brandeis Univ. Press, 1993), 234–247.

54. John Slawson, "The Quest for Jewish Identity in America," *Journal of Jewish Communal Service* 40:1 (Fall 1963), 17. Note: Slawson held a doctorate in psychology.

55. Richard Hertz, "Jewish Identity Today," Rosh Hashana sermon for Temple Beth El, Detroit, Michigan, 1964 (collection of American Jewish Historical Society). Stuart Rosenberg, "The Search for Jewish Identity," *The Reconstructionist* 30:1 (Fall 1964), 7–18; later expanded to book form as *The Search for Jewish Identity in America* (Doubleday, 1965).

56. Milton Gordon, *Assimilation in American Life: The Role of Race, Religion, and National Origins* (Oxford Univ. Press, 1964). "The Vanishing American Jew," *Look* (May 5, 1964).

57. Marshall Sklare, Marc Vosk, and Mark Zborowski, "Forms and Expressions of Jewish Identification (The Psychology of Belonging)," *Jewish Social Studies* 17:3 (July 1955), 205–218. Note: the same issue contains a critique of the Sklare study by Leibush Lehrer titled "Retention of Jewish Identity," 229–237.

58. Marshall Sklare, *Jewish Identity on the Suburban Frontier: A Study of Group Survival in the Open Society* (Univ. of Chicago Press, 1967; 2nd ed. 1979), "Preface to the First Edition (July 1966)," xii.

59. Bethamie Horowitz, "Indicators of Jewish Identity: Developing a Conceptual Framework for Understanding American Jewry," Discussion Paper Prepared for the Mandel Foundation (Nov. 1999).

60. See, in this regard, Sklare's survey questionnaire, "The Image of the Good Jew," in Sklare, *Jewish Identity on the Suburban Frontier*, 322.

61. Philip Roth, *Goodbye, Columbus and Five Short Stories* (Vintage Books, 1959). Also see Roth's 1963 essay "Writing About Jews" for his perspective on the controversy, in Roth, *Reading Myself and Others* (Vintage Books, 2001), 193–211.

62. Recent books along these lines include David Theo Goldberg and Michael Krausz, eds., *Jewish Identity* (Temple Univ. Press, 1993); Laurence Silberstein, ed., *Mapping Jewish Identities* (New York Univ. Press, 2000); Vincent Brook, ed., *You Should See Yourself* (Rutgers Univ. Press, 2006); and Susan Glenn and Naomi Sokoloff, eds., *Boundaries of Jewish Identity* (Univ. of Washington Press, 2010).

63. Laurence Silberstein, ed., *Mapping Jewish Identities* (New York Univ. Press, 2000), 2–3.

64. There is of course voluminous literature on this subject. For one useful summary, see Jonathan Freedman's introduction to *Klezmer America: Jewishness, Ethnicity, Modernity* (Columbia Univ. Press, 2008).

65. See, for example, Zvi Gitelman, ed., *Religion or Ethnicity? Jewish Identities in Evolution* (Rutgers Univ. Press, 2009).

66. Hannah Arendt, *Antisemitism: Part One of The Origins of Totalitarianism* (Harcourt Brace Jovanovich, 1951, 1968), 66.

67. Daniel Bell, "Reflections on Jewish Identity," *Commentary* (June 1961), 471–478.

68. Steven Cohen and Arnold Eisen, *The Jew Within: Self, Family, and Community in America* (Indiana Univ. Press, 2000).

69. Simon Herman, *Jewish Identity: A Social Psychological Perspective*, 2nd ed. (Transaction Pub., 1989), 31.

70. The adoption of the term was likely inspired by developmental psychologist Erik Erikson, coiner of the phrase *identity crisis*. See especially Erikson, *Identity and the Life Cycle* (International Univ. Press, 1959). Erikson was born and raised a Jew, and many commentators have read his own youthful struggles with identity as the foundation of his mature psychological theory; in a sense, therefore, the term *identity* can be said to have "Jewish roots" itself. For a brief discussion of Erikson in this vein, see Stephen Whitfield, "Enigmas of Modern Jewish Identity," *Jewish Social Studies* 8:2/3 (Winter/Spring 2002), 163–164.

71. See, for example, Albert Gordon, *Jews in Suburbia* (Beacon Press, 1959); Judith Kramer and Seymour Leventman, *Children of the Gilded Ghetto: Conflict Resolutions of Three Generations of American Jews* (Yale Univ. Press, 1961); Leonard Fein, *Studying Jewish Identity: Observations and Bibliography* (Massachusetts Insititute of Technology, 1966; unpublished study in the collection of American Jewish Historical Society); Sklare, *Jewish Identity on the Suburban Frontier*; Sidney Goldstein and Calvin Goldscheider, *Jewish Americans: Three Generations in a Jewish Community* (Prentice-Hall, 1968).

72. Stephen Whitfield, *In Search of American Jewish Culture* (Brandeis Univ. Press, 1999), 113.

73. Interview by Jason Zinoman, "At Ease in his Own Pigeonhole," *New York Times* (Sunday, Aug. 16, 2009), Arts & Leisure, 5.

74. A noted exception is intellectual historian David Hollinger. See his incisive discussion of the early 1960s as a discrete era in *Science, Jews, and Secular Culture: Studies in Mid-Twentieth Century American Intellectual History* (Princeton Univ. Press, 1996), 4–7.

75. Michael Staub, ed., *The Jewish 1960s: An American Sourcebook* (Brandeis Univ. Press, 2004), xv–xvi. Bruce's "Jewish and Goyish" routine is discussed at greater length here in Chapter 3.

76. Arthur Hertzberg, *The Jews in America* (Simon & Schuster, 1989), 377; Edward Shapiro, *A Time for Healing: American Jewry since World War II*, in Henry Feingold, ed., The Jewish People in America Vol. V (Johns Hopkins Univ. Press, 1992), 207; Jonathan Sarna, *The American Jewish Experience* (Holmes & Meier, 1997), 328.

77. Hertzberg, *The Jews in America*, 375.

78. Kirsten Fermaglich, *American Dreams and Nazi Nightmares: Early Holocaust Consciousness and Liberal America 1957–1965* (Brandeis Univ. Press, 2006), 4, 8, 9, 11.

79. Hoberman and Shandler, eds., *Entertaining America*, 274.

80. Hasia Diner, We Remember with Reverence and Love: American Jews and the Myth of Silence after the Holocaust, 1945–1962 (New York Univ. Press, 2009). Also see Lawrence Baron, "The Holocaust and American Public Memory, 1945–1960," Holocaust and Genocide Studies 17 (Spring 2003).

81. Alan Mintz makes much the same point in *Popular Culture and the Shaping of Holocaust Memory in America* (Univ. of Washington Press, 2001), 12.

82. Compare with Shandler's inclusion of Anne Frank in the "Star Gallery" section of Hoberman and Shandler, eds., *Entertaining America* (in between Sammy Davis Jr. and Barbra Streisand), 192–195.

83. Leslie Fiedler, "Jews and Jewish Writers in American Literature," *Congress Bi-Weekly* (American Jewish Congress, Sept. 16, 1963).

84. For an enlightening discussion of both *Judgment at Nuremberg* and *The Pawnbroker*, see Mintz, *Popular Culture and the Shaping of Holocaust Memory in America*.

85. Raul Hilberg, *The Destruction of the European Jews* (Quadrangle Books, 1961).

86. Jeffrey Shandler, *While America Watches: Televising the Holocaust* (Oxford Univ. Press, 1999), especially Chapter 4, "The Man in the Glass Box."

87. Mintz, *Popular Culture and the Shaping of Holocaust Memory in America*.

88. Deborah Dash Moore, "*Exodus*: Real to Reel to Real," in Hoberman and Shandler, eds., *Entertaining America*, 210.

89. David Twersky, "Novelist Leon Uris Taught Jewish Readers to Stand Tall," *Forward* (June 27, 2003), 14.

90. M. M. Silver, *Our Exodus: Leon Uris and the Americanization of Israel's Founding Story* (Wayne State Univ. Press, 2010), 22.

91. Quoted in Hoberman and Shandler, eds., *Entertaining America*, 214.

92. Philip Roth, "Some New Jewish Stereotypes," in Roth, *Reading Myself and Others*, 138. Roth was responding to the success of *Exodus*.

93. Fiedler, "Jews and Jewish Writers in American Literature."

94. Lenny Bruce, "Bruce Here," *Rogue Magazine* 5:2 (March 1960), 11.

95. Nat Hentoff, "Yiddish Survivals in the New Comedy," *American Judaism* 11:1 (1961), 18.

96. For discussion of the Hollywood conversions in the context of intermarriage, see Lila Corwin Berman, "A Jewish Marilyn Monroe and the Civil Rights-Era Crisis in Jewish Self-Presentation," Chapter 7 in Berman, *Speaking of Jews: Rabbis, Intellectuals, and the Creation of an American Public Identity* (Univ. of California Press, 2009).

97. Fiedler, "Jews and Jewish Writers in American Literature."

98. Herbert G. Luft, "Our Film Folk," *American Examiner*; for profiles of Lewis, Sahl, and Kaye, see issues of June 25, 1959; Jan. 7, 1960; and Aug. 18, 1960.

99. Herbert G. Luft, "The Jewishness of Eddie Fisher," *American Examiner* (May 28, 1959).

100. Albert Goldman, "Laughtermakers," originally published in Douglas Villiers, ed., *Next Year in Jerusalem* (Douglas Villiers Pub., 1976); reprinted in Sarah Blacher Cohen, ed., *Jewish Wry* (Wayne State Univ. Press, 1987), 85.

101. David Schwartz, "Schwartz Welcomes Goldberg to Cabinet," *American Examiner* (Jan. 5, 1961).

102. Rabbi Leon A. Jick, "Is the Jewish People Vanishing," in Jick, *In Search of a Way* (Temple Books, 1966) 45–46.

103. J. Hoberman, "Flaunting It: The Rise and Fall of Hollywood's 'Nice' Jewish (Bad) Boys," in Hoberman and Shandler, eds., *Entertaining America*, 220–243.

104. Allen Ginsberg, *Kaddish and Other Poems 1958–1960* (City Lights Books, 1961).

105. David Schiller, "'My Own Kaddish': Leonard Bernstein's Symphony No. 3," in Kugelmass, ed., *Key Texts in American Jewish Culture*, 185–196.

106. Fiedler, "Jews and Jewish Writers in American Literature."

107. Roger Bennett and Josh Kun, eds., *And You Shall Know Us By The Trail of Our Vinyl: The Jewish Past as Told by the Records We Have Loved and Lost* (Crown Publishers, 2008).

108. Ibid., 112–133.

109. Ibid., 115.

110. Herbert Gans, "Behind the Popularity of 'My Son the Folksinger'—A Sociologist Takes a Look," *The Reconstructionist* (May 3, 1963).

111. Mel Brooks interviewed by Saul Kahan in the companion booklet to Carl Reiner and Mel Brooks, *The Complete 2,000 Year Old Man* (Rhino, 1994), 17.

112. Allan Sherman, *A Gift of Laughter* (Fawcett Crest, 1965), 221, 243.

113. Stephen Whitfield, "Fiddling with Sholem Aleichem: A History of *Fiddler on the Roof*," in Kugelmass, ed., *Key Texts in American Jewish Culture*, 105–125.

114. Philip Roth, *Portnoy's Complaint* (Randon House, 1967; Vintage International ed., 1994), last line of the novel.

2. Sandy Koufax

Epigraph from the July 16, 2007, profile of Koufax on the Jewhoo!-like website, Jew Or Not Jew (http://jewornotjew.com).

1. "Remarks by the President at Reception in Honor of Jewish American Heritage Month" (May 27, 2010). Available online at http://www.whitehouse.gov.

2. Ibid.

3. Debra Rubin, "Koufax Wows White House Reception," *Washington Jewish Week* (May 27, 2010).

4. Rabbi Brad Hirschfield, "Celebrating Jewish American Heritage with President Obama and Sandy Koufax," *Jewish Journal* (June 3, 2010).

5. National Baseball Hall of Fame and Museum, Cooperstown, New York.

6. Quoted in Jane Leavy, *Sandy Koufax: A Lefty's Legacy* (HarperCollins, 2002), 6.

7. See Peter Levine, *Ellis Island to Ebbets Field: Sport and the American Jewish Experience* (Oxford Univ. Press, 1992), especially Chapter 5, "America's National Game."

8. Quoted in Joshua Halberstam, ed., *Schmoozing: The Private Conversations of American Jews,* (Perigee Trade, 1997), 101–102.

9. Norman Kleeblatt, "'Passing' into Multiculturalism," in Kleeblatt, ed., *Too Jewish? Challenging Traditional Identities* (Jewish Museum, 1996), 21.

10. Leavy, *Sandy Koufax*, xx.

11. *Heritage* magazine (American Jewish Historical Society, May 2005), 21.

12. William Simons, "The Athlete as Jewish Standard Bearer: Media Images of Hank Greenberg," *Jewish Social Studies* 44:2 (Spring 1982), 96.

13. Philip Brooks, *Extraordinary Jewish Americans* (Children's Press, 1998), 197.

14. Levine, *Ellis Island to Ebbets Field*, 245–246.

15. Ibid., 242.

16. Quoted in Simons, "The Athlete as Jewish Standard Bearer," 96–97.

17. Sandy Koufax (with Ed Linn), *Koufax* (Viking Press, 1966), 258.

18. "Down to the Wire—And Then Sandy Koufax Settled It All," *Newsweek* (Oct. 11, 1965), 70.

19. Leavy, *Sandy Koufax*, 184.

20. This journalistic debunking of the myth is a notable contribution of Leavy's biography, *Sandy Koufax*; see 183.

21. Stephen Whitfield, "In the Big Inning," Chapter 10 in Whitfield, *Voices of Jacob, Hands of Esau: Jews in American Life and Thought* (Archon Books, 1984), 175.

22. Koufax, *Koufax*, 1, 4.

23. Quoted in Whitfield, *Voices of Jacob, Hands of Esau*, 177.

24. Mordecai Richler, "Koufax the Incomparable," *Commentary* 5:42 (Nov. 1966), 87–89.

25. "The Year That Is," *Newsweek*, (March 16, 1964), 73.

26. Leavy, *Sandy Koufax*, 72.

27. Ibid., 175–176.

28. Melvin Durslag, "Sandy Koufax, The Strikeout King," *Saturday Evening Post* 235:27 (July 14–21, 1962), 69–72.

29. Leavy, *Sandy Koufax*, 190–191.

30. Ibid., 176–177.

31. Koufax, *Koufax*, 4, 5, 6, 7.

32. Ibid., 10.

33. Ibid., 6, 19, 23, 49.

34. Ibid., 258.

35. Ibid., 259.

36. "Down to the Wire," 68.

37. Jerry Mitchell, *Sandy Koufax* (Grosset & Dunlap, 1966), 9.

38. On the general subject of Jewish masculinity, see two anthologies edited by Harry Brod: *A Mensch Among Men: Explorations in Jewish Masculinity* (Crossing Press, 1988); and with Shawn Israel Zevit, *Brother Keepers: New Perspectives on Jewish Masculinity* (Men's Studies Press, 2010).

39. Daniel Boyarin, *Unheroic Conduct: The Rise of Heterosexuality and the Invention of the Jewish Man* (Univ. of California Press, 1997).

40. On Breitbart, see Sharon Gillerman, "Samson in Vienna: The Theatrics of Jewish Masculinity," *Jewish Social Studies* 9:2 (Winter 2003), 65–98. On Jewish participation in basketball, baseball, and boxing, see Levine, *Ellis Island to Ebbets Field*; and Steven Riess, "Tough Jews: The Jewish American Boxing Experience, 1890–1950," in Riess, ed., *Sports and the American Jew* (Syracuse Univ. Press, 1998), 60–104.

41. James Gilbert, *Men in the Middle: Searching for Masculinity in the 1950s* (Univ. of Chicago Press, 2005).

42. Milt Gross, "The Koufax Nobody Knows," *Argosy* (May 1964), 34.

43. Deborah Dash Moore, *G.I. Jews: How World War II Changed a Generation* (Harvard Univ. Press, 2006).

44. Jonathan Freedman, "Arthur Miller, Marilyn Monroe, and the Making of Ethnic Masculinity," Chapter 2 in Freedman, *Klezmer America: Jewishness, Ethnicity, Modernity* (Columbia Univ. Press, 2008), 110.

45. Ibid., 111.

46. The literature on Allen is voluminous, but see, for example, Gerald Mast, "Woody Allen: The Neurotic Jew as American Clown," 125–140 in Sarah Blacher Cohen, ed., *Jewish Wry* (Wayne State Univ. Press, 1987). On the broader trend of "the urban neurotic antihero," see J. Hoberman, "Flaunting It: The Rise and Fall of Hollywood's 'Nice' Jewish (Bad) Boys," in J. Hoberman and Jeffrey Shandler, eds., *Entertaining America: Jews, Movies, and Broadcasting* (Princeton Univ. Press and Jewish Museum, 2003), 220–243.

47. For a full-length treatment of this theme, see Danny Fingeroth, *Disguised as Clark Kent: Jews, Comics, and the Creation of the Superhero* (Continuum, 2007).

48. Note: the name *Koufax* is possibly a corruption of *Kovacs*, the assimilated name of choice for many Central European Jews originally named Cohen. Sandy's biological father, also Jewish, was named Braun—an even more "macho" sounding name.

49. Compare to Paul Breines, *Tough Jews: Political Fantasies and the Moral Dilemma of American Jewry* (Basic Books, 1990), 68 and following pages.

50. Philip Roth, "In Response to Those Who Have Asked Me: 'How Did You Come to Write That Book, Anyway?'" (1974), in Roth, *Reading Myself and Others* (Vintage International, 2001), 31.

51. Norman Podhoretz interview, Conversations with History series (Institute of International Studies, Univ. of California–Berkeley, 1999); available online at http://globetrotter.berkeley.edu.

52. Philip Roth, *Portnoy's Complaint* (Random House, 1967; Vintage International edition, 1994), 37. Intriguingly, an early theatrical version of *Portnoy* was titled *The Nice Jewish Boy*, and was workshopped in 1964 with Dustin Hoffman in the lead role. Roth, "In Response to Those Who Have Asked Me," 30.

53. Jesse and Roy Silver, "All-Time, All-Jewish Nine," *Jewish Digest* (May 1963), 17.

54. "Koufax is Only 2nd Jew To be 20-Game Winner," *National Jewish Post and Opinion* (Sept. 13, 1963), 8. The other was Erskine Mayer.

55. "Sandy Koufax, an American Hero," *Detroit Jewish News* (Oct. 22, 1965), 4; reprinted in Michael Staub, ed., *The Jewish 1960s: An American Sourcebook*, (Brandeis Univ. Press, 2004), 50.

56. Harold Ribalow, *The Jew in American Sport* (Bloch Publishing Company, 3rd rev. and enl. ed., 1966), 121.

57. Ibid., 124–125.

58. Ibid., 127, 131.

59. Ibid., 132, 140.

60. Ibid., 146, 154, 162.

61. Ibid., 169.

62. "Koufax, Sanford," in *Encyclopedia Judaica* (Keter Publishing House, 1972), 1225–1226.

63. Available online at http://jewishsportshalloffame.com.

64. Murray Polner, *American Jewish Biographies* (Lakeville Press, 1982), 226.

65. Robert Slater, *Great Jews in Sports* (Jonathan David Pub., 1983, rev. ed. 1992), 153–154.

66. Buddy Robert S. Silverman, *The Jewish Athletes' Hall of Fame* (Shapolsky Pub., 1989), 37.

67. Ibid.

68. Ibid., 37–39.

69. Sandor Slomovits, "Yom Kippur and Sandy Koufax: They'll Always Go Together" (Oct. 2000). Available online at http://www.jewishsports.com.

70. Ken Burns, *Baseball* (PBS, 1994). By contrast, Burns makes no such ethnic designation for Benny Goodman and other Jewish figures in his documentary on the history of jazz.

71. Seymour Brody, *Jewish Heroes & Heroines of America: 150 True Stories of American Jewish Heroism* (Lifetime Books, 1996), 230.

72. Lee Bycel, "Sandy Koufax Taught Pride to Generation of Young Jews," *Northern California Jewish Bulletin* (Sept. 20, 1996). Available online at http://www.jewishsf.com.

73. Barry Schwartz, *Jewish Heroes, Jewish Values: Living Mitzvot in Today's World* (Behrman House, 1996), 12.

74. Richard Hoffer, "Our Favorite Athletes"; and Tom Verducci, "The Left Arm of God," *Sports Illustrated* 91:2 (July 12, 1999), 82–100

75. "Sportscentury—50 Greatest Athletes (of the 20th Century): #42, Sandy Koufax," *ESPN* broadcast (March 26, 1999). Museum of Television and Radio Archive, T:57224.

76. Ibid.

77. Wladyslaw Pleszczynski, "Swung On and Missed," *The American Spectator* (March/April 2003), 82.

78. Ibid.

79. Examples include Arnold Hano, *Sandy Koufax, Strikeout King* (1964); Howard Liss, *The Sandy Koufax Album* (1966); and Jerry Mitchell, *Sandy Koufax* (1966).

80. Edward Gruver, *Koufax* (Taylor Trade Pub., 2000), 11.

81. Ibid., 46.

82. Ibid., 54.

83. Ibid.

84. Ibid., 12.

85. Ibid., 53.

86. Harvey and Myrna Katz Frommer, *Growing Up Jewish in America: An Oral History* (Harcourt, 1995).

87. Gruver, *Koufax*, 54, 48, 52.

88. J. Bottum, *Commentary* 114:3 (Oct. 2002), 74–76.

89. Leavy, *Sandy Koufax* (Perennial paperback ed., 2003), xv.

90. Ibid., xix.

91. Ibid., 71.

92. Ibid., 182.

93. Ibid., 168–169 (emphasis mine).

94. Ibid., 194.

95. Amy Essington, "Leavy, Sandy Koufax: A Lefty's Legacy," *History Teacher* 38:1 (Nov. 2004), 125.

96. Adam Langer, "Pitcher in the Rye," *Book* (Sept./Oct. 2002), 24.

97. Walter Bernstein, "Marvel on the Mound," *Los Angeles Times Book Review* (Sept. 15, 2002), 3.

98. J. Bottum, *Commentary*, 74–76.

99. Cited by Jason Reid in "Koufax Shuts Out Dodgers," *Los Angeles Times* (Feb. 21, 2003), D1.

100. Michael Plante, "Screened Identities, Multiple Repetitions and Missed

Kisses: Deborah Kass's Warhol Project," in Plante, ed., *Deborah Kass: The Warhol Project*, (Distributed Art Pub., 1999), 48.

101. Kleeblatt, "'Passing' into Multiculturalism," 21.

102. *Heritage* magazine (American Jewish Historical Society, May 2005), 24.

103. *Celebrating 350 Years of American Jewish Life* (American Jewish Committee, Nov. 2003), 35 (emphasis mine).

104. Allen Salkin, "Where Have You Gone, Sandy Koufax?" *Heeb: The New Jew Review* 5 (Winter 2004), 38. This same issue was highly controversial for its cover photo satirizing Mel Gibson's *Passion of the Christ*.

105. Martin Abramowitz, "The Making of a Card Set: American Jews in America's Game," *Heritage: Newsletter of the American Jewish Historical Society* 1:2 (Fall/Winter 2003), 10–11.

106. Card #1, "Sanford Koufax"(American Jewish Historical Society, 2003).

107. Directed by Peter Miller, written by Ira Berkow, and narrated by Dustin Hoffman, the film was widely distributed and shown during 2010–2011. *Jews and Baseball: An American Love Story* (Docurama Films, 2010).

108. Jeffrey Gurock, *Judaism's Encounter with American Sports* (Indiana Univ. Press, 2005).

109. Dovid Zaklikowski, "A Pair of Tefillin for Sandy Koufax"; the quote is translated from the Yiddish. Available online at http://www.chabad.org.

110. Faye Kranz Greene, "Tefillin On First" (Aug. 5, 2004). Available online at http://lubavitch.com.

3. Lenny Bruce

Epigraph from Gerald Nachman, Seriously Funny: The Rebel Comedians of the 1950s and 1960s *(Pantheon Books, 2003), 397.*

1. David Lyman, *The Jewish Comedy Catalog* (Jonathan David Pub., 1989), 72.

2. Gerald Nachman, *Seriously Funny: The Rebel Comedians of the 1950s and 1960s* (Pantheon Books, 2003), 397.

3. Jonathan Mark, "Yizkor for Lenny Bruce—Daughter Revisits Controversial Comedian's Legacy," *Jewish Week* (Oct. 29, 2004).

4. See, for example, David Zurawik, *The Jews of Prime Time* (Brandeis Univ. Press, 2003).

5. Sig Altman, *The Comic Image of the Jew: Explorations of a Pop Culture Phenomenon* (Fairleigh Dickinson Univ. Press, 1971), 191. On the dynamics of standup comedy, also see Phil Berger, *The Last Laugh: The World of the Stand-Up Comics* (Limelight Editions, updated ed., 1985).

6. Nachman, *Seriously Funny*, 6–7.

7. Richard Corliss, "A Tribute to Lenny Bruce," *Time* (Aug. 10, 2006). Note: the *-nik* suffix is familiar to Yiddish speakers as well, as in *nudnik*.

8. "The Playboy Panel: Hip Comics and the New Humor," *Playboy* 8:3 (March, 1961), 35 and following pages.

9. Kenneth Allsop, "Why So Many 'Sicknik' Comedians Are Jews," *Twentieth Century* (July 1961); reprinted in *Jewish Digest* (March 1962), 55–59; Nat

Hentoff, "Yiddish Survivals in the New Comedy," *American Judaism* 11:1 (Sept. 1961), 18–19.

10. Allsop, "Why So Many 'Sicknik' Comedians Are Jews," 59.

11. Hentoff, "Yiddish Survivals," 18.

12. Hentoff, "Yiddish Survivals," 19.

13. Albert Goldman, "Laughtermakers," in Sarah Blacher Cohen, ed., *Jewish Wry* (Wayne State Univ. Press, 1987), 85.

14. For a more comprehensive list, see Bill Novak and Moshe Waldoks, eds., *The Big Book of Jewish Humor* (HarperCollins Pub., 1981), xix.

15. Steve Allen, *The Funny Men* (Simon & Schuster, 1956), 212.

16. Steve Allen, *Funny People* (Stein and Day, 1981), 11.

17. Altman, *The Comic Image of the Jew*, 185–186.

18. For full-length treatments of this psychological approach, see Sigmund Freud's classic 1905 study, *Jokes and Their Relation to the Unconscious* (W. W. Norton & Co., 1960); and Theodor Reik, *Jewish Wit* (Gamut Press, 1962).

19. Irving Howe, *World of Our Fathers: The Journey of the East European Jews to America and the Life They Found and Made* (Simon & Schuster, 1976), 556.

20. Ibid., 561.

21. Albert Goldman (From the Journalism of Lawrence Schiller), *Ladies and Gentlemen, Lenny Bruce!!* (Ballantine Books, 1974), 54. The quote is also referenced by *Gerald* Nachman, *Seriously Funny*, 397; and *Barry* Rubin, *Assimilation and Its Discontents* (Random House, 1995), 111.

22. Quoted in Goldman, *Ladies and Gentlemen*, 87.

23. Goldman, *Ladies and Gentlemen*, 143.

24. The recording may be found on disc 2, cut 2 of *Lenny Bruce: Let the Buyer Beware* as "Lenny on *Arthur Godfrey's Talent Scouts* (with Arthur Godfrey & Sally Marr)—Recorded at radio station WCBS, New York City (Oct. 1948); previously unreleased." Also see Ronald Collins and David Skover, *The Trials of Lenny Bruce* (Sourcebooks, 2002), 14–15.

25. Frank Kofsky, *Lenny Bruce: The Comedian as Social Critic and Secular Moralist* (Monad Press, 1974), 74, 80.

26. Goldman, *Ladies and Gentlemen*, 131–132.

27. Lenny Bruce, *How to Talk Dirty and Influence People* (Fireside, 1992; orig. pub. by *Playboy* magazine, serialized in issues of Oct., Nov., Dec. 1963, and Jan. 1964, and published in book form in 1965), 22.

28. Marjorie Garber, *Vested Interests: Cross-Dressing and Cultural Anxiety* (Routledge, 1992), 16.

29. Bruce, *How to Talk Dirty and Influence People*, 53–71; Goldman, *Ladies and Gentlemen*, 90–91.

30. John Cohen, ed., *The Essential Lenny Bruce* (Bell Publishing Co., 1970), 39.

31. Nachman, *Seriously Funny*, 397.

32. Cohen, ed., *The Essential Lenny Bruce*, 31.

33. *Jimmy Kimmel Live!*, March 10, 2003.

34. Cohen, ed., *The Essential Lenny Bruce*, 65–66.

35. Ibid., 66.

36. Ibid.

37. *Lenny Bruce: Let the Buyer Beware*, disc 3, cut 13.

38. Cohen, ed., *The Essential Lenny Bruce*, 53–54. Compare to recorded version on *Lenny Bruce: Let the Buyer Beware*, disc 4, cut 9 (recorded 1963).

39. Cohen, ed., *The Essential Lenny Bruce*, 49.

40. Ibid., 50. Compare to recorded version on *Lenny Bruce: Let the Buyer Beware*, disc 2, cut 6 (recorded Oct. 24, 1958).

41. Cohen, ed., *The Essential Lenny Bruce*, 26–27. Compare to recorded version on *Lenny Bruce: Let the Buyer Beware*, disc 6, cut 8 (recorded Oct. 5, 1961).

42. On Joe Ancis's influence on Bruce, see Goldman, *Ladies and Gentlemen*, Chapter 4, "How Sick Humor Came Up the River to Manhattan, Along the Gowanus Parkway (42nd Street Exit)," 137–170.

43. Nachman, *Seriously Funny*, 396.

44. Lenny Bruce, "Bruce Here," *Rogue Magazine* 5:2 (March 1960), 10. The subway platform bit later reappeared in a Woody Allen routine, and the black girlfriend story showed up in Barry Levinson's film *Liberty Heights*.

45. Hentoff, "Yiddish Survivals," 19.

46. Kofsky, *Lenny Bruce*, 81.

47. Allen, *Funny People*, 83.

48. Goldman, *Ladies and Gentlemen*, 166–167.

49. Kofsky, *Lenny Bruce*, 85–86. The emphasis on "manifesto of Jewishness" is mine.

50. Ibid., 87.

51. Altman, *The Comic Image of the Jew*, 85–86.

52. Novak and Waldoks, eds., *The Big Book of Jewish Humor*, xviii.

53. Cohen, ed., *The Essential Lenny Bruce*, 194–195. Compare to recorded version on *Lenny Bruce: Let the Buyer Beware*, disc 5, cut 3 (recorded Nov./Dec. 1962).

54. Cohen, ed., *The Essential Lenny Bruce*, 32.

55. Ibid., 33; reprinted in Novak and Waldoks, eds., *The Big Book of Jewish Humor*, 260.

56. Cohen, ed., *The Essential Lenny Bruce*, 31. Compare to recorded version on *Lenny Bruce: Let the Buyer Beware*, disc 3, cut 17 (recorded Oct. 5, 1961); and disc 5, cut 6 (recorded Nov. 1961).

57. Cohen, ed., *The Essential Lenny Bruce*, 35.

58. Cohen, ed., *The Essential Lenny Bruce*, 35–36.

59. Cohen, ed., *The Essential Lenny Bruce*, 16. Compare to recorded version on *Lenny Bruce: Let the Buyer Beware*, disc 1, cut 13 (recorded Nov./Dec. 1962).

60. Cohen, ed., *The Essential Lenny Bruce*, 17–18.

61. Cohen, ed., *The Essential Lenny Bruce*, 34–35.

62. Cohen, ed., *The Essential Lenny Bruce*, 30. Compare to recorded version on *Lenny Bruce: Let the Buyer Beware*, disc 4, cut 11 (recorded 1963). **311**

63. Bruce, *How to Talk Dirty and Influence People*, 155.

64. Lenny Bruce, "Bruce Here," *Rogue Magazine* 5:2 (March, 1960), 11.

65. Bruce, *How to Talk Dirty and Influence People*, 155.

66. Bruce, *How to Talk Dirty and Influence People*, 156.

67. Ibid.

68. Cohen, ed., *The Essential Lenny Bruce*, 88.

69. Collins and Skover, *The Trials of Lenny Bruce*, 9.

70. Howe, *World of Our Fathers*, 570.

71. Ibid., 572–573.

72. Howe, *World of Our Fathers*, 572–573.

73. Cohen, ed., *The Essential Lenny Bruce*, 84. Compare to 1959 interview with Gilbert Millstein of the *New York Times* quoted in Allen, *Funny People*, 83.

74. Cohen, ed., *The Essential Lenny Bruce*, 200.

75. Ibid., 33.

76. Cohen, ed., *The Essential Lenny Bruce*, 216.

77. Cohen, ed., *The Essential Lenny Bruce*, 11. Compare to recorded version on *Lenny Bruce: Let the Buyer Beware*, disc 1, cut 1 (recorded 1963).

78. Cohen, ed., *The Essential Lenny Bruce*, 11–12.

79. Randall Kennedy, *Nigger: The Strange Career of a Troublesome Word* (Vintage, 2003), 29: "Asserting that unmentionable slurs derived much of their seductive power from their taboo status, the iconoclastic white comedian Lenny Bruce recommended a strategy of subversion through overuse . . ."

80. Lawrence Epstein, *The Haunted Smile: The Story of Jewish Comedians in America* (PublicAffairs, 2001), 171.

81. Ibid.

82. *Lenny Bruce: Let the Buyer Beware*, disc 1, cut 8 (recorded circa 1959).

83. Cohen, ed., *The Essential Lenny Bruce*, 100–101.

84. Interview with Paul Krassner, *The Realist* (Feb. 1960); reprinted in *The Almost Unpublished Lenny Bruce* (Running Press, 1984), 40. In 1962, Mel Brooks and Carl Reiner issued their third comedy album, including the routine "Adolph Hartler." A few years later, Brooks began to write a novel titled "Springtime for Hitler," which evolved into the 1967 film *The Producers*.

85. Cohen, ed., *The Essential Lenny Bruce*, 26.

86. Cohen, ed., *The Essential Lenny Bruce*, 229–230. Compare to recorded version on *Lenny Bruce: Let the Buyer Beware*, disc 6, cut 14 (recorded Nov./Dec. 1962).

87. *Lenny Bruce: Live at the Curran Theater* (Fantasy, 1999; orig. rec. Nov. 19, 1961), disc 2, cuts 2–3 (emphasis mine).

88. Bob Shayne, "What is a Lenny Bruce," *Zero: Los Angeles Free Press* (Aug. 16, 1968), 34. Compare to Kofsky, *Lenny Bruce*, 52–56, 62: "the powerful effect he has had on the generation that came to maturity during the last decade."

89. John Murray Cuddihy, *The Ordeal of Civility: Freud, Marx, Levi-Strauss, and the Jewish Struggle with Modernity* (Basic Books, 1974), 192.

90. Ibid., 191.

91. Personal correspondence with author (Dec. 20, 2008).

92. Collins and Skover, *The Trials of Lenny Bruce*, 359.

93. Abbie Hoffman, *Soon to be a Major Motion Picture* (Perigee Books, 1980), 125.

94. Ibid., xiv.

95. Collins and Skover, *The Trials of Lenny Bruce*, 309.

96. Hoffman, *Soon to be a Major Motion Picture*, 209. Note that he mistranslates the phrase. Compare to Chapter 21, "A Tale of Two Hoffmans: The Decorum Decision and the Bill of Rites," in Cuddihy, *Ordeal of Civility*, 189–202.

97. However, as Paul Krassner points out, women were instrumental as well: "Although the Yippie leadership had a male image in the media, in reality much of the hard-core organizing was done by women-—Nancy Kurshan, Anita Hoffman, Walli Leff, Judy Clavir, Ellen Maslow, Anne Ockene, and Robin Morgan." Krassner, *Confessions of a Raving, Unconfined Nut: Misadventures in the Counter-Culture* (Simon & Schuster, 1993), 164.

98. Hoffman, *Soon to be a Major Motion Picture*, 139.

99. Michael Staub, *The Jewish 1960s* (2004), xv.

100. Quoted in Nachman, *Seriously Funny*, 397.

101. Epstein, *The Haunted Smile*, 175.

102. "Playboy Panel with Mort Sahl, Steve Allen, Lenny Bruce, Jonathan Winters, Mike Nichols, Bill Dana, Jules Feiffer" (interview conducted by Paul Krassner), *Playboy* 8:3 (March 1961), 119.

103. Collins and Skover, *The Trials of Lenny Bruce*, 206, 222–223, 282; Goldman, *Ladies and Gentlemen*, 658–659.

104. Goldman, *Ladies and Gentlemen*, 519.

105. Bruce, *How to Talk Dirty and Influence People*, 5.

106. John Cohen, "Epilogue," in Cohen, ed., *The Essential Lenny Bruce*, 231–232.

107. Leonard Berry, "Will the Real Lenny Bruce Rise From the Grave?" *Rolling Stone* 85 (June 24, 1971), 1.

108. *Lenny*, "a play by Julian Barry—Based on the life and words of Lenny Bruce" (Grove Press, 1971). Gorman would later play a character based on Bruce in Bob Fosse's 1979 film *All That Jazz*.

109. The idea of Lenny as a shaman was first suggested by Albert Goldman in "The Comedy of Lenny Bruce," *Commentary* 36:4 (Oct. 1963).

110. Goldman, *Ladies and Gentleman*, 258.

111. Andrew Kopkind, "Lenny Bruce: Resurrection of a Junkie Prophet," *Ramparts* 13, (March 1975); quoted in Collins and Skover, *The Trials of Lenny Bruce*, 399.

112. For the play version, see Barry, *Lenny*, 24–27.

113. Goldman, *Ladies and Gentlemen*, back cover.

114. Goldman, *Ladies and Gentlemen*, 100.

115. Ibid., 107. Goldman also discourses on "Jewish love" on the previous page.

116. Kofsky, *Lenny Bruce*, 9.

117. Ibid., 73.

118. Allen, *Funny People*, 77. True to this statement, in 1984 Allen hosted a comedy concert dedicated to Bruce, titled "A Toast to Lenny: An All-Star Tribute to the Most Revolutionary Comic of Our Time" (Fox Hills Video, FR0008), in which not an analytical word was uttered.

119. Bruce, *How to Talk Dirty and Influence People*, vii.

120. This is also recounted by Bruce in *How to Talk Dirty and Influence People*, 147.

121. *George Carlin: 40 Years of Comedy* (broadcast Feb. 1997).

122. Richard Zoglin, *Comedy at the Edge: How Stand-Up in the 1970s Changed America* (Bloomsbury, 2008), 8.

123. The following Jewhooing-type listings give Bruce honorable mention: Martin Greenberg, *The Jewish Lists* (Schocken Books, 1979); Asher Etkes and Saul Stadtmauer, *Jewish Contributions to the American Way of Life* (Northside Pub., 1995); Philip Brooks, *Extraordinary Jewish Americans* (Children's Press, 1998); Joel Samberg, *The Jewish Book of Lists* (Carol Pub. Group, 1998).

124. However, these texts leave Bruce out entirely: M. Hirsh Goldberg, *The Jewish Connection* (Scarborough House, 1976); M. Hirsh Goldberg, *Just Because They're Jewish* (Stein and Day, 1979); Tim Boxer, *The Jewish Celebrity Hall of Fame* (Shapolsky Pub., 1987); Seymour Brody, *Jewish Heroes & Heroines of America* (Lifetime Books, 1996).

125. Darryl Lyman, *Great Jews in the Performing Arts* (Jonathan David Pub., 1999), 55.

126. Joseph Dorinson, "Lenny Bruce, A Jewish Humorist in Babylon," *Jewish Currents* 35:2 (Feb. 1981), 14–19, 31–32; and Jack Nusan Porter, *The Jew as Outsider: Historical and Contemporary Perspectives* (Univ. Press of America, 1981), Chapter 5, "The Jewish Comic," mainly about Bruce.

127. Joseph Dorinson, "The Jew as Comic: Lenny Bruce, Mel Brooks, Woody Allen," in Avner Ziv, ed., *Jewish Humor* (Transaction, 1998; orig. pub. Tel Aviv Univ., 1986). 29–43.

128. Cohen, ed., *Jewish Wry*; the volume includes Goldman, "Laughtermakers," 80–88; and Sanford Pinsker, "Lenny Bruce: *Shpritzing* the *Goyim*/Shocking the Jews," 89–104.

129. Harry Golden, *The Golden Book of Jewish Humor* (G. P. Putnam's Sons, 1972), 18–19.

130. Novak and Waldoks, *The Big Book of Jewish Humor*, 214.

131. Ibid., xvi.

132. Pinsker, "Lenny Bruce: *Shpritzing* the *Goyim*/Shocking the Jews," 89–104. In the same article, Pinsker makes a compelling comparison between Bruce and Philip Roth.

133. Novak and Waldoks, *The Big Book of Jewish Humor*, 60, 214–219, 260.

134. Epstein, *The Haunted Smile*, 171–172. Chapter 7, "'Is There Any Group I Haven't Offended?': The Changing World of Stand-Up Comedy," begins with Bruce. Note: the cover illustration (paperbook ed.) has images of Buddy Hackett, Billy Crystal, Woody Allen, George Burns, Milton Berle, Groucho Marx, Gilda

Radner, Roseanne Barr, Rodney Dangerfield, Jerry Seinfeld, Mel Brooks, and Jerry Lewis—but no Lenny Bruce.

135. J. Hoberman and Jeffrey Shandler, *Entertaining America: Jews, Movies, and Broadcasting* (Jewish Museum, 2003), 222. Though the exhibition catalogue doesn't cover standup comedy in any great depth, Hoberman and Shandler highlight the Bruce routine "How the Jew Got Into Show Business."

136. Jack Kugelmass, ed., *Key Texts in American Jewish Culture* (Rutgers Univ. Press, 2003), 5.

137. Zadie Smith, *The Autograph Man* (Vintage Books, 2002).

138. MacDonald Moore and Deborah Dash Moore, "Observant Jews and the Photographic Arena of Looks," in Vincent Brook, ed. *You Should See Yourself: Jewish Identity in Postmodern Jewish Culture* (Rutgers Univ. Press, 2006), 179.

139. Beth Wenger, *The Jewish Americans: Three Centuries of Jewish Voices in America* (Doubleday, 2007), 300; and John Efron, Steven Weitzman, Matthias Lehmann, and Joshua Holo, eds., *The Jews: A History* (Prentice Hall, 2009), 422.

140. Michael Staub, *The Jewish 1960s: An American Sourcebook* (Univ. Press of New England, 2004), xv.

141. Goldman, "Laughtermakers," 85.

142. Quoted on the back cover of the DVD *Sarah Silverman: Jesus Is Magic* (2006 Visual Entertainment).

143. Isaac Galena, "Dividing things Jewish & Goyish," MyJewishLearning. com. Reprinted with permission from Bangitout.com.

144. *Heeb: The New Jew Review*. MySpace page (emphasis mine).

145. *Heeb* 10 (Spring 2006), 24.

146. *Heeb* 19 (Winter 2008), 26.

147. Jon Stewart, *Naked Pictures of Famous People* (HarperCollins, 1998), 151–159.

148. Bittersweet Lenny's R.I.P.A. was intended as the first offering in a new line called "The Shmaltz Tribute to Jewish Stars" (2006 press release).

149. Wenger, *The Jewish Americans*.

4. Bob Dylan

Epigraph from Jay Michaelson, "He Wandered the Earth as an Exiled Man: Bob Dylan's New Book Juxtaposes Roots and Rootlessness," Forward *(Feb. 4, 2005)*.

1. Stephen Whitfield, *In Search of American Jewish Culture* (Brandeis Univ. Press, 1999), 112.

2. Nat Hentoff, "Is it Rolling Zeus?" *Rolling Stone* (Jan. 15, 1976); reprinted in Carl Benson, ed., *The Bob Dylan Companion: Four Decades of Commentary* (Schirmer Books, 1998), 147.

3. Robert Shelton, *No Direction Home: The Life and Music of Bob Dylan* (Da Capo Press, 1986; rev. ed. 1997), 344.

4. Michael Gray, "Lenny Bruce" in Gray, *The Bob Dylan Encyclopedia* (Continuum, 2006), 101.

5. Bob Dylan, "Lenny Bruce." Lyrics available online at www.bobdylan.com.

Ironically, the song is included on the third of Dylan's trilogy of Christian albums, *Shot of Love* (Columbia Records, 1981).

6. During a legendary Halloween concert in Oct. 1964 (issued on CD as *The Bootleg Series, Vol. 6: Bob Dylan Live 1964: Concert at Philharmonic Hall*, Columbia Records, 2004). Following the moody "Gates of Eden," and while tuning up for the comic number "If You Gotta Go, Go Now (Or Else You Got To Stay All Night)," Dylan wryly comments (punctuated by laughter): "Don't let that scare you . . . it's just Halloween . . . I have my Bob Dylan mask on . . . I'm masquerading."

7. Gray, *The Bob Dylan Encyclopedia*.

8. A portion of the papers presented have now been collected in Colleen Sheehy and Thomas Swiss, eds., *Highway 61 Revisited: Bob Dylan's Road from Minnesota to the World* (Univ. of Minnesota Press, 2009).

9. Clinton Heylin, *Bob Dylan: Behind the Shades Revisited* (HarperCollins, 2001), xvii.

10. John Gordon, "Dylan: A Few Years Older Than Israel (1971)"; reprinted in Craig McGregor, ed., *Bob Dylan: The Early Years: A Retrospective* (Da Capo Press, 1972), 165–166.

11. Quoted in George Robinson, "The Many Sides of Bob Dylan," *Jewish Journal* (Nov. 16, 2007).

12. David Kaufman, " 'Einstein Disguised as Robin Hood': The Enigmatic Jewishness of Bob Dylan," lecture delivered at Skirball Cultural Center, Los Angeles, California (March 30, 2008).

13. Interview with Ron Rosenbaum, *Playboy* 25:3 (March 1978), 90. Thirty years later, Rosenbaum is now working on a book-length treatment of Dylan as a Jew.

14. This headline references "Girl from the North Country," from Dylan's second album, *The Freewheelin' Bob Dylan* (1963).

15. Anthony Scaduto, *Bob Dylan* (Grosset & Dunlap, 1971); Shelton, *No Direction Home*; Bob Spitz, *Dylan: A Biography* (W. W. Norton & Co., 1989); Clinton Heylin, *Bob Dylan: Behind the Shades Revisited* (HarperCollins, 1991, 2001); Howard Sounes, *Down the Highway: The Life of Bob Dylan* (Grove Press, 2001).

16. Shelton, *No Direction Home*, 28.

17. Quoted in Phil Sutcliffe, "Bolt From The Blue: The Rolling Thunder Revue" in Mark Blake, ed., *Dylan: Visions, Portraits, and Back Pages* (DK Publishing, 2005), 165.

18. Gray, *The Bob Dylan Encyclopedia*, 595.

19. Quoted in Nat Hentoff, "The Crackin,' Shakin,' Breakin' Sounds," *New Yorker* (Oct. 24, 1964); reprinted in McGregor, *Bob Dylan*, 57–58.

20. I thank Jeff Klepper for calling this poem to my attention. An image of the original can be found on the web at http://michel.pomarede.pagesperso-orange.fr.

21. Bob Dylan, "Highway 61 Revisited," on the 1965 album of the same title.

22. Quoted in Toby Thompson, *Positively Main Street*; reprinted in McGregor, *Bob Dylan*, 11.

23. Quoted in McGregor, *Bob Dylan*, 112.

24. Ron Rosenbaum, "Born-again Bob: Four Theories," *New York Magazine* (Sept. 24, 1979); reprinted in Elizabeth Thomson and David Gutman, eds., *The Dylan Companion*, (Dell Publishing, 1990), 235.

25. Quoted in the film documentary *Hollywoodism: Jews, Movies, and the American Dream* (Associated Productions, 1998).

26. Spitz, *Dylan*, 69.

27. Stephen Whitfield, *In Search of American Jewish Culture* (Brandeis Univ. Press, 1999), 113.

28. Scaduto, *Bob Dylan* (1971), 43–44.

29. Ibid., 44–45.

30. Irwin Silber, "An Open Letter to Bob Dylan," *Sing Out!* 14:5 (1964); reprinted in Benson, ed., *The Bob Dylan Companion*, 27.

31. Morris Dickstein, *Gates of Eden: American Culture in the Sixties* (Basic Books, 1977), 192. The book is named after the title of a Dylan song.

32. Hentoff, "The Crackin', Shakin', Breakin', Sounds"; reprinted in *Younger Than That Now: The Collected Interviews with Bob Dylan* (Thunder's Mouth Press, 2004), 21.

33. Spitz, *Dylan*, 153.

34. Jeff Klepper points out that at the Woody Guthrie Memorial Concert held at Carnegie Hall in January 1968, Dylan sang Guthrie's "I Ain't Got No Home." Personal correspondence with author (Aug. 17, 2011).

35. This headline references the lyric from "Talkin' New York," one of two original compositions on Dylan's first album, *Bob Dylan* (1962).

36. Jon Pankake and Paul Nelson, "Bob Dylan," *Little Sandy Review* (circa 1962); reprinted in Thomson and Guttman, eds., *The Dylan Companion*, 59.

37. Robert Shelton, "Bob Dylan: A Distinctive Folk-Song Stylist," *New York Times* (Sept. 29, 1961); reprinted in McGregor, *Bob Dylan*, 17–18.

38. See entries for Rinzler and Yellin in Gray, *The Bob Dylan Encyclopedia*. Yellin later moved to a kibbutz in Israel, where Dylan visited him in 1971. Dylan himself has worn cowboy hats throughout his career, as when Hentoff described him in 1975: "Under the cowboy hat, the klezmer, the Jewish hobo musician with roots—roots by the centuries." Hentoff, "Is it Rolling Zeus?" in Benson, ed., *The Bob Dylan Companion*, 139.

39. A similar term is *city-billies*. There is as yet no full-length historical treatment of this phenomenon. See Ronald Cohen, "Folk Music," 113–125 in Paul Buhle, ed., *Jews and American Popular Culture Vol 2: Music, Theater, Popular Art, and Literature* (Praeger Perspectives, 2007).

40. Shel Silverstein, "Folk Singer Blues" (Hollis Music, 1962); published in *Hootenanny: The National Folk Singing Magazine* 1:2 (March 1964), 34. Continuing the theme of Jews in folk music, the magazine's editor was Robert Shelton (*New York Times* music critic), the associate editor was Natalie Goldfarb, and the music editor was Barry Kornfeld.

41. Silverstein, "Folk Singer Blues," 85.

42. Dave Van Ronk quoted in Scaduto, *Bob Dylan*, 67 (1971); also quoted in Michael Billig, *Rock 'n' roll Jews* (Syracuse Univ. Press, 2000), 124.

43. Shelton, *No Direction Home*, 104.

44. Lyrics to all Dylan songs may be found on the official Bob Dylan website at http://www.bobdylan.com.

45. A version of the song, recorded on April 25, 1962, and titled "Talkin' Hava Negeilah Blues," is included on the 1991 release *Bob Dylan: The Bootleg Series, Vol. 1–3 (rare & unreleased), 1961–1991* (Columbia Records).

46. Gil Turner, "Bob Dylan—A New Voice Singing New Songs," *Sing Out!* 12:4 (Oct./Nov., 1962), 10.

47. "Music Notes," *New York Times* (Nov. 4, 1961), 15; *New York Times* (April 24, 1962), 33.

48. Shelton, *No Direction Home*, 111 (my own emphasis on "the singer himself"). For a lengthier discussion of Dylan's takeoff of "Havah Nagilah," see David Kaufman, " 'Here's a Foreign Song I Learned in Utah': The Anxiety of Jewish Influence in the Music of Bob Dylan" in Josh Kun, ed., *The Song Is Not the Same: Jews and American Popular Music*, The Jewish Role in American Life: An Annual Review, vol. 8 (Purdue Univ. Press for the USC Casden Institute for the Study of the Jewish Role in American Life, 2011), 115–135.

49. Gray, *The Bob Dylan Encyclopedia*, 609.

50. Spitz, *Dylan*, 217.

51. The album was honored as one of the first fifty recordings included in the National Recording Registry of the Library of Congress. It is number 45 on the list, joining Bing Crosby's recording of Irving Berlin's "White Christmas" (number 33), Woody Guthrie's "This Land is Your Land" (number 34), Elvis Presley's Sun Records sessions (number 39) and Martin Luther King Jr.'s "I Have a Dream" speech (number 44). *Los Angeles Times* (Jan. 28, 2003), A14.

52. In a 1973 study of Jewish identification, sociologist Charles Liebman explains the phenomenon of *associationalism*: "The Jewish folk religion includes a commitment to Israel and to group survival, but its essence is one's social ties to other Jews. The distinguishing mark of American Jews is less and less how they behave and is certainly not what they believe; it is that they associate primarily with other Jews." Charles Liebman, *The Ambivalent American Jew: Politics, Religion, and Family in American Jewish Life* (Jewish Publication Society of America, 1973).

53. See entries for all three men in Gray, *The Bob Dylan Encyclopedia*, 371–372, 375–376, 595.

54. Dick Schaap, "I Am My Words," *Newsweek* (Nov. 4, 1963), 94.

55. Ibid.

56. Ibid., 95.

57. The headline is from "Neighborhood Bully," *Infidels* (1983).

58. Theodore Bikel, "Harold Leventhal, Folk Music Impresario," *Forward* (Nov. 4, 2005).

59. Spitz, *Dylan*, 540.

60. Rosenbaum, "Born-again Bob," 235–236.

61. Nadine Epstein and Rebecca Frankel, "Bob Dylan: The Unauthorized Spiritual Biography," *Moment* (Aug. 2005).

62. Laurence Schlesinger, "Bob Dylan's Conversion: A Noteworthy Case in Point," *Journal of Reform Judaism* (Winter 1991), 31.

63. Interview with Jeff Klepper; personal correspondence (June 12, 2009).

64. J. J. Goldberg, "Bob Dylan at 60: 'We Used To Be Young Together'; A Musical Seer Who Disdained Role of Prophet," *Forward* (May 18, 2001).

65. Interview with Klepper.

66. Quoted in Shelton, *No Direction Home*, 488.

67. Bob Dylan, *Chronicles: Volume One* (Simon & Schuster, 2004), 5, 6, 26, 73.

68. Nina Goss, personal communication with author (summer 2010).

69. Dylan, *Chronicles*, 102.

70. Ibid., 27.

71. Dylan, *Chronicles*, 92–93.

72. Ibid.

73. Dylan, *Chronicles*, 78.

74. Ibid., 79.

75. This headline references "Gotta Serve Somebody," *Slow Train Coming* (1979).

76. Jonathan Braun, "Is Bob Zimmerman Really Jewish?" *Rolling Stone* (July 8, 1971), 14; originally published as "Bringing it All Back Home . . . The Bob Dylan Rumor Machine," *The Flame* V:1 (New York Union of Jewish Students, March 1971).

77. Scaduto, *Bob Dylan* (1971), 274.

78. Anthony Scaduto, *Bob Dylan* (Abacus, rev. ed. 1973), 280.

79. Ibid., 281.

80. Ibid., 286.

81. Jay Michaelson, "He Wandered the Earth as an Exiled Man: Bob Dylan's New Book Juxtaposes Roots and Rootlessness," *Forward* (Feb. 4, 2005).

82. Alan Rinzler, *Bob Dylan: The Illustrated Record* (Harmony Books, 1978), 15.

83. Ibid., 109.

84. McGregor, *Bob Dylan*, 11.

85. Scott Marshall with Marcia Ford, *Restless Pilgrim: The Spiritual Journey of Bob Dylan* (Relevant Books, 2002).

86. Goldberg, "Bob Dylan at 60."

87. Ibid.

88. Quoted in Larry Sloman, *On the Road with Bob Dylan* (Three Rivers Press, 2002; orig. pub. 1978), 330–331.

89. Scaduto, *Bob Dylan* (1973), 287.

90. Gray, *The Bob Dylan Encyclopedia*, 538.

91. Stephen Pickering, ed., *Dylan: A Commemoration* (Nowles Pub., 1971), 47.

92. Ibid., preface.

93. Stephen Pickering, ed., *Praxis: One: Existence, Men and Realities* (No Limit Pub., Dec. 1971).

94. Pickering, *Praxis*, 3.

95. Steven Goldberg, "Bob Dylan and the Poetry of Salvation," *Newsweek* (May 30, 1970), 43.

96. Pickering, ed., *Praxis*, 64.

97. Ibid., 16.

98. Stephen Pickering (Chofetz Chaim Ben-Avraham), *Bob Dylan: Tour 1974* (Echo Limited, Dec. 1973), frontispiece.

99. Ibid.

100. Ibid., 6.

101. Ibid., 10.

102. Stephen Pickering (Chofetz Chaim Ben-Avraham), *Bob Dylan Approximately: A Portrait of the Jewish Poet in Search of God: A Midrash* (David McKay Co., 1975), 11.

103. Ibid., 14.

104. Ibid., 17.

105. Mike Metzger, "Talkin' Hava Nagila: *Bob Dylan Approximately* Reviewed," in Brian Stibal, ed., *TBZB* (*Talkin' Bob Zimmerman Blues*) 4, (March 1976), 16.

106. Ron Rosenbaum, "Bob Dylan: Messiah or Escape Artist?" *Jewish Review of Books* (Spring 2010), 48.

107. Ibid., 49.

108. Rosenbaum, "Bob Dylan," 48.

109. Scaduto, *Bob Dylan* (1973), 318.

110. Sounes, *Down the Highway*, 263.

111. Shelton, *No Direction Home*, 411.

112. Maureen Orth, "Dylan—Rolling Again," *Newsweek* (Jan. 14, 1974), 47.

113. A. J. Weberman, "Dylan Meets Weberman"; originally published in *East Village Other* (Jan. 19, 1971); reprinted in McGregor, *Bob Dylan*, 379–380.

114. Ibid., 385.

115. Ibid., 384.

116. John Lennon, "God," *Plastic Ono Band* album (1970).

117. Weberman, "Dylan Meets Weberman," 387.

118. See online at http://www.bobsboots.com.

119. Catherine Rosenheimer, "Bob Dylan Incognito in Israel," in Pickering, ed., *Praxis*, 27.

120. See online at http://www.punkhart.com. The strip is reprinted in *Guilt and Pleasure 6* (Fall 2007), 64–74. Its title, "Ventures of Zimmerman," is of course a takeoff of "The Adventures of Superman."

121. See Danny Fingeroth, *Disguised as Clark Kent: Jews, Comics, and the Creation of the Superhero* (Continuum, 2007).

122. "Son-O'-God Meets Zimmerman," *National Lampoon* (May 1974).

123. Sloman, *On the Road with Bob Dylan*, 334.

124. Sam Shepard, *Rolling Thunder Logbook* (Penguin Books, 1977), 68.

125. Dave Engel, *Just Like Bob Zimmerman's Blues: Dylan in Minnesota* (1997).

126. Sander Gilman, *The Jew's Body* (Routledge, 1991), 181. See especially Chapter 7, "The Jewish Nose: Are Jews White? Or, The History of the Nose Job."

127. Moses Hess, *Rome and Jerusalem* (1862); as cited by Gilman in *The Jew's Body*, 179.

128. Personal correspondence with author (April 10, 2008).

129. However, as Landy has described the shoot in interviews, the hat was Dylan's idea.

130. Several of these photographers have now published coffee-table volumes of their Dylan photographs: for example, Daniel Kramer, *Bob Dylan by Daniel Kramer: A Portrait of the Artist's Early Years* (Citadel Press, 1991; orig. pub. 1967); George Alper, ed., *Bob Dylan through the Eyes of Joe Alper: A Photo Essay from 1961–1965* (Joe Alper Photo Collection, 2008); and Barry Feinstein, *Real Moments: Bob Dylan* (Omnibus Press, 2008). Also see entries for Cohen, Hunstein, Kramer, and Schatzberg in Gray, *The Bob Dylan Encyclopedia*.

131. For more on the covers, see "The Other Sides of Bob Dylan," in Mark Blake, ed., *Dylan*, 218–225.

132. Kramer, *Bob Dylan by Daniel Kramer*, 111.

133. David Hajdu, *Positively 4th Street: The Lives and Times of Joan Baez, Bob Dylan, Mimi Baez Farina, and Richard Farina* (Farrar, Straus and Giroux, 2001), 237–236. Note: the cover illustration is the poster by Eric von Schmidt.

134. Quoted in Scaduto, *Bob Dylan* (1971); Engel, *Just Like Bob Zimmerman's Blues*, 16.

135. Nora Ephron and Susan Edmiston, "Bob Dylan Interview"; reprinted in McGregor, ed., *Bob Dylan*, 82.

136. Personal correspondence with the author (summer 2008).

137. Torben Bille, *Dage i Dylan* (Denmark, Informations Forlag, 2001); cover illustration is by Per Marquard Otzen, 1997.

138. Quoted in Richard Meyer, "Warhol's Jews," in Meyer, *Warhol's Jews: Ten Portraits Reconsidered* (Jewish Museum, 2008), 24. This is further discussed here in Chapter 6.

139. Beth Schwartzapfel, "Warhol's Tribe," *Forward* (Feb. 23, 2007), B1.

140. Kleeblatt, "'Passing' into Multiculturalism," 24 (emphasis mine).

141. Shlomo Ydov and Ehud Manor, "*Yaldei ha-Yareach*" (Hed Arzi, 1973; translation mine).

142. Yonatan Geffen and Dani Litani, "*Zeh haKol Beintayim, Beintayim zeh haKol*" (Phonokol Records, 2001); recorded in live performance at Tzavta theater (April 1974); quote from liner notes (translation mine).

143. Quoted in Greil Marcus, *Like a Rolling Stone: Bob Dylan at the Crossroads* (PublicAffairs, 2005), 149.

144. This headline references "Eternal Circle" (1963), *Bob Dylan: The Bootleg Series, Vol. 1–3 (rare & unreleased), 1961–1991* (Columbia Records, 1991).

145. Spitz, *Dylan*, 1–2.

146. The article is reprinted in Benson, ed., *The Bob Dylan Companion*, 170–176. See online at http://www.radiohazak.com.

147. Ibid.

148. Billig, *Rock 'n' roll Jews*; Guy Oseary, *Jews Who Rock* (St. Martin's Press, 2001); Scott Benarde, *Stars of David: Rock 'n' Roll's Jewish Stories* (Brandeis Univ. Press, 2003); and Janet Macoska, *Jews Rock! A Celebration of Rock and Roll's Jewish Heritage* (ArtVisions Exhibitions, 2008).

149. Billig, *Rock 'n' roll Jews*, 130.

150. *Jeff Klepper Live in Concert: Jewish Music for the Masses*. For liner notes, see online at http://www.kolbseder.com.

151. *Jeff Klepper Live in Concert*, liner notes.

152. Interview with Jeff Klepper, personal correspondence (June 12, 2009).

153. Interview with Klepper.

154. *Jeff Klepper Live in Concert*, liner notes. "Cantillation Row" (music by Bob Dylan [Desolation Row] Copyright © 1965; renewed 1993 Special Rider Music) New lyrics by Jeff Klepper. Recorded at Temple Micah, Washington, D.C., February 27, 1999."

155. Interview with Klepper, personal correspondence (June 12, 2009).

156. *Jeff Klepper Live in Concert*; the quote is from the song "Just Like A Chazzn."

157. Interview with Joel Gilbert, personal correspondence (June 7, 2009).

158. Ibid.

159. Ibid.

160. All quotes in this paragraph are from "The Rogovoy Report: Seth Rogovoy's Web Journal," http://rogovoy.com.

161. All quotes in this paragraph are from personal correspondence with Seth Rogovoy (May 25, 2009).

162. Personal correspondence with Seth Rogovoy.

163. Seth Rogovoy, *Bob Dylan: Prophet, Mystic, Poet* (Scribner, 2009).

164. Larry Yudelson, "Dylan: Tangled Up in Jews," *Washington Jewish Week* (1991); reprinted in Benson, ed., *The Bob Dylan Companion*, 175.

165. For a full account, see article by Louis Kemp in Gray, *The Bob Dylan Encyclopedia*, 375–376.

166. This headline references "I Feel a Change Comin' On," *Together Through Life* (2009).

167. Rebecca Goldstein, *Betraying Spinoza: The Renegade Jew Who Gave Us Modernity* (Schocken Books, 2006).

168. See, for example, John Murray Cuddihy, *The Ordeal of Civility: Freud, Marx, Levi-Strauss, and the Jewish Struggle with Modernity* (Basic Books, 1974); Peter Gay, *Freud, Jews and Other Germans: Masters and Victims in Modernist Culture* (Oxford Univ. Press, 1978); Frederic Grunfeld, *Prophets Without Honour: A Background to Freud, Kafka, Einstein and Their World* (McGraw-Hill, 1980); Yosef Hayim Yerushalmi, *Freud's Moses: Judaism Terminable and Interminable* (Yale Univ. Press, 1991).

5. Barbra Streisand

Epigraph from Alan Spiegel, "The Vanishing Act: A Typology of the Jew in the Contemporary American Film," in Sarah Blacher Cohen, ed., From Hester Street to Hollywood: The Jewish-American Stage and Screen *(Indiana Univ. Press, 1983), 258.*

1. Elliot Ratzman, "Campus Crusader: The Secular Religiosity of Camille Paglia," (interview), *Heeb* 15 (Winter 2007), 48.

2. Christopher Andersen, *Barbra: The Way She Is* (HarperCollins, 2006), ix: "She is, according to a Reuters poll, simply the greatest female singer of the twentieth century (Frank Sinatra was deemed the greatest male singer). With over thirty platinum albums, thirteen multiplatinum albums, and fifty gold albums, she is second only to Elvis in record sales—and ahead of such groups as the Beatles and the Rolling Stones."

3. "Cabaret Tonight," *New York Times* (May 9, 1961). The Bon Soir was located at 40 West 8th Street; the Village Vanguard at 178 7th Avenue. Note: Streisand was then opening at the Bon Soir for comedienne Renée Taylor (born Wechsler), who would later play the television role of Fran Drescher's mother on *The Nanny*; both women were depicted as dyed-in-the-wool Streisand fans.

4. John McPhee, "Barbra Streisand" (cover story), *Time* 83:15 (April 10, 1964), 66.

5. Anne Edwards, *Streisand: A Biography* (Little Brown & Co., 1996; rev. and updated ed. 1997), 197.

6. Liora Moriel, "Streisand, Barbra" in Paula Hyman and Deborah Dash Moore, eds., *Jewish Women in America: An Historical Encyclopedia* (Routledge, 1997), 1351.

7. Barbra Streisand, "I Was An Ugly Duckling," *Coronet* (March 1964); reprinted in Ethlie Ann Vare, ed., *Diva: Barbra Streisand and the Making of a Superstar* (Boulevard Books, 1996), 21 and following pages.

8. Quoted in James Spada, *Barbra: The First Decade: The Films and Career of Barbra Streisand* (Citadel Press, 1974), 12.

9. Ibid., 13.

10. Rene Jordan, *The Greatest Star: The Barbra Streisand Story* (G. P. Putnam's Sons, 1975), 2.

11. Vare, *Diva*, 19.

12. Camille Paglia, "Brooklyn Nefertiti: Barbra Streisand," *Sunday Times* magazine (May 30, 1993); reprinted in Paglia, *Vamps and Tramps: New Essays* (Vintage Books, 1994), 143.

13. Streisand, "I Was An Ugly Duckling," 21, 25–26.

14. See especially Sander Gilman, "The Jewish Nose: Are Jews White? Or, The History of the Nose Job," Chapter 7 in Gilman, *The Jew's Body* (Routledge, 1991); and Jay Geller, "(G)nos(e)ology: The Cultural Construction of the Other," Chapter 10 in Howard Eilberg-Schwartz, ed., *People of the Body: Jews and Judaism from an Embodied Perspective* (State Univ. of New York Press, 1992).

15. "Bea, Billie, and Barbra," *Newsweek* (June 3, 1963); reprinted in Vare, *Diva*, 27.

16. *Time* 83:15 (April 10, 1964), 62, 64.

17. Shana Alexander, "A Born Loser's Success and Precarious Love" (cover story on Streisand), *Life* 56:21 (May 22, 1964), 52.

18. Pete Hamill in Vare, *Diva*, 81–82.

19. Paglia, "Brooklyn Nefertiti," 142.

20. Lester Friedman, *Hollywood's Image of the Jew* (Frederick Ungar Publishing, 1982), 179–180.

21. Streisand, "I Was An Ugly Duckling," 21–22.

22. Hamill in Vare, *Diva*, 82.

23. Quoted in Spada, *Barbra*, 163.

24. Spada, *Barbra*, 8.

25. Arthur Laurents, *Original Story By: A Memoir of Broadway and Hollywood* (Applause, 2000), 226.

26. Henry Bial, *Acting Jewish: Negotiating Ethnicity on the American Stage and Screen* (Univ. of Michigan Press, 2005), 86–87.

27. Bial, *Acting Jewish*, 92 (emphasis mine).

28. David Samuels, "Assimilation and Its Discontents: How Success Ruined the New York Jew," *New York Magazine* (Sept. 28, 2008).

29. Kathleen Carroll, *New York Daily News*, quoted in Spada, *Barbra*, 215.

30. Ratzman, "Campus Crusader," 48.

31. Audio recording of television interview with Johnny Carson, *Tonight Show* (NBC, Oct. 4, 1962).

32. "Bea, Billie, and Barbra," 28.

33. Jordan, *The Greatest Star*, 4

34. Barbara Delatiner, *Newsday*, quoted in Spada, *Barbra*, 105.

35. Spada, *Barbra*, 91.

36. Susskind was in fact identified with the "too Jewish" complaint, once rejecting a Paddy Chayefsky script for that stated reason. David Zurawik, *The Jews of Prime Time* (Brandeis Univ. Press, 2003), 221.

37. Jordan, *The Greatest Star*, 22.

38. Mae Questel later played the role of Mrs. Strakosh in the film version of *Funny Girl* (and still later, played Woody Allen's mother in his short film *Oedipus Wrecks*).

39. According to Bugs Bunny "biographer" Joe Adamson: "Bugs was the cartoon version of the loud-mouthed but loveable Brooklynese smart-aleck who turns up in the cockpit, in the barracks, or on the battlefield in every World War II movie." Adamson, Bugs Bunny: 50 Years and Only One Grey Hare (Henry Holt, 1990), 64.

40. The Jewish population of Brooklyn was estimated at 975,000 in 1937 and 950,000 in 1950; see entry "New York City," *Encyclopedia Judaica*, 01.12, 1107. The estimate made by the *American Jewish Yearbook* for 1952 ranged from 940,000 to 1,007,000; see Jacob Rader Marcus, *To Count a People: American Jewish Population Data, 1585–1984* (Univ. Press of America, 1990), 153.

41. Edwards, *Streisand*, 28.

42. Linda Nochlin, foreword in Norman Kleeblatt, ed., *Too Jewish? Challenging Traditional Identities* (Jewish Museum, 1996), xvii.

43. For example, Irving Howe, "The Nature of Jewish Laughter" (1951);

reprinted in Sarah Blacher Cohen, ed., *Jewish Wry* (Wayne State Univ. Press, 1987), 19.

44. Sean Kelly, "What's So Funny? Only Brooklynites can laugh at Brooklyn" in Michael W. Robbins and Wendy Palitz, eds., *Brooklyn: A State of Mind*, (Workman Pub., 2001), 17–19; and David Spaner, "That's Entertainment!" in Ilana Abramovitch and Seán Galvin, eds., *Jews of Brooklyn*, (Univ. Press of New England, 2002), 323–324.

45. Introduction to "Value," track 9 on *Barbra Streisand: Just For the Record* (Sony Music, 1991).

46. *My Name Is Barbra* television special, April 28, 1965 (CBS/Fox Video Music, 1986).

47. Arthur Knight, *Saturday Review*, quoted in Spada, *Barbra*, 179.

48. Ibid., 180.

49. Ibid.

50. Bial, *Acting Jewish*, 16: "When considering the performance of Jewishness in mass culture, then, it is necessary to address the way that work speaks to at least two audiences: a Jewish audience and a general or gentile audience. This is what I mean by the term *double coding*."

51. John Murray Cuddihy, *The Ordeal of Civility: Freud, Marx, Levi-Strauss, and the Jewish Struggle with Modernity* (Basic Books, 1974).

52. Pete Hamill, "Barbra the Great: Talented Girl on a Triumphal March," *Cosmopolitan*, (Feb. 1968); reprinted in Vare, *Diva*, 74 (emphasis mine).

53. Joseph Morgenstern, "Superstar: The Streisand Story," *Newsweek* (Jan. 5, 1970); reprinted in Vare, *Diva*, 89.

54. Jordan, *The Greatest Star*, 6.

55. *Playbill* 6:21 (May 21, 1962), 30. Collection of the author.

56. Jordan, *The Greatest Star*, 15.

57. Jerome Weidman, "I Remember Barbra," *Holiday* (Nov. 1963); reprinted in Vare, *Diva*, 12–13.

58. Joyce Antler, *The Journey Home: How Jewish Women Shaped Modern America* (Schocken Books, 1997), 324.

59. Harley Erdman, *Staging the Jew: The Performance of an American Ethnicity, 1860–1920* (Rutgers Univ. Press, 1997).

60. Jordan, *The Greatest Star*, 15.

61. Ibid., 16.

62. Spada, *Barbra*, 16.

63. Laurents, *Original Story By*, 221–222.

64. Ibid., 222.

65. Weidman, "I Remember Barbra," 8–9.

66. Quoted in Spada, *Barbra*, 45.

67. On Brice's adoption of a Yiddish accent, see June Sochen, "Fanny Brice and Sophie Tucker: Blending the Particular with the Universal," in Sarah Blacher Cohen, ed., *From Hester Street to Hollywood: The Jewish-American Stage and Screen* (Indiana Univ. Press, 1983), 44–57.

68. For a general history of women's comedy, see Linda Martin and Kerry Segrave, *Women in Comedy* (Citadel Press, 1986).

69. Sarah Blacher Cohen, "The Unkosher Comediennes: From Sophie Tucker to Joan Rivers," in Cohen, *Jewish Wry*, 105–124. Also see the recent documentary film *Making Trouble* (Rachel Talbot, director; Jewish Women's Archive Productions, 2006), which profiles Molly Picon, Fanny Brice, Sophie Tucker, Joan Rivers, Gilda Radner, and Wendy Wasserstein.

70. See, for example, the deli discussion between Judy Gold, Jackie Hoffman, and others in *Making Trouble*.

71. Barry Dennen, *My Life with Barbra: A Love Story* (Prometheus Books, 1997), 186.

72. Spada, *Barbra*, 22.

73. Kathryn Bernheimer, *The 50 Greatest Jewish Movies: A Critic's Ranking of the Very Best* (Birch Lane Press, 1998), 33. For a somewhat more sophisticated reading of the Brice-Streisand connection, see Stacy Wolf, "Barbra's 'Funny Girl' Body" in Boyarin, et al., *Queer Theory and the Jewish Question*, 246–265.

74. Bernheimer, *The 50 Greatest Jewish Movies*, 35–36.

75. Friedman, *Hollywood's Image of the Jew*, 180.

76. Ibid., 183.

77. Letty Cottin Pogrebin, *Deborah, Golda, and Me: Being Female and Jewish in America* (Anchor Books, 1991), 260.

78. Ibid., 267.

79. Pogrebin, *Deborah, Golda, and Me*, 260.

80. Ibid., 269.

81. Laurents, *Original Story By*, 257.

82. Pogrebin, *Deborah, Golda, and Me*, 270.

83. Ibid., 270–271.

84. See J. Hoberman, *Bridge of Light: Yiddish Film Between Two Worlds* (Temple Univ. Press, 1991), 235–243.

85. Shaun Considine, *Barbra Streisand: The Woman, the Myth, the Music* (Delacorte Press, 1985), 305.

86. Marjorie Garber, *Vested Interests: Cross-Dressing and Cultural Anxiety* (Routledge, 1992), 79–80.

87. Moriel, "Streisand, Barbra," 1351.

88. Moriel, "Streisand, Barbra," 1350.

89. Janet Jakobsen, "Queers Are Like Jews, Aren't They? Analogy and Alliance Politics," in Boyarin, et al., *Queer Theory and the Jewish Question*, 83.

90. From the March 1997 issue of *Out*, as quoted in Moriel, "Streisand, Barbra."

91. Laurents, *Original Story By*, 226.

92. Paglia, "Brooklyn Nefertiti," 142–143. The Redford quote can be found in many sources, including Andersen, *Barbra*, 214.

93. Paglia, "Brooklyn Nefertiti," 142–143.

94. Quoted in Felicia Herman, "The Way She *Really* Is: Images of Jews and Women in the Films of Barbra Streisand," in Joyce Antler, ed., *Talking Back:*

Images of Jewish Women in American Popular Culture (Brandeis Univ. Press, 1998), 171.

95. June Sochen, "From Sophie Tucker to Barbra Streisand: Jewish Women Entertainers as Reformers," in Antler, *Talking Back*, 69.

96. Herman, "The Way She *Really* Is," 173.

97. Ibid., 172.

98. Paglia, "Brooklyn Nefertiti," 142.

99. Camille Paglia, "The Way She Was," in Vare, *Diva*, 225.

100. Calev Ben-David called Streisand the "Jackie Robinson of female Jewish performers" in "The Way She Is," *Jerusalem Report* 2 (June, 1994), 43.

101. Ratzman, "Campus Crusader," 48.

102. Paglia, "Brooklyn Nefertiti," 144.

103. Paglia, "The Way She Was," 222.

104. Sochen, "From Sophie Tucker to Barbra Streisand," 77–78.

105. Spada, *Barbra*, 151.

106. Moriel, "Streisand, Barbra," 1352.

107. Paglia, "Brooklyn Nefertiti," 142.

108. See especially Marc Dollinger, *Quest for Inclusion: Jews and Liberalism in Modern America* (Princeton Univ. Press, 2000); and Michael Staub, *Torn at the Roots: The Crisis of Jewish Liberalism in Postwar America* (Columbia Univ. Press, 2002).

109. Vare, *Diva*, xix.

110. From the *Village Voice* (review of Streisand's first television special, 1965), quoted in Spada, *Barbra*, 109.

111. From Streisand's keynote address at the Women in Film Crystal Awards, 1992; reprinted in Vare, *Diva*, 115.

112. From *Mad* (June 1971); reprinted in Spada, *Barbra*, 181–188.

113. Ibid., 183.

114. See online at http://www.kingweb.net.

115. "Who Am I, Anyway?" *Life* 68:1 (Jan. 9, 1970), 90–97: "An interview with Barbra Streisand: The brightest star of the 60s moves into the new decade, still wondering about herself and her success."

116. James Spada, *Barbra* (1974) and *Streisand: The Woman and the Legend* (1981); Rene Jordan, *The Greatest Star: The Barbra Streisand Story* (1975); Shaun Considine, *Barbra Streisand* (1985); Randall Riese, *Her Name is Barbra* (1993); Andersen, *Barbra* (2006); Tom Santopietro, *The Importance of Being Barbra: The Brilliant, Tumultuous Career of Barbra Streisand* (2006).

117. Nellie Bly (Sarah Gallick), *Barbra Streisand: The Untold Story* (1994); Allison Waldman, *The Barbra Streisand Scrapbook* (1995); Vare, *Diva* (1996); Edwards, *Streisand* (1996).

118. *Cleveland Jewish News* (May 23, 1997).

119. Available online at http://snltranscripts.jt.org.

120. See Vincent Brook, *Something Ain't Kosher Here: The Rise of the "Jewish" Sitcom* (Rutgers Univ. Press, 2003), especially Chapter 6, "Under the Sign of *Seinfeld*: The Second Phase of the Jewish Sitcom Trend," 118–128.

121. Quoted in Abigail Pogrebin, *Stars of David: Prominent Jews Talk About Being Jewish* (Broadway Books, 2005), 182.

122. Brook, *Something Ain't Kosher Here*, 131. In his chapter on Fran Drescher, "Un-'Dresch'-ing the Jewish Princess," Brook argues that the Nanny character effectively subverted the JAP stereotype by sexualizing what otherwise would have been a negative caricature.

123. Kleeblatt, *Too Jewish?* x.

124. Norman Kleeblatt, " 'Passing' into Multiculturalism," in Kleeblatt, ed., *Too Jewish? Challenging Traditional Identities* (Jewish Museum, 1996), 9.

125. Ibid.

126. Kleeblatt, " 'Passing' into Multiculturalism," 9–10.

127. Quoted in Michael Plante, ed., *Deborah Kass: The Warhol Project* (Distributed Art Publishers, 1999), 42.

128. I am most grateful to Deborah Kass for opening her studio to me and sharing her passion for Barbra Streisand. I also gladly give her credit for suggesting the "Hollywood Jew" subtitle for this chapter.

129. Kleeblatt, " 'Passing' Into Multiculturalism," 24.

130. Rhonda Lieberman, "Jewish Barbie," in Kleeblatt, *Too Jewish?* 109.

131. Joseph Albanese, "Well, The Time Has Come" (March 10, 2010). See online at http://www.amazon.com.

6. Epilogue

1. Adam Sandler, "The Chanukah Song," on *What the Hell Happened to Me?* (Warner Bros. Records, 1996).

2. Susan Glenn, "In the Blood? Consent, Descent, and the Ironies of Jewish Identity," *Jewish Social Studies* 8:2/3 (Winter/Spring 2002), 140.

3. Ibid., 148.

4. Eric L. Goldstein, *The Price of Whiteness: Jews, Race, and American Identity* (Princeton Univ. Press, 2006), 210.

5. Kurland's 1984 song can be found on the CD *Now That Sounds Kosher* (Shout! Factory, 2005).

6. Ibid.

7. Mac Davis, *They Are All Jews: From Moses to Einstein* (Hebrew Publishing Co., 1937). Also see Daniel Itzkovitz, "They Are All Jews," in Vincent Brook, ed., *You Should See Yourself: Jewish Identity in Postmodern American Culture* (Rutgers Univ. Press, 2006), 230–251.

8. Harold Ribalow, *The Jew in American Sports* (Bloch Pub. Co., 1948); Robert Slater, *Great Jews in Sports* (Jonathan David Publishers, 1983); and Buddy Robert S. Silverman, *The Jewish Athletes' Hall of Fame* (Shapolsky Publishers, 1989).

9. Ralph Schoenstein, "Let Us Now Claim Famous Men," *Village Voice* (Nov. 24, 1975); reprinted in Bill Novak and Moshe Waldoks, eds., *The Big Book of Jewish Humor*, (HarperCollins Pub., 1981), 117–120.

10. Ibid., 117.

11. For a reproduction of the handwritten list, see Richard Meyer, "Warhol's Jews," in *Warhol's Jews: Ten Portraits Reconsidered* (Jewish Museum, 2008), 23.

12. Beth Schwartzapfel, "Warhol's Tribe," *Forward* (Feb. 23, 2007), B1.

13. *Warhol's Jews: Ten Portraits Reconsidered* (exhibition catalogue).

14. David Zurawik, *The Jews of Prime Time* (Brandeis Univ. Press, 2003); see 2–3 on the television sketch "Jew, Not a Jew," 5–6 on the phrase "too Jewish."

15. Goldstein, *The Price of Whiteness*, 210.

16. Dan Bern, "Lithuania," included on *The Swastika EP* (Messenger Records, 2002). *The Official Dan Bern Lyric Archive*; http://home.earthlink.net.

17. Hoberman and Shandler, *Entertaining America* (2003), 151.

18. Goldstein, *The Price of Whiteness*, 210.

19. Ibid., 277.

20. See Arnold Eisen, *The Chosen People in America: A Study in Jewish Religious Ideology* (Indiana Univ. Press, 1983).

21. Mildred Rein, Letter to the Editor (in response to an op-ed by Michael Chabon, "Chosen, but Not Special," June 6, 2010), *New York Times* (June 8, 2010), A26.

22. Tony Karon, "How Jewish is Israel?" Haaretz.com (May 19, 2006). See online at http://www.haaretz.com.

23. For a book-length treatment of this theme, see Yuri Slezkine, *The Jewish Century* (Princeton Univ. Press, 2004).

24. Contemporary Christian statements of Jesus's Jewishness are made for various reasons, including improving Christian-Jewish relations and advocating for Messianic Judaism or "Jews for Jesus." The voluminous popular literature on the topic includes Zola Levitt, *Jesus: The Jew's Jew* (Creation House, 1973); Amy-Jill Levine, *The Misunderstood Jew: The Church and the Scandal of the Jewish Jesus* (HarperOne, 2007); Ann Spanger and Lois Tverberg, *Sitting at the Feet of Rabbi Jesus: How the Jewishness of Jesus Can Transform Your Faith* (Zondervan, 2009); Arnold Fruchtenbaum, *Jesus Was A Jew* (Ariel Ministries, 2010); and Rabbi Shmuley Boteach, Kosher Jesus (Gefen Pub. House, 2012).

25. See especially Susannah Heschel, *Abraham Geiger and the Jewish Jesus* (Univ. of Chicago Press, 1998); Matthew Hoffman, *From Rebel to Rabbi: Reclaiming Jesus and the Making of Modern Jewish Culture* (Stanford Univ. Press, 2007); and Sonja Spear, *Jesus the Jew: Jewish, Protestant, and Catholic Constructions of Jesus in an Age of Anti-Semitism, 1890–1940* (VDM Verlag, 2009).

26. Albert Schweitzer's classic work *The Quest of the Historical Jesus* first appeared in 1906, and the "Historical Jesus" school has been revived more recently by scholars such as E. P. Sanders, John Dominic Crossan, and John Meier. See, for example, James Charlesworth, ed., *Jesus' Jewishness: Exploring the Place of Jesus in Early Judaism* (Crossroad, 1991).

27. Joseph Klausner, *Jesus of Nazareth* (Macmillan, 1925); Solomon Zeitlin, *Who Crucified Jesus?* (Bloch Pub. Co., 1964); Samuel Sandmel, *We Jews and Jesus* (Oxford Univ. Press, 1965); David Flusser, *Jesus* (Herder and Herder, 1969); and Geza Vermes, *Jesus the Jew* (William Collins, 1973).

28. Written by Friedman in the early 1970s and included on his first album, *Sold American* (Vanguard, 1973). See Theodore Albrecht, "'They Ain't Makin' Jews Like Jesus Anymore': The Musical Humor of Kinky Friedman and

The Texas Jewboys in Historical and Geographical Perspective," in Leonard Greenspoon, ed., *Jews and Humor* (Purdue Univ. Press, 2011), 211–224.

29. Joseph Telushkin, *Jewish Humor* (William Morrow, 1992), 39.

30. See Henry Bial, *Acting Jewish: Negotiating Ethnicity on the American Stage and Screen* (Univ. of Michigan Press, 2005), 147: "How does the imagined community of Jews, especially American Jews, continue (however shakily) to cohere? It does so in part through the sustained and strategic project of reading Jewish."

31. Goldstein, *The Price of Whiteness*, 211.

32. *Gesher: A Journal of Outreach to Unaffiliated Jews* (Fall 1995); cited by Larry Yudelson, "Dylan: Tangled Up in Jews," *Washington Jewish Week* (1991). See online at http://www.radiohazak.com.

33. Roger Bennett and Josh Kun, eds., *And You Shall Know Us By The Trail of Our Vinyl: The Jewish Past as Told by the Records We Have Loved and Lost* (Crown Publishers, 2008), 13.

34. See Norman Kleeblatt, ed. *Too Jewish? Challenging Traditional Identities* (Jewish Museum, 1996); and J. Hoberman and Jeffrey Shandler, eds., *Entertaining America: Jews, Movies, and Broadcasting* (Princeton Univ. Press and Jewish Museum, 2003).

35. See especially Sylvia Barack Fishman, *Double or Nothing? Jewish Families and Mixed Marriage* (Brandeis Univ. Press, 2004); and Daniel Klein and Freke Vuijst, *The Half-Jewish Book: A Celebration* (Villard, 2000).

36. See: J. Hoberman, "Flaunting It: The Rise and Fall of Hollywood's 'Nice' Jewish (Bad) Boys," in Hoberman and Shandler, eds., *Entertaining America*, 220–243.

37. David Leonhardt, "A Better Way to Measure Twitter Influence," *New York Times Magazine* (March 27, 2011), 18.

38. Glenn, "In the Blood?" 141.

39. Larry Gordon, "Updated Work Has Volumes to Say about Judaism," *Los Angeles Times* (March 10, 2007), B2.

40. Jonathan Freedland, "Mag That Gives You the Heeby Jeebies," *Jewish Chronicle* (Sept. 24, 2004). See online at http://www.jonathanfreedland.com.

41. *The Daily Show* (Comedy Central, 2011).

42. "Palestinian Chicken," *Curb Your Enthusiasm*, episode 73 (HBO, 2011).

43. For further discussion of Dylan's Christmas album, see my article " 'Here's a Foreign Song I Learned in Utah': The Anxiety of Jewish Influence in the Music of Bob Dylan," in Josh Kun, ed., *The Song Is Not the Same: Jews and American Popular Music* (USC Casden Institute for the Study of the Jewish Role in American Life, 2011), 129–130.

44. As of this writing, the performance can be seen on YouTube, with close-ups of Dylan's vocals.

45. Bradley Burston, "Bob Dylan, It Turns Out, Does Live in Israel," Haaretz.com (June 21, 2011).

46. The concert has since been released on CD and DVD as *One Night Only: Barbra Streisand and Quartet at The Village Vanguard—September 26, 2009* (Columbia, 2010).

47. Interview with Deborah Kass (Sept. 16, 2011).

48. Both quotations in this paragraph come from my interview with Deborah Kass (Sept. 16, 2011).

49. Promotional letter for the National Museum of American Jewish History, June 2010.

50. All 218 candidates may be viewed on the website, grouped by the following eight categories: Arts & Entertainment; Business & Philanthropy; Literature; Performance; Politics, Law & Activism; Religion & Thought; Science & Medicine; and Sports.

51. Ibid.

52. The four are as follows: Rabbi Mordecai M. Kaplan, representing Conservative/Reconstructionist Judaism; Hazan Isaac Leeser, representing Modern Orthodox Judaism; Lubavitcher Rebbe Menahem M. Schneerson, representing Ultra-Orthodox Judaism; and Rabbi Isaac Mayer Wise, representing Reform Judaism.

53. See the NMAJH website (http://www.nmajh.org), "Mission Statement."

54. Mark Oppenheimer, "Agency's Shtick Is Jewish Humor for a Good Cause," *New York Times* (Dec. 11, 2010).

Index